The Torah, the Gospel, and the Qur'an

The Torah, the Gospel, and the Qur'an

Three Books, Two Cities, One Tale

Anton Wessels

Translated by
Henry Jansen

WILLIAM B. EERDMANS PUBLISHING COMPANY
GRAND RAPIDS, MICHIGAN / CAMBRIDGE, U.K.

First published in Dutch under the title
Thora, Evangelie en Koran: 3 boeken, 2 steden, 1 verhaal,
2010 by Kok

Published 2013 by
Wm. B. Eerdmans Publishing Co.
2140 Oak Industrial Drive N.E., Grand Rapids, Michigan 49505 /
P.O. Box 163, Cambridge CB3 9PU U.K.

Printed in the United States of America

18 17 16 15 14 13   7 6 5 4 3 2 1

Library of Congress Cataloging-in-Publication Data

Wessels, Antonie.
The Torah, the Gospel, and the Qur'an: three books, two cities, one tale /
Anton Wessels.
    pages   cm
Includes bibliographical references and index.
ISBN 978-0-8028-6908-1 (pbk.: alk. paper)
1. Sacred books — History and criticism.
2. Abrahamic religions.   I. Title.

BL71.W47   2013
208.2 — dc23

2013009749

www.eerdmans.com

For Anton Houtepen

CONNECTED FOR LIFE

In your work you have given an inspiring interpretation of "God, heaven, holy"—one can perhaps get rid of these grand words, but one cannot get rid of the desire that gave them life.

FRANS KELLENDONK, "GROTE WOORDEN"

Contents

Contents

Foreword

Jews on occasion talk about the New Testament and the Qur'an, often from a standpoint shaped and informed by their own sacred scripture, the Hebrew Bible. So too Christians talk about the Hebrew Bible and the Qur'an, often from a standpoint shaped and informed by their sacred scripture; and Muslims talk similarly about the Hebrew Bible and the New Testament.

Sometimes a member of one of these parties discusses the sacred scriptures of the other parties in order to draw contrasts: contrasts in how God is understood, contrasts in how human beings are understood, contrasts in how God's actions in history are understood, contrasts in how the life of true devotion is understood. Often the person drawing these contrasts will implicitly or explicitly find fault with the understandings of these matters in the sacred texts of the other parties; he will implicitly or explicitly indicate that, on these matters, he finds those other texts defective.

Anton Wessels's *The Torah, the Gospel, and the Qur'an* is strikingly different from such discussions. Wessels is himself a Christian missiologist. But his project here is not to talk about the Hebrew Bible and the Qur'an from the standpoint of someone shaped and informed by the Christian Bible. His project is to read these three sacred texts *together* — to discuss and explain them *in relation to each other.*

Each of these texts is exceedingly rich and complex; if one is going to read them together one has to single out some theme as one's focus. It will, of course, have to be a theme on which all three have something to say; but that still leaves a large number of different possibilities. Obvious candidates would be the theology of these three sacred scriptures, the anthropology, or the ethics.

Wessels avoids the obvious candidates; his choice is strikingly original. Pervading all three of these sacred texts is the theme of the city, more precisely, the theme of two cities: the city where corruption and injustice rule versus the city where God rules, Babylon versus Jerusalem, Mecca versus Medina. Wessels's project is to read together the Hebrew Bible, the Christian Bible, and the Qur'an as a "tale of two cities."

Given that the Christian Bible incorporates the Hebrew Bible, and that the Qur'an refers to both the Hebrew Bible and the New Testament, it turns out that these three sacred scriptures often refer to the same actual cities, Sodom, Babylon, Jerusalem. Wessels shows that the interconnections go much deeper than that, however. In these three sacred texts there are strikingly similar discussions about the founding of cities, about exile from one's city, about violence in the city, about the role of the prophet in the city, about authority in the city, about intercession for the city, about the flourishing of the city, about the city of God.

In his Preface Wessels remarks that "Religions are often cited as the cause of enmity in contemporary conflicts in the world: Judaism (in connection with the state of Israel), Islam, and the Christian West. It is very important, therefore, to ask if that political enmity can be traced back to the sacred texts to which Jews, Christians, and Muslims appeal." I find Wessels's conclusion compelling: these conflicts cannot be traced back to the sacred texts. There are indeed passages in each of these writings that, when interpreted in isolation, can be seen as justifying political enmity. But those interpretations become implausible when those passages are set within the context of the "tale of two cities" that is told by these three sacred scriptures.

These three sacred scriptures are typically read and interpreted over against each other. Anton Wessels has made a signal contribution to interfaith understanding by showing how, on the important and pervasive theme of "two cities," they can and should be read in conversation with each other, and by going on from there to show that this same theme speaks to you and me today concerning our contemporary cities.

NICHOLAS WOLTERSTORFF

Preface

Thus the founder of the earthly city [Genesis 4:17] was a fratricide [Cain]. Overcome with envy, he slew his own brother
[Abel], a citizen of the eternal city, and a sojourner on earth. So
that we cannot be surprised that first specimen, or, as the
Greeks say, archetype of crime, should, long afterwards, find a
corresponding crime at the foundation of that city which was
destined to reign over so many nations, and be the head of this
earthly city of which we speak. For of that city also, as one of
their poets [Marcus Lucanus (39-65)] has mentioned, "the first
walls were stained with a brother's blood. . . ."

Augustine, *City of God*, XV, 5

A Tale of Two Cities, Charles Dickens

The book, *A Tale of Two Cities* (1859), by the well-known nineteenth-century
writer Charles Dickens is centered around the French Revolution of 1789,
which had such an enormous influence on history. When I went to high
school, the course on modern history began with the French Revolution.
Dickens wrote about Paris and London, and his book opens with the words:
"It was the best of times, it was the worst of times; it was the age of wisdom,
it was the age of foolishness; it was the epoch of belief, it was the epoch of in-
credulity; it was the season of Light, it was the season of Darkness . . ."[1] — a

1. *A Tale of Two Cities*, ed. George Woodcock (Harmondsworth: Penguin, 1970; repr.
1985) 35.

xi

pattern of contradictions that finally exploded in the French Revolution. Dickens attempted in his books, including this one, to understand, to explain the time in which he lived and to provide insight into it. He was convinced that revolution is a monster and a nightmare. How should one respond to such a revolution? That monster cannot be fought by hanging even more people or imposing even more prison sentences. The only possible defense is to recognize what led to the revolution. And Dickens attempted to understand the serious social misery of his time: he criticized the social abuses that were only made worse by the greed that reigned at the time. Dickens understood, to quote the great poet W. H. Auden, that

> Those to whom evil is done
> Do evil in return.²

With these lines Auden condemns the Treaty of Versailles, which imposed such crushing sanctions on the defeated enemy at the end of the Great War (as the First World War [1914-1918] was initially called) that this peace was later viewed as the beginning of the Second World War.³

We live today in a time that is generally considered a time of transition, a time of, as it were, revolution. It is often said that the world changed after 9/11, the term used for change being not revolution but terrorism. There has been war against terrorism since 9/11. What is the source of that terrorism? Should we perhaps also in our times of revolution, times of terror, think hard about what Auden says, "Those to whom evil is done / Do evil in return"? Many in the West will certainly claim that evil has been done to "us." In addition to 9/11 were the attacks in Madrid and London and the murder of the filmmaker Theo van Gogh by Mohammed B. in Amsterdam. Terrible! But is it also not important for the West to ask what evil "we" have done?

The "Grand Tales of Two Cities"

Throughout history people have divided the world into two camps. In particular, in the twentieth century was what was called the East-West Conflict, which continued for decades from 1945, the end of the Second World War (1940-45) until 1989, the collapse of the Soviet Union: the capitalist world

---

2. "September 1, 1939," *Selected Poems,* ed. Edward Mendelson (New York: Vintage, 1979) ll. 21-22.

3. Woodcock, "Introduction," *A Tale of Two Cities,* 20-21.

under the leadership of the United States, Washington, on the one side, and the communist world, under the leadership of the Soviet Union, Moscow, on the other. Since the fall of the Berlin Wall in 1989 Islam has been seen as the primary enemy of the West — Islam over against the West — and the theory of a "clash of civilizations" (Bernard Lewis, Samuel Huntington) was quickly unleashed against it. This conflict between Islam and the Western world, which was thought to have existed for centuries already, was viewed by many as real and considered confirmed by the attacks on two cities, New York and Washington. Osama bin Laden was seen as the spiritual father of these attacks. Initially, the American president George W. Bush called his "war on terror," which he initiated after the 9/11 attacks, a crusade, thus confirming what Osama bin Laden saw as his aim. Bin Laden wanted a "holy war," a *jihâd* against the West, "the crusaders." Bush's war against the "axis of evil" (Iraq, Iran, and North Korea) in his January 2002 State of the Union Address was a conscious echo of the conflict with the Soviet Union, the "Evil Empire," a phrase the American president Ronald Reagan used in 1983 (having borrowed it from *Star Wars* [1977]).

This is the grand narrative or tale of good versus evil, democracy against totalitarianism. Bin Laden himself spoke of the "Zionist-crusader alliance," against which he opened "the global Islamic front against Jews and crusaders." This is the grand tale of triumphant jihâd in the sense of holy war, the tale of the "spectacular martyrdom operation," such as that of 9/11. Muslims who think like Osama explain the whole history of fourteen centuries of Islam in these categories. The first expansion of Islam is already viewed as a struggle against Zionists and crusaders, when, for example, a Berber emir from North Africa defeated the Spanish in the eleventh century, when the Kurdish sultan Saladin drove the Crusaders from Jerusalem in the twelfth, or Mehmed the Conqueror, the Ottoman sultan, captured Constantinople in the fifteenth. The conclusion is that this great Islamic civilization that destroyed Byzantium to exalt God's name is, since 9/11, on its way again to conquer the world. While American neoconservatives propagate the grand tale of the war on terror, certain groups on the Muslim side speak about the great tale of jihâd through martyrdom. The suicide bombings in Madrid and Great Britain, the murder of Theo van Gogh in Amsterdam, and response to the Danish cartoons are viewed in those terms.[4]

---

4. Gilles Kepel, *Beyond Terror and Martyrdom: The Future of the Middle East,* trans. Pascale Ghazale (Cambridge, MA: Belknap, Harvard University Press, 2008) 4, 8, 97-98, 120, 133, 136, 177, 255.

The Bible and the Qur'an as a "Tale of Two Cities"

Religions are often cited as the cause of enmity in contemporary conflicts in the world: Judaism (in connection with the state of Israel), Islam, and the Christian West. It is very important, therefore, to ask if that political enmity can be traced back to the sacred texts to which Jews, Christians, and Muslims appeal: the Tanakh (an acronym for the Torah, the Prophets [Nebi'im] and Writings [Ketubim], to which the Psalms belong),[5] or the Old Testament, the New Testament — both of which comprise what Christians call the Bible — and the Qur'an.

I will attempt to answer that question in this book. I will do so by discussing and explaining these three texts in relationship with one another. My starting point will be the idea that three texts, the Tanakh, the Bible, and the Qur'an, can also be understood as "Tales of Two Cities," Jerusalem and Babel, Mecca and Medina.

The one city, Jerusalem, is a symbol for the city of justice and peace; the other, Babel, represents the city of injustice and oppression. The ultimate future prospect is a new city, a new Jerusalem (Revelation 21–22). This vision focuses on the city whose foundations are designed and built by God himself (Heb 11:10). The expression refers to the imperishability and salvation that will be achieved in the end time. A cloud of witnesses is said to be on the way to this city that God has built for them (Heb 11:16), Mount Zion, the city of the living God, the heavenly Jerusalem (Heb 12:22).

Jerusalem is nowhere mentioned by name in the Qur'an, nor by one of the other names that were later used for the city, such as the "holy house" *(al-bayt al-maqdis)* or simply "the Holy" *(al-Quds)*. But the city and temple are clearly in view when the two destructions that God brought upon the city are mentioned (Q 17:4-8).[6]

The Qur'an can equally be described as a "tale of two cities," namely the cities Mecca and Medina. Mecca lies in a rocky valley where nothing grows and where a holy house, the Ka'ba stands (Q 14:37). Mecca, which means "sanctum," must have been a religious center years before Muhammad was born and at the same time a transfer center for the wares transported by caravans. The south-north spice road ran via this city, a station halfway between Ma'rib in southern Arabia and Gaza.

---

5. Sir Prologue; 39:1. Law, wisdom, prophecies — this has become the classic division of the Hebrew Bible.

6. Frank E. Peters, *Islam: A Guide for Jews and Christians* (Princeton: Princeton University Press, 2003).

The city of Medina/Yathrib, which lies about 400 kilometers northeast of Mecca, is an oasis. Apart from the fact that it lay on the spice route between Yemen and Syria, it is a place specially suited for the cultivation of date palms. Through the Jewish tribes present there, Banû Qaynuqa, Banû al-Nadîr, and the Banû Qurayza, the city became an important center for agriculture. Judging from their names, the Jews there must have been of Arab or Aramean descent, although their core was formed by the Jews who had found refuge in the Arabian Peninsula after the conquest of Palestine by the Romans. The Jews had probably already given the name Medina, which means "city," to the place that was later the city of the prophet Muhammad *(Madînat al-nabî)*.[7]

In Mecca, where he was born around 570, Muhammad began his activity as a prophet in 610. In the first period of this activity (610-22), Mecca was a city of injustice, oppression, and persecution. In contrast, Medina represented the city where justice was done and would be given the epithet *Madînat al-munawarra*, "the enlightened city" or "city of light." A genre of Arabic poetry consists of praise of or longing for Medina.[8]

Jews, Jewish Christians, and Christians in the Arab Peninsula

Jews and Christians are not unknown in the Arabian Peninsula. Jews came as refugees already after the first destruction of the temple (586 B.C.), again after the second destruction of Jerusalem in A.D. 70, and in the second century after the defeat of the Jewish rebellion of Bar Kokhba. The latter was sometimes viewed as a messiah: "son of the star," in line with the text "A star will come out of Jacob" (Num 24:17). In addition to the south, Jews were present at all oases in the north and in the city of Medina. There were also Arabs who had adopted Judaism.[9]

The second wave of Jewish refugees to Arabia also included Jewish Christians. This is part of the Christian church that has more or less escaped the attention of the church in the West, which consists almost exclusively of Gentile Christians. But Jewish Christians continued to play a role in the first

---

7. Philip K. Hitti, *History of the Arabs* (8th ed.; New York: St. Martin's, 1964) 102-4.

8. *Encylopaedia of the Qur'an* (hereafter *EQ*), ed. Jane Dammen McAuliffe (Leiden: Brill, 2001-6), *s.v.* "Medina, *tashawwuq ilâ l-Madîna.*"

9. *Encylopaedia of Islam* (hereafter *EI*), new ed. (Leiden: Brill, 1960-2005), *s.v.*, "al-Madîna"; D. S. Attema, *Het oudste Christendom in Zuid-Arabië* (Amsterdam: Noord-Hollandsche, 1949).

centuries of church history in the Middle East up until the time of Muhammad. The remaining Christians in the peninsula are primarily Eastern Christians, Syrian Orthodox, and Nestorian or Assyrian Christians.[10]

The Christianity present in Arabia had its direct background in the Syrian-speaking communities on the edges of the peninsula.[11] The hymns of Ephraim the Syrian (306-73), the greatest writer and poet of the Syrian Orthodox Christians, were sung by various communities in the Arabian Peninsula.[12] There is also the Melkite church, the church that is connected with the "prince" *(melkos)*, the imperial power of the emperor of Byzantium. There was even a cemetery for Christians in Mecca during Muhammad's lifetime. According to an early historian of the Muslim holy places, an icon of Mary and her son Jesus was found among the images inside the Ka'ba. When Muhammad cleansed the Ka'ba of idols after occupying the city in 630, he expressly forbade the removal of the icon.

It is important to note that Muhammad would proclaim his message in a milieu acquainted with the biblical stories. When Muhammad began his work as a prophet, he became involved in an already existing discussion among Jews, Jewish Christians, and Christians on understanding and applying what the Torah says in essence about doing justice and loving one's neighbor.

Reading the Tanakh, the Gospel, and the Qur'an Together?

Mentioning and discussing the Bible and the Qur'an in one breath will perhaps cause some surprise. Jews will hold primarily to the Hebrew Bible, Christians to the Old and New Testaments, and Muslims to the Qur'an.

Christians have sometimes rejected the Old Testament. Marcion (ca. A.D. 110-60), founder of a church named after him, held that the God of the Old Testament was not the same as the God of Jesus Christ. He therefore attached no value to the Old Testament and argued that every reference to the Old should be removed from the New. He was excommunicated by the church. Muslims view the relationship between the Old and the New Testament somewhat differently, for the Qur'an considers Jews and Christians to

---

10. Tilman Nagel, *Der Koran und sein religiöses und kulturelles Umfeld* (Munich: Oldebourg, 2010); Anton Wessels, *Arab and Christian? Christians in the Middle East* (Kampen: Pharos, 1995).

11. *EQ*, s.v. "Christians and Christianity."

12. Nagel, *Der Koran*, 195.

be "people of the Book," *ahl al-kitâb,* the Torah *(Tawra)* and the Gospel *(Injîl)* (Q 5:47; cf. 2:105). The term "Book" is thought to refer more to the word of God that is recited, or presented, than to a book that is read. Qur'an means, literally, that which is recited. While Christians acknowledged the Old Testament and included it in their Bible, the attitude of Jews and Christians to the Qur'an has usually been different. They have often denied and still deny that Muhammad is a prophet and that the Qur'an is also the Word of God. Muslims find that difficult to understand because they do not comprehend why Jews and Christians do not show the same respect for Muhammad that they themselves show for Moses and Jesus.

It is good to remember that Moses was not a Jew, Jesus was not a Christian, and Muhammad was not a Muslim. None of the three traditions and communities of Judaism, Christianity, and Islam converge with Moses, Jesus, and Muhammad. These figures, so central to the Jewish, Christian, and Muslim religions respectively, are not the possession of each tradition alone, as if each has a patent on its corresponding central figure, as if each tradition can claim an exclusive right to the full explanation of its text. The Jewish scholar David Hartman in Jerusalem once remarked trenchantly: "We — Jews — are not the only show in town."

My approach is inspired by the great Jewish philosopher Moses Maimonides. Maimonides was born in 1135 in Cordoba in Moorish Spain, al-Andalus, and died in Cairo in 1204. His grave is in Tiberias. He was also a medical doctor and in Egypt served the sultan Saladin (1138-1193) as court physician. Saladin defeated the Crusaders in 1187 at Hattin near Tiberias and conquered Jerusalem. Maimonides thus lived and worked in a world dominated by Muslims, and he wondered about the meaning of the other two traditions, Christianity and Islam, that had developed out of the same source of inspiration, namely, his Jewish religion. He declared in his work, *Guide for the Perplexed,* which was originally written in Arabic: "As a whole, Muslims are not idol worshippers, and they proclaim the complete unity of God in the proper way."[13] Elsewhere he writes:

> It is beyond the human mind to fathom the designs of the Creator; for our ways are not his ways, neither are our thoughts his thoughts (Isaiah 55:8). All these matters relating to Jesus of Nazareth and the Ishmaelite (Mohammed) who came after him, served to clear the way for King

13. Quoted by Geoffrey Wigoder, *Joodse Cultuur: Oorsprong en bloei* (Baarn: Ambo, 1994) 71.

xvii

Messiah, to prepare the whole world to worship God with one accord, as it is written, For then will I turn to the peoples a pure language, that they may all call upon the name of the Lord to serve Him with one consent (Zephaniah 3:9).[14]

The question "Is Muhammad also included among the prophets?" could also be answered affirmatively by Jews and Christians. It is of great importance for Jews, Christians, and Muslims to read the Torah, the Gospel, and the Qur'an together and attempt to understand them as much as possible in association with one another. That is more than ever the order of the day, given that those Sacred Texts have often been — and still are — read, understood, and explained by each *over against* the others. These three books demand answers from one another. They must interrogate one another and should be constantly brought into conversation and discussed with one another.

The common message of the three books is directed to all who would hear it, all who know they have been "called": those who are called by God through the service of the prophets. Historically, this concerns the three separate communities. The Jewish community is the *qahal,* which literally means "called." The Christian community is called *ecclesia,* which is the Greek translation in the Septuagint and the New Testament of the Hebrew word *qahal.* The Muslim community is called *umma.* In the Qur'an this refers to a community that shares in a communal service to God. Abraham/ Ibrâhîm was a community, an *umma,* in himself (Q 16:120), the prototype for the true believers (cf. Q 3:67; 2:128, 134, 141).[15] A messenger is sent to each community (Q 10:47). There is mention of one community of humankind, of which God is Lord (Q 23:52), and the community of prophetic messengers is seen as one community (Q 21:92). A division has emerged (Q 21:93) over the course of history in the community that was one (Q 16:120; cf. 2:213). The people belonged to one community but had different views (Q 10:19). "And from you, namely, those who have submitted to God, will come one community that enjoins what is good and forbids what is odious. These people will be successful" (Q 3:104).[16]

---

14. Quoted by Harold Kasimow and Byron L. Sherwin, eds., *No Religion Is an Island: Abraham Joshua Heschel and Interreligious Dialogue* (Maryknoll: Orbis, 1991) 20-21.

15. Rudi Paret, *Der Koran: Kommentar und Konkordanz* (Stuttgart: Kohlhammer, 1971) on Q 16:120.

16. *EI,* s.v. *umma.*

Do These Books Have a Message for Contemporary Cities?

Just as Dickens's *A Tale of Two Cities* can be used as a key to understanding the French Revolution and its consequences, so I will attempt in this book to answer the question: What do the Bible and the Qur'an, as one "tale of two cities," have to say to us concerning our contemporary "cities"? Do these prophetic tales still have meaning today? Or do our modern cities have nothing to learn from the Bible and the Qur'an? That is what many think at least: Are religions and their holy books — not only the Qur'an — not the cause of violence and terror more than they are their solution?

The title, *The Torah, the Gospel, and the Qur'an: Three Books, Two Cities, One Tale*, contains a message. In the course of this book I will show to what extent the three books are, in the end, one tale, and what the thread is that runs through them in the critical prophetic message, which is not in the last place a social-critical one, which binds these three Books. My intention in doing so is to show what relevance this one tale has for Jews, Christians, and Muslims together — and thus for all people in the world today.

Outline

The structure of this book is as follows. It begins with "'A Tale of Two Cities' in History," how historians, writers, and poets have spoken about the oppositions and conflicts between the two "realms" (Chapter 1). Then we will look at how Muhammad's call as prophet is to be understood in relation to the calls of other biblical prophets. This will demonstrate and elaborate more precisely the connection between the three Books (Chapter 2). Evidently, human beings have been faced with a choice since creation: to be the representative of God on earth, a caliph, or to be a perpetrator of injustice (Chapter 3). Abraham, Moses, Jesus, and Muhammad call people to the exodus, to emigration, *hijra*, to break with the city of injustice and to go to the promised land, the "new city," because there justice and righteousness will be done (Chapter 4). What comes of that ideal, however, if the people led by the prophet, complete the journey through the desert and so live in the promised land and promised city? Are justice and righteousness indeed done (Chapter 5)? What is the character of the good or unjust kingship according to the tale of the visitors to the great King Solomon/Sulaymân, particularly that of the queen of Sheba/Bilqîs in Jerusalem (Chapter 6)? How do the three Books deal with the questions of violence, retribution, holy war, and *jihâd* (Chapter 7)? Why are unjust and wicked cities like Sodom and Gomorrah destroyed? Is it connected with homosexuality, or is there something else going on? Abraham prays for the city (Chapter 8). In the tales on the last days, the ultimate seriousness of the whole issue arises: What threatens the city in the end? Figures who have grown into legends and symbols are discussed, such as Gog/Yâjûdh and Magog/Mâjûj, and "the man with two horns," Alexander the Great (Chapter 9). How, in the course of history, have Christians and Muslims explained and applied their tales of two cities (Chapter 10)? How, finally, must this "tale of two cities" be understood according to the three Books together? To whom, in the end, does the victory belong (Chapter 11)?

Acknowledgments

The author is grateful to the following organizations for their financial support of this translation:

VanCoeverden-Adriani Stichting, which has a close relationship with VU University Amsterdam

De Stichting Zonneweelde

Abbreviations

BE	*Bijbelse Encyclopaedie*, ed. F. W. Grosheide et al. Kampen: Kok, 1950
BW	*Bijbels-historisch Woordenboek*, ed. Bo Reicke and Leonard Rost. Vols. 1-6. Utrecht: Spectrum, 1969
EI	*Encylopaedia of Islam*, new ed. Leiden: Brill, 1960-2005
EQ	*Encylopaedia of the Qur'ān*, ed. Jane Dammen McAuliffe. Leiden: Brill, 2001-6
KBS	*De Bijbel uit de grondtekst vertaald: Willibrordvertaling*. Roman Catholic (Willibrord) translation of the Bible
NIV	New International Version
SEI	*Shorter Encyclopaedia of Islam*, ed. H. A. R. Gibb and J. H. Kramers. Leiden: Brill, 1961

CHAPTER I

"A Tale of Two Cities" in History

Nero

The people who gave him the victory should be condemned
more than Nero.

For what was Nero that they worshipped him so?
A brute blinded by power.

A dwarf lifted by them on a shield,
They knelt and he swelled with pride.

They glorified him, lengthened his shadow
So that his heinous deeds had an endless reach.

When they gave him their power he became
A true tyrant and committed violent misdeeds.

Whoever has power only uses violence
If he did not fear violence from those who gave him power.

Nero may be condemned, but I condemn the nation.
Had they resisted, he would have retreated.

Every people produces its own Nero
Whether he is called Caesar or Chosroës.

Khalil Mutran, Lebanon

Introduction

Throughout the centuries, history has been interpreted in one way or another as a "tale of two cities," two kingdoms, two powers, or power blocks that were opposed to each other: East over against West. Thus, Homer's *Iliad* is about the Greek city of Sparta over against the Asian city of Troy: Greeks versus barbarians. It is said that the Persian invasion of Greece in the second decade of the fifth century B.C. led to the invention of the concept of barbarian. Greek stereotypes of barbarians served the interest of the dominant culture. In the Hellenistic period (323-146 B.C.), which began with the death of Alexander the Great and ended with the annexation of Greece by the Roman Empire, the negative stereotypes of enemies helped consolidate the struggle against the Persians. Centuries later, during the Middle Ages, similar negative images informed the Christian attitude toward Jews and justified the social oppression of the latter. Such labels about Muslims during the whole period of the Crusades (A.D. 1095-1291) and after helped stoke Christian aggression.[1] Each side is clear on who was right and who was wrong. Writers, poets, and historians wrote their stories about them. Just as the question "Why do they hate us?" was raised after 9/11, so thousands of years ago it was already asked why the people of the West and the East found it so difficult to live in peace with each other.

One of the famous works of literature on such a conflict is the *Iliad* by Homer. Homer's tales have appealed to the imagination throughout the centuries and still do. In 1990, the Colombian Ministry of Culture set up traveling libraries that were to bring books to the inhabitants of remote areas. The books that were borrowed were dutifully returned until one day a Spanish translation of the *Iliad* was borrowed and not returned. When the books had to be returned, the villagers refused to do so. In the end, they were allowed to keep it but were asked why they wanted to have that book in particular. Their explanation was: That tale is our own tale; it is about a country torn by war in which insane gods mingle with men and women who never know precisely what the reason behind the fighting is or when they will be happy and why they die.[2]

This chapter will explore a number of "tales of two cities," starting

1. Debra Higgs Strickland, *Saracens, Demons, and Jews: Making Monsters in Medieval Art* (Princeton: Princeton University Press, 2003) 40.

2. Alberto Manguel, *Homer's the Iliad and the Odyssey: A Biography* (New York: Grove, 2007) 13.

with that of Babylon and Jerusalem. We will look at the conflicts that occurred in history when two cities, two kingdoms, stood opposed to each other: Sparta and Troy, Greeks and Trojans, as described by Homer. If the historical causes of this conflict described in such inimitable fashion have been lost in myth, the effects of those causes have not.[3]

The historical basis is more explicit with regard to the conflict between Athens and Persepolis, again Greeks and Persians: Darius I and the Battle of Marathon in 490 B.C. and the Battle of Salamis under Xerxes in 480. In the fourth century the Persians and Greeks faced each other again during the time of Alexander the Great. Finally, Rome — the new Troy — praised by the Roman poet Virgil, stands over against Carthage, a Phoenician city, and later over against Alexandria in the Battle of Actium in 31 B.C. Wherever possible and applicable, we will connect these tales to those in the Bible and the Qur'an.

Babylon

The most important cities in ancient times owe a great deal of their existence and development to their location on a river (Memphis, Thebes, Babylon), the sea (Ugarit, Tyre, Alexandria), or the major roads (Damascus, Palmyra, Dura-Europos, and Mecca). Babylon is one of the oldest cities in the country of Shinar (Sinear), a traditional name for Babylonia (Gen 10:10; 11:2; cf. Gen 14:1, 9; Isa 11:11; Dan 1:2; Zech 5:11).[4]

The Tanakh speaks of a strong awareness of the presence of Babylon internationally and the direct impact that city had on the destiny of Jerusalem. In a series of military campaigns, the Neo-Babylonian king Nebuchadnezzar II (605-562 B.C.) destroyed Jerusalem and carried off large numbers of Jews to exile in Babylon. These campaigns began at the end of the seventh century and reached a climax in 586 with the complete destruction of Jerusalem and the temple. This put an end to the kingdom of Judah and the First Temple period.

The biblical writings give us insight into Judean society, showing the conflicts between the prophets and the kings, between the true prophets and the false ones, in which the true prophets oppose the policies of the kings rather than sanctioning them.[5] One of the most important stories begins

---

3. Tom Holland, *Persian Fire* (New York: Doubleday, 2005) XV.
4. Gwendolyn Leick, *The Babylonian World* (New York: Routledge, 2007) 542.
5. Leick, *The Babylonian World*, 541-42.

with father Abraham/Ibrâhîm, who abandons his homeland, Ur of the Chaldees, to start a new nation in Canaan. But this people is later banished in stages from that land: first by the Assyrians from northern Mesopotamia and then by Nebuchadnezzar II, the king of the Chaldees, from Babylon.[6]

In the history in which the stories in the Bible and the Qur'an take place, there is a world in which two cities, two kingdoms, are constantly opposed. This history covers Assur and Babylon, the centers of the Persians (Persepolis, Ctesiphon), Egypt (Memphis, Alexandria), the Greeks (Athens, Sparta), and the Romans (Rome). During Muhammad's life, he had had to contend with the city of the Byzantines, Constantinople, and that of the Persians, Ctesiphon.

Babylon/Bâbil is built on both the left and right banks of the Euphrates River. Between 1770 and 1670 B.C. it was the largest city in the world and again between 612 (the fall of Nineveh) and 320. In 612 the Neo-Babylonian Empire began. The city fell into the hands of the Persians in 539 and was later conquered by Alexander the Great, who was initially buried there (320). For centuries beginning in 2000, the city played an important role and acquired great symbolic significance. The Babylonians considered their city to be the navel of the universe in which the world was anchored. Marduk is the most prominent god of the Babylonian pantheon. Babylon is the ideologically religious center of an imperialist world power that extended to Asia Minor, the borders of Egypt, Syria, Palestine, and western Iran. It was a multicultural metropolis with a multicultural ambience,[7] where thousands of people with different languages and cultures lived together. Even after the loss of its independence to the Persian king Cyrus the Great (559-529), Babylon[8] remained one of the most prominent melting pots in the Near East. Immigrants, slaves, exiles, and mercenaries filled its streets, the first truly multicultural city in history. From the time of King Hammurabi (ca. 1795-1750), the codifier of laws who lived in Babylon, the city became the cultural and religious center of Mesopotamia and remained that until its end.[9]

The Euphrates flows right through the city and divides it into two halves. In the center of each half is a colossal building: in the one the royal palace and in the other the temple of the Babylonian Marduk, in the middle

---

6. Leick, *The Babylonian World*, 559.

7. Joachim Marzahn et al., *Babylon: Myth and Truth*, vols. 1-2 (Munich: Hirmer, Staatliche Museen zu Berlin, 2008) 487.

8. Holland, *Persian Fire*, 40.

9. Anton Gills, *The Rise and Fall of Babylon: Gateway of the Gods* (London: Quercus, 2008) 8.

of which is a temple tower[10] in honor of this city god. Nimrod is the notorious founder of Babylon, and he is also compared with the legendary Assyrian king Ninus.

Semiramis, a legendary Assyrian queen, is supposed to have been King Ninus's wife. She ruled as queen over all of Asia and is described as the one who gave the glittering city of Babylon its hanging gardens, one of the seven wonders of the world. But she is also described as a lascivious and homicidal woman, a notorious and lusty *femme fatale*.[11]

Nimrod is called the creator of the tower of Babel. The ancient city included a temple tower of the city god Marduk in the form of a ziggurat, a terraced step pyramidal temple. The Vienna version of Peter Bruegel the Elder's (1520-1569) painting *The Tower of Babel* shows Nimrod in the lower left.[12] According to the ninth-century Muslim historian al-Tabarî, Nimrod built the tower that God destroyed, after which God confused the original Syrian language into seventy-two languages.

According to an early Arabic work, Nimrod also built the cities Seleucia and Ctesiphon. The latter was a city in Mesopotamia close to Baghdad; its ruins are 26 kilometers south of Baghdad. It was later the capital of the Parthians, and still later of the Second Persian Empire of the Sassanids. The city was occupied a couple of times by the Romans (Trajan in A.D. 116 and Septimus Severus in 197), conquered a few times by the Byzantines, but returned after peace negotiations. There was a strong Jewish district after the destruction of the Jerusalem temple in A.D. 70. In 637 the city was conquered by the Arabs. The establishment of the new capital, Baghdad, in 751, meant the end of Ctesiphon.

In the Bible, the stories about Babylon can be found spread throughout a number of books. In the Qur'an, the city Babylon, which was well known in the pre-Islamic period in the Arabian Peninsula, is mentioned only once (Q 2:102).[13] Nimrod is the king with whom Abraham disputed (Q 2:258). The ruins of the city can be found 87 kilometers south of Baghdad and are considered to be the oldest in Iraq.[14]

---

10. Marzahn, *Babylon*, 491; Moritz Wullen and Günther Schauerte, eds., *Babylon: Mythos* (Berlin: Staatliche Museen, 2008) 45.

11. Wullen and Schauerte, *Babylon: Mythos*, 75.

12. Wullen and Schauerte, *Babylon: Mythos*, 169.

13. Arthur Jeffery, *The Foreign Vocabulary of the Qur'ān* (Baroda: Oriental Institute, 1938) 74-75. *E.Q.*, *s.v.* "Bâbil."

14. *EI*, *s.v.* "Bâbil."

Truth and Fantasy about Babylon

The name Babylon calls up both positive and negative images. The positive paradisal aspects are the hanging gardens and the city's unparalleled walls, and the negative is the tower of Babel, the symbol of pride. In the eyes of the Jews, this city and tower were the evidence of that pride. The name Babylon was traced back to the Hebrew word for "to confuse," although it actually derives from a Babylonian name that means "gods' gate."[15] In Christian tradition, Babylon is connected with "the whore of Babylon" (Revelation 17) and the antichrist.

Right up until the present, the myth of Babylon has taken precedence over the truth of Babylon. Although the myth of Babylon concerns the Babylonian scenario of enslavement, oppression, and forced labor, the truth about Babylon is more nuanced. There was, for example, no mass arrest at the time of the Babylonian Exile. Rather, this was a forced exile of an elite group from their homeland to the city where the conquerer lived, a common practice in that time. Archaeological and historical discoveries show that Babylon functioned more as a multicultural and liberal melting pot. In the multiethnic Babylon, numerous minorities were treated in a sympathetic way, one that permitted the continuation of Jewish tradition and the unfolding of religious identity. But in Christian tradition, the captivity of the Israelites became a leading metaphor for persecution, enslavement, oppression, and violence.[16]

It has been noted that these stories about Babylon are like video clips. Since the early days of Christianity, Babylon has, through the Bible, gained a central place in European and world consciousness and imagination.[17] This picture has lasted for thousands of years without change: Babylon as the stage of the Apocalypse, as the seat of rulers who, like King Nebuchadnezzar II, the destroyer of Jerusalem (587 b.c.), are viewed as terrible. Every clip has had its own history of influence in the last two thousand years, constantly reflecting the time in which it arose.[18]

---

15. Remco Groetelaers and Jan van Laarhoven, *De waanzin ten top: Driezuidend jaar toren van Babel* (Nijmegen: SUN, 1998) 3, 32.

16. Wullen, *Babylon: Mythos*, 17, 27.

17. Gills, *Gateway of the Gods*, 9.

18. Wullen, *Babylon: Mythos*, 169.

The Babylonian Exile

In 722 B.C., the Assyrians conquered the city of Samaria. The Babylonians adopted the Assyrian strategy of exiling the elite of the rebellious provinces. Nebuchadnezzar II was king of Babylon (605-562 B.C.), and under his reign the Neo-Babylonian Empire reached its apex. He was known for his building projects. He conquered Jerusalem in 597 and again in 587, the second time carrying off a large portion of the population into exile. Thus, the elite of Jerusalem, including King Jehoiachin, were taken captive to Babylon by the Babylonians in 597 (cf. 2 Kgs 24:15): all the army commanders and soldiers, ten thousand people, and all artisans and smiths. Only the most insignificant of the people remained (2 Kgs 24:14). Babylon emerged as the city of slavery and exile, as the city of sin and as the whore of Babylon (Rev 17:3, 5). The writer of the book of Revelation, which dates to A.D. 90, the time of the persecutions under Emperor Domitianus (ruled 81-96), turned against pagan Rome, comparing it to the great "whore of Babylon." Babylon was characterized as the prototype of the antidivine world power, a veiled allusion to the Roman world power that had turned against the church of Christ (Rev 14:8; 16:19; 17:5; 18:2, 10, 21).[19]

Baghdad and Babylon

When Caliph al-Mansür founded Baghdad on the west bank of the Tigris in A.D. 762, he called it *Madînat al-salâm*, "City of Peace," referring to "paradise": "To the pious will fall the house of the peace of salvation *(dâr al-salâm)*" (Q 6:127). European travelers often confused the city of Baghdad with Babylon. The same also holds for exegetical literature of the Babylonian Talmud in the Abbasid period as well as that of later Jewish writers. Eden is irrigated by the Euphrates and the Tigris, both of which provide the Fertile Crescent with water. A tradition in the Talmud connects the garden of Eden with Babylon. The palms in the city of Babylon are thought to go back to the time of Adam and Eve.[20]

Baghdad is said to have been without equal in the world, called into existence by a magician's staff. The city of al-Mansûr thus became heir to the power and prestige of Ctesiphon, Babylon, Nineveh, Ur, and other cities of

---

19. *BE, s.v.* "Babel."
20. *EI, s.v.* "Baghdâd."

the ancient Near East and attained a prestige and splendor unrivalled in the Middle Ages, except perhaps by Constantinople.[21]

Jerusalem

Jerusalem is called *Yerushalayim* in the Hebrew of the Old Testament, a name suggesting "twin cities" and implying "house of peace," "established in safety." Cf. "God has laid his firm foundations on Zion's mount" (Psalm 87 in the *Psalter Hymnal*). Jerusalem is called the dwelling place of God or of his Name (Isa 48:2; Neh 11:1; Dan 9:24). The name Zion was initially nothing more than a reference to the fortress of the Jebusites or the city of David (1 Kgs 8:1). It was extended to refer to the Temple Mount and finally to the whole city of Jerusalem and its inhabitants. Salem is an abbreviated form of the name (Gen 14:18; Ps 76:3[2]). The priest-king Melchizedek from Abraham's time (Gen 14:18) is also called the king of Salem, king of "righteousness and peace" (Heb 5:6).

The Qur'an mentions various important events that occurred in Jerusalem: the condemnation of David after he committed adultery with Bathsheba, Uriah's wife (2 Samuel 12), which is understood as a test (Q 38:21-25); the announcement to the aged Zechariah about the birth of a son, John/Yahyâ (Q 3:39; 19:7); and the stay of the young Mary in the temple, where she is entrusted to Zechariah (Q 3:37).[22] In Arabic, Jerusalem is called *al-Quds*, "the Holy," or *al-muqaddas, al-muqaddis, Bayt al-Maqdis*, "House of the Holy One,"[23] because of the religious significance of the city. The latter has three meanings. First, it means the Jewish temple, the Temple Mount with the Dome of the Rock, *al-Haram al-Sharîf*, and the "Furthest Mosque" or Al-Aqsâ mosque (Q 17:1), the destination of Muhammad's nightly journey *(isrâ')* from Mecca to Jerusalem and the setting for the heavenly journey *(mi'râj)*. It is where stood the Jewish temple that was destroyed by the Romans in A.D. 70 and was the place to which prayer was directed *(qibla)* before that was supplanted by Mecca. Second, it means the city of Jerusalem. Third, it refers to the holy land *(al-ard al-muqaddasa)*. The Qur'anic text "Who is more unrighteous than those who forbid God's name from being

21. Philip K. Hitti, *History of the Arabs* (8th ed.; New York: St. Martin's, 1964) 302, 293.

22. *Protevangelium of James*. Cf. Wilhelm Schneemelcher, ed., *New Testament Apocrypha*, vol. 1, trans. R. McL. Wilson (rev. ed. Louisville: Westminster John Knox, 1991).

23. Derived from Hebrew *Bêt ha-miqdâsh* ("the temple").

mentioned in the places of worship and who are devoted to destroying them?" (Q 2:114) can be seen as a reference to the destruction of the temple by Nebuchadnezzar in 587 B.C. or Titus's destruction of the rebuilt temple in A.D. 70. The prophet Jeremiah, who weeps over the destruction of the temple, is associated with the "man" who passed by a town that he views as a ruin (Q 2:259; cf. Lam 1:17).[24]

When the Persian scholar al-Bîrûnî (A.D. 973-1048) discusses the conquest of Jerusalem by the Roman emperor Titus (39-81), he remarks that the population of Jerusalem called everyone who destroyed the city a Nebuchadnezzar. In an unusual miniature in a fourteenth-century manuscript, Nebuchadnezzar is described as the one who destroyed Jerusalem. The Dome of the Rock, which is no older than the seventh century, is clearly visible in that miniature. The association is connected with the idea that the Dome of the Rock was itself part of the temple that Solomon is said to have built.[25]

Homer: Sparta and Troy

The stories by Homer in the *Iliad* and the *Odyssey* are about the enticement of war and the striving for peace. What was the reason for the Trojan War? The son of the king of Troy (Paris) abducted Helen, wife of the king of Sparta, Menelaus. The blind singer or poet Homer narrates the destruction of the Trojan city as a result of the war that ensued. He begins with singing about the wrath of the greatest Greek hero of that war, Achilles. During the siege of Troy, Achilles is insulted by Agamemnon, king of Mycenae and brother of Menelaus. Agamemnon has taken charge of the expedition against Troy. He quarrels with Achilles over the possession of the captured slavegirl Briseis, who was taken by Achilles during the invasion of her city. But Agamemnon now takes her away from him by force, thus Achilles' grudge against Agamemnon, who says:

> I am going to pay a visit to your hut and take away the beautiful Briseis, your prize, Achilles, to let you know that I am more powerful than you, and to teach others not to bandy words with and openly defy their King. (*Iliad*, I, 184-87)[26]

24. *EQ, s.v.* Jerusalem. Other meanings are also given.

25. Irving L. Finkel and Michael J. Seymour, *Babylon: Myth and Reality* (London: British Museum Press, 2008) 149.

26. Homer, *The Iliad*, trans. E. V. Rieu (Harmondsworth: Penguin, 1950).

When Achilles is about to fly at Agamemnon with his sword, the goddess Athena suddenly appears, visible only to him:

[He] spoke out to her boldly: "And why have you come here, Daughter of aegis-bearing[27] Zeus? Is it to witness the arrogance of my lord Agamemnon?" (*Iliad*, I, 201-2)

Athena tells him to sheathe his sword and prophesies:

The day will come when gifts three times as valuable as what you now have lost will be laid at your feet in payment for this outrage. Hold your hand, then, and be advised by us.[28] (*Iliad*, I, 212-14)

Out of wrath, Achilles withdraws from the battle and only after his bosom friend Patroclus dies does he take up arms again to avenge himself on Patroclus's killer, Hector, the son of the Trojan king.

The *Iliad* opens as follows:

The wrath of Achilles is my theme, that fatal wrath which, in fulfilment of the will of Zeus, brought the Achaeans[29] so much suffering and sent the gallant souls of so many noblemen to Hades,[30] leaving their bodies as carrion for the dogs and passing birds. Let us begin, goddess of song, with the angry parting that took place between Agamemnon, King of Men, and the great Achilles son of Peleus. Which of the gods was it that made them quarrel? (*Iliad*, I, 1-7)

In his second epic, the *Odyssey*, Homer writes about the adventures of Odysseus and the aftermath of the destruction of Troy, which becomes the story of an exile. The cities are destroyed, and the survivors wander over all the earth like pirates and beggars. Achilles' mother Thetis puts the choice to her son: a happy but obscure old age or an early death with glory. Achilles does not hesitate to choose the latter. He will die young and famous.[31]

Homer has his readers and audience sympathize with both the Trojans and the Greeks, and perhaps more with Priam, the king of Troy, and his son

27. Aegis, Zeus's (Jupiter's) shield.
28. Zeus and Athena.
29. Greeks.
30. The underworld.
31. Holland, *Persian Fire*, 268.

Hector than with Achilles and Agamemnon.[32] The *Iliad* is a monument to war. As an example of the surprising didactic features one could point to the power with which the motives of the conquerors are described. It is indeed a story written by the conqueror, but perhaps the reader will remember primarily the human side of the Trojans, such as Priam and Hector and Hector's wife Andromache. There is a stubborn love for peace.[33]

Scholars have noted the feminine side of the *Iliad:* "Relations between men and women in human society are already a major theme of the *Iliad,* in spite of its military setting; in the *Odyssey,* these gender relations are at the very center of the story." Before the battle in which he will die, Hector goes inside the city of Troy and meets three women. All three give voice to the same entreaty, each with her own emotional nuance: *peace.* His mother asks him to pray with her, Helen to lie down at her side to rest, and, finally, Andromache, Hector's wife, to let his role as father and husband count for more than that of hero and warrior. Two possible worlds are opposed, and each has its own motifs: Hector's is inflexible, more shortsighted, and Andromache's modern and much more human. In countless passages of the *Iliad,* the heroes talk rather than fight. There are endless meetings, endless debates, a way of postponing the battle as long as possible. It makes one think of Scheherazade from *A Thousand and One Nights,* who escapes death by telling a new story night after night. The word is the weapon with which they cheat death. "They are all condemned to die, but they make their last cigarette last an eternity, and they also smoke them with words" (Book IV).[34]

The *Odyssey* contains a short dialogue between Odysseus and the shade of the deceased Achilles. After Odysseus first addressed Achilles in all kinds of laudatory terms, Achilles' ghost answers:

> I would rather be a serf in the house of some landless man, with little enough for himself to live on, than king of all these dead men that have done with life. (*Odyssey,* XI, 488-91)[35]

A commentary on this quotation remarks that Achilles would never have said this when he was alive. Doing so would have meant peace for Troy.

---

32. John Burrow, *A History of Histories: Epics, Chronicles, Romances and Inquiries from Herodotus and Thucydides to the Twentieth Century* (New York: Knopf, 2008) 11.

33. Andrew Dalby, *Rediscovering Homer: Inside the Origins of the Epic* (New York: Norton, 2006) 128; cf. 86-88.

34. Alessandro Baricco, *De Ilias van Homerus* (Breda: De Geus, 2004) 182-84.

35. Homer, *The Odyssey,* trans. E. V. Rieu (Harmondsworth: Penguin, 1946).

Did that great disaster for the Greeks and Trojans not occur partly as a result of Achilles' wrath about which the opening lines of the *Iliad* speak? It has been suggested that, with this outburst by Achilles in the underworld, Homer — now older and after having written the *Iliad* — is questioning, in the *Odyssey*, the whole impulse behind the *Iliad*. The latter is characterized by "the mercilessness of the young." Perhaps Homer later considered this view to be incomplete. It could be that, in the evening of his life, this widely-traveled poet returned to the world of the *Iliad*. Now he has doubts about the whole enterprise.[36] But actually, one could say, this reserve with respect to a simplistic black-and-white point of view is already absent from the *Iliad* itself, and a critical view is taken of the use of violence and war.

Herodotus's "Tale of Two Cities"

In the fifth century B.C., the Greek traveler Herodotus (ca. 485-425), often seen as the world's first historian and the "father of historiography" (Cicero), made the conflict between East and West his lifelong theme. The question of the causes of this conflict has been seen as a question from which history or historiography emerged. In his comprehensive work *The Histories*, Herodotus describes the history of the violent confrontation between East and West, between Greeks and "barbarians," which reached its apex in the Persian Wars.

Herodotus places what he understood as being Greek in the mouths of the Athenian speakers who appealed to their allies, the Spartans, at a crucial moment in the decisive conflict between the Greeks and barbarians, the non-Greek Persians, during the winter of 480/479:

> There is not so much gold in the world nor land so fair that we would take it for pay to join the common enemy and bring Greece into subjec-
> tion. There are many compelling reasons against our doing so, even if we
> wished: the first and greatest is the burning of the temples and images of
> our gods — now ashes and rubble. It is our bounden duty to avenge this
> desecration with all our might — not to clasp the hand that wrought it.
> Again, there is the Greek nation — the community of blood and lan-
> guage, temples and ritual; our common way of life; if Athens were to be-

---

36. George Steiner, "Homer and the Scholars," in *Language and Silence* (London: Faber, 1985) 200, 211, 213. Cf. Dalby, *Rediscovering Homer*, ch. 5, 111-14.

tray all this, it would not be well done. We would have you know, therefore, if you did not know it already, that so long as a single Athenian remains alive we will make no peace with Xerxes. (*Histories*, VIII, 144)[37]

Herodotus was originally from the Greek colony of Halicarnassus on the eastern coast of the Aegean Sea. He thus belonged to a part of the Greek world that had been transplanted into Asia, an area that was the source of conflict between the Greeks and the Persians. This fact played an important role in Herodotus's account of history. He was thus born as a subject of the Persian king Cyrus the Great (559-529 B.C.), who had defeated the great empire of the Medes by his conquest of their capital Ectabana (553), and subjected the Greek cities of Ionia in 546 and Babylon in 539 because the priests of the god Marduk had opened the city gates for him. This established the Old Persian Empire. He would allow the Jewish exiles to return from Babylon in 538.

Herodotus provides examples of the friction, both mythical and legendary, between Europe and Asia. With respect to the latter, one can think here of the Argonauts under Jason's leadership. These were Greek heroes who went to Colchis (modern Georgia) on the Black Sea to obtain the Golden Fleece. One can hear an echo here of the trade expeditions to the rich East. Herodotus leaves no doubt that the heart of the Greek resistance to the Persians comes from the city of Athens.

Although Herodotus never speaks contemptuously of the Persians, the political and moral differences between them and the Greeks constitute an important part of his message. He characterizes Athens as the great champion of Greek freedom over against Eastern despotism. This contrast would become a permanent theme in Western historiography and political thinking: freedom is placed over against slavery, law over against the whim of tyrants.

Herodotus saw the starting point for this conflict in the illegal acts committed by the Lydian king Croesus (ruled 560-546 B.C.), who was legendary because of his wealth. He was the richest man in the world. Lydia was a strong country between Greece and Persia, and Croesus conquered the Asian Greek cities on the coast of Asia Minor, such as Ephesus. He was the first Asian we know of to do so, and compelled the cities to pay tribute.[38]

The Persian emperor Darius I, the Great (521-486 B.C.), was the most

---

37. Paul Cartledge, *Ancient Greece: A History in Eleven Cities* (Oxford: Oxford University Press, 2009) 4-5; Herodotus, *The Histories*, trans. Aubrey de Sélincourt, rev. A. R. Burn (Harmondsworth: Penguin, 1972).

38. Holland, *Persian Fire*, xv.

important Persian ruler in antiquity. By constructing major strategic roads (2684 km, the "king's highway"), he connected the provinces of his empire from the city of Susa in Persia to Sardis in Asia Minor. From 500 to 494 Darius fought an uprising of Ionian Greeks. He demanded the total surrender of the Greek city-states on the coast of Asia. Many gave in to Darius's demand, but Athens and Sparta refused. The stage was thus prepared for the first invasion of Europe by Asia against the European Greeks, primarily directed against the Athenians and the Spartans.[39] The return of the Jews from Babylonia occurred under his reign, and the rebuilding of the temple continued. In the second year of his reign Darius permitted the temple to be rebuilt (Ezra 4:24), the costs for which were to be paid completely from the royal treasury (Ezra 6:6-15). The prophets Haggai and Zechariah appeared in that same year (Hag 1:1; 2:10; Zech 1:7) and Zechariah in the fourth year of his reign as well (Zech 7:1).

Susa was one of the most prominent cities in the Persian Empire. As the capital of the Achemenids, it was the setting for the book of Esther during the reign of the Persian king Xerxes or Ahasverosh (486–ca. 446 B.C.). It was there that in March 446, Nehemiah, the Jewish cupbearer of the Persian king Artaxerxes I (465-424), asked the king for permission, as governor of Judea, to rebuild the walls of Jerusalem (Nehemiah 2–3). During Artaxerxes' rule, the Jews were allowed to return from Babylonia and also to continue rebuilding the temple in Jerusalem. Together with the prophet Haggai, Nehemiah pleaded for the rebuilding of the temple that had been destroyed by Nebuchadnezzar in 586 (Ezra 5:1-5; 6:14). The rebuilding was permitted but only slowly got underway. Susa is where the prophet Daniel received a vision dealing with the empires of the Medes and Persians and the ascent of Alexander the Great and his successors (Daniel 8).

The Battle of Marathon (490 B.C.)

On 12 September 490 B.C., the famous Battle of Marathon took place on the eastern coast of Attica between the Persians and the Athenians who were led by the charismatic Miltiades, statesman and general (ca. 550-489). Miltiades

---

39. Burrow, *A History of Histories*, 12-13, 17-18. G. J. M. Bartelink, *Klassieke letterkunde: Overzicht van de Griekse en Latijnse literatuur* (Utrecht: Spectrum, 1989), *s.v.* "Argonauten"; Kaveh Farrokh, *Shadows in the Desert: Ancient Persia at War* (New York: Midland House, 2009) 72.

was made general in 490 because of his anti-Persian sentiment and his familiarity with Persian military tactics. It was in that role that he gained victory over the invading Persian army at Marathon in the First Greek-Persian War, during which the Persians attempted to add the Greek city-states to their empire. The Persian army was led by Datis, commander of the Persian land and sea troops. Datis was a Median admiral serving the Persian Empire under the leadership of Darius I in the first campaign against the Greeks. He brought his large armada to Marathon and had taken along marble in the expectation of celebrating a victory. Although the Persians were numerically stronger than the approximiately ten thousand hoplites, the heavily-armed Greek infantry, the Greeks were still victorious.

The marathon as known in modern athletics is derived from this event: a courier is said to have run the estimated 40 kilometers from the battlefield to Athens to bring tidings of the victory, even though it cost him his life. It could be that this is a romanticized version of the race by Militiades' main forces to protect the city of Athens from the Persians. In essence, the victory in Marathon was achieved by the hoplites led by the mastermind Miltiades.[40] Marathon proved to be the first in a series of military and political shocks that would eventually bring down the Persian Empire. Darius died in 486, four years after Marathon, and the mantle of kingship passed to his son Xerxes I. The Athenians built the Parthenon to celebrate the victory at Marathon. With his plans for the Acropolis, Pericles (490-429 B.C.), statesman and army commander, wanted to preserve the memory of that battle for all eternity, and Marathon was seen by the Athenians as the greatest victory of all time. The Persians, of course, had a different perspective.[41]

The Persian Attack on the Greek Cities

The Persian king Xerxes I (486–ca. 446 B.C.) had already been appointed successor to his father, Darius I the Great, while the latter was still alive. This Xerxes appears in the Bible as Ahashverosh, and the Jew Esther was his wife. The story of his vizier Haman is connected with these two figures. In the Qur'an, Haman called the servant or minister of the Egyptian pharaoh (Q 28:6; 28:8), who orders him to build a high palace, an allusion to the tower of

---

40. Cartledge, *Ancient Greece*, 98.
41. Holland, *Persian Fire*, 368-69, 202; Farrokh, *Shadows in the Desert*, 74, 77-79, 46; Holland, *Persian Fire*, 73.

Babel, an expression of pride (Q 28:38; 40:36, 37). Xerxes is considered to have been less gifted than his father. He was confronted with uprisings in Egypt and Babylon. The campaign in Egypt ended in 484, and he put down the uprisings in Babylon ruthlessly. The increasing alienation of the sub-jected populations as a result of repressive measures planted the seed that would lead to the decline of the Persian Empire 150 years later.

Xerxes chose to go to war again with Greece ten years after the defeat at Marathon. In Xerxes' view, the invasion of Greece was part of the unfinished task of his father. To the Persians, the Greeks had challenged the authority of the king, and they had to be brought to their knees. Xerxes invaded Greece with a huge army. A gigantic bridge over the Hellespont, consisting of two massive floating bridges of 670 ships, made it possible for his army of 120 thousand troops to cross from Asia to Europe. On 17 September 480 B.C. Xerxes approached the narrow pass at Thermopylae. Leonidas I was king of Sparta at the time, from 488 to 480. Three hundred Spartans under his com-mand, along with three hundred hoplites, fought to the last man against the superior forces of the enormous invading army. Leonidas was defeated and killed with all his men. To the Persians, the victory seemed to be their birth-right, an aura of invincibility hung over them. Despite the Greeks' heroic re-sistance, Athens was occupied and its shrines destroyed. The Persian troops occupied the heights facing the Acropolis, "High City," sometimes simply called "City" *(polis).*[42] Athens was plundered on 27 September and burned. Both the old temple of Athena and the new temple, which they had just be-gun building, called the proto-Parthenon, were destroyed by the Persians.[43]

Battle of Salamis (480 B.C.)

Ten years after Marathon, another battle took place that has also become the stuff of legend. In the Second Persian War between the Greek city-states and Persia, Persian forces were led by Xerxes I in a sea battle in the strait between Piraeus and Salamis. The Persian land forces were accompanied by a fleet of 1,207 ships. According to Herodotus, Xerxes committed the sin of hubris when he castigated the Hellespont after a storm had destroyed his bridges. The report of the disaster infuriated him, and, Herodotus writes: "He gave orders that the Hellespont should receive three hundred lashes and have a

---

42. Cartledge, *Ancient Greece,* 91.
43. Farrokh, *Shadows in the Desert,* 74, 77-79, 46; Holland, *Persian Fire,* xv.

pair of fetters thrown into it. I have heard before now that he also sent people to brand it with hot irons" (*Histories*, VII, 35).[44] In one episode Xerxes appears as very sympathetic and human. He is sitting on a throne of white marble and is able to oversee his whole army and fleet. Then suddenly, at the moment of his greatest glory, he weeps.

Xerxes now decides to hold a review of his army, at Abydos, a city on the Hellespont. On a rise of ground nearby, the people of Abydos had already specially prepared a throne of white marble for his use; so the king took his seat upon it and, looking down over the shore, was able to see the whole of his army and navy at a single view. As he watched them, he was seized with the desire to witness a rowing-match. The match took place and was won by the Phoenicians of Sidon, to the great delight of Xerxes, who was as pleased with the race as with his army. And when he saw the whole Hellespont hidden by ship, and all the beaches and plains of Abydos filled with men, he congratulated himself — and the moment after burst into tears. His uncle Artabanus, the man who in the first instance had spoken so freely in trying to dissuade Xerxes from undertaking the campaign, was by his side, and when he saw how Xerxes wept, he said to him: "My lord, surely there is a strange contradiction in what you do now and what you did a moment ago. You called yourself a lucky man — and now you weep." "I was thinking," Xerxes replies, "and it came into my mind how pitifully short human life is — for of all these thousands of men not one will be alive in a hundred years' time" (*Histories*, VII, 44-46). John Burrow comments, "It is an extraordinary moment, at which, thanks to Xerxes, or Herodotus, the political distinctions between peoples and even, for us, the gulf between ancient and modern melt away in the contemplation of a common human lot."[45]

The Athenian statesman and admiral Themistocles (524–ca. 460 B.C.), who expected that the Persians would take revenge for Marathon, argued that only a reinforced fleet could protect Athens from a complete defeat. The decisive factor in Herodotus's report is Themistocles' interpretation of the Delphic Oracle, whose prophets had declared, cryptically as usual, that "the wooden wall only shall not fall" (*Histories*, VII, 141-44). This prediction was believed to refer to the Athenian ships.

As soon as Xerxes arrived, Themistocles realized that Xerxes would choose to fight on the open sea, given his numerical superiority. Themistocles then convinced the rest of the Greeks to sail into the narrow strait of

44. Burrow, *A History of Histories*, 16.
45. Burrow, *A History of Histories*, 17.

Salamis and to entice Xerxes to follow them there. The Persians fell for the deadly ruse. The Athenians, who had retreated to the "wooden bulwarks" of their ships, waited for the Persian ships in the bay of the island of Salamis. For Xerxes, with his huge fleet, victory seemed just a matter of time. Self-confident and proud, this "king of kings" had assumed a position from which he could watch the spectacle of the sea battle between both fleets with his own eyes. It was a beautiful summer day; he had the rising sun at his back, a pleasant breeze was blowing. A kind of canopy of gold cloth had been suspended above his throne. He sat there in his golden armor, with a new, high-tapered diadem on his head. His black beard had been perfumed. He looked contentedly and benignly around him. The god of the Persians would help him and those with him. Then the battle started, and, although the Persian king's forces were superior, he misjudged the situation. By allowing himself to be tricked into sailing his large fleet into a much too narrow bay, he lost the advantage of his superior forces, and that led ultimately to his defeat. In anger he ordered a number of his Phoenician sea commanders to be executed for cowardice. This self-confident, proud king finally had to flee quickly to save his life, and did so disgracefully. The Battle of Salamis marked the turning point of the war, and the Persian advance was stopped. Herodotus placed his description of this final battle at the center of his history of the world in which he wanted to record the origins of the Greek-Persian wars.[46]

Aeschylus and Salamis

The writer Aeschylus (ca. 525-456 B.C.), himself an eyewitness of the Battle of Salamis, composed a tragedy about the event. His *The Persians* (472), the only tragedy with a historical subject that has been preserved, describes the battle and its effect on the Persians in the capital city of Susa. Aeschylus portrays the dismay that the Persian loss caused there and the reactions to the return of the defeated Xerxes. The people in Susa had awaited news of the army in Greece with some worry. The king had left Persia with all pomp and circumstance, but returned in rags. While his court thought they could welcome him back as a conquering hero, the weeping of misery could be heard on all sides. The queen mother Atossa, an Achemenid queen and daughter of Cyrus the Great (550-475), wife of Darius I and mother of their oldest son

---

46. Farrokh, *Shadows in the Desert*, 80-81; Burrow, *A History of Histories*, 15-17.

Xerxes, lived through the invasion of Greece. It was because of her position that Xerxes could succeed his father. She had a terrifying dream in which a messenger came with the report of the catastrophe. The shade of Darius appeared from the underworld to announce that the hubris of the Persians was the reason for their crushing defeat. At the end of the play, Xerxes himself appears as a defeated man.[47] Aeschylus wants to put his fellow citizens at ease and opines that Athens, the city that beat Xerxes, was now the beacon of freedom for nations everywhere: the world has been made safer for Athens and democracy.[48]

The Greeks and the Persians at the Time of Alexander the Great

After having conquered Greece shortly before, Philip II, the king of Macedonia (ruled 359-336 B.C.) and father of Alexander III (356-323), the emperor known as Alexander the Great, was given the task of going to war with Persia for revenge. This task was given not least because of the desecration of the temples in Athens during Xerxes' invasion, a war that was also seen as a "holy war." The Greeks had been pondering revenge on their archenemy for a long time. Alexander was charged with the holy war against Persia, which was led at that time by Darius III (335-330).

Among Alexander's illustrious teachers was none less than the philosopher Aristotle. When, at age twenty, Alexander succeeded his father after the latter's murder (was Alexander involved in this?), he quickly became one of the greatest conquerers the world has ever seen. Since his youth, Alexander had always had great ambitions. His favorite book on all his expeditions was Homer's *Iliad*. In 336 B.C., with an army of fifty thousand, Alexander crossed the Hellespont and invaded Asia to engage the Persian king in battle. The first thing Alexander did when he landed on Asian ground was to plant a spear in the ground near Troy as a symbol of his claim to the region. In Troy he visited the grave of Achilles, the great Greek hero from the Trojan War, his great example. He took Achilles' shield with him on his further journeys, and this shield would one time save his life. At the beginning of June 334, at the river Granicus, Alexander defeated Darius's occupying Persian forces. This was the first battle. In 333 he defeated the Persian king again at Issus, although Darius himself managed to escape. After this battle, the

---

47. Bartelink, *Klassieke letterkunde*, 51.
48. Holland, *Persian Fire*, 360.

city of Sidon in Phoenicia, modern Lebanon, surrendered voluntarily to Alexander, but the capture in 332 of the nearby island city of Tyre was more difficult. Tyre, whose name means "rock," was a trading center on an island in the middle of the sea.

Tyre flourished under the reign of Hiram I (969-936 B.C.), the friend of King David/Dâwûd and Solomon/Sulaymân, to whom Hiram sent cedars, carpenters, and stonemasons in connection with the building of the palace of David (2 Sam 5:11) and of the temple in Jerusalem by Solomon (1 Kgs 5:1-18). The king of Tyre considered himself equal to God and would therefore be brought to ruin, as a prophet foretold: "Son of man, say to the ruler of Tyre, 'This is what the Sovereign LORD says: 'In the pride of your heart you say, "I am a god; I sit on the throne of a god in the heart of the seas." But you are a mere mortal and not a god, though you think you are as wise as a god'" (Ezek 28:2). The prophets foretold the destruction of the powerful city (Isaiah 23; Ezekiel 26, 28; Amos 1:9-10). But the capture of Tyre by Alexander took a siege of seven months. Alexander had a dam 600 meters long built from the coast to the island rock on which Tyre was built: this was the end of Tyre's supremacy.

In the same year, Alexander conquered Egypt, where, in the Zeus-Ammon shrine in the Siwa oasis, he was inaugurated as a "son of the deity." He also founded the city of Alexandria. Alexander's greatest urban legacy lay in the new cities that he and his successors built: in addition to Alexandria were Antioch and Seleucia. Each of these cities was designed with an *agora*, a temple, and government buildings. Alexandria was the largest of those cities, designed as a transshipment point for trade between Africa, the Near East, and the Mediterranean area.[49] In the first century A.D., Alexandria had about one million inhabitants and was the second largest city of the world and the largest trade center, exporting papyrus, linen, and — especially to Rome — grain (Acts 27:6; 28:11). The lighthouse on the island of Pharos was one of the seven wonders of the world.

In Gaugamela, on the Mesopotamian plain of Mosul, Alexander managed once again to put Darius to flight. The city was an expansive metropolis with a good agricultural system, whereby it was able to withstand lengthy sieges. Babylon, however, did not offer any resistance: the Persians opened the gates for him. A great deal of plundered wealth was seized and divided among his troops. In 330 B.C., the city of Persepolis went up in flames after being captured. Darius I the Great had begun building the city of Parsa in

49. Joel Kotkin, *The City: A Global History* (New York: Modern Library, 2005) 24-25.

520, better known to the Greeks as Persepolis, "the city of the Persians," which was completed by his successor Xerxes (486-465) who had already supervised the construction when crown prince. In addition to Ecbatana and Susa, Persepolis also functioned as a residence of the Achemenids. The Persian name for Persepolis means "the throne of Jamshid." One of the most important functions to occur there was the Persian New Year's Festival, whose origin was ascribed to the legendary King Jamshid. *Nowruz,* literally "new year," means harmony, respect, diversity, unity, regeneration, and the exchange of gifts. The feast is still celebrated in Iran today as a New Year's feast, at the beginning of spring, and is not limited to a specific religious group. Alexander found gigantic royal treasures in Susa and Persepolis. In the latter he pondered the vicissitudes of fortune when viewing the enormous statue of the Persian emperor Xerxes the Great, who had been overthrown and beheaded by his soldiers. Alexander conquered Persia and finally reached India. He died in Babylon in 323 on the return journey during a campaign against the Arab peoples.

Nevertheless, Alexander wanted a union of the Persians and Greeks, with him as imperator. That is why he encouraged mixed marriages between his Macedonian officers and the nobility of Susa. But Zoroastrian sources see Alexander as the great destroyer because he killed the "wise people" of Persia. Many works of Persian literature, particularly scholarly works and Zoroastrian texts, were lost during Alexander's conquests. In the Islamic period, ca. A.D. 1000, the *Shahnameh Epic* was written by the poet and writer Ferdowsi (935-1020) and became the national epic of the Persians. This poem narrates the mythical and historical past of Iran from creation to the Islamic conquest in the seventh century. Here Darius and Alexander are depicted as half-brothers. Alexander may have sought revenge for Xerxes' burning and destruction of the temples of Greece, and the Zoroastrian sources may have exaggerated Alexander's destruction, but the fact remains that the Persians suffered intensely at his hands.[50]

The apocalyptic book of Daniel alludes to Alexander's empire as the "iron kingdom" (Daniel 7). In the Qur'an Alexander is called the "man with two horns *(Dhû al-Qarnayn)*" (Q 18:83-98).[51]

In A.D. 871, the historian Ibn ʿAbd al-Hakam gave an overview of the mosques in Alexandria, listing the mosque of Dhû al-Qarnayn near the Alexandrian harbor. In the following century, in 943 and 944, a commentator

---

50. Farrokh, *Shadows in the Desert*, 105-10.
51. See Chapter IX.

spoke of the existence of a modest building called "the tomb of the prophet and king Iskander."[52]

Alexander's Successors or Diadochi

Armed conflict broke out from Iran to the Balkans. Cities were besieged and pillaged, the countryside plundered by hungry armies. Alexander had scarcely acquired power before his empire was broken into pieces and divided according to the four corners of the world. His empire was not passed on to his descendants nor did his successors have the power he had, for his empire was torn apart and given to others. The rule of Alexander and his succesors form the historical context in which the events recorded in the book of Daniel occurred. Antiochus IV Epiphanes (ruled 175-164 B.C.) continued the process of Hellenization during which period Daniel was written. Epiphanes is one of the more puzzling rulers in history. He came within a hair of conquering Egypt and wandered, like the caliphs in *One Thousand and One Nights,* incognito through the streets of Antioch to gauge the opinions of his subjects. He is known primarily for his attempt to be worshipped by all peoples as a god. Antiochus is presented as evil incarnate in Jewish writings, the book of Maccabees, and Daniel, which was written shortly after his death. He was a model for the figure of the antichrist in the biblical book of Revelation.[53]

The uprising by the Maccabees (167-135 B.C.) was directed against Hellenization. The name Maccabees is probably derived from the Aramaic word for "hammer." Simon Maccabee succeeded his brother Judas as leader of the uprising. The first book of the Maccabees was written in the second century from the perspective of a rebellious province. Hanukkah, or the Feast of Lights, which lasts for eight days, was initiated to commemorate and celebrate the "miraculous conquest" of the Seleucid king Antiochus IV Epiphanes in 164 B.C. by Judas Maccabee.

After Alexander's sudden and premature death, his generals felt compelled to rule parts of the empire that had fallen apart immediately after his death: Ptolemy over Egypt, Seleucus over Mesopotamia (Babylon), and

---

52. Andrew Michael Chugg, *Alexandre le Grand: Le Tombeau Perdu* (London: Periplus, 2004) 168.

53. Rolf Strootman, *Gekroonde Goden: Hellenistische vorsten van Alexander tot Kleopatra* (Amsterdam: Amsterdam University Press, 2005) 31.

Antigonus over Asia Minor (now Turkey). Ptolemy and Seleucus established two strong empires that dominated the Middle East for a time. The Ptolemies ruled Egypt for three centuries from the city of Alexandria. The famous Cleopatra VII would be the last ruling member of this dynasty (69-30 B.C.). Seleucus moved his capital from Babylon first to Seleucia, a new city on the Euphrates, and then to Antioch. Alexander's heirs fought among themselves for Jerusalem and other cities in the area. Antiochus IV Epiphanes was one of the Seleucids, thus one of the several testators of part of Alexander's empire. Antiochus lived in Athens for a time as a devotee of all things Greek until he succeeded his murdered brother in 175. He had ambitions at ruling the world. While retreating from Egypt, where he had attempted to conquer Alexandria, he entered Jerusalem, a city that was in turmoil because of a civil war between the orthodox and Hellenistic Jews. Antiochus supported the Hellenists, who allowed him to rob the temple and steal the temple treasures to support his war.

Jason (a Greek name, rather than Joshua or Jesus) was appointed high priest in 174 B.C. by Antiochus IV because of the large gifts he promised the king (2 Macc 4:7). Jason wanted to make Jerusalem a Greek city. A Hellenistic Jew, he attempted, with the help of the majority of the inhabitants, far-reaching measures to adapt the temple state of Jerusalem to a Greek city (2 Macc 4:7-20). He began to reform his fellow inhabitants along the lines of the Greek model. In honor of the king, he called Jerusalem Antioch. In 171 Jason was pushed aside and fled to the Transjordan (2 Macc 4:24-26). After a failed attempt to win back his office, he went to Sparta, where he died. "Godless wretch that he was and no true high priest, Jason set no bounds to his impiety; indeed the hellenizing process reached such a pitch that the priests ceased to show any interest in serving the altar" (2 Macc 4:13-14). Antiochus attempted to force Hellenistic culture and religion on the Jews. The low point was reached in 168, when he erected a statue of the Greek god Zeus on the sacrificial altar in the Jerusalem temple (1 Macc 1:54). He attempted to put an end completely to the worship of the God of the Jews and, by locating the worship of Zeus Olympus in the temple, he hoped to be able to assimilate the Jews. His political purpose was "that all . . . become a single people, each nation renouncing its particular customs" (1 Macc 1:41). The placing of this altar for an idol was called "the abomination that causes desolation" (Dan 8:13; 9:27; cf. also Dan 11:31; 12:11; 1 Macc 1:54; Matt 24:15). One thing and another led to rebellion and a guerrilla war under Judas, surnamed Maccabee (166-160), and his brothers (the Hasmonean dynasty) against the political and religious oppression of Antiochus

(Dan 11:21-45; 1 Maccabees 1–6; 2 Maccabees 3–9). The temple would be re-dedicated in 164.

As one of Alexander's successors, Antiochus IV saw himself as an "epiphany of God" — hence his epithet, *epiphanes*. According to Polybius (203-120 B.C.), a Greek historian from the Hellenistic period who himself held military and political office, the name *epimanes*, "delusional," was more fitting. Antiochus is the personification of a power hostile to God. He is also called the "king of the north" (Dan 11:40).[54]

The cult of the victorious conquest was not pure bombast but a practical matter. The Hellenistic kingdoms were war machines that demanded tribute to finance the very military power that had made the tribute necessary. The church father Augustine argued that these kingdoms were nothing more than "large criminal gangs." Imitating the Assyrian and Persian kings, Alexander — and later the Seleucids — went with their armies to what was then thought to be the ends of the earth, the Caucasus, the Central Asian steppe, the Indian Ocean, in what was partly a ritual demonstration of the power they thought they had.

In the East, the cities were originally often ruled by a city king, who was also sometimes the high priest, and by the priests of the most important cultus in the city, such as that of Marduk in Babylon and Melkart in Tyre. During the Hellenistic period, the kings performed the role of city king. The name Marduk was so sacred that it was not to be spoken aloud; instead, people said "Lord [Bel]," whereas Marduk's wife was called "Lady." The Seleucid Empire was a true multiethnic state. It was so large that it included various capitals: Sardis in Lydia, Antioch and Damascus in Syria, Seleucia, Babylon, and Susa in Mesopotamia, Ecbatana in Iran, Baktra and Samarkand in the East.[55]

Rome and Carthage

In the third century B.C., during the Punic Wars, Rome carried on a long and finally successful campaign against the city of Carthage in North Africa (modern Tunisia). Punic is the western dialect of Phoenician, and it was the Phoenicians who founded this largest of all Phoenician trade centers in 814. The ruler of the city of Tyre founded Carthage/Qart Hadasht, whose name means "New City."

54. Cf. Chapter IX.
55. Strootman, *Gekroonde Goden*, 49, 55, 59-61.

Carthage served the expansion of Phoenician trade with the countries on the west coast of the Mediterranean. In the fifth century B.C., the population of Carthage was larger than that of Tyre and Sidon together. This city would become a major opponent of Rome.

The Carthaginian commander Hannibal (247-183 B.C.) left at the beginning of 218 with an army of thirty-five to forty thousand men and a number of elephants for what would become the Second Punic War (218-201). He achieved great victories against the Romans, crossing the Alps and arriving at the gates of Rome in 211: "Hannibal is at the gates *(Hannibal ad portas)!"* Cato the Elder (234-149) fought against him as a young man. In 216 Hannibal inflicted a sound defeat on the Romans at Cannae, and for fifteen years he was the greatest strategist in Italy. Carthage would finally be destroyed in 146 during the Third Punic War.

Rome and Alexandria: The Battle of Actium (31 B.C.)

After the assassination of Julius Caesar on 15 March 44 B.C., Octavian — later the emperor Augustus (63-14) — whom Caesar made his son in his will, played an important role. In 40 B.C. the senate made Herod I (Herod the Great) king of Judea. Mark Anthony was his patron in the Roman aristocracy. Julius Caesar had contact with Cleopatra VII Philopator of Alexandria (69-30), the last member of the Ptolemaic dynasty. Her family was originally Greek-Macedonian. She was the queen of old Egypt, the last Hellenistic ruler. Cleopatra had an affair with Julius Caesar and is said to have borne him a child. When he was in Alexandria, Caesar visited Alexander the Great's grave.[56] But the location of that grave is uncertain. Ptolemy I "highjacked" the body when it was being transported from Babylon for reburial in Macedonia. Or, as some have speculated, are his remains really in Venice, under Saint Mark's Cathedral? The Venetians are said to have taken the remains of Alexander from Alexandria under the presupposition that they were taking the remains of Saint Mark.[57]

After the assassination of Caesar, Cleopatra allied herself with Mark Anthony (ca. 83-30 B.C.). Anthony, Lepidus, and Octavian together formed a triumvirate that ruled the Roman Empire, and Anthony was initially the strongest of the three. He became captivated by Cleopatra, married her, and

---

56. Chugg, *Alexandre le Grand*, 105.
57. Cartledge, *Ancient Greece*, 154; Chugg, *Alexandre le Grand*, 231.

fathered children with her. This invoked the specter of Eastern despotism in Rome, and Octavian made good use of it. On 2 September 31 a sea battle took place at Actium, on the western coast of Greece, between the fleet of Anthony and Cleopatra and that of Octavian. Both Anthony and Cleopatra were defeated. In Alexandria Octavian, the victor, visited the grave of Alexander the Great.[58] Herod's position became critical because of the Battle of Actium, but he won Octavian's favor by promising to be loyal to him. He rebuilt and beautified the Jerusalem temple to appease the Jews. As imperator and commander, Octavian inherited the title Caesar from Julius Caesar, and the senate gave him a new name: Augustus. A century of prosperity and abundance was proclaimed. The city of Rome was transformed in order to become as splendid as the oldest city of the Greek east, Alexandria.[59] Jesus was born in the time of the Emperor Augustus and Herod the Great (Luke 2:1, 6).

Virgil's *Aeneid:* Troy and Rome

Virgil (70-19 B.C.) was one of the greatest Roman poets. Caesar Augustus is said to have commissioned Virgil to write the epic poem *The Tale of Aeneas,* which was intended to honor the peace and world dominion of Rome. The *Aeneid* was also intended to give legitimacy to the intense struggle that was necessary to fight for such peace.

The Trojan hero Aeneas fled the horrors of war after Troy was destroyed, only to be confronted with a new battle: the long war he had to fight in Italy to finally fulfill the divine mandate, to lay the foundations for what would become the powerful Roman Empire.

The *Aeneid* begins:

> This is a tale of arms and of a man. Fated to be an exile, he was the first to sail from the land of Troy and reach Italy, at its Lavinian[60] shore. He met many tribulations on his way both by land and on the ocean; high Heaven willed it, for Juno[61] was ruthless and could not forget her anger.

---

58. Chugg, *Alexandre le Grand,* 111-13.

59. Martin Goodman, *Rome and Jerusalem: The Clash of Ancient Civilizations* (New York: Vintage, 2008) 40-41; cf. J. C. Stobart, *The Grandeur That Was Rome* (4th ed.; New York: St. Martin's, 1987) 109-10.

60. A city in Latium, which Aeneas named after his wife.

61. Juno was the mistress of heaven, the wife of Jupiter.

And he had also to endure great suffering in warfare. But at last he succeeded in founding his city, and installing the gods of his race in the Latin land: and that was the origin of the Latin nation, the lords of Alba,[62] and the proud battlements of Rome.[63]

Virgil relates how, on the orders of the gods, the Trojan Aeneas had to found a "new Troy" in the West. Troy and Rome were thus connected. Throughout the epic he is called "devout Aeneas," who seeks peace for his people. The *Aeneid* was intended to be the equivalent of Homer's epics; it filled a national need. Virgil thus gave the Romans their own *Iliad* and *Odyssey*.

The first part of the *Aeneid*, the wanderings of Aeneas, is the counterpart of the *Odyssey*, which is about Odysseus's return to his country, and the second part the counterpart of the *Iliad*, the story of the hero Achilles who fights and finally kills his great opponent. The *Aeneid* is concerned with hegemony over Italy.

The hero of the tale is the Trojan prince Aeneas, who lands, in accordance with his fate, in Italy and after a great deal of effort and a dangerous struggle founds a new empire: Rome.

The *Aeneid* — essentially a report of wanderings and struggle — is especially impressive because of the expressions of warm humanity, of a sensitive, often melancholic understanding of human destiny, of cosmic perspective. As a result, it towers above the literature of its time. Virgil wanted to show how the founding of Aeneas's empire and the establishment of world dominion was willed by the gods. Its purpose and climax are reached in the policy of the "divine" Augustus, whose world empire was also an empire of peace.[64]

Virgil and a "Tale of Two Cities"

Aeneas, the son of Venus and Anchises, left Troy after it fell and fled with his father on his back. Leaving the city for good, his fleet is shipwrecked, and he

---

62. Alba Longa, the mother city of Rome, was situated in the Alban Hills southeast of present-day Rome, founded by the son of Aeneus. Romulus and Remus are descended from the kings of Alba.

63. Virgil, *The Aeneid,* trans. F. Jackson Knight (Harmondsworth: Penguin, 1968) 27.

64. J. Wytzes, *De Vergilius: De Dichter van het imperium* (Kampen: Kok, 1951); *Christelijke Encyclopedie,* ed. F. W. Grosheide and G. P. van Itterzon (2nd ed.; Kampen: Kok, 1956-61), *s.v.* "Vergilius."

lands in Carthage, where he first meets his mother, Venus. He sees Carthage and Dido, its queen. Mercury, Jupiter's messenger, sees to it that she welcomes the Trojans in Carthage, and Aeneas introduces himself to her. Dido was originally from Phoenicia, from which she fled after her brother murdered her husband. She promises the Trojans help, and Aeneas tells her about the fall of Troy and his adventures afterward. He goes hunting with her and is symbolically married to her during a thunderstorm by the agency of Juno. Aeneas helps Dido with building her "new city." But when Mercury sees that, he goes to Aeneas immediately and says: "What, are you siting foundations for proud Carthage and building here a noble city? A model husband! For shame! You forget your destiny and that other kingdom which is to be yours." Mercury reminds him of his task to found a new Troy in Italy. When Aeneas indicates that he will complete the task, Dido confronts him about it, and Aeneas defends his choice by saying that his love must give way to the task given him by the gods. Dido calls him a traitor: "Did you actually believe that you could disguise so wicked a deed and leave my country without a word? And can nothing hold you, not our love, nor our once plighted hands, nor even the cruel death that must await your Dido?" Aeneas answers: "If you, a Phoenician, are faithful to your Carthaginian fortress here, content to look on no other city but this city in faraway Africa, what is the objection if Trojans settle in Italy? It is no sin, if we, like you, look for a kingdom in a foreign country." Dido's sister attempts to mediate with a request that Aeneus postpone his departure for a bit. Dido wants her to convey Dido's words: "I do not now beg him to restore our honored marriage as it was before he betrayed it, or ask him to forgo his splendid Latium where he hopes to reign. I ask only the time of inaction, to give my mad mood a breathing-space and a rest, until my fortune can teach me submission and the art of grief. This is my last plea for indulgence." Dido has a funeral pyre built to destroy all memory of Aeneas. Urged by the gods to make haste, Aeneas sails away from Carthage. When Dido sees Aeneas's fleet sailing off in the distance in the morning, she does not postpone her decision to die any longer:

> That is my prayer and my last cry, and it comes from me with my life-blood streaming. From then onwards shall you, my Phoenicians, torment with acts of pursuing hate all his descendents to come, each member of his line. This service will be your offering to my shade. Neither love nor compact shall there be between the nations. And from my dead bones may some Avenger arise to persecute with fire and sword those settlers from Troy, soon or in after-time whenever the strength is given!

Let your shores oppose their shores, your waves their waves, your arms
their arms. That is my imprecation. Let them fight, they, and their sons'
sons, for ever!

These curses would become reality in the Punic Wars fought between
Rome and Carthage in the third and second centuries B.C. Hannibal is the
Carthaginian Avenger referred to here (*Aeneid*, IV, 250-441, 606-37).[65]

Hubris and Nemesis

In surveying the tales of two cities cited above, it is striking that as a rule they
are not black-and-white. They certainly are concerned with the continuing
division between East and West. Greeks certainly see themselves as opposed
to the Persians, as if it was a question here of Greeks versus barbarians, freedom and democracy versus oriental despotism (Karl August Wittvogel).
Truth and fantasy about the conflicts between the two cities are tangled up.
The dominant view among Western historians is perhaps that the Greek-
Persian wars were about an epic battle between democracy, represented by
Greece, and Persian tyranny. This explanation, as if the Greeks were doing
nothing more than defending their freedom, is an example of a certain understanding and view of what had happened in the past. In reality, the struggle between Persians and Greeks had more to do with ambitions to dominate the sea. If the Persians had succeeded in breaking the Greek sway over
the Aegean Sea, then there would have been no rivals to hold back the Persian maritime, political, and military expansion in the Mediterranean Sea.
But the Aegean Sea was the stage for the formulation of the so-called East
versus West thesis.[66]

What is striking in these tales is that a simple black-and-white perspective does not seem to be tenable, even if it was attempted. According to
Edward Gibbon, author of the well-known *Decline and Fall of the Roman
Empire*, the despotism of the Roman emperors was an important factor in
the decline of that empire.

Overconfidence and pride run through all the stories on both sides.
The Greek heroes suffered from these qualities as much as did the Persian
princes, like Xerxes. There was also no lack of self-criticism. Overconfidence

---

65. Virgil, *Aeneid*, 105-10, 116.
66. Farrokh, *Shadows in the Desert*, 69, 71.

or hubris, a concept found in Greek ethics, already played an important role in Homer's tale of the two cities, Sparta and Troy. Hubris refers to vast certainty, a feeling of good fortune, overconfident trust in one's own power. It is the transgression of the limits placed on humankind, contempt and blasphemy of the gods, which summon up divine displeasure and retribution, nemesis. Nemesis is a Greek goddess, the personification of avenging justice, which gives everybody what they deserve. It is primarily overconfidence, that transgression of the limits imposed on humankind, that she punishes. Nemesis is said to be the mother of Helen and thus the cause of all the misery that comes about because of Helen.[67]

We will see in the following chapters how that compares more specifically with the narratives in the Bible and the Qur'an.

67. Konrat Ziegler and Walther Sontheimer, eds., *Der Kleine Pauly: Lexikon der Antike in fünf Bänden* (Stuttgart: Druckenmüller, 1979), *s.v.* "hybris," "nemesis"; Eric M. Moormann and Wilfried Uitterhoeve, *Van Alexandros tot Zenobia: Thema's uit de klassieke geschiedenis in literatuur, muziek, beeldende kunst en theater* (Nijmegen: SUN, 1989), *s.v.* "Nemesis."

CHAPTER II

Is Muhammad One of the Prophets?

I love it, your Torah,
It's always on my mind.

Your word is a lamp for my feet,
A light on my path.

I have sworn, and stand by it,
that I will follow your word that guides me.

I bow and kneel to you, O Living One,
Let me live, through the power of your word.

My lips mumble to you: I will . . . I want . . .
Teach me your righteousness. You — yes, I will.

My soul lies in my hands, so trivial,
But I will not forget your Torah.

Blackguard and transgressor set their traps
— But wander away from you? Me? Not Me.

What you have arranged is my inheritance forever,
    the joy of my heart.

I will bow my heart to your words
And keep them to the very end.

Huub Oosterhuis, Psalm 119:105-12

I don't know Who — or what — put the question, I don't know when it was put. I don't even remember answering. But at some moment I did answer Yes to Someone — or Something — and from that hour I was certain that existence is meaningful and that, therefore, my life, in self-surrender, had a goal.

Dag Hammarskjöld, *Markings*

Introduction

A prophet is not someone who predicts the future, who looks into a crystal ball. Rather, a prophet is a seer, someone who points out what an event means, someone who provides insight into what is going on both spiritually and politically. A prophet is an agitator, someone who walks around temple and palace stating his criticism, who rages against the injustices political leaders are committing. A true prophet does not adopt the drab and color-less language of his society, does not speak the jargon of diplomats, the lan-guage of theologians or a priestly caste, or the rigid prose of the business world. He is and remains faithful to the language of the parable. He does not predict history but studies and analyzes it, uncovers and unmasks it.

To answer the question "Is Muhammad one of the prophets?" we should first clarify what is understood by a prophet in the Bible and the Qur'an. Thus, we will first look at a number of individuals who were called to be prophets prior to Muhammad. Who is "God" who calls them and in whose name they speak, and what does God want them to do? I will begin with the call of Moses/Mûsâ, the prophet mentioned most often in the Qur'an, and then look at the prophet Elijah/Ilyâs/Yâsîn. I will then conclude with a discussion of the call experiences of the biblical prophets in general and that of Muhammad in particular.

What Is a Prophet?

"A voice says, 'Cry out.' And I said, 'What shall I cry?'" (Isa 40:6). A prophet, *al-nabî* (in both Hebrew and Arabic), is a speaker, a proclaimer, an interpreter of the Word of God. God's words are put into a prophet's mouth, and he must proclaim them (Deut 18:18). The prophet is called by God to call or proclaim: a prophet is therefore both called and caller. "Recite *(iqra)*" is the first thing Muhammad hears (Q 96:1). He has to call, recite (from which the word Qur'an is derived) what he is to utter in the name of God. The authority of the word that the prophet speaks is based solely on his call. Prophets do not speak on their own authority (Q 53:3). Those who do are false prophets who proclaim what they themselves have thought up and concocted themselves. God asks: "What possesses those prophets, the proclaimers of their own concoctions?" He opposes prophets who mislead his people with their so-called dreams, their lies, and their flood of words. "I did not send or appoint them" (Jer 23:25, 32): in that case, it is certainly not God who spoke to such a prophet. True prophets are often confronted with false prophets. It was precisely this situation in which the prophet Jeremiah found himself when faced with the false prophet Hananiah, to whom he says: "Listen, Hananiah! The LORD has not sent you" (Jer 28:15).

The false prophets proclaim what they do for the sake of what they themselves say, to fulfill human desires. They dream and talk about their dreams or, possibly, the delusions of their hearts (Jer 23:25-27). Out of the wishes and impulses they share with the people they brew the numbing illusions that will make them forget. They say what people want to hear, what they also want to hear from their own mouths. They speak not only to please others but also for the sake of their own dreams and delusions; they do not deceive intentionally but are themselves caught up in the deception of the world of their desires.[1] Muhammad also had to deal with such a false prophet, Musaylima, in Yemen.[2]

The true prophet speaks in the name of God, which is why it is important to discern who is a true prophet. The true prophet can be recognized by his faithfulness and by when what he predicts actually happens (Deut 13:1-5; Ezek 33:33). Prophecies of disaster are often intended to bring people to repentance by pointing out the disastrous consequences of doing evil (Jer 18:7-8; Jonah). The false prophet is not sent by God (Jer 23:32); he imagines that he has seen something, claims to speak in God's name but does not actually do that, and his words do not come to pass (Ezek 13:1-8); he is following himself, does not stand up for the people, and obscures their true needs. The true prophet is sensitive to God's voice and raises a critical voice in his name: for example, issuing a threat over against the false feeling of comfort, consolation over against discouragement.[3] When false prophets arise (Rev 16:13; 19:20;

---

1. Martin Buber, *Werke*, vol. 2: *Schriften zur Bibel* (Munich: Kösel, 1964) 425.

2. *EI, s.v.* Musaylima.

3. *De Bijbel uit de grondtekst vertaald: Willibrordvertaling* (2nd rev. ed.; 's-Hertogen-bosch: Katholieke Bijbelstichting, 1996), on Deut. 18:21-22. Hereafter abbreviated as KBS.

20:10) and perform signs and miracles, they are doing so to deceive — if possible — the elect themselves (Mark 13:22).

Moses, Mûsâ, in the Holy Valley

Moses, who is grazing the sheep and goats of his father-in-law Jethro/ Shu'ayb, a Midianite priest, arrives with his flock at Mount Horeb, the "mountain of God," in the Sinai Peninsula. His eye is caught by a fire flaring up in a bush. Miraculously, the bush is not consumed by the fire (Exod 3:1-3; Q 28:29; 20:10). At first, Moses thinks that it is a kind of campfire where he can get warmth or some light for his further journey. He says to his family: "I saw a fire; I'll go see if it is only a burning piece of wood that we can warm ourselves by" (Q 27:7). Is it indeed that simple, or is there actually something supernatural involved here?

This story recalls the prophet Isaiah mocking the foolishness of worshipping idols made of wood. In that case, the story concerns people who make idols that are nothing and from whose creation nothing can be expected. And then Isaiah derides the worship of idols: someone cuts down a few cedars, chooses a pine or an oak that he let grow in a wood with other trees, or a laurel that he planted and that grew because of the rain. These trees provide him with firewood so he can warm himself or bake bread. Or he makes an idol from the wood and bows down to it. One half he burns in the fire over which he is preparing meat, roasting it, and eats his fill. He grows warm and says: "Ah! I am warm! I see the fire." He fashions the remaining piece, however, into a god and kneels before it in prayer: "Save me, for you are my god!" The idolater does not stop to think, and he lacks the knowledge and insight to say: "The one half I burned in the fire, I even baked bread over its coals and roasted meat to eat. And from what was left I made a detestable image. I'm bowing to a piece of wood!" What he cherishes is ashes. A deluded mind led him astray. He can no longer be saved, for he does not ask himself: "Is what I have in my hand actually a lie?" (Isa 44:9-20).

Thus, the real question for Moses is: Is it only a tree that is on fire, or is it truly a miracle? Only when the bush begins to speak to him, however, does he suddenly understand that it is God who is appearing to him in this form. He covers his face (Exod 3:6), just as the prophet Muhammad will do later after a similar experience (Q 73:1; 74:1). God then lets Moses approach in confidence (Q 19:52). Moses is called from the right side of the mountain (Q 19:52) to a holy place (*al-Wadi al-muqaddas*; Q 20:12), in the holy valley

Tuwâ (Q 79:16; 20:12). He is addressed from within the bush, the burning bush: "Moses, it is I, God, the Lord of the worlds" (Q 28:30). Then a voice is heard from within the bush: "Moses, Moses, 'Do not come any closer.'" God says: "Take off your sandals, for the place where you are standing is holy ground" (Exod 3:4-5). "You are in the holy valley of Tuwâ: and I have chosen you. Listen therefore to what is revealed." Moses hears: "I am God; there is no other God beside me" (Q 20:12-14; 79:16; Deut 6:4). God has seen and heard the misery and murmuring of his people about their slavedrivers: "I have indeed seen the misery of my people in Egypt. I have heard them crying out because of their slavedrivers, and I am concerned about their suffering" (Exod 3:7). God notices the cry for help from the oppressed people in the house of bondage in Egypt. Moses is then called by God to go to the pharaoh of Egypt to save his people (cf. Q 37:114-22).

The Name of God

As soon as Moses hears what God wants him to do, he is terrified and asks what he should tell the people when they ask who sent him. What is his name? The answer is that he should say "I will be there" has sent him. "I will be there" is the name written in four letters in Hebrew, YHWH, also called the Tetragrammaton, the name of God that Jews never pronounce and simply say "The NAME" to refer to God. The four letters are derived from the Hebrew word for the verb "to be." The name of God is not a philosophical statement on being. Does it provide an abstract philosophical concept of God — Somethingism, perhaps? Somethingism is a widespread belief at present in the Netherlands and apparently elsewhere: "There is something"; there must be "Something," mustn't there? But these four letters do not refer to anything like that. What do they mean then? The Name of four letters does not refer to an abstract Being; it is a verb, and it means "I will be there," I will be with You, I will be with you — Immanuel, "God with us."

But what does that mean precisely? The phrase *God met ons* ("God with us") was printed on the edge of the Dutch guilder, just as it is now on the Dutch Euro. *Gott mit uns* was inscribed on the belts of German soldiers in the Second World War. Is that the issue? Is that the meaning of the Name? If we are to hallow the Name in that way, as prayed in one of the petitions in the Lord's Prayer ("Hallowed be your name"), that would be an insult to God or a blasphemous invocation and use of the Name, the presupposition of the presence of God who can be manipulated: "God, the Netherlands, and (the House of) Orange?" or "God bless America" as a kind of self-evident prayer, as if God can indeed be used for one's own material, economic, political, and national goals or interests.

The answer Moses is to give as to who this God is who has commissioned him to liberate the people from slavery in Egypt, "'I will be there' has sent me," involves a qualified Being, a liberating presence of God (Exod 3:13-14). Why does God do that? God "I will be there" cannot watch people be threatened by nonbeing, who are not, as in Egypt, allowed to exist in the eyes of their unjust masters, not allowed to exist in freedom and justice, who have no place in society. God "I will be there" hears the cries of protest from the people who sigh as slaves in the shanty towns of the Pharaonic empire. He hears their cries. Because he cannot endure hearing or seeing this he takes action. He stands up to issue judgment, to do justice. He then descends to liberate them. "Descend" *(tanzîl)* is a word in the Qur'an for God's descent, for his Self-revelation. God "I will be there" will provide justice for the oppressed and will go with them to the land of freedom, the earth where justice will be practiced.

Thus, the Name does not describe an abstract being, separated from the hard reality of human existence, a noninvolved "Something." God "I will be there" hears the innocent blood of Cain's brother Abel that calls from the ground (Gen 4:10), crying to heaven, and does not respond as the former French president Charles de Gaulle once cynically did: "Blood dries quickly." God "I will be there" hears the cries of the victims of violence, regardless of their background. God "I will be there" sees it, hears it, knows it, and descends, for his intention is to liberate, to save. God "I will be there" remains present, is actively present, is active. Thus, it is not about God's "Being" *at the expense of* others but precisely a Being *for* others, to create room for them, to make clear that they can, may be, are allowed to be there as people. "I will be there" is the Name around which Jesus' prayer known as the Lord's Prayer (Matt 6:9-13; Luke 11:2-4) revolves, the prayer Jesus/'Îsâ taught his disciples, his "helpers *(ansâr),*" as the Qur'an calls them (Q 3:52; 61:14). The first petition of the prayer is "Hallowed be your name." The name must be hallowed, called (Exod 3:15), feared (Deut 28:58), confessed (1 Kgs 8:33), loved (Ps 5:11), exalted (34:3), praised in song (66:2), sought (83:16), praised (22:3), glorified (John 12:28), known (17:26). "Hallowed be your name," the first petition, is not a vow one makes to sanctify God's Name, nor is it a wish: "May your name be hallowed." It is a true petition that is addressed to God and of which the fulfillment is expected from him. God's name is hallowed when he establishes the Kingdom and his will is done on earth as prayed in the first three petitions of the Lord's Prayer. These three are closely connected to one another.

The Lord's Prayer is often compared with respect to its function for Christians with the meaning of *Sûra al-Fâtiha,* the "Opening Chapter" of the Qur'an for Muslims (Q 1:2-7). These petitions make an appeal first of all to God's actions in this threatened world to substantiate his name. At the same time, the human being himself becomes completely involved, as is intended with a prayer. The followers of the prophets are their helpers. This prayer cannot be without any ethical implications for all those who are taught to pray [it]. When people pray, they become involved; they can manifest the reality of the presence of God's kingdom, justice, and love. One calls God by name because in him one has a name as well: for God, a person is someone, something special. The hallowing of God's name consists in the obedience to his will, spelled out in the Ten Commandments (Exod 20:1-17; cf. Q 23:1-11; 70:22-35), summarized in the words "Love God above all and your neighbor as yourself" (Lev 19:18; Matt 5:43; 22:39; Rom 13:9; Gal 5:14; Jas 2:8).

When God spoke those words on Mount Horeb, when Moses had returned — but this time with the people of Israel who had been liberated from slavery in Egypt — those who are present on the mountain answer: "We will do everything the LORD has said; we will obey" (Exod 24:7). Special attention should be paid to the striking, perhaps even surprising, word order: action has priority over hearing. That is, only those who do it have actually heard it. Thus, the point here is not so much believing as doing. A rabbi was once asked why it had become so hard to believe in God when, apparently, it used to be much easier. He replied: "That's because no one wants to bow down as low any more." "I will be there" did and does do that. He bows down, descends to be with poor and oppressed people. The question that is constantly posed by the prophets is: Do we do that as well?

The Call of the Prophet Elijah

After the Qur'an has discussed Moses and his brother Aaron/Hârûn, it moves immediately to the commission of the prophet Elijah/Ilyâs/Yâsîn (Q 37:123-32; cf. 6:86; 38:48). Elijah, whose name means "The Lord (YHWH) is my God," is one of the greatest prophets in the Tanakh, the Old Testament. Elijah is characterized as a zealot, a people's saint, the one who initiates others into the mysteries of the Law, the Torah, and who is expected to return at the end of time. He has been called to summon the children of Israel back to the service of the God of Moses. The Qur'an includes Elijah, together with Zechariah/Zakriyya and his son John the Baptist/Yahyâ and Jesus, among the "righteous" (Q 6:85). He is one of the messengers who are called so that his people will no longer serve the idol Baal, who is seen as a parallel to the old Mesopotamian God Baal and his three daughters, the goddesses al-Lât, Manât, and al-'Uzzâ', "daughters of God" (Q 53:19-23).[4] Those gods were still worshipped in Mecca and surrounding areas at the time of Muhammad.

What kind of god actually is this Baal whom Elijah so passionately opposes? In the land of Canaan, Baal was the god of the weather and fertility. The word *baal* itself means "lord" and could be translated as "boss." *Baal* refers to having possessions, being the master of a wife, home, or animal. It becomes a god's name, denoting a bossy god with an unbridled passion for power. He represents the lust for power and for possessions that give divine legitimation to the reigning class. The worship of Baal thus has political connotations. What does that worship in the end entail? It means a return to slavery, like the slavery that existed under the pharaoh of Egypt, a politics that was at odds with the heart of the Torah God gave to Moses. Baal represents a court god who does not tolerate a God who liberates people from slavery. Many kings of Israel led the people back into slavery through their service to Baal.

It should be noted that this worship of Baal began in Israel already with King Solomon/Sulaymân and plays an important role under King Omri (ca. 876-869 B.C.), the father of King Ahab. In a secular sense, Omri was perhaps one of the more successful kings of Israel. His son continued his father's policies and reigned from ca. 873 to 851. The latter's wife Jezebel was the daughter of the king of Tyre (1 Kgs 16:31), a city well known for its pride, and would therefore be condemned. Jezebel would become the symbol of a woman who seduces people into idolatry (Rev 2:20). For the elite in the kingdom, the government of King Ahab was a period of great prosperity, for Ahab could afford the luxury of an ivory palace in the city of Samaria, the capital of Israel (1 Kgs 22:39).

Viewed on the basis of Ahab's behavior, it does indeed appear that the worship of Baal was a question of life or death. Ahab increased his holdings and did not hesitate to kill people to do so. The example of Naboth's vineyard comes to mind here, which Ahab seized literally over Naboth's dead body (1 Kgs 21:1-19). Falsely accused of cursing God and the king, Naboth

---

4. Anton Wessels, *Islam in Stories*, trans. John Bowden (Leuven: Peeters, 2002) 40-41.

was stoned to death (2 Kgs 9:26), allowing the king to appropriate his property. Jezebel, Elijah's opponent, also threatened the prophet Elijah himself with death (1 Kgs 19:1).

Elijah was active as a prophet for twenty years, between 870 and 850 B.C. He and the prophets after him opposed "false" prophets both in Samaria and in Jerusalem, the capital of Judah — prophets who deceived the people and became in fact prophets of Baal (Jer 23:13-14). Elijah announced to Ahab that God would punish Israel with a drought lasting several years (1 Kgs 17:1; Jas 5:17). When, at God's command, Elijah once again visited the king in the third year of the drought, it turned into a decisive confrontation between Elijah and the prophets of Baal on Mount Carmel, situated in the borderland between Israel and Phoenicia (Lebanon). Elijah demanded that the people choose between the city-god of Tyre, the Phoenician Baal, or the Lord. The issue in that confrontation between Elijah and the priests of Baal had to do with the fact that the little people, the widows, the orphans, and the poor, were being heavily oppressed. For Israel, the question of life according to Elijah was: Were they going to follow Baal or God?

The confrontation between both views was spectacular. Elijah proposed that he and the 450 Baal priests bring a sacrifice to, respectively, God and Baal on the mountain. The Baal priests were to call on the name of their god and Elijah on the name of his. The Baal priests began calling from morning till noon: "Baal, answer us!" But there was no response, no answer, even though they danced and skipped around the altar they had built. At noon, Elijah called out mockingly: "Shout louder! Surely he is a god! Perhaps he is deep in thought, or busy, or traveling. Maybe he is sleeping and must be awakened."[5] So the Baal priests shouted all the louder and gouged themselves, as was their custom, with swords and spears until blood flowed. They went on frantically until it was time for the evening sacrifice. But still there was no response and no answer: they were not heard. When it was time for the evening sacrifice, Elijah had the chance to show what he could achieve. He came forward and said, "LORD, the God of Abraham, Isaac, and Israel, let it be known today that you are God in Israel and that I am your servant and have done all these things at your command. Answer me, LORD, answer me, so these people will know that you, LORD, are God, and that you are turning their hearts back again." Then the fire of the Lord came down and consumed the sacrifice. Elijah won spectacularly in the confrontation with the Baal priests. When the people saw this, they fell prostrate on the

---

5. In the Qur'an Abraham also ridicules those who worship idols (Q 21:51-70).

ground and called out: "The LORD — he is God! The LORD — he is God!" (1 Kgs 18; cf. Q 3:183).[6]

The choice Elijah wanted to force the people to make was either for the God who does not hear, does not listen, or for the God who hears and thus does something, that is, saves and liberates. Not only is Baal a god who does not answer on Carmel — but he does not listen either.

But the outcome of the clash between Elijah and the Baal priests is shocking: "'Seize the prophets of Baal. Don't let anyone get away!' They seized them, and Elijah had them brought down to the Kishon Valley and slaughtered there" (1 Kgs 18:40). The Baal priests were thus killed after the confrontation, at Elijah's instigation.

Was that the intention, that the servants of the other god be slaughtered? Is God a god of thunder? Did this apparently uncompromising zealot for God properly understand who the true God is if he has the priests of Baal killed after his act? Does the story that immediately succeeds it possibly give an implicit answer to those questions?

After the events on Mount Carmel Elijah himself had to flee. Why and from what? One reason was certainly that Ahab and Jezebel wanted to make him pay. But could it not have been his own actions that led him to flee? Was it not his own fear as well that made him take to his heels? On what basis did he claim the right to kill the priests of Baal? Was unbelief to be combatted so unrelentingly and compromisingly as in this story? Was Elijah's course of action justified? Is that what had to be done? Was that God's intention, the intention of the "battle for God" (Karen Armstrong)? Or is not Elijah here acting in as terrible a way as Jezebel did with the priests of God (1 Kgs 18:13)? Does Jezebel's earlier act excuse or justify Elijah's?

Elijah did this in the extreme north of Israel, on Mount Carmel, and then fled to the extreme south, even further, to another mountain, Horeb, in the Sinai Peninsula. After a long, arduous journey of forty days and forty nights he reached the mountain where Moses had received God's revelation. Elijah took refuge in a cave, where he heard a voice: "'Go out and stand on the mountain in the presence of the LORD, for the LORD is about to pass by.' Then a great and powerful wind tore the mountains apart and shattered the rocks before the LORD, but the LORD was not in the wind. After the wind there was an earthquake, but the LORD was not in the earthquake. After the earthquake came a fire, but the LORD was not in the fire. And after the fire came a gentle

---

6. Rudi Paret, *Der Koran: Kommentar und Konkordanz* (Stuttgart: Kohlhammer, 1971) on Q 3:183.

whisper. When Elijah heard it, he pulled his cloak over his face and went out and stood at the mouth of the cave" (1 Kgs 19:11-13). When God appears, reveals himself to him, Elijah covers his face with his cloak (1 Kgs 19:13).

One could say that God revealed himself previously on Mount Carmel in the confrontation with the priests of Baal, in the fire that came down. After all, was it not in response to Elijah's prayer that the fire came down and struck the sacrifice (1 Kgs 18:38)? If, when God appears to him on Mount Horeb, God does not reveal himself in the storm nor in the earthquake nor the fire, one can ask if the statement "after the fire came a gentle whisper" in this story does not serve to correct what Elijah presupposed on that other mountain, Mount Carmel. Does God reveal himself in "a gentle voice" or the voice of a gentle stillness? Who is speaking here? What does this gentle voice say? How are we to understand it? Perhaps the mysterious words by the poet T. S. Eliot can help express this mystery: "The silence heard. The word unspoken."[7] Is there a better explanation than this paradox?

Other Call Experiences

We could point here to other call experiences of the prophets: the prophet Isaiah sees God appear in the temple, sitting on a throne, high and exalted, filling the whole temple, and Isaiah considers himself lost (Isa 6:1-5). Ezekiel is called in a vision in which God appears to him (Ezekiel 1–3), and, rendered powerless, he falls facedown to the ground (Ezek 1:28). Daniel is emotionally affected: visions confuse him, and he loses consciousness and falls to the ground as well (Dan 7:15; 10:9). In the special experience of Jesus, the transfiguration on Tabor (Luke 9:28-36), Jesus' disciples are overcome with terror (Mark 9:6), hide their faces out of fear (Matt 17:6), and fall into a deep sleep (Luke 9:32). Paul has a call vision on the road to Damascus: he is thrown to the ground and is blind for three days (Acts 9:4, 9). The seer John sees the Son of Man and falls down as if dead (Rev 1:17). In those experiences, which are described in various ways in these call narratives, the human being is faced with his limits. It is also a death experience. That is the reason for the expression "No one can see God and live" (Gen 32:30; Exod 19:21; 33:20; Lev 16:2; Num 4:20; cf. Deut 5:24; Judg 13:22; Isa 6:5). From this death the human being is raised and set upon his feet again by the Spirit of God himself (Ezek 2:2).

---

7. *Collected Poems, 1909-1962* (New York: Harcourt, Brace & World, 1963).

This is actually quite nicely expressed in the ritual of the Muslim prayer, the *salât*. This prayer begins with standing up to pray, then bowing and kneeling in complete surrender to God before rising once again. The person who surrenders to God in complete trust is enabled to stand on his or her own two feet again and thus be God's vicar or deputy on earth.

The scenes mentioned here indicate in an exemplary fashion what is the case for everyone who hears the word of God. "The human hears God through being transported by the Spirit out of himself; he hears and understands God 'in God and through God.' In these exemplary examples, they are expropriated by their 'seeing,' overcome by complete obedience, instruments of the Word and the act of God."[8]

Muhammad's Call to Be a Prophet

Muhammad is also called to be a prophet. His call involves both auditory and visual experiences: what he hears (Q 96) and what he sees on that occasion (Q 53:1-18). Muhammad's experiences are strikingly similar to the earlier prophets, such as Isaiah, who hears a voice saying, "Cry out," and the prophet asks, "What shall I cry?" (Isa 40:6). These same words are used to relate what happened to Muhammad. He retreated each year to a cave on Mount Hira' close to Mecca, his birthplace, which is similar, as far as landscape is concerned, to Mount Sinai where Moses and Elijah received their revelations of God. When he was around forty years old (ca. A.D. 610), Muhammad suddenly heard a voice in this cave, "the mountain of light," that called out: "*Iqra* — Recite, Read aloud!" Just like the prophet Isaiah, Muhammad asked, "What shall I recite? What shall I read aloud?" And Gabriel/ Jibrîl, the angel of God, said, "Proclaim! (or read!) in the name of your Lord, Who created, created man, out of a (mere) clot of blood: Proclaim! And your Lord is Most Bountiful, he who taught (the use of) the pen, Taught man what he did not know" (Q 96:1-5). When he is told to stand up and to warn others, Muhammad wraps himself in a cloak as the prophet Elijah did when he heard the "gentle whisper" of God. And Muhammad also covers his face with his cloak.

Muhammad is very shocked by the fact that God speaks to him. It is then no wonder that that first experience astonishes him greatly. He even

---

8. Hans Urs von Balthasar, *Herrlichkeit: Eine theologische Aesthetik*. Vol. 3/2: *Theologie*. Pt. 1: *Alter Bund* (2nd ed.; Einsiedeln: Johannes, 1989) 14-15.

thinks of taking his own life, fearing he may be *majnûn* — insane, or possessed. It was not least of all Muhammad's wife, Khadija, who encourages him and confirms his call. She advises Muhammad to consult her cousin, Waraqa ibn Nawfal, who, it is thought, was a Christian. He confirms Muhammad's calling and says that the same thing had been revealed to Moses: the *Nâmûs, nomos,* the law as it had formerly been revealed to Moses. "If you, Khadija, are telling me the truth, then truly the greatest *Nâmûs* that came to Moses has come to him, and then Muhammad is the prophet of this community, *umma.*"[9] Given that the Qur'an mentions no other prophet more than it does Moses (120 times), the response by Waraqa ibn Nawfal is not surprising. Moses then serves as a prefiguration of Muhammad himself, to whom an intimate encounter with God is also granted, who sees God himself, according to one interpretation, sitting on his throne (Q 53:6-7; cf. Num 12:6-8).

After an interval of perhaps six months following some revelations, Gabriel appears to Muhammad again. Muhammad sees someone on the clear horizon, God or the servant of God, Gabriel, who comes as close as two bow lengths or even closer (Q 53:1-18). Muhammad is now convinced he is not possessed (Q 81:22-23; 7:184). The heart of the prophet sees this powerful person near the lotus tree of the final border, an experience that occurs in an exceptionally elevated place, near the garden of Abode (Q 53:15; cf. 81:19-21).[10]

Muhammad is said to have had the same experience that the prophet Jeremiah had (Jer 20:7), that God was too strong for him and therefore he had to speak: "[Muhammad] was taught by One mighty in power" (Q 53:5). Just as in Jeremiah's case, what Muhammad has to proclaim goes against his own human ideas, his own human desires and preferences. It is explicitly stated that the revelation that Muhammad received did not come from his own heart nor was it his own fabrication. We hear the same thing about Moses, that it was not his own idea, he did not speak on his own authority (Num 16:28), and Ezekiel spoke out against those who prophesy out of their own imagination (Ezek 13:2). A feeling of immense gratitude overcomes Muhammad. Gratitude is the opposite of ingratitude, just as belief is the opposite of unbelief. An unbeliever is called a *kâfir* in Arabic. The original meaning of this term is "ungrateful (one)," and that accounts for the association of unbelievers with ungrateful people and believers with grateful peo-

---

9. Alfred Guillaume, *The Life of Muhammad: A Translation of Ishâq's Sîrat Rasûl Allâh* (repr. New York: Oxford University Press, 2001) 107.

10. *EQ, s.v.* "Moses."

ple. Muhammad is filled with gratitude because God is concerned about him, has taken pity on him, and has not forgotten him: "Did he not find you an orphan and give you shelter? Did he not find you wandering around, and he gave you guidance. Did he not find you in need and make you rich?" (Q 93:6-8). Muhammad is urged to warn his people: "Therefore, do not treat the orphan harshly, nor reject the petitioner; But the bounty of the Lord — proclaim it!" (Q 93:9-11). Muhammad's life and conduct would from then on be ruled by his commission by God.

Muhammad and Abraham

It is said of Muhammad that he also met Abraham when he made a mystical journey to heaven (in the spirit), *mirâj,* and met earlier prophets. It is claimed that at that time he said that he did not look like anybody so much as he looked like Abraham. Muhammad was instructed in particular to follow the religion of Abraham, who is seen as the representative of pure service to God and is contrasted with idolaters (Q 3:95; 6:79, 161; 10:105; 16:120, 123; cf. 22:31). Jews and Christians want Muhammad to become a Jew or a Christian, for only then can they accept what he says (Q 2:135). The rhetorical question then arises: Do they think Abraham, Ishmael, Isaac, and Jacob, and the children of Israel were Jews or Christians (Q 2:140)? Indeed, the church historian Eusebius (ca. A.D. 260-ca. 340) did say that Abraham could be viewed as a Christian "in fact if not in name."[11] But, Muhammad answered in the Qur'an, the Torah and the Gospel were not revealed until after Abraham (Q 3:65). Abraham was not a Jew nor a Christian, but an adherent of the true religion, a monotheist *(hanîf)* and a Muslim (Q 3:67; cf. 6:79). *Hanîf* is a loanword from Syriac, Aramaic. In the Christian vocabulary from which it is derived, it is a disparaging term meaning "heathen." The Qur'an upgrades this word: from the heathen Abraham is born the original monotheist Abraham: the meaning "seeker of God," the true believer, developed from the word *hanpa* (cf. Rom 4:10-12).[12] The combination of *hanîf* and Muslim makes clear that the term "Muslim" here does not refer to the Muslim community in the sociological sense. Here it is a matter of turning one's

---

11. *EQ, s.v.* "Christians and Christianity."

12. Martin Bauschke, *Der Spiegel des Propheten: Abraham im Koran und im Islam* (Frankfurt am Main: Lembeck, 2008) 47-48; cf. Arthur Jeffery, *The Foreign Vocabulary of the Qur'an* (Baroda: Oriental Institute, 1938) 115.

face to the true religion like a seeker of God, *hanîf.* That is the "natural religion" *(fitra)* in which God has created the human being. That is the "right" religion (Q 30:30). Natural religion means the original religion or service to God in contrast to the particular religions that arose later: polytheism on the one hand and the religions of the people of the Book on the other.[13]

Jesus Fulfills the Torah

The history of the church shows us how dangerous it is to separate the New Testament from the Old. The idea arose — and is still defended by some — that, with the coming of Jesus, his community, the *ecclesia* or the church, took the place of the Jewish people. With that, the Old Testament could be viewed as having no importance or significance for the church: "old" then takes on the suggestive connotation of "antiquated" or "lapsed." This kind of writing off of the Old Testament has certainly become one of the explanations and causes for an anti-Semitism based in Christianity: if Jews are actually no longer needed religiously or no longer even need to exist, it is a small step, it turned out, to threaten them their physical existence.

But that attitude to the Hebrew Bible is, to put it mildly, a serious misinterpretation of the life and work of Jesus. Jesus lived on the basis of the Tanakh and did not come to abolish the Torah but, on the contrary, to fulfill it (Matt 5:17). The Qur'an also states that Jesus confirmed the Torah (Q 3:50, 5:46; 61:6). The image of a leather water bag, like those still used in the Middle East, can be used to explain what "fulfill" means. Given what the water bag looks like when it is empty, one could wonder what purpose such unsightliness could serve in heaven's name. But when the bag is full, one sees immediately its purpose. Jesus fulfills the Torah, embodies it, is the Torah itself become flesh (cf. John 1:14). He shows in his life and work how the Torah should be understood — how it must, above all, be done.

This is what the discussion in the gospel stories between Jesus and the Pharisees and the experts in the law was concerned with. It is not a dispute between a Jew and a Christian, for Jesus himself was a Jew. The dispute is primarily an internal Jewish discussion on the interpretation and understanding of the Torah. When one such expert asks Jesus: "What must I do to inherit eternal life?" Jesus asks what is written in the Torah. The other answers: "Love God and your neighbor as yourself." Jesus confirms the correct-

---

13. *SEI, s.v. "hanîf."*

45

ness of that reading and says: "Do that, and you will live." But the expert in the law takes the discussion a step further, asking "Who is my neighbor?" Jesus answers in the form of a parable, "The Good Samaritan." Jews and Samaritans were on bad terms with each other. A priest and a Levite (someone whose rank was beneath that of priest) who were traveling from Jerusalem to Jericho widely skirted a robbery victim they encountered along the road. A Samaritan, on the other hand, did do something: he actually helped the victim. When Jesus finishes telling the parable, he turns the original question the expert asked ("Who is my neighbor?") around and asks him: "Who was the neighbor of the victim?" The expert in the law, who apparently cannot bring himself to say the name of the hated Samaritan, says: "The one who had mercy on him." Jesus says to him again: "Go and do likewise" (Luke 10:25-37). The expert who debates with Jesus knows perfectly well what the Torah says. There is no difference in opinion between Jesus and him on that score. But the dispute focuses on doing it. It is not orthodoxy, the right doctrine, as it were, but orthopraxis, right living, that is the rub. Jesus asks that what he himself has given as an answer be put into practice.

Muhammad and the Family of Prophets

If it can be assumed that the connection between the Old and New Testaments must remain intact for someone who wants to stand in the Christian tradition and to follow Jesus, does that obtain as well for Jews and Christians regarding the Qur'an? To answer that question properly, it is very important to understand that, in the case of Muhammad, it concerns the same Torah and observing it. The new revelation that Muhammad brought confirms the Torah (Q 3:3; 2:89, 97, 101; 4:47). Moses was a messenger or apostle or prophet (Q 19:51). Muhammad is the prophet for the "unlettered" *(al-nabî al-ummî)*, for those who were unlettered in the sense that they had not yet received any book of revelation. Muhammad inspires them to enjoin what is right and to forbid what is evil and declares what is good to be permitted and what is bad to be forbidden (Q 7:157).

Since the time of the first fratricide in which Cain killed Abel (Gen 4:1-16; Q 5:27-31) and the human race became divided and began to engage in destruction, God has sent prophets. People originally belonged to one community *(umma wâhida)*, but when they became divided God brought a Scripture, a Wisdom, to judge them (Q 2:213). The original meaning of the verb from which "wisdom" is derived is "to judge," "to govern," "to decide."

Wisdom must be understood first of all as practical wisdom.[14] One prophet after another was sent (Q 2:87; 23:44). All the prophets have the same origin: from Adam and from Abraham (Q 19:58; cf. 6:84); they make up one family of prophets connected by their descent (Q 3:33-34). Some prophets have particular characteristics. Abraham is called the friend of God, *Khalîl*[15] (Q 4:125). God allows Moses to approach him for a confidential conversation (Q 19:52), and God speaks with him (Q 4:164; Num. 12:8). Later, Muhammad is given his own title in the Muslim tradition: "God's beloved" *(habîbu 'llâh)*. God has graced some prophets above others: Jesus, called 'Isâ, was thus strengthened by the Holy Spirit (Q 2:87, 253).

One Community, *Umma*

The word "community" *(umma)* can refer in the Qur'an to all three communities: the Jewish, the Christian, and the Muslim. All three are people of the Book, respectively, the Torah revealed to Moses, the Gospel revealed to Jesus, and the Qur'an revealed to Muhammad. God teaches Jesus the Scripture, wisdom, the Torah, and the Gospel (Q 3:48; cf. Q 5:110; 57:27).[16] An Arabic Qur'an is revealed to Muhammad that confirms the previous Revelations, so that he could warn the "mother of cities" *(umm al-qurâ)*, Mecca, and its surrounding areas (Q 42:7; 6:92). Abraham and Ishmael, who together laid the foundations for the dedicated house of prayer, the Ka'ba, prayed together: "Make us both submissive and our descendants into a community that submits to you in full trust *(umma muslima)*" (Q 2:127-28). This *umma* should not be understood in the narrow sense as a Muslim community but as a community to which all three — Jew, Christian, and Muslim — can potentially belong, a community that therefore involves all three and ultimately all people. An exclusive claim to descent from Abraham is rejected (Q 3:67). Every community has had a prophetic messenger sent to it (Q 10:47) who preaches the good news and comes to issue a warning. And for every community a rite has been appointed to which the community has to adhere (Q 22:67, 34). That is, every community has its customs *(shir'a)* and a path to follow, *minhaj* (Q 5:48), its own "way of life."[17] The early Jesus movement

---

14. *EQ, s.v.* "Wisdom"; "Book."
15. Hebron in Hebrew.
16. *EQ, s.v.* "Gospel."
17. Jeffery, *The Foreign Vocabulary*, 273. E.Q. *s.v.*, "Community and Society."

was proclaimed as "the Way," and Christians were called "people of the Way" (Acts 9:2; 19:9; 22:4; 24:14, 22). The religion of Muhammad was also called a "way" (*sharī'a;* Q 5:48), in the sense that God put Muhammad on the open, clear, right way.[18]

The Gospel Confirms the Torah as the Qur'an Confirms the Torah and the Gospel

The Qur'an repeatedly emphasizes that Muhammad confirms what had been revealed prior to him. God has revealed the Scripture with the truth, the Qur'an, to Muhammad, sent down as a confirmation of the Scriptures that were revealed prior to the Qur'an to lead people in the right path (Q 3:3-4). All the Books are connected by the same chain of Revelations. Thus, Jesus confirmed the Torah (Q 5:46). Precisely because the Qur'an confirms both the Torah and the Gospel, the people of the Book, Jews and Christians, are asked to do the same in turn with the Qur'an (Q 4:47; cf. Q 2:41). Just as the Apostle Paul stated emphatically that he believed in everything that was in accordance with the law (Torah) and was written in the prophets (Acts 24:14), one also reads in the Qur'an: "We believe in God and the revelation given to us, Muhammad, in the Qur'an and to Abraham, Isma'il, Isaac, Jacob, and the tribes of Israel, and that given to Moses and Jesus, and that given to (all) prophets from their Lord: We make no difference between one and the others" (Q 2:136). At the Last Judgment people will be judged according to their belief in the messengers who were sent to them (Q 39:71; 67:8; 40:50; 6:130). The earlier Books also continue to be relevant for Muslims. The religion that was given to the earlier prophets was always the same as that now given to Muhammad: "God gave you the same religion he decreed to Noah and what he gave to you, Muhammad, by inspiration, and what we recommended before you to Abraham, Moses, and Jesus with the injunction: 'Keep the precepts of religion and make no divisions in it'" (Q 42:13). The latter sentence here alludes both to the differences between Jews and Christians and to those among the Christians themselves (cf. Q 3:105; 19:37).[19]

Muhammad is seen as a prophet whose sending goes beyond the borders of one people. He is sent as an apostle to humankind (Q 4:79), and he is a "Mercy for all creatures" (Q 21:107).

18. *EQ, s.v.* "Religious Pluralism."
19. Paret, *Der Koran,* on 19:17.

The connection Muhammad sees between the Qur'anic stories about the prophets and those from the Bible is why he calls Jews and Christians to confirm the truth of the Qur'anic allusions and references to the earlier prophets. In turn, if the Muslims do not understand or know something (Q 16:43; 21:7), they are advised to ask the people of the earlier "memory" *(ahl al-Dhikr)* for clarification. The phrase "people of the Memory" refers to those who have a high knowledge of the Torah and the Gospel, who know it best, are properly informed about the history of the prophets through the knowledge of their own "Books." "Memory" *(dhikr)* is also the label that Muhammad used for the Qur'anic stories that Muhammad recited for his audience, such as the story of the "man with two horns" (Q 18:83), Alexander the Great.[20] But the term *dhikr* is also used for the whole revelation (Qur'an) (Q 16:44). The charge to Muhammad's audience to interiorize the stories of the earlier prophets, to remember those of Mary (Q 19:16) and of Abraham (Q 19:41) can be heard. The purpose of the different calls to remember God *(dhikr Allah)* is to remember God as Creator and Preserver of both humankind as well as the whole creation. That can refer to events from the past as many examples of God's mercy and acts of kindness. The Qur'an repeatedly states that human beings continually forget God. It is characteristic of human beings, after all, as indicated by an Arabic wordplay, that the human being *(insân)* is "forgetful" *(nisyân):* "in the remembrance of God do hearts find satisfaction" (Q 13:28).[21]

Narrative units on prophets, which Muhammad is expected to recite, are also called "reports" or "tidings" *(naba', anbâ).* This is what the tales of the two sons of Adam, Cain and Abel (Q 5:27; Gen 4:1-16), of Noah (Q 10:71; Genesis 5–9), and of Abraham (Q 26:69; Genesis 12ff.) are called. The stories of what happened are told in this way (Q 20:99). Some episodes are called the "stories of what is hidden" because the events happened a long time ago and the prophet was not personally present to witness them. An example is the story of Mary: God chose Mary and made her pure, chose her above all women (Q 3:42-44; cf. Luke 1:26-38, 42; cf. Q 12:102). Aside from this story, this term also applies to the story of Noah (Q 11:49; Genesis 6–9), Joseph (Q 12:102; Genesis 37–47), Moses (Q 28:3; Exodus, Deuteronomy), David (Q 38:21; 1 Samuel 16 — 2 Samuel), and the seven sleepers of Ephesus (Q 18:9-11). The latter reference is to a Christian legend about the "Seven Sleepers of Ephesus" who survived the persecution of Christians at the time of the Ro-

20. Cf. Chapter IX.
21. *EQ, s.v.* "Remembrance." For the consequences of this, see Q 5:12-14.

man emperor Decius (A.D. 249-51). Seven young men hid in a cave near Ephesus and appeared to have slept there for 309 years. After awakening, they were discovered because they apparently tried to buy provisions with antiquated money.[22] All that information or reports of the apostles were given to Muhammad to encourage him (Q 11:120) as well as to teach his audience the bitter lesson of how unbelief and disobedience brought destruction to cities in previous times, such as Sodom and Gomorrah (Q 7:101; 9:70). But the unbelieving Meccan audience did not listen and treated the stories like fables (Q 8:31; 6:25; 23:83; 27:68; 46:17; 16:24; 25:5; 68:15; 83:13).[23] The stories of punishments visited on people and cities are, at the same time, a reflection of Muhammad's own situation in Mecca before moving from there to Medina in 622, when he himself suffered from persecution and rejection. The description of these stories of the rejection of earlier prophets was given to Muhammad during that difficult period to encourage him.[24]

Moses and Aaron were commissioned to tell the good news (*bushrâ*, from which the Islamic word for "gospel, glad tidings," is derived) to the believers (Q 10:87). Jesus confirmed the Torah, which preceded him, and proclaimed the good news of a messenger whose name is praised (Q 61:6), which is seen as the announcement of the coming of Muhammad.[25]

Prophets thus bring a double message (Q 2:213; 4:165; 6:48; 18:56): Muhammad is therefore both a bringer of good news *(bashîr)* as well as someone who warns *(nadhîr)*, two rhyming words: the good news for those who do good; the warning for those who do not (Q 2:119; 5:19; 7:188; 10:2; 11:2; 17:105; 19:97; 25:56; 33:45; 34:28; 35:24; 48:8). The warning aspect has to do with informing people of something dangerous and terrifying that can be expected, for they should be on their guard. The warning is a matter of sounding an alarm. The message of Muhammad includes a warning like those given by the earlier messengers as well (Q 53:56). The Qur'an has the same double function: glad tidings and a warning (Q 41:1-4).[26]

It is not appropriate for God to give a human being the Book/*kitâb*, wisdom/*hikma*, and prophecy/*nubûwa* and for the prophet to say: "Be my worshippers (in the sense of the person of the prophet himself) instead of God's." Rather, human beings should be satisfied to be "rabbis," the Qur'an

---

22. *EQ, s.v.* "Ashâb al Kahf."

23. Jeffery, *The Foreign Vocabulary,* 56-57; Paret, *Der Koran,* 137-38.

24. *EQ, s.v.* "Prophets and Prophethood"; "News."

25. Cf. John 14:26. This is seen as a reference to Muhammad, whose name means "praised" *(ahmadu)*.

26. *EQ, s.v.* "Good News, Warner."

says, teachers or exegetes[27] through teaching fellow believers the Scripture and even studying it. Thus, people should not view a prophet as their Lord (Q 3:79) instead of God. That is, human beings, particularly "men of God," have acquired the ability in the course of history to judge, to have the understanding required to make decisions in disputes on issues of faith and thus help the truth prevail. That is how the prophet Muhammad received the Scripture with the truth in order to be able to make such a decision (Q 4:105). Muhammad is called to pronounce a judgment on disputes with people of the Book, primarily the Jews in Medina (Q 5:48). But it is ultimately God who will pronounce his final definitive judgment *(hukm)* on whatever disagreements exist (Q 27:76, 78; cf. 5:48-49).[28]

God is the one who is wise *(hakîm)*. He possesses wisdom *(hikma)*, gives wisdom to whom he wills (Q 2:269), primarily to the prophets: Abraham and his family (Q 4:54), David (Q 2:251; 38:20), Jesus (Q 5:110; 43:63), and Muhammad (Q 4:113). Wisdom is also revealed, a revelation (Q 17:39). The Qur'an itself is also called wise (Q 36:2), for Wisdom is also on equal footing with Scripture or the Book/*kitâb*. This also applies for the Torah and the Gospel (Q 3:48; 5:110). God teaches the Scripture (Q 3:48) and Wisdom (Q 2:231). It is the task of the messenger or prophet to bring people the Scriptures together with Wisdom (Q 2:151; 43:63) or to recite Scripture and Wisdom to people (Q 33:34; 62:2).[29]

Jews and Christians on the Question of Muhammad as a Prophet

Muhammad is a link in the chain of prophets who were sent to earlier communities, a chain that includes Noah, Abraham, Moses, and Jesus (Q 33:7), and Muhammad is the seal of the prophets (Q 33:40), the one who confirms the earlier prophets.[30]

Muhammad is only a messenger who follows the messengers who preceded him (Q 3:144). In that respect, he is equal to some other messengers in the chain, such as Jesus, about whom it is also said that other messengers passed away before him (Q 5:75). Other prophets were sent with a Book of

27. Jeffery, *The Foreign Vocabulary*, 137-38. The word is probably of Syriac origin.

28. On Q 3:79, see Paret, *Der Koran*, 73-74.

29. *EQ, s.v.* "Wisdom, Book."

30. Josef Horovitz, *Koranisch Untersuchungen* (Berlin: de Gruyter, 1926), cited by Heinrich Speyer, *Die Biblischen Erzählungen im Qoran* (Darmstadt: Wissenschaftliche Buchgesellschaft, 1962) 422-23.

the truth to lead them and to resolve their disputes (Q 2:213). The purposes of revelation are equal for all: to warn and to bring good tidings to believers (Q 6:48). The model of the earlier prophets is thus continued in Muhammad's career.

All are advised to follow the prescriptions of their common religion and not to split up into different groups (Q 42:13). It is for that reason that the Qur'an insists that people believe in everything that is revealed to each of the prophets and not to make any distinction between them (Q 2:136, 285; 3:84). The message that was revealed to the prophet Muhammad is essentially the same as that found in the books that were revealed to earlier prophets. The Book that was revealed to Muhammad confirms what preceded him (Q 35:31; cf. 3:3; 5:48; 6:92). The Scripture of Moses, the Torah, had preceded him as a guideline and proof of God's mercy as revelation in order to warn people about injustice and to bring the good tidings to the righteous (Q 46:12; cf. 46:30). In the same way Jesus confirmed the Torah that had been revealed before him (Q 3:50; 5:46; 61:6; cf. Matt 5:17). In the same way Muhammad confirms the Torah and the Gospel.

In contrast, the Jews and Christians whom Muhammad had to deal with directly asked him to follow their religion. As long as that did not happen, they were not happy (Q 2:120). The unbelief of the Jews or the people of the Book in the prophetic call of Muhammad was strongly condemned primarily because the Qur'an did clearly confirm the earlier Scriptures. Why did the Jews and Christians not do the same for the Qur'an? According to the Qur'an, Jews and Christians are condemned because they consciously deny the task given in their own Books, to believe in Muhammad as a prophet (Q 2:89, 91, 101; 4:47). The Jews are reproached for having killed and persecuted their own prophets (Q 3:181; 2:61, 87, 91; 4:155; 5:70), and Christians for having rejected the prophets sent to the Jews (cf. Q 2:113). All prophets who are sent by God are and remain relevant. Apart from their persecution of prophets, the Jews are also reproached for not following their own Torah (cf. Q 62:5), which provides guidance and light for the judgments of the prophets (Q 5:44). Christians are reproached for similar things: the people of the Book do not follow the Torah and the Gospel (Q 5:68); one group has abandoned God's Scripture (Q 2:101; 3:187). But the people of the Book, Jews and Christians, are given the opportunity to be forgiven through fulfilling their commitment to the Torah and the Gospel. If the people of the Book would only believe and live devout lives, then God would forgive their bad deeds (Q 5:65-66).[31]

31. *EQ, s.v.* "Jews and Judaism."

Is Muhammad One of the Prophets?

The Qur'an acknowledges the Torah and the Gospel to be revelations of God and therefore calls Jews and Christians "people of the Book." Muhammad sees himself as belonging to the same chain of prophets. There are Jews who rejoice about what has been revealed to Muhammad, just as there are also some who reject parts of it (Q 13:36). There are Jews and Christians who believe in Muhammad's mission (Q 28:52-53; 2:121; 29:47; 3:199; 6:114). Among the people of the Book, Jews and Christians, there are those who form a community, who are attentive in prayer, who recite verses in the night and prostrate themselves while doing so. They believe in God and the day of judgment, enjoin what is right and forbid what is evil and compete in good deeds. They belong to those who are righteous (Q 3:113-14). They know Scripture (Q 13:43) and are therefore to be viewed as fellow believers (Q 29:46). Muhammad confirms the Revelations, the Torah and *Injīl*, that preceded him (Q 3:3-4). The people of the Book are charged to believe in the Qur'an (Q 4:47; 2:41). Precisely because the people of the Book were formerly the recipients of God's revelation, it is assumed that they will see Muhammad as a true messenger of God and acknowledge that he brings the same "Book," not the same text but the same message from God, the same guidance for humanity.[32]

The attitude of Jews and Christians to the Qur'an is usually different, however. The Qur'an says that the people of the Book obscure the truth with lies and deceit and conceal it (Q 3:71). In Muhammad's time, they turned his religion into an object of mockery (Q 5:57). Most Jews and Christians denied and still deny that Muhammad is a prophet and thereby also deny that the Qur'an is the word of God.

In general, it is also true today that Jews and Christians are not able to recognize the role of Muhammad as prophet. That was already the case in Muhammad's time, with a few exceptions, and not much has changed since. *Nostra Aetate*, a declaration issued by the Second Vatican Council on the relation of the church to non-Christian religions, proclaimed by his Holiness Pope Paul VI on 28 October 1965, adds after referring to the belief of the Muslims in God who is one and the Creator: "who also spoke to the people." A proposed amendment, "ad homines per prophetas allocutum" ("spoke to the people through the prophets"), was not accepted.[33]

If a Jew or Christian recognizes that Muhammad is a prophet who

32. *EQ, s.v.* "Book."
33. Bradford E. Hinze and Irfan A. Omar, eds., *Heirs of Abraham: The Future of Muslim, Jewish, and Christian Relations* (Maryknoll: Orbis, 2005) 68.

confirms both the Torah and the Gospel, Muslims usually understand this as indicating that that person has become a Muslim or should become one. In my view, there is a third way that recognizes Muhammad's status as prophet but does not require one to become a Muslim in the sociological sense by joining the Muslim *umma* in the formal sense of the word. Thus, the recognition that Jesus confirmed the Torah does not mean that I must become a Jew, just as a Jew's recognition of Jesus' fulfillment of the law does not necessarily entail that he should become a Christian in the more narrow sense of the word. The Qur'an's statement that Abraham was not a Jew and not a Christian but a Muslim (Q 3:67) has sometimes been heard or understood to mean that the Qur'an is saying that Abraham cannot be claimed by Jews or Christians but only exclusively by Muslims. But that is not what the text is saying. What it intends to say is that Abraham is the model, the example, of the true believer for all three. To all three, the Jew, the Christian, and the Muslim, this text poses the critical question: Are you really a Muslim in the true sense of the word Muslim, one who has surrendered completely to God?

There is more reason today than ever before, and it is long overdue, to involve the third shoot of this trunk of Abraham, who is seen by all three as "the father of all believers," in the discussion. Muslims see themselves even — like Jews and Christians — as descendants, either physically or spiritually (or both) of Abraham, for Abraham's oldest son Ishmael is seen as the patriarch of the Arab peoples and thus of the Muslims, and Isaac as the patriarch of the Jews. The prophet Muhammad sees himself as descending from Ismâ'îl.

The point of the story of the three Books concerning the example of Abraham is that it concerns his faith. Abraham's faith was expressed in deeds and was perfected by his deeds (Jas 2:22). In that he is an example for all believers. "Descent from Abraham alone, in whatever sense, is not only not enough and is ultimately not the point. Faith in God in general and prophethood in general is not an automatism, and it is also not automatically left to descendants."[34]

The Qur'an says: "Abraham's family are those who follow him, as are this Messenger and those who believe" (Q 3:68). They "follow in the footsteps of the faith that our father Abraham had," as the Apostle Paul says (Rom 4:12). It is not the descendants of Abraham who are the true believers but, as the Dutch poet and theologian William Barnard wrote in a poem, "Only those who believe are Abraham's descendants."[35]

---

34. Bauschke, *Der Spiegel des Propheten*, 123.
35. Hymn 3, *Liedboek der kerken* (Protestantse Kerk in Nederland, 1973). Wessels, *Islam in Stories*, 180.

CHAPTER III

The Choice before the Human Being: Caliph or King?

Justice being taken away, then, what are kingdoms but great robberies? For what are robberies themselves, but little kingdoms? The band itself is made up of men; it is ruled by the authority of a prince, it is knit together by the pact of the confederacy; the booty is divided by the law agreed on. If, by the admittance of abandoned men, this evil increases to such a degree that it holds places, fixes abodes, takes possession of cities, and subdues peoples, it assumes the more plainly the name of a kingdom, because the reality is now manifestly conferred on it, not by the removal of covetousness, but by the addition of impunity. Indeed, that was an apt and true reply which was given to Alexander the Great by a pirate who had been seized. For when that king had asked the man what he meant by keeping hostile possession of the sea, he answered with bold pride, "What thou meanest by seizing the whole earth; but because I do it with a petty ship, I am called a robber, whilst thou who dost it with a great fleet art styled emperor."

Augustine, *City of God*, IV, 4

Kings detest wrongdoing,
for a throne is established through righteousness.

Proverbs 16:12

Introduction

On 13 April 1975, the Lebanese civil war began. A very extensive book was written about that war — which is often portrayed as nothing more than a war between Muslims and Christians — by a British journalist, Robert Fisk, called *Pity the Nation: Lebanon at War*. The title is taken from a poem by the famous Lebanese poet Khalil Gibran (1883-1931): "Pity the nation that is full of beliefs and empty of religion." Our family was in Lebanon when war broke out and for the first few years of the war. Our apartment in Beirut was hit one Sunday afternoon by a rocket; fortunately, we were not home. Although that sounds cynical, it is true: it was a Jewish (Israeli) rocket, fired by Maronite Christians at the Muslim district in West Beirut where we lived. At that time, people were harassed haphazardly at checkpoints, set up by different factions, simply because of their Christian or Muslim identity. Christians could, solely for that reason, be kidnapped, tortured, or killed, and Muslims could be treated in the same manner at a Christian checkpoint. We lost friends and acquaintances on both sides in the war that way.[1] I remember that a nun, dressed in the recognizable attire of her order, was stopped at a Muslim checkpoint and asked: "Whose side are you on?" "To which party do you belong?" The question was, of course, stated in Arabic: "Which *Hizb?*" To which her spontaneous answer was: "Hizbollah." She was allowed to pass. Why was she spared? Because the people serving that post thought she was a follower of Hizbollah? Or perhaps because they understood that she truly was of the party of God?

What was God's intention in creating humankind? Was it to make human beings God's representatives, caliphs, on earth? In contrast, the devil wants human being to be kings, people who shed blood and bring destruction on the earth. How do the caliphs and kings succeed one another in history? What position do the prophets, Abraham, Moses, Jesus, and Muhammad, take over against the unjust kings and what choices do we people make?

1. I think of Marie Rose Boulos and Shaykh Subhi Salih and the Jesuits Nicolaas Kluiters and Michel Allard. I dedicated my book, *Twee watermeloen in één hand* (Amstelveen: Luyten, 1986), to the latter two.

The Creation of Humankind

The creation story in the Qur'an begins, as does the biblical book of Job, with a "prologue in heaven." One day, the angels, the inhabitants of heaven, including Satan, are paying their respects to God. Satan functions as the accuser in a heavenly court (Job 1:6; 2:1). Later on, the seventeenth-century Dutch poet Joost van den Vondel would use this as a theme in his play *Lucifer* (1654). Out of blind love for himself, Lucifer, the archangel, the chief and most illustrious of all the angels, haughty and desiring a higher position, is envious of God's unlimited greatness and is also jealous of the human being, who has been created in God's image and endowed with dominion over the earth in a luxuriant paradise. This haughty and envious angel attempts to make himself equal with God and to keep humankind out of heaven. That is also a theme in *Paradise Lost* (1667) by John Milton (1608-74), the story of a rebellion in heaven led by Satan and the revenge of Satan and the fallen angels on newly-created humankind in paradise.

The Bible states: "Then God said, 'Let us make mankind in our image, in our likeness'" (Gen 1:26). The Qur'an relates how in his meeting with the angels God revealed his plan that he would create humankind (Q 2:30; cf. 38:69; 37:8; 15:28; 38:71).[2] The angels are very much opposed to this plan. They find it a particularly bad idea, for, they respond, humankind will only bring destruction and bloodshed on the earth (Q 2:30). They sense what will happen: God's "human project" will lead to bloodshed on earth. Shedding blood and bringing destruction on the earth are closely connected, as is quickly apparent as soon as the first human being to be born, Cain, kills his brother Abel and thus literally sheds blood. Abel's blood calls out to God from the ground (Gen 4:10); it cries out to heaven. Nevertheless, God keeps a level head, does not let himself be talked out of his wisdom, and says to the angels: "I know what you do not know" (Q 2:30). One can indeed ask what God does know that the angels do not. It is hard to imagine that God did not know that humankind would bring destruction on the earth. No direct answer is given to the question of what the angels do not know. However this may be, God apparently has confidence in his own plan to create humankind, despite his knowledge of the risks it entails, and he carries out his plan.

But what is God planning, in heaven's name? That is stated emphatically: He wants to make humankind, male and female, his representatives,

---

2. Heinrich Speyer, *Die Biblischen Erzählungen im Qoran* (Darmstadt: Wissenschaftliche Buchgesellschaft, 1962) 52-53. *EQ, s.v.* "Adam and Eve."

his vice-regents, on earth. The word "caliph" is used here. Another term used in the Qur'an, in addition to caliph, is *imâm,* the word for "leader." This term means "model," "ideal," "example," or "guide." The term is used later especially in the Shi'ite tradition as an alternative title to caliph for the successor to Muhammad.

God carries out his intention and creates humankind (Q 55:3; Gen 1:26-27), man and woman (Q 49:13), who live in the garden of Eden/'Adn (Q 2:35; Gen 2:15-17). The story of the creation of the woman from the rib of Adam (Gen 2:21-22) does not appear in the Qur'an, and thus the story that has so often led to a woman-unfriendly interpretation is missing here as well.

Humankind and the Earth

Humankind is formed from clay (Q 15:26; 17:61). The first humans enjoy living in the paradisal garden and do not suffer from hunger, nakedness, thirst, or pain occasioned by the heat of the sun (Q 20:118-19). The human being is created from the earth and will return to it and rise up from it another time, at the resurrection of the dead (Q 20:55; cf. 71:18). God has made the earth an assembly point for the living and the dead (Q 77:25-26).

In the creation story, the human being is granted an extremely high position. In any case, he is the perfect work of God, living by God's breath, who reflects God's attributes like a mirror. A tradition, one of the *hadiths,* the second most important source — after the Qur'an — of stories ascribed to the prophet Muhammad, says that God created Adam in his image. Adam is the prototype of the perfect human being. He is blessed with the special grace of knowledge: God, after all, teaches Adam the names (Q 2:31). To know or be acquainted with the name of a thing is to be able to control it, to use it for oneself. Because of his knowledge of the names, Adam becomes the master of all created things. God makes humankind his caliph, his vice-regent on earth, and commands the angels to bow down before him (Q 2:34; 20:116; 20:65; 18:50; 38:71-73) since the human being is superior to the angels — the secret of the names is not given to the angels. They do nothing else but worship God in perfect obedience, whereas the human being enjoys — or suffers from — the choice between obedience and rebellion.

After completing the work of creation, God first wanted to entrust responsibility for that to the heavens and the mountains, but they refused to accept or bear such responsibility, flinching at the idea. But humans accepted the responsibility without a moment's thought. "[The human being] was indeed unjust and foolish" (Q 33:72), the Qur'an adds soberly.

The Role of Satan/Iblîs

As soon as humankind is created and placed in the garden, Satan appears on stage. He is first and foremost the tempter of the human being, the one who led human beings to eat from the tree of immortality (Q 20:120). In that role he is called Satan (Q 2:36). Satan, or the devil, has the ability to incite fear (Q 3:175), to lead human beings into making mistakes (Q 2:36; 3:155), to lead them astray (Q 4:60), to sow hostility and hatred between people (Q 5:91), to lead them into temptation, to raise false hopes (Q 7:27; 47:25), and to provoke people (Q 17:53). Satan lies in wait (Q 7:16; cf. Gen 4:7). He is a deceiver (Q 31:33; 35:5) and sneaks around (Q 114:4).[3] In the Qur'an he appears primarily in the early history of the world (Q 2:34; 7:11; 15:31ff.; 17:62; 18:50; 20:116; 38:73ff.) at the creation of humankind as a rebel and as a tempter in paradise. Humans are warned about the devil as their enemy (Q 20:117) or an avowed enemy (Q 7:22). The devil refuses to bow before Adam (Q 2:34; 7:11; 15:31; 17:61; 18:50; 20:116; 38:74) and is then banished from heaven (Q 7:13; 38:77; 15:34). Out of rage and envy, he swears to lead Adam, his wife, and descendants on the wrong path (Q 7:16-17). This image of the wrong path is borrowed from the imagery of the desert. In contrast, God wants humankind to travel the right or straight path, and that is why the opening chapter of the Qur'an, *Sûrat al-Fâtiha*, contains the prayer: "Show us the straight way" (Q 1:6; cf. Ps 1:6). This prayer's status among Muslims is comparable to that of the Lord's Prayer among Christians.

Because Adam and Eve eat from the forbidden tree at the instigation of Satan they are banished from the garden (Q 20:122-23), just as Satan is thrown out of heaven. From that moment on, the earth will be the dwelling place of humankind. There they will live and die, and from the earth they will rise up from the dead (Q 7:24-25). But the people are then comforted. Whenever God sends the right guidance, those who follow it need not be afraid, sad, or unhappy (Q 2:38; 20:123).[4]

Another name for Satan is Iblîs, which is derived from Greek *diabolos*, that which wants to make havoc or a complete mess of everything or muck

---

3. *EQ, s.v.* "Devil."
4. *EQ, s.v.* "Fall of Man."

everything up, a "sower of discord" who starts a rebellion against God (Q 7:12-19, 31-33; 17:61-65; 38:71-85). Iblîs can be characterized as proud and disobedient.

Satan's Temptation

If God wants humankind to be his vice-regent, Satan wants to try something else. The way in which he wants to test humankind seems to correspond precisely to one of the three temptations of Jesus, who is often seen as the second Adam. After Jesus' stay in the desert and his fast of forty days and forty nights, he becomes very hungry. The devil first tempts him to turn stones into bread, then to jump from the highest point of the temple and to ask God to catch him, literally, and third, to worship the devil in order to gain dominion over all kingdoms of the earth: "Again, the devil took him to a very high mountain and showed him all the kingdoms of the world and their splendor. 'All this I will give you,' he said, 'if you will bow down and worship me'" (Matt 4:9). These temptations revolve around the understanding of and primarily acting in accordance with the Torah/*Tawra,* the Book in which God points out the way people are to live. These three temptations have to do with "bread," economic power and how to exercise that, "holy" or religious power, and "kingdoms," political dominion. But Jesus resists these temptations one by one. He wants to worship and honor God alone. Jesus turns to the Torah here: "Away from me, Satan! For it is written: 'Worship the Lord your God, and serve him only'" (Matt 4:8-11; Luke 4:8; cf. Deut 6:13).[5] It is stated in the Qur'an that God, not Satan, showed Abraham that he would have dominion over heaven and earth. In contrast to his father, Abraham is convinced of the truth of this (Q 6:75): "So glory to him in whose hands is the dominion of all things: and to him will ye be all brought back" (Q 36:83). The temptation Satan presents the first human being in the Qur'an narrative is the third temptation of Jesus. He offers the human being an imperishable kingdom *(mulk).* Satan whispers evil thoughts to him and says: "O Adam! shall I lead thee to the Tree of Eternity and to a kingdom that never decays?" (Q 20:120).

---

5. Huub Oosterhuis and Alex van Heusden, *Het Evangelie van Lukas* (Vught: Skandalon, 2007) 100.

God Is King

To understand what one should understand by this temptation to be king, it is first of all important to know that in the language of the Bible and the Qur'an kingship is not a neutral or innocent concept. According to the Bible and the Qur'an, only God is the true king: "The LORD is King for ever and ever" (Ps 10:16). "Now to the King eternal, immortal, invisible, the only God, be honor and glory for ever and ever" (1 Tim 1:17). "Whose will be the dominion on that Day? It is God, the One the All-Conquering!" (Q 40:16). "Blessed be he who has Dominion [kingship]; he has power over all things" (Q 67:1). God is the true king (Q 20:114), the holy king (Q 59:23). To him belongs dominion over heaven and earth, and he alone exercises this dominion (Q 17:111). On the last day dominion will belong to God (Q 22:56), to the Merciful, Rahmân (Q 25:26), an important name for God that was used in southern Arabia by Christians and Jews already before the time of Muhammad.

Earthly Kings

But what is precisely going on with those who are kings or are called kings on earth? In the view of the Bible and the Qur'an, kings are seldom examples of those who do justice. They are, rather, those whom the angels warned God would bring destruction and bloodshed on the earth. Examples of such kings who are evil, unjust, proud, and become haughty and bring destruction on earth are Nimrod the king of Assur and Babel (Q 2:258); Pharaoh/ *Firawn* of Egypt; Agag the king of the Amalekites; or Goliath/Jâlût, who was a Philistine and also called king of the Canaanites or the Amalekites.[6] Goliath thus becomes a collective name for the oppressors of the people of Israel.[7] But most of the rulers of the kingdoms of Judah and Israel fall under this category of unjust kings as well: they "did evil in the eyes of the LORD" is a constant refrain in the book of Kings (1 Kgs 11:6, passim).

If Satan thus directs humankind to the tree and imperishable kingship, he in fact suggests to humans that they assume an authority that belongs only to God. Satan thus suggests that the human being can become God's equal. That kingship, of which Satan holds out the prospect, therefore stands

6. *EI, s.v.* "Tâlût."
7. *EI, s.v.* "Djâlût."

diametrically opposite to the vice-regency of the position of caliph that God intended for humankind, to be God's representative on earth, which entails doing justice, following the way of the Torah, fulfilling the Torah, the *shari'a*.

Vice-Regents, Caliphs, after the Deluge

The course of human history shows, in a sufficiently shocking way, that the angels were right. Humankind has brought much destruction on earth and shed copious amounts of blood. That began already with the first children of men, Cain and Abel — the first fratricide: Cain kills his brother Abel (Genesis 4). Cain is also the first person to build a city. Right from the start, therefore, the city has a stigma. In the Qur'an, in the singular, the term "city" refers to an important city: Mecca (Q 48:24), Medina (Q 9:101), Sodom (Q 21:74; 25:40), and Nineveh (Q 10:98). Mecca is called the "mother of cities," a metropolis. Most references in the Qur'an to cities in the plural are negative: cities that will be destroyed by God because their inhabitants reject the message of the prophet or their leaders. They wallow in excesses and destruction, abandon their religious obligations, and persecute God's prophets.[8]

When God sees how great injustice on the earth has become, he decides to eradicate humankind from the earth by a great flood (Gen 6:5-7). Only Noah/Nûh and his family and representatives of the animal kingdom will escape. God wants to start anew with Noah. After saving Noah and his family in the ark, God makes the survivors his vice-regents, caliphs, on the earth (Q 10:73). But as quickly becomes apparent, history repeats itself. The story of Noah (Q 7:59-64; cf. Genesis 6–9) is followed by a number of similar stories about the so-called Arab prophets, who were sent to their own people. The leaders *(al-mala')* of the people of Thamûd became haughty and asked those who were oppressed or those among them who believed if they were all that certain that Sâlih had been sent by God. They were also judged and punished by an earthquake (Q 7:73-79). The prophet Hûd was also sent to the people of 'Ad, a powerful people that existed shortly after Noah and was proud of their great kingdom. Hûd says that they have to remember how God had appointed them, the people of 'Ad, to be vice-regents after the people of Noah and had given them a colossal stature and great physical strength. But they say, "Who is superior to us in strength?" (Q 41:15; cf. 7:69; Gen 6:4). If they turn away from God, however, God will appoint another people as vice-regents (Q 11:57).

8. *EI, s.v.* "Karya"; *EQ, s.v.* "City."

Moses then says to his people, the children of Israel, that God will perhaps destroy their enemy, Pharaoh of Egypt and his people, and make the Israelites vice-regents on earth and will then see how they do in that role (Q 7:129). The rhetorical question is posed: Is it not God who appoints people as vice-regents on earth (Q 27:62)? Thus, the idea is expressed repeatedly that if the caliphs do not act like caliphs, true vice-regents, but like unjust kings, they will be punished and replaced by those who will act justly, will act like caliphs on earth.

Muhammad proclaims that God thus chose the Meccans, after he had punished earlier nations for their unbelief, to be his vice-regents on earth (Q 10:14). God promised those among them who believe and do good works in Medina that he would make them vice-regents on the earth as he did those before them. Those who reject faith after this are rebellious and sinful (Q 24:55).[9]

Thus, the fixed pattern is: all human beings and the peoples are called to cultivate and preserve the earth (Gen 2:15) and to be vice-regents or caliphs on earth. If they nevertheless bring destruction on the earth, they are replaced by others, although there is always the added clause that the replacements will be watched as well to see if they in turn will act as real caliphs.

Kings and the Worship of Moloch

Since the tenth century B.C., when kings reigned in Israel, there were indeed kings who were considered good, such as David (1 Samuel 16–2 Samuel 23), Hezekiah (Isaiah 36–39), and Josiah (2 Kings 22). Most of them, however, were evil, as we will discuss more extensively below.[10] A king and kingship are almost always unjust. *Melek* in Hebrew or *malik* in Arabic are connected with the word "Moloch," which is the name of a god to whom children were sacrificed (Lev 18:21). These human sacrifices were not only performed in non-Jewish cults (Ezek 23:37ff.; Ps 106:37-38) but even in Israel. Jephthah, one of the judges in the time that there were no kings in Israel, sacrifices his own daughter because of an oath he swore too rashly (Judg 11:30ff.).[11] But a

---

9. *EQ, s.v.* "Punishment Stories," "Generations."

10. Cf. below in this chapter.

11. It is possible that she was not killed in the end, but is the intended meaning that she remained a virgin?

serious change occurs as soon as kingship is instituted in Israel. Already the third king, Solomon/Sulaymân, it should be noted, has sacrificial sites, high places, built for Moloch on the mountain east of Jerusalem (1 Kgs 11:7). Already early on people set up a holy site in Hinnom Valley near Jerusalem, a sacrificial site where people would have their children burned in sacrifice to Moloch (Jer 7:31-34; 19:6; 32:35). High places for Baal were built in that same valley. People burned and sacrificed their sons and daughters there before Baal (Jer 19:5) or before Yahweh (7:31), even though God did not want such an outrage to be done (32:35; cf. Deut 12:31; 18:10). Ahaz, king of Judah, even sacrificed his own son according to "the detestable practices of the nations the LORD had driven out before the Israelites" (2 Kgs 16:3; cf. also King Manasseh, 2 Chr 33:6). The prophet Ezekiel, who belonged to the elite of ten thousand people who had been exiled and who worked in Babylon (Ezek 3:15), denounced such horrible acts. It was the just king Josiah who put a stop to this. He desecrated the furnace of Moloch in the Ben Hinnom Valley so that no one would be able to burn his son or daughter again (2 Kgs 23:10). Nevertheless, after Josiah's death, the sacrificial practice was resumed (Jer 7:31-32; 19:5-15). Because of the terrible acts that occurred on that spot and the curse that the prophet Jeremiah pronounces over this valley of murder (Jer 7:32), the name Hinnom Valley comes to represent in Judaism the place where the definitive last judgment will occur: Gehinnon or Gehenna; the Arabic word for hell, *jahannam,* often used in the Qur'an as a synonym for fire, is derived from that (Q 2:206).[12] For that matter, in the Septuagint Greek translation of the book of the prophet Amos (5:25-27), the worship of Moloch is seen as something that already happened during the Israelites' wandering in the desert.

Human Kingship

That, according to the Bible and the Qur'an, God alone is king is not, obviously, intended to mean that God cannot and does not in fact give kingship to human beings, including in the sense of appointing them. God does grant the kingship to whomever he wills and takes it away from whomever he wills (Q 3:26). It is possible to be king — but then it is a matter of being king "by the grace of God." God can grant kingship to those to whom he is favorably disposed, such as Joseph, David, and Solomon. But it is striking that none of

12. *EI, s.v.* "Djahannam."

64

those three are specifically called king in the Qur'an. Joseph turns to God with gratitude for the sovereignty that God has given him. He prays: "O my Lord! You have indeed bestowed on me kingship, and taught me something of the interpretation of dreams and events, O Thou Creator of the heavens and the earth! You are my Protector in this world and in the Hereafter. Take my soul (at death) as one submitting to thy will (as a Muslim) and unite me with the righteous (*sâlihîn*)" (Q 12:101). Here the word "muslim" is used, which should not be understood in the contemporary sense of the term but in the proper sense of those who submit to God in complete faith. Solomon prays: "O my Lord! Forgive me, and grant me a kingdom that (perhaps) is not suited to another after me" (Q 38:35; cf. 1 Kgs 3:5ff.; 11:11-13).[13]

Nevertheless, it is again and again apparent from the stories in the Bible and the Qur'an that a tension exists or remains between kingship, which belongs solely to God, on the one hand and those who desire or are thought to exercise kingship or do exercise it on the other hand. The Qur'an speaks just like the Bible about kings in the sense of human rulers. But it is and remains highly dangerous to be king. If the term "king" is used not for God but for a human being, then it usually has a negative ring to it. When a king enters a city, it is obvious that he is consigning it to destruction (Q 27:34). But in all these cases, the issue is what the true nature or character of kingship is or should be. That can best be illustrated by the example of King David/Dâwûd. After David defeated Goliath (1 Samuel 17), he receives the kingship and wisdom from God and God teaches him what he will do (Q 2:251; cf. 38:20). But David is expressly appointed by God as vice-regent or caliph on earth. Other than Adam, he is the only one in the Qur'an, also the only king, who is called that (Q 38:26). It is then clearly stated what this being king entails: he must judge justly between people, not follow his own desires, for that leads away from the path God indicates (Q 38:26).[14] Thus, David is a good king insofar as he exercises kingship like a caliph.

Abraham, Moses, Jesus, Muhammad, and the Kings

Now we will discuss the important stories of prophets who were confronted in exemplary fashion by kings with divine pretensions; Abraham and Nimrod in Assur and Babel, Moses and Pharaoh in Egypt, Jesus and the Herods

---

13. Speyer, *Biblischen Erzählungen*, 383-84.
14. *EI*, s.v. "Dâwûd"; *EQ*, s.v. "David."

and Pilate, the representative of the Roman emperor, and Muhammad and the leaders of Mecca.

Abraham versus Nimrod

Nimrod/Namrûd is seen as the first potentate and tyrant on earth (Gen 10:8; 1 Chr 1:10). He is called the son of Cush in the Table of Nations (Gen 10:8). Cush was the oldest son of Ham, one of Noah's sons, and the name is usually a reference to Ethiopia. Nimrod is the famous ruler of Babel and the founder of Nineveh (Gen 10:10-12), two powerful cities. Assur is called the land of Nimrod (Mic 5:6). Nimrod is thus portrayed as the king of Babylon and Assur in the primeval age. These cities are also imperial centers, areas where injustice and oppression reign. Nimrod's dominion includes war and terror; he has been connected with the god of war and hunting (Gen 10:9), but he does not only hunt animals. Nimrod is the first biblical example of a prince who demands the kingship from God for himself. He also engages in aggression toward people and claims that God made him king. The evil Nimrod stands over against righteous Abraham.

Abraham lives and works in the land where Nimrod is king. The Bible mentions King Nimrod but does not speak of any encounter between him and Abraham as do the Jewish and Muslim traditions. The first-century Jewish historian Flavius Josephus (A.D. 37–ca. 100) relates that Nimrod opposed his will to God's and was worshipped by his subjects.

Nimrod becomes involved in a dispute with Abraham about his kingship. When Abraham says: "My Lord is the One who gives life and death," Nimrod replies: "I give life and death." Then Abraham says: "But it is God who causes the sun to rise from the east: Do you cause it to rise from the west?" He thus confounds and shames the unbeliever (Q 2:258).

Nimrod in the Tradition

In the Jewish and Christian tradition Nimrod is a model of the evil person, the archetype of an idolater and tyrannical king. In rabbinic literature Nimrod is called "the evil one." In the Muslim version Nimrod is called the tyrant, the oppressor, the "obstinate transgressor" (Q 11:59). His name is derived from a verb meaning "to rebel," namely, against God. It is also suggested that the name designates a female panther, which would entail that Nimrod was suckled by this animal, reminding us of the later story of Romulus and Remus who were suckled by a wolf. Another story is told in which Nimrod, raised by an unknown person, first kills his father and then marries his mother, which brings to mind the story of Oedipus.[15]

When Nimrod throws Abraham into the fire, an angel intervenes to cool the fire. Here the Qur'an intends to say: "The one whose heart burns for the one God is indifferent to the fire of men."[16] Nimrod is amazed by that, just like Nebuchadnezzar, the later king of the Neo-Babylonian Empire, who conquered Jerusalem (587 B.C.) and exiled some of the people to Babel. He had a golden image of himself set up, and everyone was required to bow before it. But when the companions of the prophet Daniel, Shadrach, Meshach, and Abednego, refused to do so, they were thrown into a fiery oven. To the king's amazement, they remained unhurt and could move freely about in the midst of the flames and honor and praise God (Dan 3:1-24). Nimrod is thus given the features of two archetypal cruel and oppressive kings: Nebuchadnezzar and Pharaoh.

That Nimrod is killed by a gnat which entered his brain through his nose is based on a Jewish story. His death was painful as that of the Roman emperor Titus (A.D. 39-81), who met his end in a similar fashion. Titus led the war in Judea and conquered and destroyed Jerusalem in the year 70. The gnat tortured Nimrod for four hundred years before the latter died. Nimrod finds his way into the late Jewish legend of Abraham. It is indisputable that the Jewish stories, the Haggadah, and the Muslim legends influenced each other. Nimrod is also seen as having built the tower of Babel because he wanted to see Abraham's God. This story is parallel to the story of Pharaoh, who had a high palace built with the same objective, so that he could peer at God (Q 28:38). Nimrod's tower is destroyed by a heavy storm (Q 16:26). The names of Nimrod and Pharaoh are thus interchangeable. Nimrod even attempted to kill Abraham's God, ascending to heaven in a cart carried by eagles, and when the arrow he shoots comes back with blood on it, he thinks he has killed God.[17]

Abraham has to separate himself from the injustice of such kingship and leave. Over against this king, Abraham is called an *imâm* ("leader"), an alternative title for caliph(!), of humankind (Q 2:124). Following him, Isaac

---

15. *EI, s.v.* "Namrûd."

16. Martin Bauschke, *Der Spiegel des Propheten: Abraham im Koran und im Islam* (Frankfurt am Main: Lembeck, 2008) 42.

17. *EI, s.v.* "Namrud"; *EQ, s.v.* "Nimrod."

and Jacob will also be appointed leaders, will let themselves be led by God's command (Q 21:72, 73; cf. 32:34). God has given dominion, kingship, to the family of Abraham (Q 4:54) clearly in another sense than what Satan intended. This is dominion in the sense of caliph and imam, which entails doing justice and righteousness.

Moses versus Pharaoh

Moses/Mûsâ appears in another setting, Egypt. Egypt is the kingdom to which the pharaohs belong (Q 43:51), the country where Joseph would be viceroy (*'aziz*, Q 12:78, 88), a title meaning "the powerful person of Egypt," which appears to refer to the position of first minister under Pharaoh.[18] Egypt is the arena in which the struggle of Moses and Aaron/Hârûn on behalf of the children of Israel will take place (Q 10:75; 23:45ff.). Jesus and his mother would later seek refuge there (Matthew 2; Q 23:50). Even though Egypt is cited only five times by name in the Qur'an, it is the city or country most frequently mentioned, as is also the case in the Bible.[19]

Pharaoh rules in Egypt and is an outstanding example of an unjust ruler. He is a model of the arrogant ruler who claims, with pride, the kingship over Egypt (Q 43:51). The image of the pharaoh is that of a tyrannical leader (Q 79:17; cf. 20:24, 34). As an indication of the typical arrogant and unashamed tyrant, the term has led to a verb in Arabic that means "act like a hardened tyrant" *(tafar'ana)*.[20]

Pharaoh employs violence throughout the whole land and knows no limits (Q 10:83). He brings destruction on the earth (Q 28:4) and deceives his people (Q 20:79). Just like King Nimrod, he also claims to be God (Q 26:29; 28:38), saying to his own people: "I am your Lord, Most High" (Q 79:24). Those who claim any other to be God are thrown into prison (Q 26:29). To those in high positions in his empire he says that he acknowledges no other god than himself. It is not difficult to see here how the ruler calls people to an attitude that is precisely the opposite of what would later be formulated in the Islamic confession of faith. Whereas the latter states, "There is no other God than God," the arrogant, proud ruler states: "There is no other God than me" (Q 28:38). He therefore requires absolute subjection from his

18. *EI, s.v.* "'Azîz Misr."
19. *EQ, s.v.* "Egypt."
20. *EI, s.v.* "Fir'awn."

people and unquestioning obedience. Moses is sent to Pharaoh to save his people (Q 37:114-22) and assumes the leadership of the children of Israel (Q 10:83-87; 26:52).

The Child Jesus versus Herod the Great

Jesus lived and was active in the time that the Roman Empire ruled Palestine. Around the time of his birth Palestine was governed by King Herod (37-4 B.C.), called "the Great" by the Jewish historian Flavius Josephus because he was "the Elder." One of the gospels, Matthew, is called the gospel of the Kingdom. In that gospel two kings stand opposed to each other: Herod, the king of the Jews, and Jesus, also called the king of the Jews (Matt 2:2; 27:11, 29, 37; cf. Mark 15:2; Luke 23:3; John 18:33). This gospel revolves around the question: Who is the true king of the Jews and what is the nature of true kingship?

Shortly after Jesus' birth, magi come from the east to King Herod in Jerusalem to ask him where the king of the Jews had been born, for they had seen his star. The high priests and experts in the law, summoned by Herod, tell him that the expected messianic king was to be born in Bethlehem. Herod communicates that information in secret to the magi with the explicit request that they report to him if they find the child in Bethlehem (thus not in Jerusalem!) so he can pay his respects to this messianic king as well (Matt 2:1-8). But when they find the child and have worshipped him, they are warned in a dream not to return to Herod. As soon as Herod notices that he has been mocked by the magi, he gives the order to have all the children two years old and younger in Bethlehem killed.

Thus, the gospel begins with a report of how, already as a child, Jesus had his life threatened by King Herod, who wanted to kill him. He is just barely born, still an "innocent" child, before Herod begins with killing: the slaughter of the Innocents in Bethlehem (Matt 2:16-18).

Jesus versus Pilate and Herod Antipas

At the beginning of Jesus' public ministry, when he was about thirty years old, he went to the desert for forty days (Luke 4:2). Those forty days correspond to the forty years Israel wandered in the desert before they crossed the Jordan to take possession of the land. When Jesus later stands before the judgment seat of Pilate, the Roman procurator and representative of the emperor in Rome, he is asked: "Are you the king of the Jews?" (John 18:33). Jesus answers that his kingdom is not of this world (18:36). When Pilate then says that he is a king, Jesus says that those are Pilate's words (18:37). When Pilate has him flogged and a crown of thorns is pressed on to his head, Jesus is hit in the face and clothed with a purple cloak — thus dressed up like a mock-king. Then Pilate says, "Here is the man (*Ecce homo*)" (John 19:5). The chief priests and officers begin to cry out: "Crucify him, Crucify him" (19:6). After Pilate has sat down on his judgment seat, he says to the Jewish leaders: "Here is your king." Their answer is to scream that Jesus should be crucified. When Pilate then asks if he is to crucify their king, the chief priests answer: "We have no king but Caesar" (19:13-15). When they say this, they therefore deny in so many words what the Torah says: Only God is king. The Roman emperor is as unjust a ruler as were Nimrod and Pharaoh.

Before his condemnation, Pilate sends Jesus to King Herod because Jesus comes from Galilee, the area under Herod's jurisdiction. This Herod is Herod Antipas (4 B.C.–A.D. 6), tetrarch of Galilee and Perea, the Transjordan, who founded the city of Tiberias, named after the Roman emperor Tiberius (emperor from 13-37), on the Sea of Galilee. He was married to Queen Herodias, previously his brother's wife, the granddaughter of Herod the Great. She has a great desire for power and convinces her half-brother to divorce his wife and marry her. John the Baptist/Yahyâ, who strongly condemns the marriage, is executed by Herod at Herodias's instigation (Matt 14:3-12). Herod and those in his court ridicule Jesus by dressing him in clothes befitting a king. But when Jesus says nothing to Herod, he is sent back to Pilate (Luke 23:6-11).

When Jesus is crucified, the Roman soldiers place a sign above his head with the charge against him: "This is Jesus, the king of the Jews" (Matt 27:37), in three languages, Hebrew, Latin, and Greek (John 19:19). While Jesus is hanging there between two other crucified criminals, the chief priests, the experts in the law, and the elders mock him and say: "He saved others, but he can't save himself! He's the king of Israel! Let him come down now from the cross, and we will believe in him. He trusts in God. Let God rescue him now if he wants him" (Matt 27:42-43; cf. Ps 22:8). Pilate had already mocked Jesus by crowning him with a crown of thorns, and Herod mocked him by dressing him in an elegant robe.

In the gospel narratives the question is: Who is the true king — Herod or Jesus? Herod the Great does not let himself be mocked and thus becomes a child-killer. The other king of the Jews lets himself be mocked. He does not save or liberate himself but others: he is a caliph, a messianic king, as God intended.

Muhammad versus the Unjust Leaders of Mecca

In his time, the prophet Muhammad did not have to deal with kings in Mecca. But the equivalent of kings were there: *al-mala'*, the aristocratic leaders in the city who held all authority. In the period A.D. 610-22, Muhammad had to deal with these unjust leaders of Mecca who resisted him and his message. To properly understand their position, we should note what the opponents of the other prophets whose stories Muhammad sees reflecting his own situation are often called. In the stories of the earlier messengers, *al-mala'* ("prominent people") represent the stereotype of unbelieving leaders, such as those Muhammad had to endure in Mecca. Thus, Muhammad sees his own confrontation with the leaders in Mecca in the confrontation with leaders of the people of Noah; the people of ʿAd and Thamûd; the prominent leaders of the people of the Arab prophet Hûd, who was sent to the people of ʿAd; Sâlih, who was sent to the people of Thamûd; and Shuʿayb/Jethro, who was sent to the people of Midian/Madyan (Q 7:90). Moses also had to deal with such prominent people among the people of Pharaoh (Q 7:109, 127).

It is such leaders, kings, of a city or tribe that constitute the largest obstacle to the success of the prophetic mission.[21] Such leaders mock and threaten Muhammad and want to kill him. The prominent or notable individuals of the people time and again represent the party of unbelievers, the ungrateful, those who commit injustices, who bring destruction, who shed blood, who advance over dead bodies. It was that kind of injustice done by such leaders that the prophet Muhammad had to deal with.

The First Caliphs

The first successors to Muhammad after his death were not called kings but caliphs. The tradition refers to the first four as the "rightly guided caliphs," who were Abû Bakr (A.D. 632-34), ʿUmar (634-44), Uthmân (644-56), and ʿAlî (656-61). But the tensions between caliph and king can also be seen in

---

21. *EQ, s.v.* "Chastisement and Punishment."

these individuals. Caliph 'Umar once asked Salmân the Persian, who was such an intimate companion of Muhammad that he was considered a member of his family: "'Am I a king now or a caliph?' Salmân answered: 'If you tax the land of the believers in money, either a little or much, and put the money to any use the law doth not allow, then thou art a king and no caliph of God's apostle.' 'By God!' said 'Umar, 'I know not whether I am a caliph or a king, and if I am a king, it is a fearful thing.'"[22]

After 661, the center of the caliphate shifted from Medina to Damascus. Mu'âwiyya, a son of Abû Sufyân who had led the opposition to Muhammad, was initially governor of Damascus under the third "rightly guided" caliph, 'Uthmân. After the death of the fourth caliph, 'Alî, Mu'âwiyya became the first caliph of the Umayyad dynasty. The Umayyads believed that they were connected with the line of descent from the biblical prophets.[23] Hasan (625-70), 'Alî''s son, the eldest grandson of the prophet Muhammad, transferred all power to Mu'âwiyya without a fight. "'I do not use my sword when my whip will do,' was one of his [Mu'âwiyya's] sayings; 'nor my whip when my tongue will do. Let a single hair still bind me to my people, and I'll not let it snap; when they slack, then I pull, but when they pull, then I slack.' 'What's approved today was reproved once,' he said; 'even so things now abominated will someday be embraced.' 'Abû Bakr sought not the world, nor did it seek him. The world sought 'Umar for all that he sought it not. But ourselves are sunk in it, to our middles.' 'I,' said he, 'am the first king (in Islam).'"[24]

The 'Abbasids' defeat of the Umayyads was cheered as representing the reinstatement of the true view of the caliphate, the notion of a theocratic state instead of the purely secular or worldly state *(mulk)* of the Umayyads. The caliph of Baghdad turned out, in fact, to be as worldly as the one of Damascus he had replaced.[25]

Thus, after the four so-called "rightly guided" caliphs, the other rulers continued to call themselves caliphs. In Baghdad, some of them even began to see themselves as the caliph of God, "the shadow of God on earth." But is that what they were? People quickly learned, in line with the prophetic critique in the Qur'an, whether talking about a caliph or a king, to make a sharp distinction between these rightly guided caliphs and secular kingship. The caliphate began, in fact, to show all the signs of pharaonic injustice and oppression. As

22. Cyril Glassé, *The Concise Encyclopaedia of Islam* (rev. ed.; London: Stacey International, 2001), *s.v.* "'Umar"; cf. "Salmân the Persian."

23. *EQ, s.v.* "Prophets and Prophethood."

24. Glassé, *Concise Encyclopaedia of Islam, s.v.* "Mu'âwiyya."

25. Philip K. Hitti, *History of the Arabs* (8th ed.; New York: St. Martin's, 1964) 288-89.

soon as a new caliphate arose in Damascus (the Umayyads, A.D. 661-750), the caliphs began to be characterized by devout Muslims as unjust *kings*.

Kings and Pride

The actual intention of a central story of the Three Books is to make clear that the unjust princes of Assur, Babel, and Egypt are all connected ideologically and are all characterized by pride, thinking themselves to be like God. The theme returns again and again in the stories of how princes become haughty, prideful, for which the Greek translation, the Septuagint, uses the term *hubris*. Humans have the inclination to transgress boundaries set by God. Pride is often seen as a sin because it makes one equal to or involves an aspiration to be like God in his greatness. Warnings are issued constantly against the pride and arrogance of priests and kings: Nimrod, Pharaoh, Nebuchadnezzar, and Herod, who make themselves equal to God, to be the son of God, such as Alexander the Great, who thought he was the epiphany of God, as Antiochus IV Epiphanes once did. That lasted until the time of Muhammad, whose unbelieving opponents thought rather highly of themselves (Q 25:21). Such rulers are constantly attempting to make themselves great *(istikbâr)*, whereas only God is great *(Allahu al-akbar)* (Q 59:23), the Most High (Q 22:62).[26]

Pride is the preeminent sin of all who refuse to submit to God. It is the sin of those who have not listened to the message of the prophets throughout history. Reference is often made to communities, groups, and individuals who proudly and arrogantly rejected God's word. They are the "prominent people," the aristocratic leaders in all kinds of situations who are so prideful or arrogant (Q 7:75; 34:31-33). That was the case in Noah's time: his contemporaries hardened themselves in uncompromising arrogance (Q 71:7): the people of ʿAd to whom the Arab prophet Hûd was sent behaved arrogantly throughout the land or on the earth (Q 41:15); the leaders of the people of Thamûd of the Arab prophet Sâlih were proud and did not believe in what he believed in (Q 7:75-76); the leaders of the Midianites of the prophet Shuʿayb, Jethro, Moses' father-in-law, were proud and said: "We shall certainly drive thee out of our city" (Q 7:88).

Pride is the preeminent sin of the pharaoh of Egypt. Haman and Korah

---

26. Nebuchadnezzar serves as the model for Nero, Caligula, right up to the English king Henry VIII and the Russian czar Ivan the Terrible. The negative meaning of the tower as a cathedral of the evil one, stamped by the delusion of greatness and pride of the legendary builder King Nimrod, lives on in popular pop culture. Cf. Moritz Wullen and Günther Schauerte, eds., *Babylon: Mythos* (Berlin: Staatliche Museen, 2008) 45.

are both seen as ministers in service to Pharaoh and behave arrogantly on earth (Q 29:39). Pharaoh and his highest civil servants are arrogant (Q 10:75; cf. 23:46), although one should note that Moses and Aaron are reproached themselves by Pharaoh for wanting to be achieve greatness in the land (Q 10:78). In contrast, Moses prays for protection from all haughty people (Q 40:27). Despite the plagues that Egypt has to suffer, Pharaoh and the people remain arrogant (Q 7:133). He is a mirror image of Satan when he rejects the message Moses brings (Q 28:39) and deceives his own people by acting arrogantly (Q 7:133; 10:75; 23:46; 29:39). Satan, the archenemy of humankind, refuses out of arrogance to bow before Adam at God's command. That is why he has to descend from paradise to earth and can no longer behave arrogantly in paradise. He belongs among the meanest of creatures that are despised (Q 7:10-13; cf. 38:74-75). Satan and Pharaoh are thus called the two representatives who symbolize the disastrous consequences of arrogance and pride.

Pride makes people blind, which makes them unable to recognize the signs of God. People are called to see the signs of God in nature, human history, and individual experience. The signs of God that can be seen in the world can lead to faith (cf. Q 58:22; 6:103). Blindness is the metaphor for deliberate unbelief and is often also connected with deafness (Q 7:179; 11:20; 47:23). "Seeing is believing." Seeing physically is a metaphor for faith: seeing with the heart (Q 7:179; 11:20; 47:23). Hearing is obeying God's commands: "We hear and obey" (Q 2:285; 4:46; 5:7; 24:51; cf. 24:47). It is possible to have ears and not hear (Q 7:179), but it is also possible to hear without accepting what one hears: "We hear, and we disobey" (Q 2:93). Believers are exhorted not to be like those who have heard but did not really listen (Q 8:21). Deafness means that God's commands can be rejected. Those who are deaf and dumb and do not understand are like the worst animals (Q 8:22). Just as hearing and seeing go together, which in turn go together with understanding and accepting, so deafness and blindness go together (Q 5:71; 11:24; 25:73; 43:40; 47:23). Deafness is often caused by sticking one's fingers in one's ears (Q 2:19). Those who do evil are truly blind: not their eyes, but their hearts. They reject God's signs and act arrogantly (Q 7:36; cf. 6:93; 7:40; 40:60).[27]

Pride and Wealth

Pride and prideful, arrogant people are often presented in association with wealth and the rich. Hoarding and greed go hand in hand with pride. God

27. *EQ, s.v.* "Pride"; "Vision and Blindness"; "Hearing and Deafness."

does not love the pompous braggart, who is avaricious and urges people to be avaricious (Q 57:23-24). The fundamental error of greed is the claim to self-satisfaction and smugness (Q 92:8). The price of greed is one's own self: one is greedy toward oneself. Greed is to one's own disadvantage (Q 47:38). Conversely, giving something good is to one's own advantage. It will go well with those who are protected from innate human greed (Q 64:16). It is difficult for the rich to enter the kingdom of God: a camel can pass through the eye of a needle more easily than a rich man can enter the kingdom of God (Mark 10:25; Matt 19:24; Luke 18:25). The same image is used in the Qur'an, but the third facet of the comparison in the Qur'an is not the rich man who seeks to enter eternal life, true life, but those who arrogantly reject God's signs (Q 7:40; cf. Matt 19:24; Mark 10:25).

Despite the many risks that wealth entails for people, one can purify oneself by spending one's wealth without any ulterior motive to be paid back (Q 92:18-19). Acts of charity must not be spoiled by a demand for gratitude or out of hope of being seen by others (Q 2:264; cf. Matt 6:5). Only if one acts without that expectation can that wealth resemble God's original gift to humankind, which was given in the same way without any expectation that it should be returned to the original giver. Piety is a matter of giving one's money, despite one's love for it, to relatives, orphans, and the poor and for ransom, setting slaves free (Q 2:177), and to feed a poor person, orphan, or prisoner (Q 76:8; cf. Matt 25:31-46). If the individual believes in God and is god-fearing, "He will grant you your recompense, and will not ask you (to give up) your possessions." People are asked to give for God's sake. If this message is not heard, God will have another people take their place who will obey the call to salvation (Q 47:36-38).[28]

Parables on Pride and Wealth

From the Gospel:

> Someone once asked Jesus to tell his brother to share his inheritance with him. Jesus then says: "Watch out! Be on your guard against all kinds of greed; life does not consist in an abundance of possessions." And then he tells this parable: "The ground of a certain rich man yielded an abundant harvest. He thought to himself, 'What shall I do? I have no place to

28. *EQ, s.v.* "Wealth." Cf. also: "Poverty"; "Water"; "Blessing"; "Avarice"; "Gift"; "Path or Way"; "Astray"; "Arrogance"; "Virtue."

store my crops.' Then he said, 'This is what I'll do. I will tear down my barns and build bigger ones, and there I will store my surplus grain. And I'll say to myself, "You have plenty of grain laid up for many years. Take life easy; eat, drink, and be merry."' But God said to him, 'You fool! This very night your life will be demanded from you. Then who will get what you have prepared for yourself?' This is how it will be with those who store up things for themselves but are not rich toward God." (Luke 12:13-21)

From the Qur'an:

There were once two men. To one God had given two gardens with vines surrounded with date palms and in between grain fields where a river flowed through them. When the owner has a good harvest, he begins to brag to the other man without land about the products of his orchard and expresses his confidence that his future is certain and assured. He fears neither God nor the day of judgment. The other man, who confesses that he had never made someone equal to God, warns him that his pride amounts to nothing more than unbelief. Although poor in this world, this good man will receive God's reward in the coming life. He warns his rich colleague that his gardens can be destroyed. And when that does actually happen, the owner is beside himself and expresses his regret that he did not trust in God. The moral of the story is clearly that possessions and children are the fake gold of contemporary life. The only things that have permanent value are one's good deeds, one's acts of justice. These will be rewarded better and are the foundation of hope. (Q 18:32-46)[29]

The Choice for Everyone: Caliph or King?

Human beings, all of them individually, are intended by God to be God's vice-regents, God's representatives on earth. Thus, it not only concerns the first people to be created. What is said about Adam and Eve in the creation story applies to everyone, man or woman. It holds for Everyman. God wants every person to be his vice-regent, caliph, representative on earth (Q 6:165; 35:39).

God's opponent and the enemy of humankind, Satan, wanted from the start to seduce human beings into being kings. The human is thus faced with

29. *EQ*, s.v. "Parable."

a choice: What does he or she want to be — a caliph or a king? Does he or she want to do what God's intends for humankind, or does he or she want to be an unjust king who brings destruction and sheds blood, just as the angels predicted and God's opponent suggests with everything that that entails: exploitation, oppression, injustice? What does the human being choose? Is he or she a believer, grateful, or an unbeliever, ungrateful? Does he or she follow the right path or a wrong path? Will he or she become a leader, an imam of justice, or a leader of injustice? A leader of faith or an immoral leader of unbelief? A leader of justice according to God's command (Q 21:73; 32:24) or a leader of injustice, of unbelief (Q 9:12)?[30] Will he or she belong to the party of God *(hezbollah)* or to the party of Satan *(hizb shaytan)?* Those who are in the power of Satan and forget God are of the party of Satan (Q 58:19; cf. 4:119; 8:48). God is pleased with those who have God written in their hearts. They belong to the party of God, and it will go well with them (Q 58:22). Whoever chooses God and his messenger and those who believe have made the right choice. They belong to the party of God and will be conquerors (Q 5:56).

The Prophet Jeremiah and the Tale of the Caliph or King

The well-known Lebanese poet Khalil Gibran, whom I quoted at the beginning of this chapter and who wrote the beautiful work *The Prophet,* wrote: "Pity the nation that is full of beliefs and empty of religion." What is the true religion to which human beings are called? How can that be established, and what are the criteria for that? The answer is given clearly by the prophets who, after all, are those *par excellence* who speak in the name of God, who address the spiritual ("temple") and political ("kings") leaders critically. The prophet Jeremiah acted very specifically on that issue when he addressed King Jehoiakim and contrasted his conduct with that of his father, Josiah.

King Josiah, the Father

Josiah was king of Judah from 640 to 609 B.C. He ascended the throne when he was eight years old and reigned for thirty-one years. In the eighteenth year of his reign, the book of the Law, of the covenant, was discovered (2 Kgs

---

30. *EQ, s.v.* "Imam."

77

22:8). That book of the Law could be our present book of Deuteronomy ("Second Law"), in one form or another, and was the catalyst for reform in the land (2 Kgs 23:1-24). Josiah fills the role of the pious king. He is remembered in songs (2 Chr 35:25) and is probably the last king of significance in Judah (2 Kgs 21:24–23:30). Only David exceeded him in fame and praise. Before Josiah there was no king who turned to God according to the Law with all his heart, soul, and strength, nor were there any after him who matched him in this (2 Kgs 23:25). He carried out important religious and political reforms. Josiah's grandfather, King Manasseh, was a king who did evil in the sight of God (2 Kgs 21:2) by reintroducing the worship of idols. He had the shrines to Baal rebuilt and images of the goddess Asheroth set up. He sacrificed his son on one of the many altars to the idols that he had built (2 Chr 33:6), whereas his own father was the pious king, Hezekiah. When he was sixteen, Josiah began to seek the God of his (fore)father David (2 Chr 34:3). Four years later Josiah issued a command against all worship of idols and had the altars that had been built for them, images, and high places destroyed. He was twenty-six years old when he decided to have the long neglected and dilapidated temple in Jerusalem restored and collected money at the entrance for that purpose. During the restoration, the high priest found the book of the Law from ancient times. Reading this book made such a deep impression on Josiah that he tore his clothes in despair when he learned that the whole people of Judah would be destroyed as punishment for their sin. The prophetess Huldah, whom Josiah immediately consulted, confirmed that this would indeed happen but that he would personally be spared having to witness it because he had acknowledged God and his Torah (2 Kgs 22:3-30). The king therefore summoned the priests, elders, and all inhabitants of Jerusalem, "from the least to the greatest," to the temple, where he personally read the book of the Law. Then Josiah and his subjects made a covenant before God that they would follow the Lord (2 Kgs 23:2-3). He had all sacrificial altars outside the temple destroyed, particularly the altar at Bethel set up by King Jeroboam in 922 after the establishment of the northern kingdom of Israel. The celebration of Passover after this had all been accomplished was the symbol of Judah's devotion to God: such a Passover had never been celebrated during the time of the judges and during the time of the kings of Israel and Judah (2 Kgs 23:22), for four hundred years.

King Jehoiakim, the Son

Jehoiakim, Josiah's son, was twenty-five years old when he was chosen to be king in 609 B.C. and reigned for eleven years until 598. He was said to have done evil in the sight of God, just as his fathers had done (2 Kgs 23:37): he committed murder, incest, rape, theft, and mocked the Torah. Jeremiah's preaching in Jerusalem is directed at this last king, even though he is not mentioned by name: "Woe to him who builds his palace by unrighteousness, his upper rooms by injustice" (Jer 22:13). Jeremiah compares him with his father, and thus a clear and sharp picture emerges of what is a true king or caliph (in the language of the Qur'an) and what is a bad king.

Jeremiah's Message: Caliph or King?

What I found particularly salient during the war in Lebanon in the 1970s was the striking correspondence that seemed to exist between the social, economic, political, and religious situation then and the situation at the time of the prophet Jeremiah. When I read Jer 22:13 at that time in Beirut during the civil war, my first reaction was: How applicable to what is happening now in Lebanon! "Woe to him who builds his palace by unrighteousness, his upper rooms by injustice." If there was anything that caught one's eye in Beirut, it was the beautiful homes, the most luxurious residential areas that had been built right next to the most grinding poverty. The slums of the Palestinian camps and the homes of the impoverished Lebanese were even visible from the exorbitant and luxurious buildings. "Woe to him who [makes] his own people work for nothing, not paying them for their labor" (Jer 22:13). At that time there were about three hundred thousand Syrian guest workers in Lebanon who had to work for minimum wage. Because they were foreigners or resided illegally in the country, they often worked for even less. "But your eyes and your heart are set only on dishonest gain, on shedding innocent blood and on oppression and extortion" (Jer 22:17). One only needed to read those words aloud, as I once did there, without any further commentary, and everyone understood immediately what it was about. What struck me so much was not only that these words seemed applicable to the situation in Lebanon but that Lebanon is even mentioned further on in this text. And when one sees the unbridled destruction, the buildings and houses set on fire and blown up, story by story, and how people were killed, then the words of the prophet are like a shock: "Go up to Lebanon and cry out . . . for all your allies are crushed. I warned you when you felt secure, but you said, 'I will not listen!'" (Jer 22:20-21).

But it is not a question of simply applying names from then to today in the sense of giving someone, in this case, the Lebanese, a piece of one's mind. The word of the prophet is not intended to be viewed as applicable to the other, our neighbor next door or on the other side of the world. It is intended in the first place for oneself, for one's own situation. It involves understanding what the prophet's concern is, in this case Jeremiah's. The existence of tiny Judah is threatened; its destruction is nigh, caught, as it were, between the super powers of that time. King Jehoiakim is made king by Pharaoh of Egypt. He is the son of Josiah, under whom reforms occurred (Jer 22:15). His father did what was right in the sight of the Lord, we read, and now Jeremiah compares father and son with each other. Two kinds of kingship are placed over against each other, two ways of governing. Despite the poverty that grips the city of Jerusalem, Jehoiakim the son lives in luxury. Like a true Oriental despot, he forces the laborers in his service to work without paying them the wages they are owed. He has his palace embellished and the newest gadgets installed. He does not think it is large enough and has some walls knocked down, spacious upper rooms built, special windows with cedar frames installed, using forced labor to do this. Jeremiah does not mince matters and states clearly what is going on here: it is an abuse of power and injustice. The king is going to such lengths not for the sake of public housing, for example, but only for his own private gratification. And in that case Jehoiakim's father is the better king, a completely different kind of king. The justice and righteousness that the son tramples underfoot were food and drink for his father, Josiah. As much as he ate and drank every day, so he followed daily the requirements of justice and righteousness. Certainly, he enjoyed the good things of life. That is not the point here — to forbid that. The son's mistake lay in the fact that doing justice and righteousness were not his daily food and drink. Josiah's reign was aimed at achieving justice for the oppressed, and in that he showed that he directed himself to God, knew God. That is the core of what a good king is and what the prophet actually wants to say. "'He defended the cause of the poor and needy, and so all went well. Is that not what it means to know me?' declares the LORD" (Jer 22:16). That is the true knowledge of God; that is the true religion to which the poet Khalil Gibran points. God is truly known, justice is truly done to God when justice is done to the human being. That is the profound difference between the two ways of governing, of ruling. The son abuses the administration of justice to fatten his own pocket. He does not hesitate to trample over dead bodies, just like King Ahab in his time, to seize illegally the land of another, Naboth (2 Kgs 9:26).

If one asks what the prophets still have to say today, it is clear that two ways of governing, of exercising dominion, are placed over against each other. The names of those kings possibly say little to us anymore. Jeremiah himself does not mention them by name. But the issue then is still an issue today. For what wages should workers, the weakest in society, work, if they can still get work? For that matter, they are not called workers but neighbors: "making his [neighbor] work for nothing" (Jer 22:13). And the neighbor is oneself. Apparently, that is what the relationship between employer and employee must be, according to the prophet.

The issue here, both in society and in one's personal life, is that one understand what "religion" means; what knowing God ultimately signifies. "Therefore do not let sin reign in your mortal body so that you obey its evil desires. Do not offer any part of yourself to sin as an instrument of wickedness, but rather offer yourselves to God as those who have been brought from death to life; and offer every part of yourself to him as an instrument of righteousness" (Rom 6:12-13), the Apostle Paul writes. Just like Jeremiah, he is concerned about two things: serving desire or knowing and thus serving God. People are often privileged satisfiers of the desires of their own bodies. Not that the enjoyment of food and drink is condemned as such. But, apparently, the question that everyone must ask is and remains: Who satisfies the desires of the body at the expense of whom? Usually, people only ask: What shall we eat, what shall we drink, what shall we wear, how will we enjoy life, build houses, how will we see to it that we don't run short? How will we feel safe? But that is not all that one should do.

One cannot live alone in safety. Safety is indivisible: the safety of the one is the safety of the other. But the prophet and the apostle ask what it truly means to know and serve God: offering one's body as an instrument of righteousness, so that one learns to ask: What will others eat? What will others drink? How will others find homes? How will justice be done to others? How will others feel safe?

That is the question for our leaders. That is the question for ourselves: Will we be caliphs or kings?

CHAPTER IV

Exodus from Babel to Jerusalem, Hijra from Mecca to Medina

Exodus
When Pharaoh forbade the people to go, a staff divided the
    waters, and the current ceased.
Dry-footed, they reached the bank, the reeds of the Red Sea.
    That was how the exodus occurred.
Late every night, in a dream,
I see the waters standing curved back.
We walk amazed, hand in hand.
And high above the strip we are walking along, high above
    the wall of water and wall of water,
There is a strip of noise and the bustling beat of birds' wings.
    Migrating birds, their path right above us, on their way
    to the promised land.

Ida Gerhardt

A Muslim tradition says: "The call to *hijra* does not end until
the sun rises from the place it set."

Introduction

What do people understand by exodus, departure, and *hijra*, emigration?
The story of the liberation from Egypt under the leadership of Moses/Mûsâ
is projected back into the past of Noah/Nûh, Joseph/Yûsuf, Abraham/

Ibrâhîm, as well as into the future of Jesus/ʿÎsâ and Muhammad. We will look more deeply at the individual exoduses of Abraham, Moses, Jesus, and Muhammad.

Finally, we will ask why Jews, Christians, and Muslims cannot remember and celebrate the feast of the exodus, the liberation, together.

Exodus, Departure; *Hijra,* Emigration

Exodus — the term refers in the first place to the exodus of the children of Israel, the Banû Isrâʾîl, from Egypt, the house of slavery and oppression, under the leadership of Moses. The preamble to the Ten Words, usually called the Ten Commandments, that God gave to the Israelites on Mount Sinai, reads: "I am the LORD your God, who brought you out of Egypt, out of the land of slavery" (Exod 20:2). The children of Israel receive the Torah in the desert (Exod 32:15-16; Q 7:145-54). The word Torah was translated into Greek by *nomos,* "law," which is often viewed as connoting legality or even legalism. The word *shariʾa* has suffered a similar fate; usually translated as (Islamic) law, its primary meaning is "path to the source," namely of water that is so necessary for survival on one's way through the desert. But Torah also means the signpost. It is the way pointed out to humankind. There are ten signposts that function like bread for a journey, manna that gives life, enough for every day so that no one has to suffer want. The children of Israel are granted this "bread from heaven" on their journey through the desert (Exod 16:13-36). The Torah, briefly put, is about "doing justice and loving one's neighbor." To do justice and to show love is their daily bread. The Torah teaches people to share everything with one another. One of the most revolutionary testimonies to the Torah says that God will take away the burden that Egypt laid upon the people and redeem and liberate them from their existence as slaves (Exod 6:6). God is able and ready to intervene against all oppressive and alienating circumstances and powers that stand in the way of the people's well-being. The Old Testament, or Tanakh, uses different verbs to indicate the exodus, and God is always the subject, the agent, of these verbs: "bring out of," "liberate," and "redeem." This is, in the first place, a matter of "bringing them out of" Egypt in a geographical sense (Exod 12:41; 13:3; 14:8; Deut 16:3, 6) and liberating them from the oppressive power of Pharaoh (Exod 3:8; cf. 5:23; 6:6; 18:9), in that sense also taking them physically out of danger, like "a burning brand plucked from the fire" (Amos 4:11 KJV). Thus, God liberates Israel from the danger of Egyptian slavery. The word "redeem" is used, with the connotation connected with family solidarity, such as when some-one going through bad times has to sell his land but is redeemed from that situation. God sees to the well-being of the family (Lev 25:25-28). Other syn-onyms can also be mentioned: "save," "buy back," and "bring up." God's powerful deeds of salvation put an end to a situation of fear, suffering, and hopelessness and create the possibility for an alternative life. It is an action, a deed, whereby God fights against the forces that threaten the well-being of the people. This salvation happens very concretely in actual history and is something that Israel was not able to do itself (Exod 14:30; cf. Ps 106:8, Exod 14:13; 15:2). Buying back, redeeming, is an economic transaction in which someone is bought back out of slavery (Exod 13:15; cf. Deut 7:8; 15:15; 24:18; Ps 78:42).

When God sees the misery of his people, hears their cries, and knows how much they are suffering, he descends to "bring them up" out of the land of oppression (Exod 3:8, 17). The fact that the people go up out of slavery to freedom, from the land of oppression, Egypt, to a promised land makes that word more than simply what the geographical term suggests. By bringing Is-rael up out of the house of slavery, the people are lifted up into better cir-cumstances. In the transitive sense as well, it can concern a personal salva-tion, being raised up, being lifted up out of the depths: "Though you have made me see troubles, many and bitter, you will restore my life again; from the depths of the earth you will again bring me up" (Ps 71:20).[1]

Retelling the Exodus

Experiences of what occurs in other times, other places, and in other cir-cumstances are (re)told in the Bible through the lens of the memory of that special departure, liberation, and salvation from Egypt. God does what is ex-pressed by these verbs not only at the beginning but all through history. That is how he acts before and after the exodus from Egypt and will continue to do so in the future — that is the constant message. The salvation of Moses' people is also portrayed in terms of a typological repeat of the story of the flood. After the flood, Noah goes to "dry land"; he and his family settle in an inhabitable country (Q 7:59-64; 10:73; 11:36-48; 21:76-77; 23:27-29, 26:119; 29:15, 54:13). He is mentioned among the prophets with whom God made a

---

1. Walter Brueggemann, *Theology of the Old Testament: Testimony, Dispute, Advocacy* (Minneapolis: Fortress, 1997) 173-76.

covenant — Abraham, Moses, and Jesus (Q 33:7). He is called a liar (Q 22:42) and is saved by the ship, the ark (Q 7:64). Before he lands, he prays for a blessed landing (Q 23:29), like the children of Israel who inhabit the land after Pharaoh's death (Q 17:104; cf. 14:14).

Abraham's departure from the city of Ur of the Chaldees sounds like an anticipation of the later exodus from Egypt (Gen. 12:1; 15:7). God leads Abraham out of Ur, out of the land of the Chaldees or Babylonians, so that he could give him the promised land as a possession (Gen 17:8; cf. Neh 9:7). Abraham goes obediently to the place that was intended for him and his descendants. He left without knowing where he was going (Heb 11:8).

When Israel enters the land of promise after crossing the Jordan River, that event happens in a way similar to the crossing of the Red Sea immediately after the departure from Egypt (Josh 4:22-23; cf. Exod 14:29). The crisis in which the people find themselves in the land with respect to the Philistines is seen from the perspective of the exodus from Egypt (1 Sam 4–7:1): the Philistines pray to be saved from the power of that great God who had brought plagues on the Egyptians (1 Sam 4:7-8). Just as Pharaoh had to let the people go in the end and the Egyptian gods were defeated (1 Sam 6:6; cf. Exod 12:12), so the gods of the Philistines are defeated as well. After the fall of Jerusalem to Nebuchadnezzar in 587 B.C. and the Babylonian Exile that followed, this same God is able to liberate Israel from the hegemony of Babylon (Deutero-Isaiah).

It is important to realize that that memory of the exodus of the children of Israel from Egypt was, as the prophet Amos emphasizes, not purely and simply for the people of Israel. Amos, who came from Tekoa in Judah, where he bred small livestock, kept cattle, and raised sycamore figs, was called around 769 B.C. to leave his cattle behind immediately and become a prophet. He had to preach against the violation of justice rampant in Israel, the extravagant city life, and the many sacrifices that were brought without paying heed to God. King Jeroboam had turned a shrine near Bethel into the national shrine of the northern kingdom of Israel, founding his own cultus with sacrificial high places and priests chosen from ordinary people. This cultus was appealing because it involved the Eastern bull cultus (the bull was a symbol of fertility) (1 Kgs 12:29-32). This cultus was viewed as "Jeroboam's sin."[2]

Amos comes into conflict with the high priest, who betrays him to the king, and he therefore has to flee. He condemns the attitude of those who

---

2. KBS on 1 Kgs 12:28-29; Exod 32:5.

boast about being chosen by God, emphasizing that there are other peoples who also underwent an exodus. He then mentions three outstanding enemies of Israel: the Cushites, the Philistines, and the Arameans. Abraham's brother, Nahor, was the ancestor of a group of Arameans. At the time of the patriarchs, the Arameans lived, among other places, in Harran (Haran), Abraham's second hometown. Certain petty kingdoms made life difficult for Israel, going to war with Saul, David, and Solomon. Amos denies that the liberation movement of the exodus is something that applies exclusively to Israel. The prophet expresses a castigating reproach when Israel misuses this election for particularistic propaganda. God has also granted other peoples, even those most hostile to Israel a departure, an exodus: "'Are not you Israelites the same to me as the Cushites?'[3] declares the LORD. 'Did I not bring Israel up from Egypt, the Philistines from Caphtor and the Arameans from Kir?'" (Amos 9:7). The God who brought Israel out of Egypt also performs similar acts of liberation elsewhere. The same God brought about the exodus of the Philistines and the Arameans, Israel's obstinate opponents. It is characteristic of God that he performs exoduses, liberations, savings, redemptions — everything that is indicated by the verbs cited above — and he does that in many places, if not everywhere. Where peoples or individuals find themselves in oppressive and hopeless situations, God becomes involved in their liberation from those situations.[4] Thus, the Qur'an also says that the people of the Book do not have a monopoly on the mercy or grace of God, for God shows grace to whomever he wills (Q 57:29).[5]

I will now look in particular and more extensively at the stories of the exodus of Abraham, Moses, Jesus, and the Hijra of Muhammad.

Abraham's Exodus from the Land, the City of Nimrod

The tales about Abraham take place in three locations according to the Qur'an. The first is in Mesopotamia, the land of the two rivers, the Euphrates and the Tigris, the land of Abraham's birth. The second is in the neighborhood of Jerusalem, Salem, and the third is in Mecca. Abraham came from the city of Ur, at that time a city of some size with a highly-developed civili-

---

3. *Bijbels-historisch Woordenboek*, ed. Bo Reicke and Leonhard Rost, vols. 1-6 (Utrecht: Spectrum, 1969), *s.v.* "Kush." Hereafter cited as *BW*. KBS on Amos 9:7 adds: "een zwarte bevolking [a black people]."

4. Brueggemann, *Theology of the Old Testament*, 178-79.

5. *EQ*, *s.v.* "Jews and Judaism."

zation. As a sheik of nomads and a shepherd, with flocks of sheep and goats, Abraham would come into the city to sell his products and buy goods he needed. It is said that Abraham and his father Terah — Âzar in the Qur'an, another form of the name Eliezer, one of Abraham's most prominent servants (Q 6:74; cf. Gen 15:2-3) — worshipped other gods when they lived in Mesopotamia (Josh 24:2). The shining moon-god Sin was the most prominent god in Ur.[6]

As far as the route of the exodus of Abraham and his household from Ur is concerned, various stops are cited on the way to the land God will show him: Harran, Egypt, and Mecca.

It is striking that the Jewish thinker Martin Buber used the term *hijra* for Abraham's exodus: "The whole *hijra* of Abraham is a 'religious' event."[7] He points out in that context that the cities of Ur and Harran were both centers of the Syrian-Babylonian worship of the moon. The name of the city Harran, where Terah died, means "way" as well as "caravan" and is thus the place where the caravans meet and from which they leave. The moon-god of Harran is also called Bel-Harran, which can be understood as "lord of the way," "the intersection." In one hymn, the moon-god is called "the one who opens the way." He is the pathfinder, literally, the one who illuminates the way for the caravan traveling by night across the steppes to avoid the heat of the sun; he is the god of the Mesopotamian nomads. In the Nile region, it was apparently the sun-god Amon who was the god of the road and gave his representatives his image, "the Amon of the road," as a heavenly ambassador. But in the Euphrates region, it was the moon-god.[8]

Abraham is said to have left Ur, together with his father, his wife Sarah, and his nephew Lot/Lût (Gen 12:1). They go together to Canaan, stopping in Harran (Gen 11:31), which lay on the intersection of the caravan routes from Nineveh in northwestern Mesopotamia on the eastern bank of the Euphrates, to Asia Minor, Syria, and Egypt. They settle in Harran (Gen 11:31), and only after his father dies does Abraham move on to the land of Canaan (Acts 7:2, 4).

The reason for this departure from his country of origin, also called the land of Nimrod in addition to Babel in the Qur'anic account, is that Abraham confronts his father and his people with the idolatry prevalent

---

6. *BE, s.v.* "Ur."

7. Martin Buber, *Het geloof der profeten* (Wassenaar: Servire, 1972) 39, 42; *Werke*, Vol. 2: *Schriften zur Bibel* (Munich: Kösel, 1964) 271-74.

8. Buber, *Geloof,* 207; *Schriften zur Bibel,* 425.

there. When he was still a youth, Abraham understood naturally that neither the idols nor the sun or moon could be divine. When he sees a star arise in the night, he thinks he has seen God. But he no longer believes that when the star sets. The same applies to the sun rising and disappearing. Even though the sun is larger, it still sets (Q 6:74-83; cf. Gen 15:5). Abraham asks his father about the worship of idols (Q 6:74; 21:51ff.), which he himself rejects, asking him why he serves what cannot hear and cannot see and cannot help him very much at all (Q 19:42). Abraham then destroys his father's idols and those of his countrymen (Q 21:57-58; 37:93). Despite his father's enmity toward him (Q 19:46), Abraham does pray for forgiveness for his father for worshipping idols (Q 9:114; 14:41; 19:47; 26:86; 60:4). (Muhammad wanted to do the same for his polytheistic ancestors who worshipped idols.)

Abraham is also called to break with the unjust King Nimrod, the ruler of Assur and Babel, and to leave. Abraham declares himself free of his people (cf. Q 60:4); he leaves his country and people so that he can worship the One God and to practice religion as it should be practiced. His emigration is cited or presupposed in the Qur'an (cf. Q 19:48-49). God thus saves Abraham and Lot as well in the land that he has blessed, Palestine (Q 21:71; cf. 29:26; 37:99; Gen 12:1). Abraham then goes to Egypt, where he encounters another unjust tyrant, Pharaoh. There he had his wife pass herself off as his sister out of concern for his safety. When Pharaoh has Sarah move into his palace, he is visited with plagues. At Pharaoh's command, Abraham is then deported out of Egypt with his wife and all his possessions under escort (Gen 12:10-20; 20:1-18).[9]

According to the Qur'an, Abraham completes his emigration by building the Ka'ba (Q 2:125, 127; 3:97; 22:26), the ultimate result and purpose of his life of trial.[10] Mecca is mentioned as the first house of God that was built for people, in Bakkah (another name for Mecca), a blessed place, a true guidance for humankind (Q 3:96). One of the psalms says: "Blessed are those whose strength is in you, whose hearts are set on pilgrimage. As they pass through the Valley of Baka, they make it a place of springs" (Ps 84:5-6). "Valley of Baka" is also translated as "dry valley" or "vale of tears" and is brought into connection with Bakkah/Mecca. Mecca is also the place that is connected with the tears of Hagar, Ishmael's mother.[11]

---

9. *EQ, s.v.* "Abraham."

10. *EQ, s.v.* "Kings and Rulers."

11. Cf. "They throw themselves weeping to the ground" (Q 17:109). When Muslims recite the Qur'anic verses, they throw themselves weeping to the ground (Q 19:58).

Moses' Exodus from the Land of Pharaoh

At the end of his life, Joseph, his father Jacob's favorite son, already spoke of the departure, the exodus, of the children of Israel and commanded them to take his bones with them when they left Egypt (Heb 11:22).

It is in Moses, who was already placed in the river Nile as a child and miraculously saved (Q 20:37-39), that the people of Israel are given their future liberator (Exod 2:1-10). He is entrusted to the river in a basket of rushes but saved and raised by Pharaoh's daughter or wife (Q 26:18; 28:7-13). Âsîya, as Pharaoh's wife was later called, thus plays the same role that Pharaoh's daughter plays in the biblical story.[12] In the Muslim tradition, she is a virtuous and devout woman whose actions are used by God to fulfill his plans for Moses. She convinces Pharaoh, her father or husband, not to kill the child. "Moses could be useful for us, so it will help us to accept him as our son" (Q 28:9). She was a friend to Moses while he was growing up and disapproved of her husband's evil acts. According to many commentators, she was a martyr. Her resistance to Pharaoh's oppression made her an example for those who believe, an honor she shares with Mary, the mother of Jesus (Q 66:11-12). Next to Mary and Khadija, the wife of the prophet Muhammad, and their daughter Fatima, she is seen as the fourth perfect woman.[13] Because Moses grew up, defended his oppressed people, and killed a man (Q 20:40; 26:14, 19, 20; 28:14-21, 33; Exod 2:11-15), he has to flee to Midian (Q 28:22-26), where he is called by God to liberate his people (Q 26:17; 7:105; 20:47). Moses is sent by God to Pharaoh and his people (Q 11:96) to save his own people (Q 37:115). With signs to accompany him, God sends Moses with the task: "Bring your people from the darkness to the light" (Q 14:5).

Moses then returns together with his wife and sons to Egypt and does indeed become their savior and liberator (Exod 2:11–4:31). Pharaoh and the leaders among the Egyptians *(al-mala')* reject the signs (Q 7:103). Pharaoh is one of those who bring destruction upon the earth (Q 28:4; cf. 10:83; 44:31; 23:45-46). When the first negotiations with Pharaoh (Exod 5:1-6:1) do not yield any positive result, for Pharaoh cannot let them leave, a number of disasters or plagues follow (Exod 7:8-10:29; Q 7:127-35). In the Qur'an, the plagues are called "signs": God sends Moses and Aaron to Pharaoh, who is extraordinarily hostile toward them, with God's revelations and signs (Q

---

12. *EI, s.v.* "Âsîya."

13. Oliver Leaman, ed., *The Qur'an: An Encyclopedia* (London: Routledge, 2006) *s.v.* "Asiyya."

7:103; cf. Q 20:43; 10:75; 11:96-97; 23:45; 28:32; 29:39; 43:46). Here the signs are not intended so much as punishment as testimonies to God's power and presence, which Pharaoh does not want to acknowledge.[14]

Moses and Aaron have to go to Pharaoh and tell him: "We are the servants of the Lord of the worlds. Send the children away with us" (Q 26:17). Moses and his people must, just as Abraham must break with Nimrod in Mesopotamia, break with Pharaoh and leave (Q 7:105; 7:134; 20:47; 26:17; cf. Exodus 1, 4).

Night of the Exodus/*Isrâ'*

Finally, the night of the exodus arrives, Passover (Exod 11:1–13:16). Moses is charged with leading God's servants out of Egypt at night (Q 20:77; 26:52; 44:23; Exodus 14–15). He is ordered to lead his people through the sea, and they are brought through the sea in a miraculous way (Exod 13:17–15:21; Q 20:77; 26:52; 44:23-24). A way is opened for him and his people, and they do not have to fear that the Egyptians or Pharaoh will catch up to them (Q 20:77; cf. 26:52; 44:23). That this happens at night reminds us of the story of Lot, who was also told to leave Sodom at night (Q 11:81). Moses has to strike the sea, which then divides into two to let the people pass through. But when the sun rises, Pharaoh pursues them with his armies (Q 26:60). The family of Pharaoh, who leads his own people astray and not on the right path (Q 20:77-79), is destroyed because of Pharaoh's misdeeds (Q 8:54). Pharaoh and those with him drown (Q 26:66; Exodus 15) in the flood (14:28) because they declared God's revelation to be a lie (Q 7:136-37; cf. 8:54; 10:90; 17:103; 20:78; 28:40; 43:55; 44:24; 51:40). God saves the children of Israel from their enemy, Pharaoh (Q 7:141; 20:80), and his humiliating torture (Q 44:30). Moses is saved with his people (Q 2:50; 7:138; 26: 65), and Moses and Aaron along with their people are thus liberated by God (Q 37:115).

Jesus' Exodus from Egypt

The New Testament contains the same "Exodus grammar."[15] Joseph and Mary must flee to Egypt with the child Jesus to escape King Herod the Great,

---

14. *EQ, s.v.* "Plagues."

15. Brueggemann, *Theology of the Old Testament*, 179.

so that Jesus would not be killed like the other children in Bethlehem. Jesus stays in Egypt until Herod dies. After having found asylum in Egypt, Jesus is then led out of Egypt to fulfill the word of the prophet. God led the people of Israel out of Egypt by a prophet (Moses); Israel was looked after by a prophet (Hos 12:13). The prophet Hosea (750-722 B.C.) had experienced the flourishing of the kingdom and its decline, although not the fall of the capital Samaria in 722. The words of his prophecy are seen as being fulfilled in Jesus: "When Israel was a child, I loved him, and out of Egypt I called my son" (Hos 11:1; Matt 2:15). Thus, the old traditions of exodus are seen as being realized in Jesus. Salvation lies in the new exodus, the new covenant, the new David.[16] Prophets witness to a God who remains faithful to himself and who still leads his community *(qahal, ecclesia, umma):* "But I have been the LORD your God ever since you came out of Egypt" (Hos 13:4; Amos 3:1).

Jesus' Exodus from Jerusalem

The Bible relates how Jesus once ascended a mountain with his most intimate disciples. Since Origen (A.D. 185-254), an important early theologian, this high solitary mountain (Matt 17:1) in the Plain of Jezreel has been identified with Mount Tabor. While Jesus is praying, his face changes and his clothing becomes dazzling white. Suddenly, there are two men talking to him (Luke 9:28-31): Moses and Elijah, who appear in heavenly splendor. Moses is the one who had to lead his people out of slavery and right before his death was allowed to see the promised land but expressly forbidden to enter with the people. He himself could not experience the fulfillment of the exodus from Egypt (Deut 34:1-5). When the prophet Elijah, in his turn, was speaking at the end of his life to his successor Elisha, a chariot of fire with horses of fire appeared and took Elijah to heaven (2 Kgs 2:11).

There, on that mountain of the transfiguration (metamorphosis) of Jesus, both Moses and Elijah speak to him about the end of his life: his leaving, departure, or, as it is written literally in Greek, his *exodus* from Jerusalem (Luke 9:30-31). Jesus has to undergo this exodus because Jerusalem has become a city of injustice. The approaching of the kingdom is connected directly with Jesus' going up to Jerusalem and thus also the political judgment he will pronounce over those in power who have made common cause with the Romans. Very concretely, Jesus has to break with the injustice of the cor-

16. Kurt Frör, *Biblische Hermeneutik* (Munich: Kaiser, 1961) 214-15.

rupt political and spiritual leaders of the city of Jerusalem and achieve liberation for his people. He accomplishes this exodus by saving not himself but others and bringing them redemption and liberation. What is characteristic of the exodus tradition comes out in Jesus' deeds of transformation in solidarity with the blind, the lame, the deaf, the dead, and the poor (Luke 7:18-23). His miracles are performances or depictions of that exodus, manifestations of God's power and love. The name of Jesus reflects his ability to save people from the powers of destruction, for his name means "God redeems or liberates." The story of Jesus' life and works is thus transparent when compared with the story of Israel's exodus, the liberation from the slavery and oppression in Egypt. His treacherous betrayal, suffering, and death in the house of slavery that was Rome finds its ultimate end when he is sacrificed outside the walls of Jerusalem (Luke 9:31).[17]

When it is time for Jesus to be taken from the earth, he sets out resolutely to Jerusalem (Luke 9:51). The raising or lifting up of Jesus means both death and ascension. The words "exodus" and "lifting up" supplement each other. Just as the prophet Ezekiel directs his gaze at Jerusalem to indict or curse the sanctuary and to prophesy against the land of Israel (Ezek 21:7), so Jesus goes to Jerusalem to pronounce a political judgment over the government of the city, the holy temple, and the people.

Examples are given of what awaits people when they want to follow Jesus in his exodus (Luke 9:57-62): foxes may have holes to which they can flee, but the Son of Man has no place to lay his head. If someone first wants to bury his father, he is told to let the dead bury the dead. When Elisha assumes the prophet's mantle from Elijah and wants to say good-bye to his father and mother, Elijah tells him it would be better for him to go back. Apparently, haste is needed. The hour is approaching. Whoever has put his hand to the plow should not look back (1 Kgs 19:19-21; Luke 9:60).[18] Jesus is walking in the footsteps of Moses and other prophets and sees himself as joining those prophets who are killed because of their message.

Muhammad and the Hijra from Mecca

In Mecca, Muhammad, who also sees himself standing in the tradition of the earlier prophets, is, like them, oppressed, called a liar, mocked (Q 9:65; 25:41;

---

17. Huub Oosterhuis and Alex van Heusden, *Het Evangelie van Lukas* (Vught: Skandalon, 2007) 138, 102; Brueggemann, *Theology of the Old Testament*, 179; *BW, s.v.* "wonder."
18. Oosterhuis and van Heusden, *Lukas*, 104.

36:30; 37:12), not believed because he is merely human (Q 17:94; 21:3; 74:25), threatened, and persecuted. Attacks were plotted against him to keep him in prison, to drive him out or to kill him (Q 8:30).[19] Muhammad reminds his hearers in his sermons how many cities that were stronger than Mecca and drove him out were eradicated by God without anyone being able to do anything about it (Q 47:13).[20] Already before Muhammad, the Qur'an says, prophets had to break with the injustice that occurred in their respective cities. Abraham had to break with King Nimrod and his city, and Lot, Abraham's nephew, with the cities of Sodom and Gomorrah (Q 21:74; 26:170; 27:57; 29:33; 37:134; 51:35; 54:34). Lot had to flee; he had to become an emigrant and move to another place (Q 29:26; cf. Gen 19:12ff.).

Those who want to follow the prophets and act like them are humiliated and oppressed and also expected to leave, emigrate from, the country where they are persecuted. To be able to do so but not leave puts salvation in danger. Muhammad's Meccan followers say that if they follow the true guidance with him, they will be removed violently from their land (Q 28:57; 8:26; 29:67). Muhammad is first called to have patience, but also to carry out an internal exodus there already, distancing himself in an appropriate way from whatever injustice happens there (Q 73:10). This internal *hijra* ends in territorial, physical exile (Q 9:40-41).[21] The exodus that Muhammad must perform is that from Mecca to Medina. This is denoted by the term *hijra* and also becomes the example for the believers for their leaving oppressive, unbelieving rulers.[22]

Just as the prayer is found in the Psalms that God watch over one's coming and going both now and forevermore (Ps 121:8), so the Qur'an calls for us to pray to God to ensure a good exit and entry (Q 17:80). The exit has to do with leaving the godless city of Mecca by means of the Hijra in the year 622. The oppressed men, women, and children who remain in the city pray: "Lord, bring us out of this city whose inhabitants are criminals and raise up for us one from yourself who will be a friend or helper" (Q 4:75; cf. 17:80). The prayer for a good entry has to do with entering Medina.[23]

Muhammad's own understanding of his task is influenced by the exodus of other prophets and colors his own experience of the emigration/*hijra*.

19. *EQ, s.v.* "Emigration."

20. *EQ, s.v.* "Salvation."

21. *EQ, s.v.* "Geography."

22. *EQ, s.v.* "Ascension"; "Myths and Legends."

23. Cf. Rudi Paret, *Der Koran: Kommentar und Konkordanz* (Stuttgart: Kohlhammer, 1971) 305-6.

Those experiences of other prophets gave Muhammad heart during a time of social and economic oppression by a boycott in Mecca that became increasingly intolerable for him and his followers. That was true already at the time of the first *hijra* of a number of his followers to Ethiopia. In 615, in the fifth year after the beginning of the revelation of the Qur'an, a number of Muhammad's followers left Mecca for Christian Abyssinia. Different groups left with and without their families. The number eighty-two is given for those who left at various times for Abyssinia. The emigration was the consequence of a pagan Meccan persecution that became stronger, and Muhammad found it increasingly difficult to protect his followers. He advised them to go to "the land of trust," where the Christian ruler, the negus, was a just person who would provide a refuge for them. The emperor of Ethiopia did indeed receive the Muslim emigrants hospitably. The negus asked about their new religion and about their understanding of Jesus, the son of Mary. In answer, Ja'far, the leader of the delegation, recited the announcement of Jesus' birth to Mary, a passage in the Qur'an that was revealed shortly before their departure from Mecca (Q 19:16-21). Content with this answer, the negus allowed them to stay. That was the first emigration. Before the year 622, these emigrants returned to Mecca, and the earlier experiences in Ethiopia were also one motive for the second emigration to Medina.[24]

The Night Journey/Isrâ' of Muhammad to Jerusalem

The situation for Muhammad and his followers in Mecca worsened after the death of his wife Khadija and his uncle Abû Talib. The latter was the head of the clan of the Banû Hashim to which Muhammad belonged. Until his death, he protected the prophet against the enmity of his own tribe, the Quraysh. He was also his guardian after the death of Muhammad's grandfather, who had cared for Muhammad after the death of his mother. Abû Talib had always supported Muhammad, even though he himself never became a Muslim. When he died in 619, Abû Lahab, the leader of the clan and an uncompromising enemy of Muhammad, revoked the protection and thus placed Muhammad's life in danger. He even tried to kill Muhammad. Just as Lot had to make his exodus from Sodom and Gomorrah at night and Moses

---

24. *EQ, s.v.* "Oppression"; "Emigation"; "Abyssinia"; Alfred Guillaume, *The Life of Muhammad: A Translation of Ishâq's Sîrat Rasûl Allâh* (repr. New York: Oxford University Press, 2001) 358.

had to leave Egypt at night, so in 622 Muhammad had to leave for Medina at night. But before that, in 621, Muhammad's night journey (Isrâ') to Jerusalem and his journey to heaven (Mi'râj) occurred. This night journey can, in fact, be seen as a mystical exodus experience that precedes the physical experience of the 622 journey, the Hijra, to Medina, just as Jesus meets Moses and Elijah during the transfiguration on the mountain and speaks with them about his own exodus out of Jerusalem. This journey serves as the prototype for the spiritual and the concrete exodus of the prophet Muhammad and the Meccans from their local situation of oppression and misery in Mecca and serves to give them a vision of the holy land and to have them direct themselves in prayer *(qibla)* to Jerusalem (Q 17:1).[25]

Hijra to Medina

Just as in the Bible the experience of the exodus from Egypt is projected onto such experiences as Abraham's departure from Mesopotamia, so the Hijra, Muhammad's experience of leaving Mecca for Medina, is understood in terms similar to those of Abraham and Lot leaving their respective cities. Like the other prophets, Muhammad must also lead his people out of the city of injustice, Mecca, and the old contexts of paganism, idolatry, and the injustice that accompanied those practices, and go to Medina, the city where justice will be done.

According to one of the prophet's cousins, Muhammad arrived in Medina on the Jewish Day of Atonement (Yom Kippur), an annual feast on the tenth day after the Jewish New Year, a day of fasting from sunrise to sunset, a day of penance for Jews (Lev 16:27-31; 23:27-30). That was an occasion for Muhammad to ask the Jews why they fasted and did penance. To their answer, "We celebrate the liberation by Moses from Egypt," Muhammad is said to have declared the day, *'Ashûrâ'* in Arabic, to be a day of fasting for his community, the *umma.* "We fast because Moses and the Israelites were liberated from Egypt on that day with God's help." Muhammad sees himself as a bearer of the legacy of Moses. A connection can be made between fasting and the reception of the Revelation in the month of Ramadan (Q 2:185).[26]

---

25. *EQ, s.v.* "Mozes"; cf. Chapter X.
26. *EQ, s.v.* "Fasting"; *EI, s.v.* "'Ashûrâ'."

Badr and the Exodus

The rescue, liberation, and salvation that takes shape in the history from Abraham up to and including Jesus is clearly continued in the understanding of the life and actions of Muhammad as a prophet. The Battle of Badr and the miraculous rescue of the Muslims who fought with Muhammad against a superior enemy is related in such a way as to link up clearly with the history of the exodus (Q 8:5-18).[27] The Battle of Badr occurred in the month of Ramadan in 624, the second year after the Hijra from Mecca to Medina — in the spring. The battle was fought just after Muhammad had broken with the Jewish tribes in Medina and changed the direction of prayer *(qibla)* from Jerusalem to Mecca. Initially, the prayer, the ritual *salât*, was done facing Jerusalem, as do Jews who are in a strange land (1 Kgs 8:48; Dan 6:10). At the Battle of Badr, a small group of Muslims even managed, despite their few numbers, to defeat the superior power of their Meccan opponents and gain a major victory. Because of that victory, Muhammad and his followers were confirmed in the rightness of their cause.[28]

The fight was led on the Meccan side by Abû Jahl, one of Muhammad's archenemies who was called the "father of foolishness." Abû Jahl's influence rested on his power in the area of trade and finance. He was behind the boycott in Mecca that was initiated against Muhammad and his followers, and he also tried to kill Muhammad. He was blamed for many of the persecutions of Muhammad and his followers. Abû Jahl led the Meccan force of about one thousand men at this battle.[29]

A parallel can now be drawn between Muhammad and Moses on the one hand and Abû Jahl and Pharaoh on the other (Q 20:79). In both cases God intervened. In the confrontation with Pharaoh's pursuing army, Moses announces in God's name to the people: "Do not be afraid. Stand firm and you will see the deliverance the LORD will bring you today. The Egyptians you see today you will never see again. The LORD will fight for you; you need only to be still" (Exod 14:13-14). Similarly, God makes it rain during the Battle of Badr, which makes it difficult for the Meccans to move, giving the Muslims an advantage (Q 8:11; cf. 3:154).[30]

This event at Badr is called the Day of Distinction, *furqân* (Q 8:41).

27. Angelika Neuwirth, *Studien zur Komposition der Mekkanischen Suren* (Berlin: De Gruyter, 1981) 135.
    28. *EQ, s.v.* "Badr."
    29. *EI, s.v.* "Abû Djahl."
    30. *EQ, s.v.* "Hidden."

This expression is translated variously as "criterion," "separation," "liberation," and "redemption."[31] The Arabic verb *faraqa,* from which it is derived, means "to separate, divide, distinguish."[32] Calling the event by this term means that a separation of ways is truly occurring (Q 8:41), that between believers and unbelievers, a distinction between good and evil (Q 8:29). It could also be said that the "hour of truth" has dawned; truth and falseness can be distinguished. After Badr, it is clear who is truly Muslim, who has truly entrusted himself to God and who has not, who the enemy is and who is not. In a number of respects, Badr is the turning point. After Badr, both fasting in the month of Ramadan and "an exertion on the path of God" *(jihad)* form an integral part of Muslim practice. The word *furqân* is used in the sense of "distinction" and "liberation" as the central idea in the Jewish Passover. The aspect of liberation is expressed most clearly in the words: "If you fear God, he provides liberation *(furqân)*" (Q 8:29). Muhammad has to remember how he was a minority in Mecca and was oppressed on earth or in the land, and had to fear that people would remove him forcibly (Q 8:26). In Mecca he had only a few followers, but God brought him many. "See how it ended for those who bring destruction upon the earth" (Q 7:86). God helped them in Badr when they were insignificant (Q 3:123).

Revelation of the Qur'an and the Victory at Badr in the Month of Ramadan

The victory of liberation in Badr occurs, just like the Revelation of the Qur'an itself, during the month of Ramadan, the ninth month of the Islamic (lunar) year. The Muslim calendar begins in the year 622, the year of the Hijra. The word *furqân* is always used only in connection with the giving of the divine Revelation to Moses and Aaron (Q 2:53; 21:48) and to Muhammad (Q 2:185; 3:4). One of the Meccan chapters is called *Furqân* (Q 25): "Blessed is he who has sent down or revealed the distinction, the criterium to his servant, so that Muhammad could be a warner for the people in the world" (Q 25:1). In the case of Moses and Aaron, there is a connection between the "Book" and the "Distinction" (Q 2:53; 21:48). Because Moses is both liberator and someone to whom the Revelation is given, there is a clear link between liberation and revelation. The same double emphasis is found in Muham-

---

31. Cf. Aramean *purkan* with the same meaning.
32. *EQ, s.v.* "Forgiveness."

mad, and, thus, there is a close connection between Moses and Muhummmad as liberators and as receivers of the Revelation, the Torah and the Qur'an, respectively. With respect to Muhammad, the Revelation (Q 97) and the liberation in Badr occur in the month of Ramadan. Badr is for Muhammad's prophethood what the exodus is for Moses: a radical break with the past, the injustice of Pharaoh and the injustice in Mecca, respectively. From now on, it is clear who the enemy is. The exodus marks that point in Moses' story. The Egyptians of Pharaoh represent for Moses what the polytheistic Meccans represent for Muhammad. The victory at Badr means the liberation of the Muslims and the separation of the unbelievers from the believers, the assurance of divine approval and confirmation.

The Prophets and the Exodus

The major prophetic figures in the Bible and the Qur'an since Abraham — Moses, Jesus, up until and including Muhammad — are commanded to break with unjust leaders and the injustice in their respective cities. Abraham had to break with Nimrod, king of the oppressive empires of Assur and Babel in Mesopotamia and leave. Moses stood up to Pharaoh of Egypt and had to break with his injustice and leave with the children of Israel. Jesus opposed the spiritual and political leaders of Jerusalem, which had become unjust, and had to perform an exodus from that city. Muhammad preached against the wicked and egotistic leaders of Mecca and eventually had to leave that city. The expression that is used for that "breaking with" and "leaving from" in the Bible is exodus, and in the Qur'an the word is "emigration" *(hijra)*.

Abraham, Moses, Jesus, and Muhammad all had to go to the land God would show them, the promised land, the promised city, the new Jerusalem, Medina, the city of light, the city of the future, the place (Makom, the "Place," a Hebrew name for Jerusalem), Mokum, "Great Mokum." The latter is the honorary name the Jews who took refuge in Amsterdam gave to that city, sometimes also called the Jerusalem of the West.

Can Jews and Christians Celebrate the Exodus Together?

Years ago, I visited the excavation site of a Byzantine monastery in the Judean desert in the company of a group of British Anglican vicars. This excursion was led by the Jewish Israeli archeologist who was in charge of the dig. He was thoroughly acquainted with the Byzantine Christian tradition, which was connected with the ruins of this old monastery from the sixth century in Palestine. Among the buildings that had been excavated was the chapel. At the end of the excursion, the Anglicans suggested celebrating the Eucharist or Communion, the celebration to commemorate the last Passover meal Jesus ate with his disciples (Matt 26:20-29; Mark 14:17-25; Luke 22:14-20), a celebration that has found its way into the liturgy of Christian churches around the world. The Passover feast is connected with the memory of and the commemoration of the liberation of the children of Israel from the slavery of Egypt (Exod 12:12-51).

The Jewish archeologist was very impressed by this proposal at that time and at that place, especially with the notion that this would be the first time that it had happened there since the sixth century. One of the priests led the celebration. The bread and the wine were passed around. The person on my right gave me the cup at a certain moment and said: "The blood of Christ." I took the cup and drank but had to think for a few seconds what I wanted to say when passing the cup to the person on my left, the Jewish archeologist. When I passed the cup to him, I said: "The cup of thanksgiving" (1 Cor 10:16).[33] He took the cup and drank.

As a rule, it will seldom or perhaps never occur that a Jew will show such candor in taking part in a rite celebrated in a "Christian" way. But, I asked myself later on and again now, why should Jews not be able to participate in a rite, a commemoration of their liberation from slavery in Egypt, which was originally a Jewish rite? This is not to suggest, explicitly or implicitly, that the Jewish participant should actually become a Christian any more than the Christian participant must become a Jew if he does that. Indeed, I deliberately did not use the phrase "The blood of Christ" spoken by the person on my right. It was not that I was not willing to do so, but I am very aware of how charged that phrase has become throughout history, certainly for the Jews, and loaded with theological baggage and misunderstandings, such as the idea that God required blood for reconciliation and that is why Jesus had to die. For myself, I think one could use such an expression if the words "Greater love has no one than this: to lay down one's life for one's friends" (John 15:13) could be heard in it. In his fulfillment of the Torah, Jesus is the example of someone who is ready to sacrifice all, to let his own blood be shed, for another.

33. Cf. Ps 116:13.

Can Muslims Celebrate the Exodus, Good Friday, and Easter with Christians?

But can we go a step further? If it is possible for Jews and Christians to celebrate the Passover together, why should Muslims not be able to celebrate the Passover, the feast of the exodus, together with Jews and Christians as well?

I was asked to give a lecture on Holy Saturday of Holy Week in 2009 for an almost exclusively Muslim audience at the Islamic University of Rotterdam, the Netherlands. I accepted the invitation and discussed primarily the obstacles that appeared to exist in conceiving of the option of a common celebration.

I remembered to begin with the fact that the day before, all over the world, Christians had commemorated the crucifixion of Jesus, Good Friday, and that Easter would be celebrated on that same (Saturday) evening and night of Holy Week. But does the Qur'an not deny that Jesus was crucified? After all, it is written: "They did not kill him, Jesus the son of Mary, they did not crucify him" (Q 4:157). Can Muslims then remember and celebrate these days with Christians?

This Qur'anic text just cited (Q 4:157) is almost always explained by Muslims as a denial of the historical fact of Jesus' crucifixion. But does the Qur'an have to be understood in that way? This question is posed not only because that idea goes so clearly against what is narrated in the New Testament but also for the sake of understanding and interpreting the Qur'an itself. Is it also possible to read the three Books together in this respect as well?

In the first place, as far as the Qur'an itself is concerned, it is striking that the presupposed denial of the crucifixion, "They did not kill him, they did not crucify him," does not arise in the context of a discussion with Christians but with claims made by Jews, what Jews said. There are various aspects that are striking here. As is always the case with exegesis, a text must be understood in terms of its context. It is said about Jews in the context of this text that they broke the covenant, that they killed the prophets (cf. 1 Kgs 19:10, 14; Rom 11:3), that their hearts were uncircumcised (cf. Lev 26:41; Jer 9:25; Q 4:155), and that they slandered Mary, the mother of Jesus (Q 4:155-56). And then follows the text about the apparent negation and denial of the crucifixion.

To understand the apparent denial (Q 4:157), it is important that we not skip the introduction to the verse: "As far as what they (namely, the Jews) say," or "what they (the Jews) say."[34] There are many references in the Qur'an

---

34. Jews are accused of such things in Syrian texts. *EQ, s.v.* "Christians and Christianity."

to what can be caused by something someone says, by something that, for example, hypocrites say with their mouths but not what is in their hearts (Q 3:167; cf. 48:11). There are Jews who compete with Muslims in unbelief, primarily those who say with their mouths that they believe but do not believe in their hearts (Q 5:41; cf. 49:14; 5:61; 2:8-9, 14; 3:119; 9:8). Jews are repeatedly accused of twisting the words of God or the words of Scripture — the *Tawra,* the *Injîl,* or the Qur'an (Q 2:75-79). Jews in Medina were reproached for twisting the verbatim content of the text during the reading of the Scripture, so that one might think that what was not part of Scripture had to be viewed as Scripture (Q 3:78; 5:13, 41). Sometimes it can be a kind of tinkering with words so that the sense is turned into its opposite (Q 4:46; 5:13, 41).

The text is not stating, as is often presupposed, that Jesus was not killed because it was thought that prophets of God could not be killed, according to the Qur'an. The idea that a prophet of God can be killed is clearly acknowledged in the Qur'an. The prophet Muhammad was himself threatened with death in Mecca. In the same context of this text, the Jews are accused precisely of having killed prophets in line with what is also said in the Bible (Q 4:155; cf. 2:61; 3:112; 3:21, 181; 2:91; cf. Matt 23:37; Luke 13:34).

But even more important perhaps is that the Qur'an does speak candidly about Jesus' death. Jesus says: "Peace be upon me the day that I was born, the day that I shall die, and the day I shall be raised again" (Q 19:33). Elsewhere, God says to Jesus, "I shall let you die and I shall raise you to me" (Q 3:55; cf. 5:117). That means that God took Jesus to himself in the form of his dying.

What is the apparent discrepancy between these texts, which clearly speak of the death and dying of Jesus, and the text that apparently denies his death and resurrection? Was Jesus killed and crucified or not according to the Qur'an? Aside from there being a reason to wonder if this text can be explained in a different way on the basis of the unanimous witness of the New Testament, there is thus also a clear reason on the basis of the Qur'an itself to think that there may be another explanation than the usual one offered by Muslims.

To that end, I will first refer to an important passage from the Qur'an that has to do with the above-mentioned Battle of Badr, where the Muslims managed to defeat a superior force despite their own few numbers. There we read: "You have not killed your opponents; God killed them" (Q 8:17).[35] There is no doubt at all in the text that Muhammad's opponents were de-

---

35. Cf. Paret, *Der Koran: Kommentar,* on this verse.

feated and killed by Muslims in the battle. But what is denied is that Muhammad and his followers can claim the victory for themselves. The Qur'an intends to make clear that this victory is not to be attributed to their own merit but only to God himself. It is God who brought about the victory; God gave them the victory in Badr (Q 3:123). Thus, the text does not deny an actual historical event; what it denies is that they achieved the victory through their own strength. In other words, such a text about Jesus' alleged crucifixion is concerned with what people have done and what God himself has done. That is why it is not too much to assume that the apparent denial of the crucifixion does not refer to the actual event but is intended to deny that the Jews are to be held responsible for that. "They did not do it." But who did it then? The answer is: God did it. God took Jesus to himself. God lifted him up to himself. God raised him up to himself (Q 4:158).

Before explaining further what the Qur'an means precisely by the latter, "raising," I want to first refer to the New Testament, the *Injîl*.

One of the most prominent of Jesus' disciples, Peter, preached on the first Pentecost, fifty days after the Passover. He relates how the following people conspired, successively, against God's holy child Jesus in this city of Jerusalem: King Herod, the Roman governor Pontius Pilate, with the Gentiles and the peoples of Israel (Acts 4:27). It is clear that everyone, without exception, is held responsible for the death of Jesus.[36] But Peter follows that statement immediately by the declaration that they did it so that what God's hand intended to do and what he decided in his counsel to do would in fact happen (Acts 4:28).

Thus, there were various actors in the drama of Jesus' execution. It is not denied that plans were devised by people, that lawless people had a hand in Jesus' death. At the the the same time, it is said that God had a hand in Jesus' death in that what happened was what God's power[37] and will had decided beforehand should happen (Acts 4:28). God's counsel is fulfilled. The responsibility for this crime of condemning and executing an innocent person is still to be imputed to those bodies or people mentioned, but in the end it was God's counsel and his hand that decided the course of events.

It becomes evident in other biblical stories as well that there can be two sides to one and the same event. That is very clear in the story of Joseph, the son of the patriarch Jacob/Ya'qûb, and his brothers. Because Joseph is fa-

---

36. Muhammad Kamel Hussein elaborates how everyone betrayed his conscience that day; *De stad des verderfs: Een vrijdag in Jeruzalem* (Amsterdam: De Brug-Djambatan, 1991).

37. The KJV has "hand" here, which is a standard metaphor for God's acts of power.

vored by his father, his brothers sell him into slavery out of jealousy and Joseph thus ends up in Egypt (Q 12:8-22). But there he manages to ascend to a position of honor. He even rises to the position of viceroy and administrator of the storage barns that were filled during the seven good years of abundance to assist people when the lean years would arrive (Genesis 41; Q 12:54-57). Because of a great famine in their land, Joseph's brothers go to Egypt to buy food. There Joseph meets his brothers again (Genesis 42; Q 12:58-62). Put in charge of the provision of food by Pharaoh, Joseph twice gives his brothers food to take home (Genesis 43). At first, however, they do not recognize him as their own brother, but only in the final instance that they come to buy food does Joseph reveal himself to them. The brothers are now afraid that he will make them pay for their crime. But Joseph says to them: "You intended to harm me, but God intended it for good to accomplish what is now being done, the saving of many lives" (Gen 50:20). Here as well there is no denial of the brothers' bearing responsibility for the crime they committed with their own hands. But something good has come out of this crime: Joseph has climbed to such a high position in Egypt. Now he can be their savior. God has intended one and the same act for good. The story of Joseph is an example (Q 12:111). The whole narrative of Joseph in the Qur'an is accompanied by interpolations that urge believers to see the hand of God in human affairs (Q 12:6, 7, 56, 57; Genesis 37–50).

The Lifting Up, Raising, of Jesus/'Îsâ

Thus, the Jews did not kill and crucify Jesus (Q 4:157). "Now, it was not the Jews who crucified [you, Lord Jesus]" (Jakobus Revius); God killed him (Q 5:117). What is meant by the latter? To answer that question, it is important to look closely at the expression "lifting up": "Truly they have not killed him, but God has lifted or raised him up to himself" (Q 4:157-58). To explain what is meant by lifting or raising up, we should look again at the story of Joseph. That image of lifting up is borrowed from that story. When Joseph is sold by his brothers and arrives in Egypt, he ends up in prison because of the charge of adultery with the wife of his master, Potiphar/Azîz (Q 12:25). In the prison Joseph must, when asked, interpret the dreams of two other prisoners, Pharaoh's butler and baker. They are suspected of wanting to kill Pharaoh and have both been imprisoned. Both have now had dreams and ask their fellow prisoner, Joseph, to interpret them. The butler dreamed of a vine on which there were three clusters of grapes. He picks some of the grapes, presses them, and hands the juice to Pharaoh. The baker has a similar dream: he dreamed of three baskets on his head filled with white bread. In the topmost basket are all kinds of bread of the finest quality, intended for the Pharaoh, but birds come and devour it (Gen 40:6-17).

Joseph explains the butler's dream as follows: "Within three days Pharaoh will lift up your head" (Gen 40:13). And to the other, the baker, he says: "Within three days Pharaoh will lift up your head" (Gen 40:19). The explanations sound almost identical but mean precisely the opposite: for the butler, it means that Pharaoh will restore him to his position as butler, whereas for the baker it means that he will be hanged from a tree in three days. Thus, the expression "lift on high," "raise up," is ambiguous. It can mean both promotion and execution: lifting up, raising, glorification, or destruction.

It is striking that the gospel of John speaks of the crucifixion as lifting up: "Just as Moses lifted up the snake in the wilderness, so the Son of Man must be lifted up" (John 3:14). Here John refers to the event during the wanderings of the children of Israel in the desert when the people became impatient and asked why they had been brought out of Egypt. In other words, they placed the whole exodus undertaking in question. Then poisonous snakes were sent among them, and many died from being bitten. As soon as they confessed to having sinned and asked Moses to deliver them from the poisonous snakes, Moses had a snake made of bronze and fixed to a pole. Everyone who had been bitten and looked on that snake would live (Num 21:4-9). Thus, John says, the Son of Man, Jesus, will be lifted up on a pole, halfway between heaven and earth, but that lifting up is also another kind of lifting up: it is his ascent to the Father, which means salvation for humankind (John 3:14-15). Death and lifting up therefore belong together. None other than God is guiding events: "I am" (Exod 3:14; cf. Isa. 43:10). The meaning of the person of Jesus is clear from his exaltation, by his being lifted up on the cross: the love of God for the world, as well as Jesus' faithfulness to his mission and God's faithfulness to his messenger *(rasûl)*, the one he sent (John 8:24, 29). Looking on the cross can bring salvation: "They will look on the one they have pierced" (John 19:37).[38] This is a reference to what the prophet Zechariah says about the messianic king, the representative of God whom his people would not accept (Zech 12:10, 8).[39] Good Friday, the day of the crucifixion, and the ascension, Jesus' being lifted up to God, fall on the same day. Jesus' crucifixion, Good Friday, is his being lifted up, his ascension. The

---

38. KBS on John 8:24.
39. KBS on Zech 12:8, 10.

being lifted up explains the crucifixion, states its meaning. In the words of the Qur'an, "God killed him" and "God lifted him up" (Q 4: 157); Jesus' being lifted up thus also revolves around one and the same event viewed from different sides.

Are Jews, Christians, and Muslims Not All Emigrants?

Let us ask the question once again: "Why should Muslims not be able to celebrate the feast of the exodus, the Passover, with Jews and Christians?" Abraham was told to leave Ur, the capital city of the Sumerian civilization. He is described as the ancestor who used to live on the other side of the river, from where God took him (Josh 24:2-3). The river, it is assumed, is the Euphrates. The epithet that Abraham is given, the Hebrew *(ha-Ibri)* (Gen 14:13), has been explained as a reference to someone whose roots lie on the other side. In Hebrew, an *ibri* is someone who crosses to the other side. According to the Haggadah, this passage from the book of Joshua is read during the celebration of the Jewish Passover meal. In the *Prager Haggadah* from 1526, one can see an illustration of Abraham crossing the Euphrates in a rowboat. In a later illustration, the crossing is elaborated even more, with the boat having the form of a Venetian gondola. In the latter, Abraham goes aboard the ship with his whole family, while the idols worshipped by the people on the bank are going up in flames.[40]

After traveling around Asia Minor for a long time, the book Acts of the Apostles tells us, the Apostle Paul arrives in Troas, better known as Troy. His original goal was obviously Ephesus, the capital of the Roman province of Asia, the western part of Asia Minor. The route he followed went first in a northern direction and then westward to Troas.[41] Not knowing where he had to go next, Paul received a vision of a Macedonian man who called: "Come over and help us" (Acts 16:9). He then decides, on the basis of that dream, to cross over from Asia to Europe. Paul also calls himself a Hebrew (2 Cor 11:22). Hebrews are immigrants and emigrants, God's nomads, pilgrims, those who go on pilgrimage to the other side. That vision leads Paul to an understanding of his goal, his internal vocation. The name Hagar, the mother of Ishmael, means "emigrant." The name can be connected with the

---

40. Moritz Wullen and Günther Schauerte, eds., *Babylon: Mythos* (Berlin: Staatliche Museen, 2008) 191-92.

41. KBS on Acts 16:6-8.

Arabic word for "emigration," *hijra*. Hagar is thus the migrant *par excellence*. Hagar is the one driven out and threatened twice with dying of thirst in the desert. But she is saved by the well that God shows her (Gen 16:13). She is later saved by God again, together with her son Ishmael (Gen 21:19). God looked after her, just as he looks after his humble servant Mary (Luke 1:48). Hagar can be seen as a foreshadowing of that woman in the final book of the Bible who flees into the desert: "The woman fled into the wilderness to a place prepared for her by God" (Rev 12:6).[42] From ancient times, the desert has been a place of refuge for those fleeing: Moses fleeing from Egypt to Midian (Exod 2:15) and Elijah fleeing from Israel to Mount Horeb in the Sinai Peninsula (1 Kgs 19:1-8). In the biblical narrative, Hagar and Ishmael are the first, since the exodus of Eve from paradise, to undertake the *hijra*, the "emigration in tears." "These tears are holy and redemptive."[43] According to Muslim tradition, both Hagar and Ishmael stayed in Mecca and were buried in one grave, Hijr Ismail,[44] close to the Ka'ba, which Abraham had once built with his son Ishmael (Q 2:127). Even before the exodus of the people of Israel from Egypt, Ishmael is the first voice to cry in the wilderness, "Prepare the way of the Lord" (cf. Isa 40:3). That would be applied later to John the Baptist/Yahyâ (Matt 3:3; cf. Q 6:85). Thus, there is already a connection with this voice of fear that announces the day of the exodus.[45]

Petra Sijpesteijn, a scholar working at Leiden University, is studying Arabic papyri from the early period of Islam in Egypt. It is striking that she has discovered that there is no mention of Muslims in them. Rather, Muslims are indicated by two different Arabic expressions: "believers" *(mu'minûn)* and "emigrants" *(muhajirûn)*. These two expressions are, of course, taken from the Qur'an. Christian Syrian writers used the expression "emigrants" *(mhaggrâyê)* to distinguish Muslim Arabs from Christian Arabs.[46] The term *mhaggrâyê* in Syrian and *agarenoi, magaritai* in Greek were used by non-Muslim writers at that time for the children of Ishmael, son of Hagar. Obviously, it was also how they then referred to themselves.[47] The early Muslim

---

42. Michel Hayek, *Les Arabes: ou, le baptême des larmes* (Paris: Gallimard, 1972) 232.

43. Hayek, *Les Arabes*, 220.

44. *EI, s.v.* "al-Hidjr." Richard F. Burton, *Personal Narrative of a Pilgrimage to al-Madinah & Meccah* (New York: Dover, 1964) 2:305-6.

45. Hayek, *Les Arabes*, 19.

46. Robert G. Hoyland, *Seeing Islam as Others Saw It: A Survey and Evaluation of Christian, Jewish, and Zoroastrian Writings on Early Islam* (Princeton: Darwin, 1997) 148.

47. Hoyland, *Seeing Islam as Others Saw It*, 547-48; Fred M. Donner, *Muhammad and the Believers: At the Origins of Islam* (Cambridge, MA: Belknap, 2010) 86.

garrison cities, *dûr al-hijra,* were called cities of emigration.[48] The fundamental attitude, the essential characteristic of the Muslim, is that he or she is an emigrant, a *muhajir.*

Abraham is the leader of the exodus, the liberation from Mesopotamia, Moses of that from Egypt, Jesus of that from Jerusalem, and Muhammad of that from Mecca. Each of these cases involves the predecessors of emigrants from oppression on their way to the new land, the new city, where the oppressed will receive justice. The call to *hijra,* according to a tradition about the prophet Muhammad, does not end before the sun rises from the place where it sets. All of the above examples are about liberation. Why should Jews, Christians, and Muslims not be able to celebrate the exodus, the *hijra,* together and travel together toward a world where there are justice and peace and bread enough for all? Are they not all three *muhajirûn?*

---

48. *EQ s.v.,* "Emigrants and Helpers"; Hoyland, *Seeing Islam as Others Saw It,* 548.

CHAPTER V

The Ideals and the Reality of the Promised City, the Land, and the Earth

He has shown you, O mortal, what is good. And what does the Lord require of you? To act justly and to love mercy and to walk humbly with your God.

Micah 6:8

Introduction

Once the exodus, the *hijra,* has begun, what happens on the way to and when the people arrive in the promised land? What happens to the ideals after the liberation from oppression? Do those who are liberated from oppression finally receive justice? Do the oppressed people truly become the leaders, imams (Q 28:5)?

What happens when Abraham/Ibrâhîm and Lot/Lût arrive in the land God has shown them? What is Abraham's relation to the city of Salem/Jerusalem and Lot's to the cities of Sodom and Gomorrah? How does Joseph function as the viceroy of Egypt? What happens during the trek through the desert when Korah/Qârûn challenges Moses' leadership? How do the first leaders, the judges like Gideon, act in the new land once they have entered it? And what can we say about the kings Saul/Tâlût, Samuel/Shamwîl, David/Dâwûd, and Solomon/Sulaymân when it is precisely the whole notion of kingship that the prophets preach so fiercely against in the name of God? To whom, finally, is the land, the earth, the city actually promised?

A "Tale of Two Cities": Sodom and Salem

Abraham comes across all kinds of cities when he enters the land of Canaan. Sodom and Gomorrah were two of them, but Salem, which later became Jerusalem, is one of those cities as well. God's "tent is in Salem, his dwelling place in Zion" (Ps 76:2), Mount Zion. Salem is the residence of the priest-king Melchizedek (Gen 14:18). Abraham's nephew Lot, the son of Abraham's brother, chooses Sodom as the place where he will live.

When a war between various cities breaks out, the kings of Sodom and Gomorrah are forced to flee. Their opponents seize all their possessions, including their entire supply of food provisions. Lot and all his possessions are seized as well. As soon as Abraham hears about this,[1] he takes up arms and sets out with 318[2] men in pursuit. He defeats the kings and thus rescues his nephew Lot (Gen 14:8-16).

On his return, Abraham meets the king of Salem, Melchizedek, who gives Abraham's men bread and wine. His name has been interpreted as meaning "king of righteousness and peace" (Heb 7:2). Righteousness/justice and peace kiss each other, as it were, in him (cf. Ps 85:10). Melchizedek shows Abraham Eastern hospitality, as a result of which he enters into a relationship of peace with him. Actually, Melchizedek does not do anything special insofar as it was usual to provide troops who were passing through with food (cf. 1 Sam 25:18; 2 Sam 16:1; Judg 8:4-5). But there is more going on here. Melchizedek is not only a king but also a priest: he is called a priest of God, El, 'Elyôn, "the Most High God." In the Qur'an, God is also called the Most High, and that is also the title of one chapter (Q 87:1). This name El for God appears in various composite names, such as Israel ("one who wrestles with God") and Bethel ("House of God"; Genesis 28). Melchizedek blesses Abraham and says "Blessed be Abram by God Most High, Creator of heaven and earth. And praise be to God Most High, who delivered your enemies into your hand." In turn, Abraham gives Melchizedek a tenth of everything he had seized, a kind of tax (Gen 14:20). This blessing formula is substantial, for it is formulated in analogy with the formula in which God the Lord (YHWH) is praised: "Praise be to the LORD, who rescued you from the hand of the Egyptians" (Exod 18:10). Abraham has no difficulty in allowing him-

---

1. According to legend, Og/'Udj, a refugee, brought Abraham the news of Lot's capture. He was rewarded with a long life. *EI, s.v.* "'Udj."

2. The numerical value of the name of Abraham's loyal servant, the Damascene Eliezer (Gen 15:2-3).

self to be blessed by Melchizedek, despite the fact that he has already been blessed by the Lord (Gen 12:2). Abraham obviously acknowledges the God of Melchizedek, El, as his God as well. He obviously sees El, the Most High God whose priest is Melchizedek, as the same God who called him from Ur of the Chaldees and blessed him (Gen 12:1-2).

In discussions the prophet Muhammad had with the Jews after his emigration (Hijra) from Mecca to Medina in A.D. 622, he says that God also granted Abraham and his descendants, in addition to Scripture and Wisdom, an immense "kingship" (Q 4:54), just as he would later grant kingship to Saul (Q 2:247-48), then to David (Q 2:251; 38:20) and to Solomon (Q 38:35). Abraham and Lot were first called leaders (imams) who were liberated for the land that God blessed for all of humankind (Q 21:71). And God made them examples for those who let themselves be guided by God's commandment (Q 21:73).

Joseph as King

The tension that Joseph feels concerning the office of kingship can be clearly discerned in the Joseph narrative. Already as a young man, Joseph dreamed that he would rule. He tells his brothers what he has dreamed: when they were busy tying up their sheaves in the field, his sheaf stood upright while his brothers' gathered around and bowed before his. His brothers then ask him if he wants to be their king or rule over them. They hate him intensely. Joseph has a similar dream: "I saw the sun, moon, and eleven stars bow down to me." When he tells this dream to his father and brothers, his father scolds him: "What is this dream you had? Will your mother and I and your brothers actually come and bow down to the ground before you?" These dreams make his brothers jealous (Gen 37:5-11; Q 12:4-5).

When Joseph ends up in Egypt after being sold by his brothers, he manages to rise to the position of viceroy. Apparently, Pharaoh has a favorable view of him because of Joseph's interpretation of his dream about the seven prosperous years and seven lean years that Egypt would undergo. Joseph interprets it as meaning that supplies should be stored in the seven years of prosperity that would come first, to be used for food during the following seven lean years. Joseph himself is then placed in charge of the grain barns. Thus, in Egypt of all places, which the narratives usually depicted as oppressive, he is granted kingship. Joseph governs the country (Gen 42:6). Pharaoh gives him power and standing in the country, and Joseph enjoys his trust (Q 12:54-57; cf. 12:21). Apparently, Joseph has learned from experience, so when he is actually given political power he looks at the nature of kingship differently. It is no longer a boy's dream of power but authority granted by God. Joseph thanks God, not Pharaoh, for this kingship (Q 12:101). God can, after all, give the kingship to someone else or take it away, as he wills (Q 3:26). Joseph expresses this thanksgiving after he has placed his parents, Jacob and his mother Rachel (who in the biblical account has died [Gen 35:19]), on the throne. That is in absolute contrast with his dream in which his parents bow down to him and about which his father had scolded him. That Joseph places his parents on the throne is an illustration of giving heed to the criticism that his father expressed when he was still young. It is apparent from this that Joseph has become conscious of the ambivalent side of kingship, the possession of power, and the temptation to misuse it, which is so often expressed by the prophets.

Muhammad was inspired later by Joseph's example when he himself became a leader. He also was accused by his fellow tribesmen of seeking superiority over others for personal reasons, just as Joseph was by his brothers. Just as Joseph received his leadership to save his own people, so Muhammad saw that applying to himself as well. He was given his leadership position to save his people. He also later followed Joseph's example in forgiving his brothers in Egypt. When Joseph reveals himself to his brothers in his position as viceroy in Egypt and his brothers fear that he will now seek revenge for the evil they did to him when they sold him as a slave, he says: "And now, do not be distressed and do not be angry with yourselves for selling me here, because it was to save lives that God sent me ahead of you" (Gen 45:4-5). Muhammad also displays such a forgiving attitude when he returns to his hometown Mecca, after capturing it in 630. Although the Meccans had conspired against him before the *hijra* to Medina, heaped up insults on him, and punished his family and friends to the point of driving them away, Muhammad is able to greet the Meccans on the day of their capture with a message of forgiveness. He praises and glorifies God and says: "I speak to you now like my brother Joseph. Peace be upon him. Today you suffer no reproach. God has forgiven you" (Q 12:92). This recalls how Joseph received his once treacherous brothers and became reconciled with them.[3] The idea behind this story is that, given that even Muhammad followed Joseph's example here, how much more ordinary "political" leaders should do the same.

---

3. John Renard, *Seven Doors to Islam: Spirituality and the Religious Life of Muslims* (Berkeley: University of California Press, 1996) 263.

Joseph in the Mirror of Princes

It is interesting to refer, in this context, to the "Mirror of Princes" genre. These are works in which a mirror is held up before a prince or king to indicate how he should act. The law for the king in the Torah (Deut 17:14-20), which was the rule for the kings of Israel, is an outstanding example. Al-Tha'âlibi (A.D. 961-1038), a prominent Muslim scholar, later wrote a similar mirror of princes,[4] in which he cites a tradition about Muhammad that relates how the prophet Joseph, when he departed from this world, was carried to Abraham's tomb to be buried near his ancestors.[5] In this story, the angel Gabriel appeared and said: "Stop where you are. This is not his place, for at the resurrection he will have to account for the kingship he practiced." Joseph will be stopped at the gates of paradise for five hundred years and not admitted until the tainting of a worldly kingship will be completely removed from him. Apparently, Joseph's role as a temporal ruler makes some devout people suspicious and thus he needs to undergo purging before he is admitted into paradise. The message is: if that is the case for Joseph, how much more so for others?[6]

ERASMUS'S MIRROR OF PRINCES FOR CHARLES V

Commissioned by the Chancellor of Brabant and the Lord High Chancellor of Burgundy, Erasmus wrote a "Mirror of Princes" for the future Emperor Charles V (1500-58). In that work he drafted the education of the ideal Christian prince, intended to make Charles V aware of the dignity of his position and to point to his duties toward his people, rather than his rights. In that respect, the treastise is directly opposed to Machiavelli's *The Prince*, written in 1513. For Erasmus, the ideal training of the *princeps Christianus* and the unbreakable bond between prince and subjects were central. Erasmus's political leitmotif is: the authority of the prince must rest on the consensus of the subjects, be bound by the law, and may be used only for the advancement of the common good. He based his deep hostility to the use of violence as a political instrument on the original Stoic doctrine: if all people are

---

4. *Adâb al-mulûk. EI, s.v. "Al-Tha'âlibi."*
5. This calls to mind the parable of the rich man and Lazarus. After his death, Lazarus is carried by angels to Abraham's bosom (Luke 16:22).
6. Renard, *Seven Doors to Islam*, 263.

brothers, then all war is fraticide. Erasmus's pacifism is rooted in his opposition to the doctrine of the just war *(bellum justum)*, the Christian hypocrisy of holy war, which is not conducted out of necessity but out of fear, ambition, and stupidity. In the end, *humanitas* is lost in every war: "Whoever proclaims Christ proclaims peace."*

De Institutio principis Christiani (1516). Cf. *Erasmus: Een portret in Brieven*, trans. and ed. Jan Papy, Marc van der Poel, and Dirk Sacré (Amsterdam: Boom, 2001) 74-75.

Moses and Korah/Qârûn

The people of Israel leave Egypt after the exodus under Moses' leadership. During the journey through the desert, they live in huts or tents *(sukkot)* as is typical for people who are traveling, wandering. The Hebrew name for one of the books of the Bible, Numbers, is translated "In the Desert," and the book is devoted entirely to that journey.

The people who have been liberated from slavery do not immediately enter a land "flowing with milk and honey" (Exod 3:8; Deut 31:20; Josh 5:6; Jer 11:5; 32:22; Ezek 20:6, 15), as the promised land was characterized. These products were precious commodities, and basic needs for nomads (Gen 49:12; Judg 5:25; Isa 55:1; Song 4:11; 5:1, 12). There is enough to meet everyone's need but not everyone's greed, as Mahatma Gandhi would later say. Moses' leadership was challenged during the journey through the desert, however. Korah, Dathan, and Abiram, together with 250 prominent leaders in the community (Num 16:1–17:13), stirred up religious and political opposition to the leadership and authority of Moses and his brother Aaron/Hârûn. They thought that Moses had not led them to a land flowing with milk and honey and that they had not received a field and vineyard.

Who is Korah/Qârûn (Q 28:76-84) actually? Korah is an Israelite, but he desires power over that people himself. He is presented as someone who, as a leader, acts like Pharaoh. He is also called Pharaoh's treasurer and oppresses the people and treats them unjustly. God gives Korah enormous wealth; he is a kind of Croesus figure, on the order of the king of Lydia (561-542 B.C.) who was famous for his legendary wealth. Korah has so many treasuries that it requires several strong men to lug just the keys around. The people warn Korah not to take pride in his wealth and to display it, as he apparently did: "Be generous and don't bring destruction upon the earth." When people urge Korah to use his wealth for God's purposes, with the attendant reward or retribution in the next world, he answers that the only reason he is wealthy is because of his knowledge. When Korah visits his people in all his finery, there are, apparently, people who are receptive to that display, have a weakness for it, and who crave this life and say: "If only we had as much money and possessions as Korah. He's very lucky." But those who have true knowledge *('ilm)*, a type of knowing that differs from that to which Korah appeals, say: "Woe to you, God's reward is better for those who believe and do justice" (Q 28:80).[7] When God threatens to destroy the whole people in an instant because of the uprising by Korah and and his followers, Moses and Aaron throw themselves to the ground and say: "O God, the God who gives breath to all living things, will you be angry with the entire assembly when only one man sins?" Through this mediation Moses and Aaron manage to prevent the whole assembly of Israel from being destroyed, but the ground does open up in punishment under the feet of Korah, Dathan, and Abiram, and they go down, together with everything they possess, alive into the realm of the dead (Num 16:31-33; 26:9-10; Q 28:81-82; cf. 29:40).[8]

The Korah figure is primarily a symbol for the power of money that brings destruction upon the earth. The theme of pride and arrogance that accompanies that wealth emerges in the stories about Pharaoh and Korah and explains why Haman is mentioned along with them as one who becomes proud as well. In the Bible, Haman is a servant of the Persian king Ahashverosh, the husband of Queen Esther. Esther manages to prevent Haman's plan to exterminate the Jews, an incident that takes place centuries later and in a different place (Persia rather than Egypt). In the Qur'an, Haman/Hâmân is associated with Pharaoh (Q 29:39). There he is one of Pharaoh's ministers, and Pharaoh tells him to stoke the fire for baking clay bricks (cf. Exod 1:14). This will enable a high palace to be built for him, undoubtedly a reference to the tower of Babel (Genesis 11), so that he can ascend to God (Q 28:38; 40:36).[9] Moses is sent with God's signs and clear authority to all three, Pharaoh, Haman, and Korah, but they call him a magician and liar.

A series of figures are mentioned as guilty of pride (Q 3:46; 10:75), including Pharaoh, Korah, and Haman. The prominent individuals of various peoples become arrogant (Q 7:75-92). The source of Korah's arrogance is his wealth (28:76-82), and Haman's is his ambitious building projects, the build-

---

7. Heinrich Speyer, *Die Biblischen Erzählungen im Qoran* (Darmstadt: Wissenschaftliche Buchgesellschaft, 1962) 342-44.

8. *EQ, s.v.* "Korah."

9. *EI, s.v.* "Fir'awn"; "Kisrâ"; "'Amâlîk."

ing of a high palace or the tower of Babel (Q 28:38-39; 40:36-37).[10] In the Qur'an the story of that arrogance, pride, and Pharaoh's equating himself with God is connected to the story of that other arrogant prince in Persia, Xerxes/Ahashverosh, and his minister. Obviously, the Qur'an is not making a historical connection, but a thematic, spiritual or ideological connection between various enemies of the people of God, between the same kind of people who bring destruction on the earth, between Pharaoh, Haman, and the building of the tower of Babel, where the issue is also one of a proud attempt to take the place of God. This is something that constantly repeats itself in history: rulers who grasp after the power and glory that only belongs to God.

The Spies Sent into Canaan

On the evening before they enter the promised land, Moses tells his people to remember the grace of God, namely that God sent prophets among them and made them kings, and gave them what he had not given any single person in the world. He asks them to enter the land and then not to continue in their old ways (Q 5:20-21). The "old ways" is a reference to the ways of Pharaoh and Korah, ways of the abuse of power and of wealth. When they arrive in the promised land, God sends some leaders to spy out the land. This refers to the twelve spies, one for each of the twelve tribes of the children of Israel (Q 5:12; Num 13:2). But once the spies have explored the holy land, the children of Israel no longer want to enter it (Q 5:21-26). When Moses commands them to do so, they refuse, because the report by the spies has made them afraid. The spies told of violent people or giants, the children of Enak who live in the land, and declared the Israelites could not attack them. Next to them, they feel like puny grasshoppers and surmise that that is how those living in the land see them as well (Num 13:28, 31, 33). They clearly think about entering the land in terms of power and violence.

Two of the spies, Joshua and Caleb, have a completely different view of the situation and ask the people to enter the land anyway. According to them, it is an exceedingly good land, a land flowing with milk and honey, a land that can provide for the people's basic needs. "If the LORD is pleased with us, he will lead us into that land, a land flowing with milk and honey, and will give it to us. Only do not rebel against the LORD. And do not be afraid of the people of the land, because we will devour them. Their pro-

---

10. *EQ*, s.v. "Authority."

tection is gone, but the LORD is with us. Do not be afraid of them" (Num 14:7-9).

In the Qur'anic account of the entering of the promised land (Q 5:21), the two god-fearing spies give the people more specific instructions: Enter through the gate of the land, whereby obviously the idea here is more one of a city(!), an enclosed settlement. "When you enter it, you will be victorious" (Q 5:23; cf. 2:58; 7:161).[11] But the Israelites still refuse to enter the land through the gate of the city. By way of punishment, the land will be forbidden territory for them for forty years. They will wander around in the desert for that entire period and will finally die there as well (Num 14:33; Q 5:21-26; 5:20-26; cf. Num 32:13).

Moses May Not Enter the Land

It is very striking that Moses himself is barred from entering the land. The reason for that is the following. One day, the people grumble against Moses and Aaron for leading them out of Egypt and into the desert where there are no figs, vineyards, pomegranates, or even water to drink. God tells Moses to summon the people and in their presence command the rock to provide water. The location where this occurred is not precisely known but would be called Meriba ("quarrel"). Instead of simply speaking to the rock, however, Moses strikes it twice with his staff. Water does flow out of the rock, but God is angry at Moses for not following his orders down to the last detail. He then says to Moses that, because they, Moses and Aaron, did not trust in him and did not show respect in the presence of the Israelites and did not honor him highly enough as holy, Moses himself would not be allowed to lead the community into the land (Num 20:12).

When the generation of the children of Israel that did not want to enter Canaan has died and the succeeding generation has arrived at the promised land, Moses must climb Mount Nebo, which faces Jericho and from which he can at least see the land (Deut 32:46-52; 34:1). He will die on that mountain and be united with his ancestors (Deut 32:49-50, 52; 34:1-4). It is God himself who buries Moses, and no one knows where his grave is (Deut 34:6). The Israelites will enter the land under Moses' successor, Joshua.

---

11. Speyer, *Biblischen Erzählungen*, 337-38; Rudi Paret, *Der Koran: Kommentar und Konkordanz* (Stuttgart: Kohlhammer, 1971) 19.

Israel and the Judges

In the first period of the children of Israel's stay in the land of Canaan, the people were led by leaders called judges, precursors in a certain sense of the later kings. One of the judges was Gideon (Judges 6–8), who led the people in war against the Midianites, a nomadic tribal federation of camel nomads. Camel nomads are reputed to have been much more aggressive than donkey nomads.[12] There were good relations at first between the Midianites and the Israelites — Moses' fleeing to Midian and marrying a Midianite woman testifies to this. His wife was Zipporah, one of the daughters of Jethro (Exod 2:21; 18:1)/Shu'ayb, the priest of Midian (Q 7:85-93). Gideon scores a major victory over the Midianites, but the victory must actually be ascribed to God (Judg 7:1–8:3). When the Israelites propose to Gideon: "Rule over us — you, your son and your grandson — because you have saved us from the hand of Midian," Gideon says: "I will not rule over you, nor will my son rule over you. The Lord will rule over you" (Judg 8:22-23). This is a response in the spirit of the prophets: after all, only God is king. It is not without reason that this story is included in a biblical book among the "former prophets." Gideon does indeed refuse the title of king; but he does accept the power that goes with being king, and he is succeeded by one of his sons after his death (Judg 9:2-3), which already points to a kind of dynasty. This entails that there has been a certain tainting by "kingship."

A Request for a King

Not long after the time of the judges, the people explicitly stated their wish to have a king like other peoples. The prophet Samuel/Shamwîl, the last of the judges who marked the transition to the kingdom of Israel, protested vehemently from the beginning against this desire (1 Sam 8:1-6),[13] as many later prophets would continue to do: "They set up kings without my consent; they choose princes without my approval. With their silver and gold they make idols for themselves to their own destruction" (Hos 8:4). Samuel warns the people against what it would mean to have a king: the king would take away their sons and use them for chariots, cavalry, or personal bodyguards. He would demand that their daughters make ointments and cook

---

12. D. S. Attema, *Arabië en de Bijbel* (The Hague: Van Keulen, 1961) 50.
13. *EQ, s.v.* "Samuël."

and bake, and he would demand a tenth of the produce of their fields and vineyards as tax. He would take their best slaves and strongest laborers so that they could work for him. He would demand a tenth of their sheep and goats. And if they then called to God for help against the king, which they themselves wanted, God would not hear (Q 8:11-18). Having chariots and horses is an expression for the potential use of excessive violence(!), which is flatly rejected by the prophets. When the Qur'an talks about the Israelites' desire for a king, the children of Israel ask Samuel to give them a king so they could fight in God's way (Q 2:246).[14] In the Qur'an, Saul is called Tâlût, the "Tall." God chose him above the people and increased his wisdom and physical stature (Q 2:247): he stands head and shoulders above everyone else in Israel (1 Sam 9:2; 10:23).

But Saul comes from the smallest tribe in Israel, Benjamin. He himself says that he belongs to the most insignificant clan in his tribe (1 Sam 9:21). But the mystery of his election lies precisely in that: God often chooses the smallest (cf. Mic 5:2). God makes it clear to Samuel that it is not he (Samuel) they have rejected but God. But the people must and will have a king, and that is what they get (1 Sam 8:5-22).

As soon as the people's wish for a king is satisfied, they refuse to recognize Saul's authority. They consider his origins to be too common (Q 2:247): they reject him as king because he is poor, a herder of donkeys, a water carrier or tanner. He comes from the tribe of Benjamin, which had produced neither prophet nor king.[15] They say scornfully: "How can this fellow save us?" They despise him and do not offer him any gifts as a sign of acknowledgement of his kingship. But Saul acts as if he does not notice (1 Sam 10:27).[16]

The Ark with the Torah Is the Sign

The prophet Samuel makes clear that it is nonetheless Saul whom God has sent as king (Q 2:247). The evidence, the sign of Saul's authority, is the ark[17] that represents the "presence" *(sakîna)* of God (Q 2:248). In order to understand what is meant by this, it is good to realize that this ark, called "the ark

14. *EQ, s.v.* "Path, Fighting, War."
15. *EQ, s.v.* "Kings and Rulers"; "Tâlût."
16. *EQ, s.v.* "Samuël."
17. *EQ, s.v.* "Faith, Belief."

of the covenant," was carried from Mount Sinai by the Israelites on their journey through the desert. During the day there was a pillar of cloud above the ark and at night a pillar of fire that told the Israelites when they were to move and when to rest. In this way, this ark indicated the route the people were to follow (Num 10:33-36): When the pillar of cloud rose, the people followed, and when it came down, they set up camp. The presence of that ark, especially during campaigns, was manifested in an exceptional way in the land of Canaan during the war between Israel and the hostile Philistines (1 Sam 4:3ff.) who lived in the coastal cities.[18]

King Saul came from Gibeah and lived there as king (1 Sam 10:26; 11:4-5). When Nahash, the king of the Ammonites, marched to and besieged Jabesh Gilead, the citizens proposed a covenant with him and agreed to serve him. But Nahash would agree only on condition that they all poked out their right eye. Then the city's inhabitants, who were at their wits' end, sent messengers to Saul to free them (1 Samuel 11). Saul defeats Nahash in the battle that follows (1 Sam 11:1-15) and then has the ark brought to Gibeah when he goes to fight the Philistines (1 Sam 14:18).

When the Philistines capture the ark the Israelites had taken with them into battle, they carry the trophy back to the city of Ashdod and place the ark in the temple of their god Dagon, a fertility god (Judg 16:23). The latter's image falls down time and again, however, because of the presence of the ark in the temple; on one occasion it is found facedown, with its head and both hands broken off and lying on the threshold. When the people in Ashdod see what is happening, they say: "The ark of the god of Israel must not stay here with us, because his hand is heavy on us and on Dagon our god." When the ark is then taken to Gath, another Philistine city, and something similar happens, the ark is moved to the city of Ekron where the same thing occurs. Then the Philistines decide to return the ark to Israel (1 Sam 5:1-12). The ark is kept for some time in Beth Shemesh, a city connected with Israel, until King David finally brings the ark to Jerusalem (2 Samuel 6). The ark is later placed in the temple built by King Solomon, in the holy of holies, in Jerusalem (1 Kings 8). Even while the ark was placed in the temple, it was remembered that the ark constantly went ahead of Israelites and then rested. The poles used to carry the ark through the desert (Exod 25:13-15) could be seen in the space before the holy of holies, called the holy place, because the poles were so long (1 Kgs 8:8). The ark was probably destroyed or brought to Babylon in 587 B.C. after the destruction of the Jerusalem temple by Nebuchadnezzar.

18. *EQ, s.v.* "Shekhinah."

The ark contained in particular the tablets of the law (Deut 10:1-5; cf. 9:9, 11), "the testimony that I (God) have given you," or "law of covenant" (Exod 25:16, 21). The important point is that the Ten Words, which embody the instruction of the Torah, lay in the ark. This law was also to remain there as a witness against this people (Deut 31:25-26). The "remnants" of Moses and Aaron that the Qur'an speaks about are understood to be referring to the Torah (Q 2:248).[19]

David and Goliath/Jâlût

According to the Qur'an, one of the reasons the children of Israel ask God for a king is so they can fight in God's way (Q 2:246). The prophet then asks them if they promise that they will fight if fighting is prescribed for them. "Why not" they answer, "since we have been driven out by the people of Goliath, the Philistines?"[20]

Before Saul engages Goliath in battle, the Israelites are first tested by a river. This story is connected thematically with what is narrated in the Bible about the judge Gideon. Everyone who is afraid or anxious is allowed to return home so that others will not lose heart because of their attitude. Whoever drinks from the river does not belong with those who are able to fight, and they can return home. But those who do not drink, no more than a handful, can continue with Gideon (Q 2:249; Judg 7:5ff.). This means that only a small group remains. The primary reason for this selection is that God does not want the army to be too large and that it thus be forgotten that God is the one who brings salvation. The reduction of the army to only three hundred men (Judg 7:2-8) emphasizes precisely that victory can only be ascribed to God: "I cannot deliver Midian into their hands, or Israel would boast against me, 'My own strength has saved me'" (Judg 7:2). "How often has a small group been victorious over a large army by God's leave" (Q 2:248-49)? This is the tale of the victory of the small Gideon gang, which has now become proverbial (cf. Isa 9:4; 10:26; Ps 83:9).

After Saul has crossed the river with a small group, the Israelites are afraid of the great power of the army of the giant Goliath, for he is a huge champion of the Philistines. He probably came from Gath and is one of the Anakitim, a "long-necked" person. The spies had viewed the inhabitants of the

19. *EQ, s.v.* "Saul."
20. *EI, s.v.* "Djâlût."

land, after all, as giants, Enakites. Two of the twelve spies, however, trusted that a small army could beat a superior force, just as the small David beat the giant Goliath. Saul's army is victorious, despite the fear of the children of Israel: when they fight, it is David who, with God's help, defeats Goliath (Q 2:251).[21]

That same motif will play a crucial role in the Qur'anic story of the struggle of the Muslims at Badr in March 624. A comparably small number of Muslim fighters under Muhammad's guidance had to defend themselves against a large force of Meccan opponents. The story of David and Goliath thus becomes a foreshadowing of the victory at Badr.[22]

"Chariots and Horses," "Silver and Gold"

David is the recipient of the divine book of the *Zabûr*, the Psalms (Q 17:55; 4:163; cf. Mark 12:35-37). After Saul — and again after David, his son Solomon — God grants the office of king and wisdom (Q 2:251; cf. 38:20; 27:15).[23] Solomon receives a kingdom like none other (Q 38:35). He is the one beloved of God, known nationally and internationally as a just and wise king. His reign of forty years was a golden period of stability, prosperity, and national unity. On the other hand, his rule was considered disastrous because of his oppression of the people. It is said that Solomon modernized the army and, to accomplish that, did not hesitate to participate in an arms race and trafficking. If other nations had "chariots and horses," chariots pulled by horses, then why not Israel? Before Israel formed a kind of unified state, those horses were not used, at least initially, by David. David had the horses he captured in battle crippled. He disabled the chariots of the Philistines and hamstrung all but a hundred horses (2 Sam 8:4). Already during David's reign, horses and chariots began to make up part of the royal army. David's sons Adonijah and Absalom purchased them (1 Kgs 1:5; 2 Sam 15:1). But it was Solomon in particular who saw the military advantage of having chariots and horses. He introduced them and acquired thousands for astronomical amounts. He imported them — one could say of course(!) — from Egypt (1 Kgs 10:28) — precisely from the place from which the people had been liberated by Moses, and built cities with stables for his chariots (1 Kgs 9:17-18). He introduced cavalry and used war chariots, which until then had only

21. *EI, s.v.* "Tâlût."
22. *EI, s.v.* "Tâlût"; "Djâlût."
23. *EQ, s.v.* "David."

been used in the field by the Canaanites and the Philistines (Josh 11:4; 17:16; Judg 1:19; 4:3, 13; 1 Sam 13:5; 2 Sam 1:6). When things clearly went wrong for the first king, Saul, the kingship was taken from him by God by means of the prophet Samuel (1 Sam 15:26). With Solomon things also began to go seriously wrong: he did everything that God had forbidden in the Torah according to the law for kings, the biblical "Mirror of Kings" that had actually been written with primarily him in mind: the king was not to acquire great numbers of horses for himself or cause the people to return to Egypt for that purpose. The king was never to take that route, never turning back to slavery out of which the people had just been liberated. Nor was the king permitted to have several wives, for that could lead his heart astray, nor accumulate large amounts of silver and gold (Deut 17:16-17; 1 Kgs 11:1-13).

Later prophets issued similar warnings. Isaiah says that there is no end to their chariots, and his contemporary Micah says: "'In that day,' declares the LORD, 'I will destroy your horses from among you and demolish your chariots. I will destroy the cities of your land and tear down all your strongholds'" (Mic 5:10-11). Chariots and horses mean power for the nations, but Israel's strength is in its God: "Some trust in chariots and some in horses, but we trust in the name of the LORD our God" (Ps 20:7).

But Solomon's heaping up of "silver and gold" (1 Kings 10) is a symbol of wealth, just as chariots and horses are symbols of power (Deut 17:16-17). Gold is the symbol of wealth (Job 3:15; Jas 2:2) and can serve as a symbol of all that is earthly, worldly, and therefore fleeting (Eccl 12:6; Acts 17:29; Jas 5:3; 1 Pet 1:7, 18). Silver, which can also mean "money," plays a major role as accumulated wealth (Exod 22:7). It cannot help save someone on the day of the wrath of the Lord (Zeph 1:18). The Qur'an also warns those who heap up treasures of gold and silver (Q 3:14) and points to the dangers of fraud, greed, and wrong behavior caused by hoarding gold and silver for personal use (Q 9:34; cf. 4:161).[24]

In contrast, wisdom cannot be bought for any amount of gold, cannot be paid for with silver (Job 28:15). The word of God is pure, like silver purified in a crucible (Ps 12:6). Wisdom, understanding, instruction, and God's promises are better than silver. The law, the Torah from God's mouth, is worth more than a treasure of silver and gold (Ps 119:72). It is better to acquire insight than silver and better to gain wisdom than gold (Prov 3:14). Instruction in wisdom should be accepted more readily than silver, and the knowledge of wisdom is to be preferred above the purest gold (Prov 8:10).

---

24. *EQ, s.v.* "Gold."

Gaining wisdom is so much better than gaining gold and precious silver (Job 22:25). God himself is not made of silver (Acts 17:29).[25]

Slavery in the Promised Land

Other than in a few instances, it goes very wrong with most of the kings in the promised land. Slavery, of all things, arose already during the reigns of the first kings in Israel. The lines between forced labor and slavery are fluid. In the memory of the children of Israel, the forced labor they had to perform in building cities in Egypt was a true period of slavery (Exod 20:2; Deut 5:6). After the conquest of the land, however, they themselves compelled the Canaanites to do forced labor (Gen 9:25; Josh 16:10), which could also often have been equated with complete slavery. Apparently, they quickly forgot that they themselves had been slaves in Egypt (Exod 23:9). To summon people to servitude, slavery, was a special right of the king. The prophet Samuel warned about that already when the people wanted a king (1 Samuel 8). David began the hunt for slaves when he needed builders for his ministries, for the splendor of his state administration. David and Solomon forced large groups into performing such services and did not exclude their own people (1 Kgs 5:13-18). Solomon especially is known for developing a harsh forced-labor policy: workers from the north had to work on the temple, and this was a source of growing resistance among the population.

A certain Adoniram was made head of forced labor in the kingdom first under David and then under Solomon (1 Kgs 4:6; 5:14) and was still the commander of the hated forced labor department under Solomon's son and successor Rehoboam. He was the first to be stoned as soon as Rehoboam assumed power, while the king himself managed to narrowly escape (1 Kgs 12:18). A few centuries later, the Babylonian Exile would be viewed by the Israelites as another time of their own servitude (Isa 40:2), like what they had once endured in Egypt.

The conclusion should be clear. Solomon's politics introduced a fundamental social change into the promised land. The rural population was bled dry to finance the military budget. Solomon's choice for the most modern military equipment of his time turned him into a despot. The great "prince of peace" Solomon had in turn become a pharaoh![26]

25. *BW, s.v.* "zilver and goud."
26. Bas Wielenga, *It's a Long Road to Freedom: Perspective of Biblical Theology* (Madurai: Tamilnadu Theological Seminary, 1988) ch. 4.

That is why the kingdom would be torn into two immediately after Solomon's death: Judah and Israel. While Solomon was still alive, the prophet Ahijah from Shiloh informed Jeroboam that he would become king. Ahijah wore a mantel that he tore into twelve pieces and said to Jeroboam: "Take ten pieces for yourself, for this is what the LORD, the God of Israel, says: 'See, I am going to tear the kingdom out of Solomon's hand and give you ten tribes. But for the sake of my servant David and the city of Jerusalem, which I have chosen out of all the tribes of Israel, he will have one tribe." One tribe, under which Benjamin would be subsumed, would remain for Solomon's successor (1 Kgs 11:29-40). Solomon's son and successor, Rehoboam, is advised immediately after ascending the throne to lighten the yoke that his father had imposed. He ignores the advice, the counsel of the elders, however, and follows instead that of the young men who told him: "My father laid on you a heavy yoke; I will make it even heavier. My father scourged you with whips; I will scourge you with scorpions" (1 Kgs 12:11). The people, however, will no longer tolerate the yoke of Pharaoh (1 Kgs 12:16).

To Whom Are the City, the Country, the Earth Promised?

What is now the message from Abraham up to and including Muhammad regarding the promised city, land, and earth? Right from the beginning it was recognized, and continues to be, that the earth is the Lord's (Ps 24:1). The land or earth is God's (Q 7:128; 23:84). God has blessed the earth and determined the measurement of food for both humankind and the animals (Q 41:10). God has made the earth a place where humankind can live and prosper (Q 55:10).

The promise of inheriting the land was already made to the patriarchs and their descendants: God promises Abraham that he will give the land inhabited by the Canaanites to his descendants (Gen 12:6-7; cf. 24:7). "All the land that you see I will give to you and your offspring forever. I will make your offspring like the dust of the earth, so that if anyone could count the dust, then your offspring could be counted" (Gen 13:15-16). The land is promised to Abraham's son, Isaac (Gen 26:2-3), and the land is also promised forever to Isaac's son, Jacob (Gen 48:4). When Moses is called again,[27] the promise is made again to the descendants of the patriarchs: "And I will bring you to the land I swore with uplifted hand to give to Abraham, to Isaac and to Jacob. I will give it to you as a possession. I am the LORD" (Exod 6:8). Moses speaks

27. Cf. Exodus 3 for the first time.

about this in his prayer: "Remember your servants Abraham, Isaac and Israel, to whom you swore by your own self: 'I will make your descendants as numerous as the stars in the sky and I will give your descendants all this land I promised them, and it will be their inheritance forever'" (Exod 32:13).

Included emphatically among those descendants of the patriarchs is Ishmael, thus also the Arabs. Abraham prays that his son Ishmael may live under God's blessing (Gen 17:18). Ishmael's name means, remarkably, "God hears." Ishmael is regularly mentioned in the Qur'an with Abraham, and if Isaac and Jacob are mentioned, Ishmael is listed first (Q 2:136; 3:84; 2:140; cf. 2:133).[28] Abraham praises God, who has given him Ishmael and Isaac despite his advanced age: "My Lord hears when men pray to him" (Q 14:39). Ishmael is referred to as someone who keeps his promises, a messenger and a prophet who commands people to perform their prayers *(salât)* and to give alms *(zakât),* in other words, to observe their religious and social obligations (Q 19:54-55; cf. 6:86; 38:48; 21:85). The prophet Muhammad sees himself as Abraham's descendant via the latter's son Ishmael.

What Land?

What land is it that is promised? Moses, who liberated his people from the house of slavery and oppression, must go to the promised land, where the oppressed will receive justice (Ps 146:7). Even though the name of the land is not mentioned, one thinks first of Canaan, the "holy land"; the Qur'an speaks of "the east and west of the land that God has blessed" (Q 7:137; cf. 17:1; 21:71, 81; 34:18). The expression recalls texts such as: "The LORD said to Abram after Lot had parted from him, 'Look around from where you are, to the north and south, to the east and west. All the land that you see I will give to you and your offspring forever'" (Gen 13:14-15). One can also think of the expression "From the rising of the sun to the place where it sets [i.e., east, west], the name of the LORD is to be praised" (Ps 113:3).

The Oppressed Become Leaders, Imams

After the children of Israel left Egypt, they went to the land that God would give them (Q 26:59). God wanted to do good to those who were oppressed in

28. Paret, *Der Koran,* 29. Cf. Q 14:39, where Jacob is not mentioned.

Egypt: the oppressed will inherit the land (Q 28:5). The oppressed refers especially to the children of Israel: "And we gave to the people who were oppressed the east and west of the land, Palestine, which we had blessed, as an inheritance" (Q 7:137).[29] But the oppressed, of which the children of Israel are an example, is extended and applied to all those who are socially and economically oppressed. What is said about the children of Israel does not hold exclusively for them, but applies *pars pro toto:* the part stands for the whole. That concerns, for example, the lowest layer of the Meccan population (Q 4:75; 2:282).[30] It is the good news of redemption and liberation that is intended for all who are oppressed: all the oppressed will inherit the land, the earth, the city. The oppressed are the subservient people and the lowest on the social scale, who have no political power: the weak, the poor, children, and women (Tabari).[31]

Conditions for Living in the Land, on the Earth

It will be a good land if the commandments of God and his Torah are not forgotten. At the end of the wandering in the desert and having arrived at the border of the land, Moses gives a long speech with a view to the imminent entry into the land, as recorded in the book of Deuteronomy, the last of the five books of Moses, viewed as a "copy" of the law (Deut 17:18). It is clearly stated in the Torah that God will bring the people into a good land, a land of rivers, brooks, and streams that gush out in the valleys and on the mountains. When they live there in abundance, they must thank God for the good land that he has given. They must take care that they do not forget God nor neglect his commandments, laws, and regulations that Moses presents to them today. When they have enough to eat and have built nice houses to live in and their possessions increase, they must not become arrogant and forget God. Moses reminds them of where they have come from: "The LORD your God . . . brought you out of Egypt, out of the land of slavery. He led you through the vast and dreadful wilderness." If they thrive, it is not because of what they themselves did or do. They must understand that it is God who makes them prosper, because God intends to keep his promises that he swore to their forefathers, as he has done until now. But if they do forget

---

29. *EQ, s.v.* "Oppression."
30. Paret, *Der Koran,* 59 on Q 2:282.
31. *EQ, s.v.* "Oppressed on Earth, Rebellion"; "Economics."

God and follow other gods and worship and bow down to them, Moses warns them in advance that they will surely die. What happened to the peoples whom God eradicated for their sake will happen to them. They will die because they did not listen to God (Deut 8:7-20).

There is thus no reason at all for self-exaltation or the idea that the people themselves deserved it, that God was obligated to them to give them the land as a possession. God drove the previous inhabitants out because they were evil and because he wanted to keep the promises he had made to the patriarchs (Deut 9:4-6). If the people do not behave, they will be spewed out by the land (Lev 18:25), like other peoples before them (Lev 18:28; cf. 20:22).

This line of thought is confirmed by the Qur'an. God does look at how the people act in the land. Those who are liberated from oppression must observe their spiritual and social obligations (Q 21:73). God will look at how they act (Q 7:129). God has exterminated families before. God then made the Meccans and the nations, whom God had punished in earlier times for their unbelief, to be governors or caliphs to see how they would act (Q 10:13-14; cf. 6:165).

The Borders of the Land: Dimensions and Number

What are the dimensions of the land? Does it have specific boundaries? All Israel is denoted as extending from Dan, on the northern border, to the southernmost border at Beersheba (Judg 20:1; 1 Sam 3:20). That covers more or less the territory which roughly coincides with the frontiers of present-day Israel and Palestine. But dimensions are also mentioned that speak of Israel as extending from the Nile to the Euphrates, more or less the whole known world at that time. "When the sun had set and darkness had fallen, a smoking firepot with a blazing torch appeared and passed between the pieces. On that day the LORD made a covenant with Abram and said, 'To your descendants I give this land, from the Wadi of Egypt to the great river, the Euphrates'" (Gen 15:8-21). Thus, it was later said of King Solomon that he ruled over all the kingdoms between the Euphrates and the land of the Philistines and the border of Egypt. He ruled over the whole area west of the Euphrates to Gaza, over all the kingdoms west of the river (1 Kgs 4:21, 24). Apparently, one should understand that it was not so much a matter of a land with geographical boundaries. It is no coincidence that the word *eretz* in Hebrew and *ard* in Arabic can be translated both as "land" and as "earth" and can thus refer to the whole earth! That the Qur'an does not mention any name for the land of Palestine should not be seen as a denial that it concerns this land primarily, but all the more allows the meaning to emerge that the message is directed in the end at every land, at the whole earth.

In this context, it is also good to note the designation of the number of the descendants: like the stars of the heavens and the sand of the sea. The number of the stars should often be seen as a symbol for an innummerable multitude (Gen 15:5; 22:17; 26:4; Exod 32:13; Deut 1:10). The "sand" in the promise of the patriarchs is a symbol for indicating a remarkable quantity (Gen 22:17) and extent of the people (Josh 11:4), as well as of the number of enemies (Rev 20:8), the grain (Gen 41:49), or the divine thoughts (Ps 139:18). That in the promise to Abraham it has to do with a number that cannot be counted indicates that it concerns the whole inhabited earth.

The Righteous Will Inherit the Earth

When the prophet Isaiah speaks of the "new Jerusalem," he says: "Then all your people will be righteous and they will possess the land forever" (Isa 60:21). The earth will be inherited by God's servants (Q 21:105; 39:74). Those who do evil, the wicked, will be exterminated or cut down, but whoever hopes in God will possess the land, the earth. It is the righteous who will inherit the earth, and they may live there forever. That is why one can hope in the Lord and why one is urged to remain on the path he indicates (Ps 37:9, 29, 34); "The meek will inherit the earth and rejoice in great peace" (v. 11). It is the final verse of this Psalm, which is attributed to David, that is cited by Jesus in one of the Beatitudes: "Blessed are the meek, for they will inherit the earth" (Matt 5:5). It is striking that precisely that verse is quoted literally by the Qur'an and confirmed: "And we [God] have written in the scripture [Zabûr, Psalms] . . . that the earth will be inherited by my righteous servants" (Q 21:105).

Pray to God for help and be patient. The earth belongs to God alone. He gives it to servants of his choosing as an inheritance. The final outcome favors those who fear God (Q 7:128). They in turn say: "Praised be God who has kept his promise and given us the earth as an inheritance!" (Q 39:74).

To whom is the land, to whom is the earth promised? To those who do justice on earth. In you — Abraham — all nations of the earth will be blessed (Gen 12:3). Just like the Bible, the Qur'an strikingly enough emphasizes that God has blessed the land, the earth, for all humankind (Q 21:71; Gen 12:3).

CHAPTER VI

Solomon and the Queen of Sheba/Bilqîs in Jerusalem

[Solomon], after good beginnings, made a bad end. For indeed, "prosperity, which wears out the minds of the wise," hurt him more than that wisdom profited him, which even yet is and shall hereafter be renowned.

Augustine, *The City of God*, XVII, 20

Introduction

In this chapter we will discuss a king, Solomon/Sulaymân, and a queen, the queen of Sheba or Saba, also called Bilqîs, and the meeting between the two in the city of Jerusalem. The question of whether one is a caliph or king, a proper representative of God on earth or a king in the sense of one who brings destruction, is given a striking illustration and pregnant focus in this tale. The story is about the important choice placed before every person, but, more specifically, every ruler or person in power. The elements in this tale that recur again and again are: power, wealth, and wisdom in their mutual relationships. To which do the king and the queen and the other visitors to King Solomon in Jerusalem give priority?

This chapter will first discuss the tales about King Solomon and will then turn to the kingdom of Saba and the visit of the queen of Sheba to Solomon in Jerusalem, as well as the many others who come to Jerusalem because of him. Why do they come? What is the purpose of their visit? Do they come because of Solomon's power, wealth, or his wisdom?

The tale of the queen of Sheba has been treated extensively in the Arabic, Ethiopian, and Jewish traditions. Persian art depicts the scene in which she stands with exposed legs in the water before Solomon's throne. The same scene appears in a window of King's College Chapel in Cambridge. The queen has been portrayed in popular art in a wide variety of forms in the West since the nineteenth century right up to our time. For Western artists, the eroticism surrounding her is a natural byproduct of her Eastern heritage. The British painter and designer Sir Edward John Poynter (1836-1919) depicts her in a racy way in his painting *Visit of the Queen of Sheba.* Gina Lollobrigida played her in a Hollywood movie.

One could ask why should not this erotic side have played a role. It is stated in the story, after all, that she presented Solomon with a large quantity of spices, an amount that was never given again (1 Kgs 10:10). Does this not contain sexual allusions for alert readers and therefore a license to see the queen in that light? In the many retellings of the tale it is suggested that a great deal more occurred between Solomon and her than just an exchange of goods and wisdom, that their relationship went beyond that. The Ethiopians hold that their rulers emerged from the intimate relationship between Solomon and this queen. According to the Ethiopian national saga, it was Menelik I who started the royal dynasty: he was said to be the child of the union between Solomon and the queen of Sheba. Haile Selassie (1892-1975) was the last negus or emperor of this house, ruling from 1941 to 1974.[1]

The Kebra Nagast or "The Glory of Kings," which includes the story of the origin of this dynasty and is viewed as reliable by Ethiopian Christians, also tells how Menelik accompanied the ark of the covenant from Jerusalem to Ethiopia. It contains a report of the conversion of the Ethiopians from the worship of the sun, the moon, and the stars to the God of Israel. For the Ethiopians, the Kebra Nagast is what the Old Testament is for the Hebrews and the Qur'an for the Muslims.[2]

Solomon is thought to be the author of the book Ecclesiastes (Eccl 1:1) and of a collection of love songs, Song of Songs (1 Kgs 4:32). Solomon loved many foreign women and had a harem of one thousand (1 Kgs 11:1-8). Presented as a royal lover in the Song of Songs (Song 1:4; 3:7, 9, 11), he is said to have been so struck by the beauty of the queen that he wrote a series of eroti-

---

1. *EI, s.v.* "Bilqîs"; James B. Pritchard, ed., *Solomon and Sheba* (London: Phaidon, 1974) 104-14.

2. Edward Ullendorff, *Ethiopia and the Bible* (Schweich Lectures 1967; Oxford: Oxford University Press, 1968) 75.

cally tinted poems about her attractiveness: "A woman's voice says: 'Dark am I, yet lovely, daughters of Jerusalem'" (Song 1:5). The latter is thought to refer to the queen of Sheba, which then means that she had to have been of Arab or African ancestry. Both could be true, given the age-old close connections between Ethiopia and the southern part of the Arabian Peninsula.

The Reports about Solomon

God gave kingship *(mulk)* to Solomon in a way that he never did to any other (Q 38:35), as well as knowledge *('ilm)*, just as he did to David (Q 27:15), and wisdom (Q 21:79). Solomon became David's heir (Q 27:16), exceeding his father David in the practice of righteousness (Q 21:78, 79), and he possessed other special gifts. God gave Solomon great wisdom, esoteric knowledge, comprehensive knowledge of things. He exceeded all people of the East and all Egyptians in his wisdom. People, including the emissaries of kings, who had heard about his wisdom came from the surrounding countries to listen to his wise words (1 Kgs 4:21, 24-25, 29-30, 34).

- It is above all God who possesses wisdom, which he gives to whomever he wants (Q 2:269), primarily to prophets: Abraham and his family (Q 4:54), David (Q 2:251; 38:20), Solomon (Q 21:79), Jesus (Q 5:110; 43:63), and Muhammad (Q 4:113). Luqmân, a legendary, long-lived hero from pre-Islamic Arabia and said to be a son of 'Ad, was given wisdom by God (Q 31:12).* In the Qur'an, Luqmân appears as a monotheist and wise father who gives devout advice to his son (Q 31:13; cf. Prov 1:8). Wisdom is a revelation (Q 17:39), and the Qur'an is also called "wise" (*al-Qur'ân al-hakîm,* Q 36:2; cf. Proverbs 8–9). Wisdom is on the same level as Scripture, the Book, including the Torah and the Gospel (Q 3:48). God sends the Scripture and wisdom down (Q 2:231), and it is the job of the messenger or the prophet to bring the Scriptures and wisdom to the people (Q 2:151; 43:63), to present them together to the people (Q 33:34; 62:2).**

- Solomon's fame reached to the ends of the earth. He is famous especially for his superlative wisdom. When God asks him in a dream what he wants, he promises to fulfill all his wishes. Solomon wishes to have a "discerning heart" so that he can govern the people and distinguish between right and wrong, for how else would he be able to administer justice? And because Solomon does not ask for long life or wealth or the death of his enemies, he is given the ability to listen as well as wisdom, unparalleled by any before or after him.

BE, s.v. "Lukmân."
**EQ, s.v.* "Solomon, Wisdom."

Solomon's dominion is said to have extended to all kingdoms between the Euphrates and the land of the Philistines and up to the border of Egypt. As long as he was alive, these areas were subject to him and paid him tribute. He ruled over the area west of the Euphrates, up to Gaza, and he lived in peace with all the surrounding countries. As long as he lived, the inhabitants of Judah and Israel, from Dan to Beersheba, could sit, worry-free, under their vines and their fig trees, an outstanding symbol of peace and prosperity (Mic 4:4).

Included among the marvelous abilities given to Solomon (Q 27:15) are command over the winds (Q 21:81; 34:12; 38:36) and the ability to understand the language of ants (Q 27:18-19; cf. Prov. 6:6), just as he does that of the birds (Q 21:79; 27:16, 19). Those abilities help him to resolve various crises. For example, it is said that his troops, which consisted of *jinns*, people, and birds, were gathered for a campaign and marching in battle formation. When they finally entered the valley of the ants, one ant said, "O ants, go into your homes because Solomon and his troops will unwittingly trample you." Solomon laughed when he heard that, because he understood the language of the ants. He said: "Lord, remind me that I am grateful for your grace that you have shown me and my parents, and that I do what is right and what pleases you! And let me be taken by your mercy into the multitude of your righteous servants" (Q 27:16-19).

- The Qur'an repeatedly summons people to notice the signs *(âyât)* in the creation, the same term that is used for the (revelatory) verses of the Qur'an (Q 2:164, passim). The Bible also speaks of the heavens as proclaiming the glory of God and the Law, the Torah, which gives a reliable testimony to God (Ps 19:1, 7). It is often maintained that making the signs in nature less significant than the revelation in Scripture would lead to opposition. That is apparent in Psalm 19, at least in the 1773 Dutch rhymed version. The first line of the first couplet reads: "The great heavens gladly tell of God's glory and splendor." The first line of the seventh verse says: "The law of the Lord, nevertheless, shows a more perfect sheen, converting the heart." There is no trace of this "nevertheless *(nochtans)*" in the original text, which, rightly so, does not appear two centuries later in the 1973 rhymed version of this psalm. God speaks, reveals himself, both in creation and in the revelation of the Word. In that sense religion is a natural religion *(dîn al-fitra).*

• What is observed in nature, in both the animal world and the plant world, is viewed as a lesson and instruction for people. Ants, for example, teach diligence: "Go to the ant, you sluggard; consider its ways and be wise" (Prov 6:6). They also show what an orderly society looks like. They may be among the smallest animals and not very strong, but they are exceptionally wise (Prov 30:24-25): "It has no commander, no overseer or ruler, yet it stores its provisions in summer and gathers its food at harvest" (Prov 6:7-8). Was Solomon himself guided by the wisdom he could learn from animals? In any case, he does pray for it.

The Kingdom of Sheba/Sabâ'

Saba or Sheba is a country and a people in the southern part of the Arabian Peninsula. It lies in an area that is called the "Happy Arabia," *Arabia Felix*. It is reasonable to suppose that there was a flourishing commercial region in southern Arabia around 1000 B.C. The wealth of Saba was based on trade, and the Old Testament frequently mentions a kingdom famous for its commercial spirit (Ps 72:15; Jer 6:20; Ezek 27:23; Joel 3:8).[3] One chapter in the Qur'an is called "Sabâ'" (Q 34:15). The term calls to mind particular images of the city and trade culture of the Sabeans. Just like most Semitic peoples, the Sabeans originally worshipped the moon, sun, and morning star. Because of astronomical properties, phases, spots, eclipses, positions, the moon occupied a particularly important place. People were convinced that the moon influenced birth, life, development, and death. The ancient centers of this worship were located in Babel, Ur, Harran, and Ma'rib in South Arabia.[4]

Sabâ' was called a "good land." The Qur'an relates that the people of this land had beautiful gardens and good fruit. But when the people turned

3. D. S. Attema, *Arabië en de Bijbel* (The Hague: Van Keulen, 1961) 41-43.
4. *BE, s.v.* "maan"; Wendell Phillips, *Qataban and Sheba: Exploring the Ancient Kingdoms on the Biblical Spice Routes of Arabia* (New York: Harcourt, Brace, 1955).

their back on God, he punished them by washing away the dam, producing a flood that caused their splendid gardens to become ones producing bitter fruit. History records that the Ma'rib Dam broke in A.D. 542, twenty-five years before the birth of Muhammad (Q 34:15-17). This dam served as the central means to control the masses of water that flowed down from the mountains of Yemen. From this location, water was distributed for miles around to create green fields. The breaking of the dam had serious consequences for the irrigation system in Yemen. Inscriptions from that time mention repair work on the dam. In pre-Islamic history, hardly any other event was so embellished by imagination or passed on in so many versions as this breaking of the Ma'rib Dam.[5]

Ma'rib was the capital of the region of Saba, one of the most important stops on the old caravan route that maintained connections with the areas that produced incense in southern Arabia (Matt 2:11; Rev 18:13). The most important and oldest trade route, the incense route extended from the southeastern coast to the north, between the land of the Sabeans and Palestine and possibly Mecca as well. Between Saba and Jerusalem God built visible cities or "places to spend the night" so people could conduct business in peace and safety (Q 34:18).

The end of the Sabean kingdom can be determined with some certainty to have occurred in A.D. 525. The last kings converted to Judaism, the very last of whom was Dhû Nuwâs (reigned 517-25), who after his conversion took the name Joseph. He is known primarily for his persecutions of Christians, including an event ca. 520 in the city of Najran, an important center of Eastern Christianity, in which four hundred men and women died. It is also known that, at the request of the emperor of Constantinople, Yemen was invaded from Ethiopia, which led to a restoration of Christianity and heralded a golden period for an Arabian "city of martyrs," which was a holy city for Arabs for one hundred years. The great Martyrion, the Ka'bat Najrân, became a center for pilgrimage. It is thought that this city was connected with "cities that God blessed" mentioned in Q 34:18. In 630 the prophet Muhammad would receive a delegation of Christians from this city under the leadership of their bishop in the mosque of Medina (cf. Q 3:61). The first treaty was concluded with this city.[6]

5. *EI*, s.v. "Ma'rib"; Phillips, *Qataban and Sheba;* W. Montgomery Watt, *Companion to the Qur'an: Based on the Arberry Translation* (London: Allen and Unwin, 1967) 196-97; Heinrich Speyer, *Die Biblischen Erzählungen im Qoran* (Darmstadt: Wissenschaftliche Buchgesellschaft, 1962) 392-93.

6. *EI, s.v.* "Dhû Nûwâs"; *EQ, s.v.* "Najrân, Religious Pluralism." But see Rudi Paret, *Der Koran: Kommentar und Konkordanz* (Stuttgart: Kohlhammer, 1971) on Q 34:18.

The Queen of Sheba/Bilqîs[7] and Solomon

Who is the queen of Sheba? She is not given any name in the Bible and the Qur'an but is called Balkis in Christian tradition and Bilqîs in later Islamic tradition. The explanation of the name as "concubine" was taken to be unacceptable[8] and says more about those exegeting the texts than about the queen. This nameless queen makes a state visit to the legendary King Solomon in Jerusalem, coming from the southern limits of the world as it was known at that time. She was probably quite famous herself. Jesus, reverential and with great respect, calls her "the Queen of the South" (Matt 12:42; Luke 11:31).

The queen came north with a camel caravan. Her visit to Solomon was undoubtedly also of great commercial importance.[9] Solomon's attempt to acquire all kinds of products himself through regular shipments on the Red Sea would possibly have incited the Sabeans, who wanted to retain control of the trade in these goods themselves, to seek contact with him, and to arrange good commercial relationships (1 Kgs 9:26-28).[10] The exchange of gifts points to this.

But there is deeper significance to the tale of this visit. The queen's bold confrontation with the great King Solomon is explained in different ways by later Jewish, Christian, and Islamic writers. In the Qur'an's account of the celebrated visit to Solomon's court by this powerful and intelligent ruler, she is not called a queen, but "someone who ruled over them" (Q 27:23). This is explained as a condescending way of speaking about her as a woman. How could a woman possess so much power? As a result, scholars have recently emphasized how this legendary queen tested or challenged the "time-honored" gender rules.[11]

The *Targum Sheni,* an Aramean translation and elaboration of the book of Esther in which apocryphal material expands the biblical account, contains a report of the visit of the queen of Sheba to Solomon that is similar to the story in the Qur'an (Q 27:20-44). This version of the tale in Esther describes a terrifying army of animals, birds, and demonic spirits under Sol-

---

7. Cf. Barbara Freyer Stowasser, *Women in the Quran, Traditions, and Interpretation* (New York: Oxford University Press, 1994) 62-66.

8. Pritchard, *Solomon and Sheba,* 99, 139.

9. Phillips, *Qataban and Sheba.*

10. Attema, *Arabië en de Bijbel,* 42-43.

11. Jacob Lassner, *Demonizing the Queen of Sheba* (Chicago: University of Chicago Press, 1993) 1. Cf. *EI, s.v.* "Sulaymân B. Dâwûd"; Q 21:82; 38:36.

omon's command. The queen asks him several riddles before paying him honor.[12] When Solomon is reviewing the birds one day, he says: "Why do I not see the hoopoe?" The hoopoe, which is ritually unclean (cf. Lev 11:19), breeds in all areas of Palestine and migrates to southern countries in the fall and is recognizable by the plume on its head. Solomon asks if the hoopoe may hide sometimes or if it is simply not present: "I will punish him myself if he doesn't have a good explanation for his absence." The hoopoe does not remain absent for long and then reports: "I have seen something special about the Sabeans and I will tell you about it. I have discovered that a woman reigns over the kingdom of the Sabeans and that all kinds of things are given to her and that she has a wonderful throne. I have discovered that she and her people fall down in worship before the sun instead of God. Satan has shown their actions in the best possible light and kept them from the right path. There is no God but God; He is the Lord of the immense, powerful throne" (Q 27:20-26).

The Meaning of the Throne

Having a throne is the symbol of the authority of a king or, in this case, a queen. The throne is symbolic of royal dominion but also betrays the fact that this possession of royal power can stand in a tensive relationship with God's power, his throne. The Arabic word for throne, *'arsh,* appears twenty-five times in the Qur'an with reference to God as the Lord of the throne (Q 17:42; 21:22; 23:86, 116; 27:26; 43:82; 81:20; 85:15), the immense throne (Q 9:129; 23:116), and possessor of the throne (Q 17:42; 40:15). After creating the world, God sat down on this throne to rule (Q 7:54; 10:3; 13:2; 20:5; 25:59; 32:4; 57:4). God's throne is situated on water at creation (Q 11:7). The ark, a sign of God's presence, is called the throne of God (Jer 3:16-17). After Solomon built the temple, the ark was placed in the temple in the holy of holies and the city of Jerusalem takes over the role of throne of God. That is why, from that time on, the city would be called "The Lord is There" (Ezek 48:35). The term "seat" *(qursi)* for throne is used twice in the Qur'an and refers at one time to the throne of Solomon and at others to the throne of God: "God's seat extends over heaven and earth" (Q 2:255).[13]

Solomon wants to know the facts concerning the queen and her power of which her throne is a symbol. That is why Solomon answers the hoopoe:

12. Lassner, *Demonizing the Queen of Sheba,* 14-17.
13. *EQ, s.v.* "Throne of God."

"We'll see if you're telling the truth. Take this letter from me to her and give it to them. And then wait to see what they, the queen and her retinue, respond." The hoopoe carries out his orders. After receiving Solomon's letter, the queen asks for quick advice from the prominent people around her *(al-mala')*, her ministers. She tells them first that she has received a letter from Solomon that starts: "In the name of God the Compassionate, the Merciful." With one exception, this is how all chapters of the Qur'an begin, and it has become customary among Muslims to begin a letter or a book or other projects in this way. "The Compassionate," Rahmân, is the name of God that was known in the area from which this queen came, according to inscriptions found there. In Sabean texts God is called Rahmânân, the Compassionate, the master of heaven and earth. An inscription by the Ethiopian viceroy and later king of Sabâ', Abraha (ca. 525-75), begins with the formula "In the name of Rahmânân and his Messiah and the Holy Spirit."[14]

The letter from Solomon reads: "Do not be proud toward me and come to me as 'one who surrendered' *(muslim)*." Here the term is used in its original sense and not as it was later used. Her advisors say: "We have power and a great army and are prepared for everything. But you tell us how to respond and what to do." Thus, they leave it up to her as to how to answer Solomon's letter. This now touches on the theme of the relationship between power, wealth, and wisdom and what they think about that. The queen's own response and commentary to the letter shows what, in her view, can be expected from kings: "Whenever kings enter a strange city, they destroy it and humiliate those among its inhabitants who are powerful." It is possible that she says this to test Solomon, just as she does with her intention to send a gift to Solomon and his court to see what the emissaries will bring back in answer. The latter concerns the theme of wealth. When the messenger returns to Solomon, he says: "You want to shower me with gifts of money! But you cannot satisfy me with that. What God has given me with respect to money and wealth is better than what he has given you." And it seems that the queen is not far off in her negative view of the usual nature of kings. Solomon says: "Go back to them and tell them: 'We will come to you with troops, against which nothing can be done, and we will drive you out of the city and humiliate you and cut you down to size.'"

Then Solomon says to his own leaders: "Who will bring me the throne of the queen [the symbol of her power] before she comes to me as 'one who

---

14. St John Simpson, ed., *Queen of Sheba: Treasures from Ancient Yemen* (London: British Museum Press, 2002) 165.

surrendered'?" Here one can clearly hear the tension between the kingship that ultimately belongs to God and the kings to whom God can grant kingship and also actually does do so. But the question that keeps coming up is: Do the kings observe the Torah, in particular the "law for kings" (Deut 17:14-20), the mirror God holds up to all kings beginning with Solomon? This tale is about two monarchs: the queen and Solomon. The question Solomon asks, "Who will bring me her throne?" (Q 27:38), actually has to do with the question of how both view the nature of kingship.

A *jinn*, an invisible spirit or genie, assumes the task of bringing Solomon the throne but cannot do it quickly enough. Someone who knows Scripture *('ilm min al-kitâb)* says, however: "I will bring the throne here in the wink of an eye." And so it happens. When Solomon then sees the throne before him, the symbol of the queen's power and authority, he says: "This has happened through God's grace to test me to see if I am grateful, a believer, or ungrateful, an unbeliever." It is apparent from Solomon's reaction that it has to do with a test of his faith. But now Solomon wants to test the queen and says: "Make her throne unrecognizable, so that I can see if she is guided by justice." When she arrives at Solomon's court, she is asked if this is her throne. "It could be," she responds cautiously (Q 27:42). That means that she has gained true insight into the nature of true kingship before coming to Jerusalem. That was apparent from her first response to Solomon's letter when she so clearly rejects the use of violence, which her counselors had advised and which was so characteristic of (bad) kingship (Q 27:33-35).

She is then told: "Enter the palace." When she does, she thinks that the glass floor is water and so uncovers her ankles. In this episode, it seems that she has mistaken appearance for reality. She understands that she is wrong and draws the appropriate conclusion with respect to her faith.[15] When Solomon tells her that the floor is really a terrace covered with glass plates, she says: "I have sinned against myself because I did not believe. I surrender *(aslamatu)* together with Solomon to the Lord of the worlds" (Q 27:44). She thus submits not to Solomon, who suggested earlier that she do this, but to God, which is what being "muslim" really means: finding peace *(salam)* with God and one's fellow human beings, together with Solomon. What holds for her holds just as much for Solomon. It means that there is no place for a true king on a throne if he worships any other god than God.[16]

---

15. Oliver Leaman, *Islamic Aesthetics: An Introduction* (Notre Dame: University of Notre Dame Press, 2004) 132-36.

16. Lassner, *Demonizing the Queen of Sheba*, 38.

What Is Her Conclusion Concerning the Visit to Solomon?

At the reception that Solomon prepares for the queen of Sheba in Jerusalem, she moves from one surprise to the next. At the royal dinner, she is struck by the costly food, the abundance of drink, and the beautifully-attired servants. For her, it is literally and figuratively breathtaking.

She wants to test Solomon with riddles during her visit. She asks various questions she has devised, thereby involving him in a kind of riddle match. At Solomon's court riddles are part of the practice and display of wisdom. The riddle is a special form of wisdom, which can be tested by other riddles. These riddles are cryptic questions that have long been pondered, and the questions themselves testify in turn to wisdom and life experience. A riddle completely conceals but at the same time may reveal one's whole heart (cf. Ps 49:4). "The riddle is, after all, in the last resort, playing at discovering the truth. One person hides or disguises the truth, the other brings it out of concealment into the light."[17] The queen speaks to Solomon about everything she has in her heart or on her mind. And Solomon knows the answers to all her questions; there is no single question he cannot answer. He explains "all her words" to her, lays out the meaning of her questions, the power of her desires, and the purpose of her existence. "There was nothing that remained veiled for the king: the whole of human existence was unfolded between the two of them" (1 Kgs 10:1-13; cf. 2 Chr 9:1-12).[18] How she ultimately experienced and evaluated her visit to King Solomon emerges from her thanksgiving to God: "Praise be to the LORD your God, who has delighted in you and placed you on the throne of Israel. Because of the LORD's eternal love for Israel, he has made you king to maintain justice and righteousness" (1 Kgs 10:9). That is what she concludes from her visit to Solomon in Jerusalem before returning home.

A Kingdom of the Beast

The queen of Sheba is, however, not the only one who visits Solomon. People come to him from all over the world to listen to the wisdom God gave him. What does that wisdom actually entail? Because he did not ask for power or

---

17. Gerhard von Rad, *Wisdom in Israel* (Nashville: Abingdon, 1972) 37.

18. *BE, s.v.* "raadsels"; T. J. M. Naastepad, *Salomo: Verklaring van een Bijbelgedeelte* (Kampen: Kok, 1975).

wealth but for wisdom, God nevertheless did give him the power and wealth he did not ask for in addition to wisdom. But there is no end to Solomon's acquiring of wealth. Apparently, he does not know when to stop. One can detect a certain ostentation in Solomon with respect to his wealth and possessions: Solomon's income was 666 talents of gold a year, a number that is both telling and ominous. That number is later called the number of the false prophet, the beast from the abyss (Rev 13:11, 18)! The beast represents injustice and unrighteousness. It appears in various times and places, villages, and cities. The archetypal beast, *dabba*, also appears in the Qur'an: "And when the judgment, the punishment of God, comes upon the unbelievers, God will let a beast come from the earth" (Q 27:82). The coming of the beast is a sign that precedes the final judgment. The use of that number in this story can be explained as indicating that Solomon's kingdom is that of the beast.[19]

The income of 666 gold talents a year does not include the tax revenue from the traders, the trading rights of the merchants, and everything that the kings of Arabia and the governors of the land produced. Solomon had two hundred large shields of beaten gold made from that gold. He had another three hundred small shields made. In so doing, he took that gold off the market. In other words, he did nothing useful with it except to use it for parade shields and to hang them in the royal treasury, in the House of the Forest of Lebanon. He also made a throne of ivory (2 Chr 9:17), covered in fine gold, something that had never before been made in any kingdom: an ostentatious display of power and wealth. All that gold began to dominate his kingship: he drank out of a golden cup, not one of silver, for that was not worth as much in that time, as was remarked with disdain. Silver was as common in Jerusalem as stones. Every three years a ship loaded with gold, silver, elephant tusks, peacocks, and monkeys would sail into port. The whole world wanted to visit and to listen to the wisdom with which God had gifted, so they all brought more gifts: silver and gold objects, clothes, weapons, perfumes, and horses. And so it went, year in, year out (1 Kgs 10:14-22, 27).

Solomon and Horses

With respect to the horses, one could think that they had to do with something innocent like parades that were organized for the visitors. The Qur'an

---

19. Paret, *Der Koran;* Watt, *Companion to the Qur'an; EI, s.v.* "Dabba"; David Cook, *Studies in Muslim Apocalyptic* (Princeton: Darwin, 2002) 120-22.

states that Solomon had thousands of horses that he had captured in wars. The power of the horses, however, was not pleasing to God, nor was the strength of soldiers. The Lord is pleased with those who worship him and who put their hope in his love and faithfulness (Ps 147:10-11). But Solomon had more than four thousand stalls for his chariot horses as well as twelve thousand horses (1 Kgs 4:26). He purchased chariots and set up a cavalry, with four thousand chariots and twelve thousand men, which he kept in chariot cities and near his palace in Jerusalem (1 Kgs 10:26; 2 Chr 9:25).

One can see the danger of having and keeping these horses from the following story. One evening before sunset, Solomon has his racehorses paraded before him and becomes completely absorbed in admiring them. He strokes their legs and necks and becomes so preoccupied that he forgets about the time of prayer at sunset, so he thus neglects to think about God. He loves his horses, the possession of worldly goods, more than he does thinking about God, until the sun is concealed behind the veil of night (Q 38:32).[20] Like every other person, he is filled with intense love for the goods of this world (Q 100:8); indeed, he is someone who loves possessions very much (Q 89:20). When he realizes this, he asks for forgiveness (Q 38:35) and, by way of penance for his neglect, sacrifices all of his horses except for one hundred.[21]

It is quite conceivable that in the Qur'anic text one can hear an echo of what a later, good king of Israel did — Josiah, the king who found the book of the Torah and obeyed all the words of the book of the covenant, which he read to the whole community (2 Kgs 22:8; 23:2). One of Josiah's responses to that discovery was to remove from the temple the horses that the kings of Judah had devoted to the sun-god and to burn the chariots dedicated to that god (2 Kgs 23:11). For it was not the power of horses nor the strength of soldiers that pleased the Lord (Ps 147:10).

That the king was not allowed to keep many horses is stipulated in the law for kings in the Torah: for him to purchase a great many horses was seen as returning to Egypt. But Solomon did import horses from Egypt and other countries (2 Chr 9:28), and he obtained weapons, as well as his hundreds of wives, from Egypt, the country that represented slavery and oppression. Solomon thus started acting like Pharaoh (Deut 17:16), a ruler who committed injustice and brought ruin on the earth.

---

20. According to Paret's translation, *Der Koran*.

21. Watt, *Companion to the Qur'an*, 208. Arabian horses today are descended from these hundred horses that Solomon kept; Brannon M. Wheeler, *Prophets in the Quran: An Introduction to the Quran and Muslim Exegesis* (London: Continuum, 2002) 272.

Power, Wealth, or Wisdom?

Why do so many others, in addition to the queen of Sheba, come to visit Solomon? Do these people come from all over the world to gaze upon his unparalleled wealth? Is that what the world comes to gape at? Is that the wisdom people are looking for? The issue in this tale revolves around the nature of kingship, wisdom, in addition to wealth and power, the meaning of sitting on a throne. After the letter that the queen of Sheba receives from Solomon in which he asks her to submit to him, she emphatically rejects the advice of her counselors to go to war with Solomon. Kings, after all, destroy cities merely to make the powerful submit (Q 27:34). That is quite different from submitting or surrendering to God. When the queen sends gifts, Solomon rejects them because the ones God has given him are better (Q 27:36). Solomon apparently feels her gifts are beneath his dignity, and his response seems to betray arrogance with respect to wealth and power, considering also that he immediately threatens violence. Obviously, that is what the queen of Sheba was already afraid of, because that is what kings usually do, bring destruction on the earth. When she arrives in Jerusalem and sees Solomon enthroned in peace and righteousness, performing good deeds of just kingship, she praises God: "Praise be to the Lord your God, who has delighted in you and placed you on the throne of Israel. Because of the Lord's eternal love for Israel, he has made you king to maintain justice and righteousness" (1 Kgs 10:9). She thus chooses to occupy the throne herself and to possess power for the sake of justice and righteousness, thus for the caliphate instead of kingship.

The other visitors are concerned with an entirely different side of Solomon. They see Solomon turning to stone like an image, becoming whole with the lifeless throne. He becomes like a divinity, an idol, a lump of gold. One can think here of the head of the image of Nebuchadnezzar, which was also made of gold (Dan 2:32). Gold has become his god, as the psalmist says: "But their idols are silver and gold, made by human hands. They have mouths, but cannot speak, eyes, but cannot see. They have ears, but cannot hear, noses, but cannot smell" (Ps 115:4-6). Did the other visitors come for a king turned to stone, one who had merged with his throne? Did they find what they were really looking for, an idol to kneel down before?

Solomon, who began so promisingly as a king, falls, as evidenced in the horses and chariots, in the gold and silver, the worship of power, the ivory throne. This account of the visit of the queen of Sheba to Solomon concerns the search for the other Solomon for which she had come. There she praises God who has appointed a king to execute justice and righteousness (1 Kgs 10:9).

Solomon is often regarded as the author of the book of Ecclesiastes, which opens with the words "'Meaningless! Meaningless,' says the Teacher. 'Utterly meaningless! Everything is meaningless'" (Eccl 1:2). Originally, the Hebrew word *hebel* ("meaningless") meant "breath," "gust" (cf. the significance of the name Abel). It denoted a lack of value, meaninglessness and uselessness.[22] Solomon's neglecting to think about God at sunset because of his admiration for his horses (Q 38:31-32) leads to the insight that the sun rises and sets and always hastens to the place where it will rise, where its course begins (Eccl 1:5). Ecclesiastes reflects the sense of a king who has enjoyed all the goods the earth can give but has come to sense their emptiness,[23] an insight that the real historical Solomon, as described in Kings, had once possessed. The present life is nothing but a game and amusement. Life in the hereafter is truly better for those who are devout. "Do you have no understanding?" (Q 6:32; cf. 29:64; 47:36; 6:70).

The Coming of the Messianic King

The story of Solomon and the queen of Sheba leads one to reflect on the present and the future. Justice and righteousness will be performed in the world at some time. The story is also written to encourage: so it will be, so it will happen, because it had once actually happened on earth. That appearance of the queen in Jerusalem did take place, and the insight was there "once, just for a moment" in Jerusalem, with King Solomon and the Queen of the South, just as it happened again with the appearance of Jesus in Jerusalem. The Queen of the South says that what she had heard in her country about Solomon's words and wisdom has become confirmed. The legend about Solomon is true, just as the acts of God in Jesus are true. Jesus says, "The Queen of the South will rise at the judgment with the people of this generation and condemn them, for she came from the ends of the earth to listen to Solomon's wisdom; and now something greater than Solomon is here" (Luke 11:31; Matt 12:42).

Those who have knowledge of the Book (Q 27:40), the readers of Moses, the Torah, and the prophets, Jews, Christians, and Muslims — in fact, ev-

---

22. *KBS* on Eccl 1:2.
23. Watt, *Companion to the Qur'an*, 208; Speyer, *Biblische Erzählungen*, 398-99.

eryone — should be convinced again today by the testimony of the Queen of the South. It will happen because it did happen once. The Queen of the South — this Arabian queen — will judge and condemn this generation. She obviously understood what the psalm ascribed to the ideal King Solomon says:

> May the kings of Sheba and Seba
> present him gifts.
> May all kings bow down to him
> and all nations serve him.
> For he will deliver the needy who cry out,
> the afflicted who have no one to help.
> He will take pity on the weak and the needy
> and save the needy from death.
> He will rescue them from oppression and violence,
> for precious is their blood in his sight.
> Long may he live!
> May gold from Sheba be given him.
> May people ever pray for him
> and bless him all day long. (Ps. 72:10-15)[24]

---

24. *EI, s.v.* "Sulaymân b. Dâwûd"; *EQ, s.v.* "Sheba"; Naastepad, *Salomo,* on 1 Kings 10.

CHAPTER VII

Violence in the City

The heroine in Dickens's novel on the French Revolution, *A Tale of Two Cities,* has the evocative name Lucy (light). In answer to the question why political novels have heroines, it has been suggested these figures are needed not so much for resolution as for relief; their presence enables a novelist to substitute the narrative of the conventional heroine for one of political violence. Domestic ideology becomes the primary containment strategy by which Dickens attempts to morally manage and ultimately repudiate the forces of revolution.

Peter Merchant

Introduction

My starting point in this book is to read the three Books, the Torah, the Gospel, and the Qur'an as a single tale: breaking with the city of injustice (Assur, Babel, Sodom) and heading for the city of justice and peace (Jerusalem, Medina). What, then, is the one story concerning violence, retribution, and war (holy war and *jihâd*)? After I present the reason for discussing this subject, we will first look at the story of Cain/Kâbîl and Abel/Hâbîl. Who is the enemy, and how does one — or how must one — deal with them, with enemies such as Satan, Iblîs (snake, dragon), one's own brother (Abel, Esau, Edom), Amalek ('Amâlîk), the giants or Anakites, the Philistines (Goliath), the unjust king (Nimrod, Pharaoh, Agag, Nebuchadnezzar, Gog and Magog)? How do these books view vengeance and retaliation?

145

Holy War or *Jihâd*?

It is asserted quite often that the cause of wars fought today can ultimately be found in the religions: Christianity vs. Islam, Islam vs. Judaism and Christianity. That is why some think it would be better to ban their sacred Scriptures. After all, these books have long been used to justify or legitimate violence. This was also done during the American Civil War, which lasted from 1861 to 1865 between the northern states, the Union, and the southern states that had seceded, the Confederacy. Casualties are estimated at 618 thousand.

In the winter of 1861 the American writer Julia Ward Hove visited a Union military camp outside Washington, D.C., and wrote what would become known as *The Battle Hymn of the Republic*. This hymn incorporated the biblical vocabulary of her generation. She saw divine judgment at work in the battles that took place during the American Civil War.

> Mine eyes have seen the glory of the coming of the Lord;
> He is trampling out the vintage where the grapes of wrath are stored;
> He hath loosed the fateful lightning of His terrible swift sword;
> His truth is marching on.
>
> I have seen Him in the watchfires of a hundred circling camps;
> They have builded Him an altar in the evening dews and damps;
> I can read His righteous sentence by the dim and flaring lamps;
> His day is marching on.
>
> In the beauty of the lilies Christ was born across the sea,
> With a glory in His bosom that transfigures you and me;
> As he died to make men holy, let us die to make them free,
> While God is marching on.[1]

The Qur'an is often perceived by Westerners as legitimating violence against the West. In 2008, for example, the Dutch parliamentarian Geert Wilders produced the movie *Fitna* ("rebellion, sedition") on Islam, attempting to show what in his view is the inherent violence of that religion. Around seventeen minutes in length, *Fitna* shows excerpts from the suras of the Qur'an, accompanied by media clips and newspaper cuttings depicting or describing acts of violence and/or hatred by Muslims. Wilders thus attempts

---

1. Peter Partner, *God of Battles: Holy Wars of Christianity and Islam* (London: HarperCollins, 1997) xv.

to demonstrate that the Qur'an motivates its followers to hate all who violate Islamic teachings.

The Qur'an is, in fact, used today by some Muslims to defend the use of violence. One example is the use of the following Qur'anic text, which is also quoted in the film *Fitna:* "Prepare your strength to the utmost of your power against them, including steeds of war, to strike terror into (the hearts of) the enemies, of God and your enemies, and others as well, whom you may not know but God does" (Q 8:60). "To strike terror" is understood as "to terrorize" the enemy. On the basis of such a text, terrorism is seen as commendable and something of which the so-called *jihadists* can be proud; they can appeal to this text to give their use of violence legitimacy. The jihadists are those Muslim groups who interpret Islam in a radical way and have added a sixth pillar, *jihâd*, to the five basic pillars (the confession of faith, prayer, social obligations, fasting, and making the pilgrimage to Mecca). This, in their view, is true holy war — a view that, as a rule, classical Islam rejects. Terrorism is then seen as a religious obligation and gains legitimacy, just as suicide bombings are legitimated with the Qur'an in hand.

May we read and use the three Books in that way? Do these three Books say that the final victory will be won by the destruction of the hostile city of injustice through violence and war? Do those three Books call people to engage in war, in wars of the Lord, a holy war? Throughout the course of history, not only have wars arisen around the biblical and Qur'anic accounts, but these stories have also been used to defend the theory of just war, crusades, or a *jihâd*.[2] Is this indeed justified by the holy Books? That does sometimes seem to be the case. Thus, at the time of the Crusades no Scripture was cited more often for the sake of carrying out those wars than the opening words of a psalm: "O God, the nations have invaded your inheritance; they have defiled your holy temple" (Ps 79:1). At that time the text was interpreted as referring to the Muslims in Palestine.

The Goth Ulfilas (ca. A.D. 310-83), a bishop, missionary, translated the Bible from the Greek Septuagint into Gothic. Fragments of this translation have been preserved in the Codex Argenteus now in Uppsala, Sweden, the oldest surviving document in a Germanic language. He translated all the books of the Bible except for 1 and 2 Kings, omitting them because they "were nothing more than stories of military undertakings, and the Gothic

---

2. Anton Houtepen, *Geloven in gerechtigheid: Bijdragen tot een oecumenische sociale ethiek* (Zoetermeer: Meinema, 2005) 131ff.

tribes were fond of war and had more need of restraint to keep their pas-
sions in check than to be urged to engage in war."[3]

But the difficult questions of war and violence for all three traditions
should not be resolved by banning the Books or leaving passages out. Rather,
we should attempt to listen to the Bible and the Qur'an as a "tale of two cities."

Enemies of God and People?

The first enemy with whom humankind is confronted is Iblîs, the *diabolos,* Satan, or the devil. He is viewed symbolically as a snake (Gen 3:14-15), which is
the embodiment of malevolent temptation (Gen 3:1, 4-5; 2 Cor 11:3; cf. Q 31:33;
35:5; 57:14). He is also called the dragon. Adam and Eve are warned about the
enemy (Q 20:117), who should be viewed (Q 35:6) as an obvious enemy (Q 12:5;
17:53; 36:60; 43:62). People should not follow in his footsteps (Q 24:21). After
being cursed by God, Satan wants to lead people astray (Q 4:118-19).

Cain: The First to Build a City

The first human child to be born is Cain, who is also the first fratricide. In Islamic tradition Cain and Abel are prototypes of good and evil.[4] Cain is also
said to be the first to build a city (Gen 4:17). The "city of man" is connected
with violence from the very beginning. The legendary founder of Rome,
Romulus, killed his twin brother Remus and was thus able to have only his
name associated with the city of Rome. When the city of Jericho is taken,
Moses' successor, Joshua, places a curse on whoever attempts to rebuild the
city: "At the cost of his firstborn son he will lay its foundations; at the cost of
his youngest he will set up its gates" (Josh 6:26). And this does indeed happen later (1 Kgs 16:34; cf. 2 Kgs 3:27). Supposedly, it was customary to do
something horrible such as sacrificing one's own child in connection with an
important event like building a city, temple, or house.[5]

Cain kills Abel because the sacrifice of the one brother is accepted, but
not that of the other (Q 5:27-32). According to a Jewish story, as soon as Cain
kills Abel, he no longer knows what he is to do. God then has two birds ap-

---

3. Philostorgius (A.D. 368–ca. 439).
4. *EQ, s.v.* "Adam and Eve."
5. Josh. 6:26 KBS.

pear to him, one of which kills the other and digs a hole in the ground with his claws and buries the other one. The crow digging in the ground shows Cain how he can hide his victim (Q 5:31).[6] It is immediately apparent in the story of the first human children how human beings bring destruction and shed blood on earth — something the angels warned God about, even before humans were created (Q 2:30).

God calls Cain to account for his act: "What have you done? Listen! Your brother's blood cries out to me from the ground" (Gen 4:10). God hears the voice of the victim. Cain does not want to be his brother's keeper (Gen 4:9). According to an Islamic exegetical tradition, Adam gives Cain responsibility *(amâna)* for his brother, but Cain breaks his word and kills the very brother who had been entrusted to his care (cf. Q 33:72).[7] Although one could perhaps expect that Cain would be punished with death in retaliation for this murder, the deed is not avenged on him by killing him, despite Cain's fear of that: "I will be a restless wanderer on the earth, and whoever finds me will kill me" (Gen 4:13-14). But it is poignant that God does not abandon him, does not give up on him. Cain who is afraid that he will be killed out of revenge is given a mark by God so that people would not kill him (Gen 4:15). What kind of mark was it? The "mark of Cain" *(Kaïnsteken)* has entered the Dutch language in the sense of everyone being able to see what a scoundrel, a villain, a person is.[8] But the mark of Cain is actually a sign of protection, for God stands by him.[9] God does, after all, make the sun rise on both the bad and the good and rain to fall on the just and the unjust (Matt 5:45), as Jesus says later in the Sermon on the Mount.

The Qur'an says with reference to the Torah, and also in agreement with Jewish exegesis,[10] that because of Cain's murder of Abel God has ordained for the children of Israel that if someone killed another for any reason other than for retaliation for murder or to prevent destruction on the earth, it would be as if he killed the whole people. But if someone saved just

6. *EI, s.v.* "Hâbîl wa Kâbîl"; Heinrich Speyer, *Die Biblischen Erzählungen im Qoran* (Darmstadt: Wissenschaftliche Buchgesellschaft, 1962) 86.

7. *EI, s.v.* "Hâbîl wa Kâbîl," states incorrectly that there is no serious basis for this explanation.

8. *Van Dale Nederlandse Woordenboek* ('s Gravenhage: Nijhoff, 1961), *s.v.* "Kaïnsteken (Mark of Cain)": "One can see what a scoundrel, what an evildoer he is."

9. The "mark" on the forehead of the righteous person saves him from death (Ezek 9:4); the angel of destruction will pass over the houses that have blood on the doorposts (Exod 12:23).

10. And with the Mishnah, *Sanh.* 4:5. Cf. *EI, s.v.* "Hâbîl wa Kâbîl."

one life, it would be as if he had saved all the people. Those who war against God and his messenger and bring destruction on the earth can expect severe punishment or banishment from the land unless they repent: "Know that God is All-forgiving, Most Merciful" (Q 5:33-34). People are called to fear God and to heed the prophet and not to obey those who cannot control themselves, bring destruction on the earth, and do not work for peace and order (Q 26:150-52).

What the angels once said to God when he announced he was going to create humankind now becomes a warning for everyone, namely, not to choose what Satan places before human beings: "O you who believe! All of you, throw yourselves into the arms of peace. Do not follow Satan's foot-steps" (cf. Q 24:21). "He is definitely your enemy; if you abandon the way of God's peace, after having been given clear signs, know that God is mighty and wise" (Q 2:208-9; cf. 12:5; 17:53; 35:6, 36:60; 43:62).

One's Own Brother as the Enemy

While the story of the first children of mankind, Cain and Abel, is a story of a fratricide, the tensions between brothers emerge again in the stories of the children of the patriarchs. Let us begin with the tension between Jacob, Abraham's grandson, and his older brother Esau. Jacob represents the shepherd culture and Esau the hunter culture. The latter is a "skillful hunter, a man of the open country." Isaac, their father, favors Esau, for he likes venison and wild game, but his mother Rebecca loves Jacob more (Gen 25:27-28).

Jacob's descendants and Esau's clashed in Palestine, in the area east of the river Jordan, and the hunters won their independence from the shepherds (Gen 27:40). The Edomites, who saw Esau as their forefather, apparently set-tled in the Transjordan towards the end of the thirteenth century B.C. and al-ready before David had set up a kingdom without a hereditary monarchy. Perhaps there is a connection between life at court that had already developed early and the special wisdom that was accorded the Edomites and for which they were famous (cf. Jer 49:7; Job 2:11; 15:8; cf. Obad 8).

The growth of a very expansive kingdom in Israel led to conflict with the Edomites, whose copper mines and strategic position invited conquest. Under King David, Israel would overshadow the older state of Edom (Jer 49:8-10; Mal 1:2-5). Edom would thus be degraded to a province with an Isra-elite viceroy. All Edomites would become David's subjects (2 Sam 8:14).

When the kingdom of Judah collapsed in 587 B.C. after Jerusalem had been captured by the Babylonian king Nebuchadnezzar, the Edomites avenged themselves because of their previous humiliation and thus profitted from the fall of Jerusalem. That is why the prophets later directed several prophecies at the land of Edom (Isa 34:5; Ezek 25:12-14):

> Because of the violence against your brother Jacob, you will be covered with shame; you will be destroyed forever. On the day you stood aloof while strangers carried off his wealth and foreigners entered his gates and cast lots for Jerusalem, you were like one of them. You should not gloat over your brother in the day of his misfortune, nor rejoice over the people of Judah in the day of their destruction, nor boast so much in the day of their trouble. You should not march through the gates of my people in the day of their disaster, nor gloat over them in their calamity in the day of their disaster, nor seize their wealth in the day of their disaster. You should not wait at the crossroads to cut down their fugitives, nor hand over their survivors in the day of their trouble. (Obad 10-14)

> Remember, LORD, what the Edomites did on the day Jerusalem fell. "Tear it down," they cried, "tear it down to its foundations!" (Ps 137:7; cf. Lam 4:21)

Conflict with the Philistines

When the Israelites arrived at the borders of the promised land they were terror-stricken, for the inhabitants of the land seemed like giants to them. These inhabitants were the Anakim, "giants with long necks" (Josh 11:22; Num 13:22). Eventually Joshua would drive them out, with a remnant living among the Philistines, who had originally come from Caphtor, probably a reference to Crete, and settled in the southwest of Palestine. They did not form a state but did have a confederacy of five cities, a pentapolis, consisting of Gaza, Gath, Ashdod, Ashkelon, and Ekron. Dagon, the god of fertility, was worshipped in Ashdod, where a important temple was located. Baalzebub, the "Lord of the flies," was worshipped in Ekron, and Astarte, a fertility goddess, the equivalent of the Babylonian Ishtar, "queen of heaven" (Jer 7:18; 44:17), was worshipped in Ashkelon. Astarte's cult was sexually oriented, with high places for sacrifice that Solomon had built for political reasons east of Jerusalen (2 Kgs 23:13). Astarte was the patron goddess of the city where the Philistines deposited the armor of the dead King Saul (1 Sam 31:10).

The Israelites considered the Philistines as "strangers." With the coastal areas as their base, they attempted to conquer the area west of the Jordan. Just like the Israelites, the Philistines had come from outside the land of Canaan and were fighting for the same area: for the Israelites, the struggle for liberation was also the struggle against the Philistines. They were a constant threat to the Israelites, driving out one of the twelve tribes, the Danites, from their land. During the time of the judges, the period prior to the establishment of the monarchy in Israel, the Philistines actually dominated much of the Israelite territory. The battle between David and Goliath was symbolic of the struggle between the Philistines and Israel. Goliath, the Philistine's giantlike champion, is assumed to have come from Gath and was one of the Anakim. His Arabic name Jâlût has possibly been influenced by the Hebrew word for "exile," *galût,* an expression that must have been on the lips of the Jews often in the Arabian Peninsula. In the Muslim stories of the prophets *(qisâs al-anbiyâ),* Goliath is identified with the Amalekites, who were also associated with the Arab tribes of the ʿAdites to whom the prophet Hûd had been sent and the tribe of the Thamudites to whom Sâlih was sent. Jâlût became a collective name for the oppressors of the Israelites before David.[11]

Amalek: "The Most Hostile of All"

The Amalekites were the Israelites' major enemy, apart from their "brothers," the Edomites, and the Philistines. They were a nomadic tribe that ca. 1000 B.C. lived in the area of Kadesh in the Sinai Peninsula, in the Negev Desert, and in the southern reaches of Palestinian civilization (Gen 14:7; Num 13:29), and were related to the Edomites (Gen 36:12-16). The Israelites encounter the Amalekites when they cross the Red Sea after leaving Egypt[12] (Q 7:138).

Amalek, which is not mentioned by name in the Qur'an, was connected in Muslim tradition genealogically with Shem or Ham. The children of Ham settled in Egypt, Ethiopia, and Arabia (Genesis 10) and took the place of the Philistines, the people of Jâlût/Goliath, and of the Midianites.[13] The pharaohs were also considered to have descended from them. In the time of the Arabian prophet Hûd, they lived in Hijâz, but the same prophet

11. *EQ, s.v.* "Goliath"; *EI, s.v.* "Djâlût."
12. Cf. the song by Miriam, Moses' sister, after crossing the Yam Suph (Sea of Reeds) (Exodus 15).
13. The non-Jewish prophet Balaam led the Israelites to commit adultery (Numbers 22–24).

is thought to have preached to them in the city of Babel. Hûd was sent to the people of ῾Ad, with whom the city of Iram near Aden is associated.[14] Ishmael's first wife, whom he later repudiated, was an Amalekite. Moses' successor, Joshua, fought against the Amalekites. The settlement of Jewish tribes in Yathrib, later Medina, is said to have been the unforeseen result of the war of extermination fought at Joshua's command. This extermination was not carried out completely. David had to war against them as well.[15] The Amalekites became one of the peoples most hostile to the children of Israel. Agag is the name or title of the king of the Amalekites, and the Greek Septuagint reads Gog here instead of Agag (Num 24:7).[16]

Saul and Amalek

It is asserted that the Amalekites' moral ruin meant that they deserved to be destroyed. Why did they earn such a bad reputation? They attacked the rear of the people of Israel on their journey in the desert from Egypt to Canaan in a very cowardly way. They were thus targeting the weak, women, and children (Deut 25:18). Since that time, God fought against Amalek in each generation (Exod 17:16b). The children of Israel were given a task with respect to Amalek: when they entered the land that God would give them as an inheritance, they were to "blot out the name" of Amalek from under heaven and were not to neglect that task (Deut 25:19).

The prophet Samuel/Samwîl apparently was charged with reminding the Israelites of their duty to blot out all memory of Amalek. Samuel gave King Saul the divine task of carrying out the sentence against them: "Now go, attack the Amalekites and totally destroy all that belongs to them. Do not spare them; put to death men and women, children and infants, cattle and sheep, camels and donkeys" (1 Sam 15:3).

The stories about Saul remind one of a "Greek tragedy."[17] First of all, Saul became a king reluctantly. It did not matter to him — in fact, when he was to be presented, he initially hid among the supplies. When he was nevertheless crowned king, he did very well as a commander of armies and initially carried out a successful campaign against his opponents (cf. 1 Samuel 11).

14. Cf. Chapter VIII.
15. *EI, s.v.* "'Amâlîk."
16. See Chapter IX.
17. Gerhard von Rad, *Wisdom in Israel* (Nashville: Abingdon, 1972).

Nonetheless, Saul does not prove to meet the requirements of kingship. In Samuel's view, the breaking point, where everything goes wrong, is Saul's refusal to eradicate the Amalekites completely. He does attack the city of the Amalekites and defeats it, but captures King Agag alive and does not put him to death. Although he completely destroys the people by the sword, he and his men spare the king and the best and fattest sheep, cattle, and lambs — everything that was valuable. Then God speaks to Samuel, telling him he regrets having made Saul king, for Saul has turned away from him and has not carried out his command. Samuel is deeply dejected and cries out to God all night. Samuel then goes to Saul, and Saul tells him that he has carried out God's command. But Samuel asks: "What then is this bleating of sheep in my ears? What is this lowing of cattle that I hear?" Saul answers that he spared them to worship God and to sacrifice to him.

Nevertheless, because he did not obey God, Saul is rejected and may no longer continue as king. Saul confesses that he has sinned, but asks Samuel to accompany him so he can bow down before God, which Samuel at first refuses to do. Then Agag is brought to Samuel. Encouraged, Agag approaches him and says: "Surely the bitterness of death is past." But Samuel says: "As your sword has made women childless, so will your mother be childless among women." Then he cut Agag to pieces "before the LORD." Samuel leaves and does not see Saul again before his death (1 Samuel 15).

One could argue that the Torah speaks of continuing to remember what Amalek has done to the people. As soon as the people have found rest, the memory of Amalek must be blotted out (Deut 25:19). Is that remembering and not being allowed to forget intended by God to mean the destruction of Amalek, as it is understood in this story of Samuel's actions? Is it acceptable to put men, women, and children to death? That conclusion does not seem to do justice to the complexity of the story. We cannot simply build a complete theology, theory, or ideology around this, not to mention applying it directly to combatting contemporary enemies in the present. There are tensions in this story that should not be ignored: it is a real tragedy that is being described.

One can see in this story that the prophet himself has great difficulty with the word of God he has to communicate to Saul. It hits home very hard with the prophet, and he is completely distraught. When he hears from God that God has rejected Saul because he did not obey his command, Samuel is deeply dejected and cries out the whole night to God (1 Sam 15:11). But however much Samuel prays and whatever Saul does, the judgment has been made and remains in force: "Because you have rejected the word of the LORD, he has rejected you as king" (1 Sam 15:23). It should be noted that Samuel himself had appointed Saul as the first king, against all expectation and against Saul's own wishes. Thus, Samuel experiences the termination of Saul's kingship as a personal loss as well. At the end of the story we hear that the prophet Samuel suffered under Saul up until his death and continued to mourn for him (1 Sam 15:35). But the story does not show any curiosity as to why the repentant Saul cannot be forgiven, whereas David, who is also repentant about what he has done wrong, is forgiven (1 Sam 30:19-20; 2 Sam 12:13).[18]

There are other tensions or apparent contradictions in the story. On the one hand, we hear that the God of Israel does not lie and does not have regrets, for he is not a human being that he should have regrets (1 Sam 15:29). But the prophet has heard earlier that God did regret making Saul king. So, one could ask: Does or does not God regret things? Samuel first refuses to accede to Saul's request to return with him, apparently to do penance for not carrying out the command, and to bow before God, so that Saul does not lose face with the people (1 Sam 15:24-25, 30). Samuel at first refuses but then gives in and goes back with the king and thus does not abandon him completely. Is this response then not more human than it initially appears? Does the charge not to forget what Amalek has done and to remember it (Exod 17:14; Deut 25:17) have to be understood as eradication? Does blotting out the remembrance of Amalek and what he has done to Israel entail the extermination of Amalek? The Jewish philosopher Martin Buber relates in his autobiographical notes that an old Jew once asked him when he was young, "What do you think about this chapter from the book of Samuel?" Without any hesitation, Buber answered: "I think the prophet misunderstood God." The old Jew was silent for a long time and then said: "That is what I think too." Buber continued: "I have done a great deal in my life on the translation of the Bible. Always in fear and trembling. What is the word of God? What is the word of man?"[19]

The charge could be understood and explained in such a way that the children of Israel have been given the task to blot out the name of Amalek from under heaven, from among the peoples, in the sense that they must correct the notion of "might makes right," of "the survival of the fittest." In contrast, God wants the weak to survive. The name of Amalek is sought in

---

18. Walter Brueggemann, *Theology of the Old Testament: Testimony, Dispute, Advocacy* (Minneapolis: Fortress, 1997) 370.

19. Martin Buber, *Voordrachten over opvoeding: en autobiografische fragmenten* (Utrecht: Bijleveld, 1970) 134-38.

vain in the Table of Nations in which the peoples known at that time are grouped according to their place in history and where they live (Genesis 10). That name representing "might makes right" has already been erased there.[20] The Torah states that it is God who fights anew in each generation (Exod 17:16). Does that not mean that vengeance is God's (Deut 32:35-36; cf. Isa 35:4; Rom 12:19; Heb 10:30)?

Haman and Amalek

The enmity towards Amalek runs from the period of the wanderings in the desert throughout the whole history of Israel. After Saul, David took up the struggle against the Amalekites (2 Sam 8:12), and Hezekiah (king of Judah ca. 725-697 B.C.) killed the remaining Amalekites who had escaped (1 Chr 4:43). Centuries later, at the time of the exile and the Persian Empire, we find mention of Haman, the vizier of the the Achaemenid king Xerxes or Ahashverosh of Persia (486-465). Haman is called a descendant of King Agag (Esth 3:1): his ancestry automatically evokes the memory of the struggle between Israel, under Saul's leadership, and Agag (1 Samuel 15). During Queen Esther's time, Haman has it in for the Jews in Persia. Esther is a young Jewish woman, the foster daughter of Mordecai, her cousin and guardian, who was deported with King Jehoiakim to Babylonia (Esth 2:5-7), and she becomes the consort of Ahashverosh. (It is a matter of dispute if she is indeed a historical figure because there is no known Persian queen of that name. Her name is connected with the Akkadian goddess Ishtar, but it is possibly also derived from the Old Persian *stara*, "star.") Out of personal feelings of vengeance toward the Jew Mordecai, Haman wants to kill all Jews living in the Persian Empire. At the instigation of Mordecai, Esther manages to thwart this plot, and Haman is brought down by Esther and finally impaled on the pole he himself had set up for Mordecai (Esth 7:10). In the Qur'an Haman is called a servant or minister of Pharaoh (Q 28:6; 28:8; 29:39; 40:24). Despite what is often claimed, the Qur'an is not confusing the stories here.[21] It is not drawing any historical lines but connecting, as the Bible often does, the motifs from different periods concerning powers hos-

---

20. According to T. J. M. Naastepad, *Van horen zeggen: Uitleg van het boek Deuteronomium* (Baarn: Ten Have, 2001) 289. Cf. Brueggemann, *Theology of the Old Testament,* 369-72.

21. *EI, s.v.* "Haman."

tile to God. In Muslim exegesis a connection is made between Amalek and Goliath/Jâlût and the Midianites, whereas the pharaohs are thought to stem from an Amalekite group.

Is Purim a Feast?

A Jewish feast is connected with the saving of the Jews under Ahashverosh, and the book of Esther intends to explain the origin of this feast. The feast is called Purim, "lots" (Esth 3:7; 9:24, 26), or Feast of Mordecai (2 Macc. 15:36), because Haman has cast the lot to hunt down and eradicate Jews (Esth 9:24). The feast keeps alive the memory of the saving of the Jews who at the time of Ahashverosh had been threatened with death by Haman: "These days should be remembered and observed in every generation by every family, and in every province and in every city. And these days of Purim should never fail to be celebrated by the Jews — nor should the memory of these days die out among their descendants" (Esth 9:28). The command to exterminate the Jews was issued on 13 Nisan, the first month of the Jewish calendar (Esth 3:12), the day before Passover, at the evening twilight at the full moon (Exod 12:6). That establishes a connection with the exodus from Egypt. The Sabbath that precedes it is called the Sabbath of Remembrance *(Shabbat Tsadoor),* which is derived directly from the command not to forget the cited crime of Amalek. The scriptural passage from the prophets *(haftara,* after the passage of the Torah that is read on that Sabbath) is the chapter on Saul's struggle against the Amalekites described above.

Just as Buber raised critical questions concerning the explanation of the war between Amalek and Saul (1 Samuel 15), Schalom ben-Chorin (1913-99), a scholar in religious studies and a journalist, comments on the book of Esther and the events in the Purim feast. Ben-Chorin calls the chapter that records that King Ahashverosh cannot repeal his decree for a pogrom the most offensive passage in the whole book (Esth 8:8). The decree carried out by Haman is irrevocable, "written in the laws of Persia and Media" (Esth 1:19). The king then leaves it up to Esther and Mordecai to put an end to the catastrophe he himself had caused. And Mordecai proves to be a "worthy successor of Haman." He is the flipside of Haman. Ahashverosh decides to honor Mordecai in a pompous way (Esth 6:7-11), and what does Mordecai do? He accepts the honors from his mortal enemies. He is not only vain — he is also stupid: he does not oppose the honors. He does not appear before the king to say: "I thank you for the royal garments and the horse, but I wish to protect the naked existence and life of my people." He sits conceitedly on the royal horse and enjoys his private triumph.

Does Mordecai forgive his enemies generously and grant anmesty for the violent acts committed? He does nothing of the kind, but engages in a revolution with the permission of the government. That is the most deadly form of terror that can be conceived: terror without risk. A pogrom covered by the government is no better if carried out by a Jew. As for Esther, one pogrom day is not enough terror. She wants a second and is given permission for that. It is not enough that the ten sons of Haman are killed: the bodies have to be hung up as well. The Jews in the capital and the monarchy exact a very bloody vengeance from their enemies, and the chronicler remarks tastelessly enough: "In every province and in every city to which the edict of the king came, there was joy and gladness among the Jews, with feasting and celebrating. And many people of other nationalities became Jews because fear of the Jews had seized them" (Esth 8:17).[22]

"We do not," Ben-Chorin concludes, "celebrate the heroine of the book of Esther but only God to whose gracious guidance this, like every other rescue from threatening danger, is owed." What is revealed is eternal, and it is not given to us to add or subtract from that. The divine decrees should be adhered to: "Do not add to what I command you and do not subtract from it, but keep the commands of the LORD your God that I give you" (Deut 4:2). Purim, however, concerns a foundation by people (Esth 9:20-32), in which the question, according to Ben-Chorin, arises: Can this be seen as "exemplary," as an example of how we should act? Ben Chorin, of course, does not think so.[23]

Radical Rereadings of the Bible and the Qur'an Regarding Amalek

Modern violent rereadings and applications of texts from the Bible and the Qur'an can be found among Jews, Christians, and Muslims. Certain Israeli zealots in the 1960s began to say that it was a religious duty to destroy "Amalek." When the first Gulf War in 1991 ended around Purim, the Iraqi president Saddam Hussein was compared with Haman.

22. With an allusion to the liberation from Egypt: "In your unfailing love you will lead the people you have redeemed. In your strength you will guide them to your holy dwelling. The nations will hear and tremble; anguish will grip the people of Philistia" (Exod 15:13-14).

23. Schalom ben-Chorin, *Kritik des Esther-buches: Eine theologische Streitschrift* (Jerusalem: "Heatid," Salingré, 1938) 9-11.

"A new Amalek is coming," the Israeli premier Benjamin Netanyahu stated in January 2010 during a commemoration ceremony of the Holocaust at Auschwitz. Although he did not indicate whom he had in mind, it was clear to the Israeli media that Netanyahu was talking about Iran. It was not coincidental that he chose the place and the biblical reference to the people of the Amalekites, the biblical archenemy of the Jewish people. He has more often called the Iranian president Mahmoud Ahmadinejad the new Hitler, who intends to use his nuclear program for a new holocaust. "We will not permit that," Netanyahu said at Auschwitz.[24]

To assert — as do certain Zionists, neoconservative Christians (in the United States), and contemporary Islamists — that committing acts of terror could be legitimated by such texts is simply incorrect. Such a reading does not hold water if one listens closely to the texts from the three Books that are cited. How much this reading is a distortion and adulteration of the exegesis of these texts is apparent when one realizes what terrorists (and thus also the movie *Fitna*) omit. The text used to legitimate terrorism is this: "Prepare your strength to the utmost of your power against them, including steeds of war, to strike terror into (the hearts of) the enemies, of God and your enemies, and others as well, whom you may not know but God does" (Q 8:60). What they do not quote, however, is the following verse: "But if the enemy incline towards peace, do thou (also) incline towards peace, and trust in God" (Q 8:61).

Retaliation and Blood Feuds

It is said that giants walked the earth before the deluge. These giants are the notorious tyrants from the primeval age, the offspring of marriages between earthly creatures and heavenly beings. The mixing of the divine and human spheres illustrates the depravity of the people and serves to introduce the story of the flood.[25] In the eyes of God, the earth became depraved and full of violent deeds; all people on earth were following the wrong path. This is the reason for the flood (Gen 6:4, 11-13; cf. Q 23:23-30).

It is helpful to reflect on how the Bible and Qur'an speak about retribution and vengeance. Apparently, people were allowed to kill in retaliation. Vengeance was once a form of retaliation. We read in Genesis: "Whoever

---

24. Guus Valk, "Steeds meer twijfel Israël over nut aanval tegen Iran" ("More and more doubt in Israel on the point of an attack against Iran"), *NRC Handelsblad*, 11 May 2010.
25. KBS on Gen 6:1-4.

sheds human blood, by humans shall their blood be shed; for in the image of God has God made mankind" (Gen 9:6). That notion stems from a time in which individuals still lived within the family and clan. Vengeance was thus presupposed as an existing custom (Num 35:19ff.): good order in society, which did not as yet have an extensively developed central authority, demanded that a murder be punished by the closest blood relative (Judg 8:18-21; 2 Sam 3:27; 21). Vengeance would be taken by a son, brother, or kinsman. When there was as yet no government to guarantee life and honor, vengeance had an important social function. Vengeance was intended to prevent excessive violence and abuse, and there were attempts very early on already to limit vengeance. Those who did not kill on purpose could flee to a free city and there find sanctuary (Deut 19:4; Num 35:11-29). These free cities protected the guilty parties against arbitrariness. Sometimes, instead of retaliation, damages or redemption money could be paid (Exod 21:30).

The prescriptions in the Torah are connected with the notion that every transgression requires punishment and reconciliation. That is why satisfaction that corresponds to the damage suffered is set. A free man is entitled to retaliation in the form of the law of retaliation *(jus talionis):* spilled blood requires the life of the killer as reconciliation (cf. Exod 21:22-25; Lev 24:19). The Torah thus respects the principle of equality: "life for life, hand for hand, foot for foot, burn for burn, wound for wound, bruise for bruise" (Exod 21:24-25; Q 5:45).[26] The same holds for the Qur'an (Q 2:178): a proportionality between crime and punishment.[27]

A rule such as "eye for an eye, tooth for a tooth" sounds very harsh to modern people. But one should pay close attention and understand its original intention. Such laws were intended to put a check on unbounded, unlimited retaliation. If someone knocks another person's tooth out, the second person is not allowed, out of vengeance, to knock out all the teeth of the other. Lamech/Lamak, one of Cain's descendants, is an example of the latter recourse (Gen 4:18). His name possibly means "powerful young man." One of his sons, Tubal-Cain, was the father of smiths, of those who forged copper and iron (Gen 4:20-22). This entails not only tools but also weapons. The invention of music is ascribed to another of Lamech's sons, Jubal. A popular history of the prophets[28] by a certain exegete of the Qur'an and collector of stories tells the Hebrew legend of how Lamech, completely blind, acciden-

---

26. *EQ, s.v.* "Vengeance."

27. *EI, s.v.* "Retaliation, Blood Money."

28. *Qiṣâs al-anbiyâ'. EI, s.v.* "Al-Tha'labi (d. 1035)."

tally killed his father and then his beloved son who accompanied him on the hunt. Following these events, he recited the first biblical lamentation. Music is connected with excesses and the deception of Satan.[29] Lamech sings a song about excessive vengeance: "I have killed a man for wounding me, a young man for injuring me. If Cain is avenged seven times, then Lamech seventy-seven times" (Gen 4:23-24). That indicates how violence on earth increased: from one fratricide it spreads to a sevenfold, no a seventyfold, vengeance. It is such excessive violence, "overkill" in Lamech's case, that the rule "eye for an eye" is intended to curb. The law of equal retaliation limits the retaliation to the restoration of balance: whoever injures a member of one's own people must himself undergo what he did to the other: wound for wound, eye for eye, tooth for tooth. The injury he caused the other he must himself undergo (Lev 24:19-20). No pity was to be shown here (Deut 19:21). Vengeance is thus limited.[30] Regarding the time before the coming of Islam, called the "time of ignorance," Arabic poetry shows that the attitude of mercy, of moderation and compromise, was looked upon with contempt. In that age violence, even to the point of murder and the desire for battle and vengeance, was glorified. If someone was injured by another, he was to respond twice as hard. The practice prior to Islam of resolving tribal disputes with disproportionate retaliation was abandoned by the Qur'an.[31] The Qur'an also warns against a lack of moderation in taking vengeance (Q 17:33).

But the Torah clearly took the first step in curbing blood vengeance: parents could not be killed because of their children's acts, and children could not be held responsible for the acts of their parents. A person could possibly be put to death only for what he himself did (Deut 24:16; cf. 2 Kgs 14:5-6). The prophet Ezekiel would later emphasize the personal responsibility of each individual: "The one who sins is the one who will die. The child will not share the guilt of the parent, nor will the parent share the guilt of the child. The righteousness of the righteous will be credited to them, and the wickedness of the wicked will be charged against them" (Ezek 18:20). In his justice God judges each transgression, both that of the people and of the individual, and punishes accordingly.

If the Ten Commandments say that the guilt of the fathers will be visited on the children (Exod 20:5-6), it should be noted that "visiting" is not the same as vengeance! The father embodies and represents the family, and

---

29. *EI, s.v.* "Lamak."
30. KBS on Exod 21:24-25.
31. *EQ, s.v.* "Vengeance, Retaliation."

his guilt extends to his descendants, who share in his punishment (Exod 20:5; Deut 5:9).[32] The text continues immediately: God will have mercy on the children of those who love him (Exod 20:6). The Lord is a merciful and gracious God, patient, great in love and faithfulness, who shows goodness to the thousandth generation (Exod 34:6-7). Here one sees immediately that God's mercy is infinitely greater than his visiting. It is stated here that God's mercy exceeds his justice. For the judgment (of God) is unmerciful to those who show no mercy; mercy triumphs over judgment (Jas 2:13). If someone does a good deed, God will show him goodness. God is willing to forgive and appreciates people for their good deeds (Q 42:23).

The people are called to responsibility for the injustice already committed (Amos 3:2), and the judgment is accompanied by the call to penitence and repentance: "But you must return to your God; maintain love and justice, and wait for your God always" (Hos 12:6). If the people repent, then God will relent concerning the disasters that he threatened (Jer 18:8). "But if a wicked person turns away from all the sins he has committed and keeps all my decrees and does what is just and right, that person will surely live; he will not die" (Ezek 18:21). God is ready to forgive those who repent, believe, and do what is right (Q 20:82). "The Lord of heaven and the earth, and all between — Great in Might and able to enforce his will, forgiving again and again" (Q 38:66). "Is not he exalted in power — he who forgives again and again?" (Q 39:5).

Do Not Repay Evil with Evil

Actually, and this is very important to note, it is God himself to whom retaliation, judgment, vengeance, and punishment alone belong. This is not a concept that can be found only in the New Testament and not until then. When Paul states that God says: "It is mine to avenge; I will repay," he is quoting the Torah (Rom 12:19; Deut 32:35). Vengeance is an attribute of God, according to the Qur'an (Q. 3:4; 5:95; 14:47; 39:37). "The Avenger" (*al-Muntaqim*) is considered to be one of the "beautiful" names of God.[33]

"Do not hate a fellow Israelite in your heart. Rebuke your neighbor frankly so you will not share in their guilt. Do not seek revenge or bear a

---

32. N. A. Schuman, *Gelijk om gelijk: Verslag en balans van een discusie oer goddelijke vergelding in het Oude Testanment* (Amsterdam: VU Uitgeverij, 1993).

33. *EQ, s.v.* "Reward and Punishment."

grudge against anyone among your people, but love your neighbor as yourself. I am the LORD" (Lev 19:17-18). On the basis of such ideas, and continuing in this line, blood vengeance and the retaliation associated inseparably with it were abandoned by Jesus in the Sermon on the Mount: "You have heard that it was said, 'Eye for eye, and tooth for tooth.' But I tell you, do not resist an evil person. If anyone slaps you on the right cheek, turn to them the other cheek also" (Matt 5:38-39). The same notion, the same attitude, is also supported and confirmed by one of Jesus' disciples, Peter: "Do not repay evil with evil or insult with insult. On the contrary, repay evil with blessing, because to this you were called so that you may inherit a blessing" (1 Pet 3:9). Paul confirms this as well: "Make sure that nobody pays back wrong for wrong, but always strive to do what is good for each other and for everyone else" (1 Thess 5:15), and "Do not repay anyone evil for evil. Be careful to do what is right in the eyes of everyone" (Rom 12:17; cf. Deut 32:35). That statement does not imply that God ignores evil or simply takes it lying down or that people are asked to do so. God will demand satisfaction, but apparently without any attempt by ourselves to prove ourselves right or to justify ourselves. The principle in question here is: evil cannot and never will be overcome by evil, but simply and only through a greater good. Paul goes a step further by saying: "Do not take revenge, my dear friends, but leave room for God's wrath, for it is written: 'If your enemy is hungry, feed him; if he is thirsty, give him something to drink. In doing this, you will heap burning coals on his head'" (Rom 12:20).

It is very important to see where Paul derives this idea. It is often claimed or thought that this is certainly a Christian idea, that the Old Testament and the Qur'an are violent, whereas the New Testament differs on that score. Paul's idea certainly emerges from and is borrowed from the example of Jesus: "If anyone slaps you on the right cheek, turn to them the other cheek" (Matt 5:39; Luke 6:29) and not to take up the sword, "for all who draw the sword will die by the sword" (Matt 26:52). But at the same time, it is also derived from Jesus' and Paul's "Bible," the Tanakh! Paul bases his view on a story in the Former Prophets, the book of Kings, and a wisdom book, Proverbs. This shows how much the Bible is a "philosophy in narrative form."[34] The story is that of the prophet Elisha, al-Yasa', the successor of the prophet Elijah/Ilyâs or Yâsîn.

---

34. "Erzählende Philosophie" ("narrative philosophy"), an expression of Eugen Rosenstock-Huessy (1888-1973).

Enemies: "Give Them Food"

In the time of Elisha, there was war between the king of Israel, whose capital was Samaria, and the hostile Arameans. Saul, David, and Solomon had all fought wars in the past with this people. The king of the Arameans sent a great army, with horses and chariots to Samaria. They arrived at night and surrounded the city. Elisha's servant got up early in the morning and saw the army surrounding the city and cried out: "What shall we do?" (2 Kgs 6:14-15). The prophet gave a remarkable answer: "Don't be afraid. Those who are with us are more than those who are with them [the Aramean enemies]." And the prophet prays that the eyes of that servant may be opened. God did so, and the servant "looked and saw the hills full of horses and chariots of fire all around Elisha." It is important to understand what is happening here and what this story is intended to say. If there had been journalists there to photograph this event in order to record it for the newspaper *Haaretz* of the Israel of that time, the photos would have been blank. It is striking that, in the story of Jesus in Gethsemane, Peter threatens to intervene with the sword when Jesus is about to be arrested. Then Jesus says: "Put your sword back in its place, for all who draw the sword will die by the sword." He then adds: "Do you think I cannot call on my Father, and he will at once put at my disposal more than twelve legions of angels?" (Matt 26:52-53). One could ask here: But where were those legions? Why did they not come? Obviously, Jesus did not see violence as a real choice. Elisha prays that the eyes of the servant may be opened. Apparently, these legions can be seen only with the eye of faith and trust.

When the Arameans come toward him, the prophet asks God: "Strike this army with blindness." God does what Elisha asks. Then Elisha says to the blinded army: "This is not the road and this is not the city. Follow me, and I will lead you to the man you are looking for." Then — one can feel it coming — he leads the enemy to Samaria. The prophet manages to guide the Arameans into the city. Then God opens their eyes so that they can see where they are: between being tricked and being taken prisoner in the enemy city. The king of Israel asks Elisha: "Shall I kill them? Shall I kill them?" This is, after all, a golden opportunity. But Elisha answers: "Do not kill them. Would you kill those you have captured with your own sword or bow" — not to mention those whom one has tricked into entering the city?

What does the prophet advise instead regarding the question of what is to be done with the enemies who have been captured? What does he tell the king to do? "Set food and water before them so that they may eat and drink and then go back to their master." And it is no sooner said than done.

The enemies, the Arameans, are treated to a large feast, after which they are allowed to return to their homes. And how does the story conclude? From that time on, they did not raid Israelite territory (2 Kgs 6:8-23). In other words, showing their enemies hospitality, giving them food and drink, had an explicitly good effect so that they were spared further hostility.

The Inversion of Revenge

Paul derives the wisdom "If your enemy is hungry, give him food to eat; if he is thirsty, give him water to drink," the story about what was done in the besieged Samaria, from the book of Proverbs (Prov 25:21-22). There it is indicated what the result will be if one acts in that way: "In doing this, you will heap burning coals on his head." This saying alludes, strikingly enough, to a practice that stems from two of the archenemies of Israel: the way in which Assyrians punished someone by pouring pitch on his head and the Egyptian custom of penance whereby someone carried coals on his head. This is the origin of the expression "bring their own deeds down on their heads" (Ezek 9:10). Paul's point is that we should do precisely the opposite of what one's enemies suggest doing: "Instead of pitch and burning coals, let goodness come down on someone's head." Let that goodness be the punishment, the punishment that will overcome evil.

Paul appeals explicitly to a statement found in the book of Proverbs, 25:21-22. In other words, Paul intends to say: "If you're wise, you'll break through the deadly and destructive circle of vengeance and retaliation." That is why he advises: "Do not be overcome by evil, but overcome evil with good" (Rom 12:21). With that, Paul refers implicitly to what Jesus not only proclaimed but also practiced. Only by turning the other cheek can that vicious circle be broken. Only nonviolence can stop evil.

"Resist (Evil) with What Is Better"

The Qur'an confirms the message of the Old and New Testament regarding not repaying evil with evil: let good prevail over evil. Doing good is the answer to evil, for such actions have a healthy effect on those who do evil: "Nor can goodness and evil be equal. Resist (evil) with what is better: Then he between whom and you hatred existed will become, as it were, your friend and confidant!" (Q 41:34). "Resist evil with that which is best" (Q 23:96). A believer is described as someone who averts evil with good and repays the bad deed with good (Q 28:54). Believers are those who turn away evil with good (Q 13:22). The task of the believer is to call others to the way of God with wisdom and beautiful or fine preaching. Here the Arab word for wisdom, *hikma,* which is cognate with Hebrew *hokmah,* is used. People are advised to debate with them in the finest way (Q 16:125). The explicit advice is also given not to engage in dispute with the people of the Book, Jews and Christians (aside from those among them who do evil), except in the best way (Q 29:46). But if the enemy rejects such goodness, then the use of violence is allowed if it accords with the demands of justice. But in that case the Qur'an advises one to be mild or lenient with respect to those who have done evil. If such a person repents, he must be forgiven. What should the characteristic attitude of the believers be with respect to injustice? Those who believe and trust in God are:

> Those who avoid the greater crimes and shameful deeds, and forgive even when they are angry; those who obey their Lord, and perform prayer *(salât);* who (conduct) their affairs by mutual consultation; who spend what we bestow on them for sustenance; and those who (are not cowed but) help and defend themselves when an oppressive wrong is inflicted on them. The recompense for an injury is an injury equal to it (in degree): but if a person forgives and is reconciled with the other, his reward comes from God. God does not love those who do wrong. (Q 42:37-40)

With respect to how reward and punishment are related in this and the future life, the well-known and oft-quoted text is: "Then anyone who has done an atom's weight of good will see it! And anyone who has done an atom's weight of evil will see it" (Q 99:7-8). Everyone will be judged in the hereafter according to what he or she has done. No injustice will be done to such a person (Q 46:19). Not possessions or children, but whoever believes and does what is right will receive a double reward (Q 34:37). God does not perform the slightest injustice. And if a good deed should be repaid, God will multiply it and grant rewards from on high (Q 4:40; cf. 4:173). While punishment is equal to the deed, reward is more than double: "He that doeth good shall have ten times as much to his credit: He that doeth evil shall only be recompensed according to his evil: no wrong shall be done unto (any of) them" (Q 6:160). God's mercy is immeasurable.[35]

35. *EQ, s.v.* "Reward and Punishment."

"Compete in Good Deeds"

To summarize how the three Books tell the story of retaliation, punishment, and reconciliation, it will be good to cite the text from the fifth chapter of the Qur'an, which is among the texts that were revealed last.[36] In that text, the message common to the Torah, the Gospel, and the Qur'an is treated in relation to all three. The message of the prophet Muhammad is directed in the same chapter that talks about Cain and Abel (see above), first to the Jews, then to the Christians, and then to the Muslims, and finally to all three simultaneously. The context is the question of violence and retaliation in response to questions that the people of the Book, the Jews in Medina, asked Muhammad.[37]

The Qur'an first addresses the Jews, "the people of the Torah":

> We ordained for them in the Torah: "Life for life [cf. Deut 19:21], eye for eye, nose for nose, ear for ear, tooth for tooth, and retaliation for wounds." But if any one remits retaliation by way of charity, it is an act of atonement for himself. And if any fail to judge by (the light of) what God has revealed, they are indeed wrongdoers.

And then the Qur'an turns to the Christians, "the people of the Gospel":

> And in their footsteps we sent Jesus the son of Mary, confirming the Torah that had preceded him: We sent him the Gospel in which was guidance and light,[38] and confirmation of the Torah that had preceded him: a guidance and an admonition to those who fear God.

> Let the people of the Gospel judge by what God has revealed in it. If any do fail to judge by (the light of) what God has revealed, they are (no better than) those who rebel.

The following is addressed to the Muslims:

> We sent the Scripture in truth to you [Muhammad], confirming the scripture that came before it, and keeping it safe: so judge between them

---

36. Fred Leemhuis, "From Palm Leaves to Internet," in *The Cambridge Companion to the Qur'ân*, ed. Jane Damme McAuliffe (Cambridge: Cambridge University Press, 2006) 154. *EQ, s.v.* "Law and the Qur'ân." Cf. Régis Blachère, *Le Coran: Traduction selon un essai de reclassement des Sourates* (Paris: Maisonneuve, 1951).

37. Cf. *EQ, s.v.* "Torah."

38. Q 6:91: "Say: Who was it who revealed the Book that Moses brought, a light and guidance to mankind . . . ?"

by what God has revealed, and do not follow their vain desires, diverging from the truth that hath come to thee.

Then all are addressed:

> For every community we decreed a law and a way of life.[39] If God had so willed, he would have made you a single people, but (his plan is) to test you in what he has given you: so compete with one another in good deeds in all virtues [cf. Q 3:114; 21:90; 23:61]. The goal of you all is God. To God you will all return and he will make you understand what you disagree about. (Q 5:45-48)[40]

The three Books originated and have been written in a world full of war and violence. In that sense very realistic and authentic stories are told. One does not simply have to take the evil that happens to one lying down. There are, apparently, situations in which it is conceivable for one to want to repay someone else. There are three possible responses: retaliation, vengeance, and forgiveness.[41] Even if one is allowed to retaliate, all three Books state emphatically that it is nevertheless better to choose a different way, the way of compensation, reparation, and reconciliation. Aside from the right to retaliation, an act of neighborly love is recommended and obtains as reconciliation. A voluntary, praiseworthy deed can function as reconciliation for a sin. Thus, the breaking of an oath can be reconciled by giving ten needy people food or clothing or giving a slave his freedom (Q 5:89).[42] Forgiveness and offering compensation is preferred — it entails respect for life (Q 2:178, 179).[43]

That means, in modern or practical terms, if someone knocks another's tooth out, that the latter demand retaliation as punishment, that he demand that the other pay for a new crown as compensation. Thus, however understandable and comprehensible retaliation may be, all three Books nevertheless advise the other way.

---

39. *Shir'a*; cf. *shari'a*.
40. Cf. also Q 2:178-79, 194.
41. According to Muslim jurists. *EI, s.v.* "Retaliation."
42. *EQ, s.v.* "Atonement."
43. *EQ, s.v.* "Life."

The Jerusalem City Group

Such an appeal to reconciliation rather than retaliation and nonviolence, in particular the reference to Jesus' Sermon on the Mount and the possible relevance of such for politics, is shrugged off as naive, "hippie" thinking, dim-witted "flower-power" stories. But it is not a dim-witted story at all. Nor is the Qur'an. When the Qur'an first cites the Old and New Testaments and ends with its own advice that all three, Jew, Christian, and Muslim (cf. Q 2:148), compete with one another in good deeds, it is a very powerful story — one of the gentle power of love. And in that it is just as *goochem* ("sly, smart"). That "naive faith" rests solely on the trust that God's mercy will ultimately embrace all people. God has prescribed mercy for himself (Q 6:12; 6:54).

When Theo van Gogh, director, screenwriter, television producer, and columnist, was killed 2 November 2004 in Amsterdam and his killer, Mohammad B. (Bouyeri), was tried, there was talk of the so-called Hofstad group. That is the name given by the Internal Intelligence Service (AIVD) in the Netherlands to a group of radical Islamic youths. Members met regularly, it was claimed, in the Amsterdam home of Mohammed B., who felt that he, acting on God's orders, had to take revenge on Van Gogh for his insult of the prophet in the movie *Submission.* Van Gogh had produced the movie together with a right-wing Dutch politician, Ayaan Hirsi Ali, who wrote the script and provided the voice-over for the movie, which criticized the treatment of women in the Islamic world. She had renounced the Islamic faith of her birth and had received death threats after the movie debuted. During the second day of the court session Mohammed B. stated: "I was guided by the law that commands me to cut off the head of everyone who insults God and the prophet." He wanted to defend and avenge Islam with violence. In the same year of the murder, on 2 July 2004, he had translated a document from the fourteenth-century godfather of fundamentalism, Ibn Taymiyya:[44] "Verplichting van het doden van degene die de profeet ('Vrede zij met hem') uitscheldt" ("The Duty to Kill Those Who Revile the Prophet ('Peace Be upon Him')."

One could say that Jews, Christians, and Muslims belong to or are members of the "Jerusalem City Group." This terminology would group together, for instance, an Isaac A., a Mohammed B., and a Christian C. All

44. Anton Wessels, *Muslims and the West: Can They Be Integrated?* trans. John Bowden (Leuven: Peeters, 2006) ch. 6.

three believe, on the basis of, respectively, the Torah, the Qur'an, and the Gospel, in the story of breaking with injustice and traveling toward the promised land, the promised city, a promised world, where justice and righteousness are done, where the Torah, the *sharia,* is observed and kept — where justice and love are implemented.

If we listen to the one story of all three Books, as described above regarding the question of violence and retaliation, then we must draw the conclusion that if an Isaac A., a Mohammad B. or a Christian C. believe today that they can and should seek vengeance "in God's name," then this is not done as something the God of Abraham, the God of Jesus, or the God of Muhammad commanded. Rather, it is done in the name of the god that person has conjured up himself (which is very easy to do at present via Google). At Mohammad B.'s trial an expert witness testified extensively concerning the material he found on the accused's personal computer: Mohammed B. "googled" for his knowledge of God, religion, and violence. Dutch has the word *goochelen* ("juggle"). One could say that Mohammad B. googled/ *goochelt*/conjured and juggled for his concept of God.

For all three, the final key word is and remains reconciliation and non-violence. "There is no violence in God" (Diognetus, one of the second-century apostolic fathers). In the century of our father and mother (or grandfather and grandmother), that idea was the inspiration for such "naive people" as Leo Tolstoy, Mahatma Gandhi, and Martin Luther King, Jr. They dared to follow that path and to enter into that competition of doing good deeds. If there is ever to be any justice and peace in our world, then the world leaders need to appropriate this wisdom *(hokmah, hikma)* and thus be that *goochem* ("sly"). But then these leaders have to be (M. L. Jr.) King size, as it were.

CHAPTER VIII

Prayer of Intercession for the City of Sodom

The kingdom of God is this world turned inside out.

Huub Oosterhuis

[God:]
But, father Abram, do you dare
to stand before God — one man —
and plead that he this city spare,
the worst in Canaan's land?

[Abraham:]
When I think of who lives there,
on every street and in each house,
there is no one he will spare,
It's people I'm concerned about!

[God:]
But they're wicked, father Abraham!
They've abandoned human law,
and, joined together, they have damned
and turned the world into a hell!

[Abraham:]
Although it's evil what happens there,
murder and fire and tyranny,

Although all are led to despair,
They are still people like us!

[God:]
But Abram, poor intercessor,
mere man of flesh and blood you are,
Would take the place of God's transgressor?
The Judge knows what he's doing?!

[Abraham:]
A mere man of dust and ash. . . .
My hand already on my mouth.
I wait for Him, who came before,
For Him, who will come after me.

[God:]
Hail Abram! The time of your reward
For your great faith will come indeed:
A human who suffered, who implored
for all inhabitants of earth.

Jan Wit

Introduction

The cities of Sodom and Gomorrah appear in the Bible and the Qur'an. In the latter they are called the "overthrown cities" (Q 53:53). What is said about these cities, and what are seen to be the reasons for their destruction? Abraham's nephew Lot/Lût, along with his family, are also among the inhabitants of the cities. Abraham managed to save his nephew in a war that broke out between various cities, including Sodom and Gomorrah. The king of Sodom was grateful that Abraham intervened (Gen 14:1-17). And when Sodom was threatened with destruction, Abraham pleaded with God to spare the cities: "Can the cities not be spared if ten righteous people are found in them?" (Gen 18:32).

The reason the cities were destroyed is usually connected with sex, primarily with the "sin" of homosexuality, in the Jewish, Christian, and Islamic exegetical traditions. No extensive commentary is necessary to show how

172

great the consequences of that understanding have been (and still are). The American writer, playwright, essayist, and political activist Gore Vidal (b. 1925) wrote *The City and the Pillar* (1948), which was severely criticized because of its unambiguous homosexuality.

We will first look at the cities Sodom and Gomorrah themselves and then the tale of Abraham and Lot in connection with them, and thereupon the question of the true reason for the destruction according to the three Books.

Sodom and Gomorrah

Sodom and Gomorrah were Canaanite cities (Gen 10:19; 13:12; 14:2-17) that are generally thought to have been situated near the Dead Sea, in an area on the southeastern side that is now covered by water. Their destruction allegedly took place during the Middle Bronze Age, sometime between 2000 and 1600 B.C., when the earth's crust sank as a result of an earthquake accompanied by gas explosions (cf. Gen 19:24-28). The "glow" of the destruction of Sodom flickers throughout all of Scripture. Strabo (ca. 64 B.C.–A.D. 19), Greek historian, geographer, and philosopher, and Tacitus (ca. 56-117), Roman historian, writer, and rhetorician, refer to it. The area of the cursed cities may have been an abandoned, inhospitable desert for centuries afterwards (Zeph 2:9), its burned ruins covered by the sea.[1]

Before Sodom and Gomorrah were destroyed, this area was known to be well watered "like the garden of the LORD, like the land of Egypt" (Gen 13:10). It is striking that both these cities, along with Egypt, which are usually treated negatively in the Bible and the Qur'an, can also be compared to paradise! Muslim exegetes call Egypt the holy and blessed land, *al-ard al-muqaddasa al-tayyiba al-mubâraka.*[2] When Abraham and Lot wonder where they should settle, Lot emphatically chooses to live in Sodom and Gomorrah. It is stated immediately that the Sodomites did evil and sinned greatly against God (Gen 13:13). The narratives that follow elaborate on this (Gen 18:20-21; 19:4-11).

Lot/Lût, Inhabitant of Sodom

Lot was the son of Abraham's brother (Gen 11:27, 31), who together with him left Harran (12:4), the area in northwestern Mesopotamia that lay on the car-

1. *EQ, s.v.* "Clay."
2. *EQ, s.v.* "Egypt."

avan route from Nineveh to Asia Minor. After a dispute between Abraham and Lot, the two part, and Lot chooses the best part of the Jordan Valley with grazing pastures and springs: Sodom and Gomorrah. With the destruction of Sodom, he loses all of them (Gen 19:1ff.).

Lot is called the ancestor of Moab and Ammon. The popular etymological explanation of these names traces their origin to Lot's incest with his daughters (Gen 19:30-38; cf. Deut 2:9; Ps 83:8). The name Moab means, literally, "seed of the father." The Moabites derived from the incest committed in a cave where Lot sought refuge with his daughters after fleeing from Sodom and Gomorrah.[3] Such tales are told primarily to explain or excuse the enmity toward and dislike of neighboring peoples, here the Moabites and Ammonites. The historical explanation for the dismissive attitude toward them was motivated by the fact that, when the children of Israel left Egypt, these peoples did not supply them with food and drink during their journey (cf. Numbers 22–24; Deut 23:3-6; Neh 13:1-3).

Abraham's Plea for Sodom

The story of the actual judgment of both overthrown cities (Q 11:77-83; cf. Genesis 18–19) is preceded in the Qur'an by the account of the visit of the messengers from God to Abraham at Mamre: the announcement of the promise of the birth of a son, Isaac/Ishâq, to Abraham and Sarah (and, in turn, Isaac's son, Jacob/Ya'qûb) and Abraham's dispute with the messengers about the punishment of Lot's people in Sodom (Q 11:69-76). All these events constitute an introduction to that story of judgment.

One day Abraham is visited by three men, strangers whom he hospitably receives (Gen 18:16-33). Strangers are often symbolic of God himself. First, the messengers bring Abraham the good news of the approaching birth of Isaac, at which his wife laughs (Gen 18:13).[4] They also tell Abraham that the sin of the city of Sodom is exceedingly great and the cry for vengeance is rising up from Sodom and Gomorrah. It is striking that, when the

---

3. A monastery in Jordan is dedicated to the devout Lot, Deir Ayn Abata, where, according to tradition, Lot and his daughters fled after the destruction of Sodom. From the end of the eighth until the ninth century it was a place of worship shared by both Christians and Muslims. Tilman Nagel, *Der Koran und sein religiöses und kulturelles Umfeld* (Munich: Oldebourg, 2010) 154.

4. The preceding chapter reports that Abraham laughed at the announcement (Gen 17:17).

strangers announce that they will inspect Sodom, Abraham seems to be convinced already that God will carry out a judgment, even though God speaks only about the great sin of the city (cf. also Gen 13:13). One can wonder if, according to the story, God was planning beforehand to destroy Sodom. Or is that simply Abraham's conclusion? Whatever the case, Abraham pleads for the inhabitants of Sodom. Will God really eradicate the righteous with the wicked (Gen 18:16-23)? Suppose there are fifty righteous people in the city — do the good have to suffer with the wicked? No one should be put to death for the sins of another (Deut 24:16). If there are fifty, forty, thirty, twenty, or even only ten people in the city, can the city not be spared? Abraham prays for God's mercy. Does mercy not triumph over judgment (Jas 2:13)?

It does indeed appear that God can be made to relent. In response to Abraham's insistent prayer, God answers that he will not destroy Sodom and Gomorrah if there are ten righteous people in the city: "For the sake of ten, I will not destroy it" (Gen 18:23-32). Why, one might ask, does Abraham not press God further to spare the city if there are less than ten? Has God had enough? Does the biblical writer not dare to have Abraham bargain further until perhaps there is only one righteous person for whose sake God will not destroy the city? Who can put limits on the patience, forbearance, long-suffering of God, to God's being "slow to anger" (Jer 15:15; Rom 2:4): God or the believer, in this case, the "father of all believers" (cf. Q 11:69-76; 15:57-60; 29:31-32; 51:31-34)? The prophet Jeremiah would later be given the task: "Go up and down the streets of Jerusalem, look around and consider, search through her squares. If you can find but one person who deals honestly and seeks the truth, I will forgive this city" (Jer 5:1). Later Jewish writers did dare to go that far — see the moving book by André Schwarz-Bart, *The Last of the Just*. In that novel there is only one righteous person for whose sake the world is not destroyed. One is enough. There was also one in Sodom — Lot!

Lot Has Visitors in Sodom

Lot, the righteous man, suffers because of the loose life of the lawless people in Sodom. He lives among them and is tormented in his righteous soul day in, day out when he hears and sees how they ignore God and God's commands (2 Pet 2:7-8). Lot, who was sent to Sodom as a prophet, warns them not to commit immoral acts that no one ever committed before: "You play around, in sensual desire, with men instead of women" (Q 7:80-81). The people of Lot regard God's messengers as liars. Lot asks them if they do not fear

God: "In me you have a reliable messenger. Fear God, then, and obey me. Do you want to play around with people of the male gender and neglect what God has given you in your wives? No, you are criminals." They say to him then: "If you don't stop talking like that, you will certainly be driven out" (Q 26:160-69; cf. 27:54-56; 29:28-30).

As soon as the strangers who had earlier visited Abraham (Gen 18:1-5) arrive at Lot's in Sodom, he acts just as had Abraham, who is called the "father of the guests."[5] When they arrive, he lays out a meal for them with unleavened bread he had made, and they eat (Gen 19:3). An important characteristic of nomadic life is the high appreciation for hospitality. "The guest will be more precious to you than your father," according to one desert proverb. Even the poorest person will slaughter his last sheep for his guest and not reveal anything of his own possible misery. People do not expect gratitude. They want nothing more than to serve the guest and make his temporary stay one of ease. Everything they have is given to the guest. During his stay, the stranger will be under the protection of his host. That obligation to hospitality and protection is taken so seriously that sometimes means are used that seem to be or are completely unacceptable, as in what happens between Lot and his daughters (Gen 19:30-38; cf. Judg 19:5-22).[6] Lot's behavior is completely the opposite to that of the Sodomites. Before they go to bed, all the men from every district in Sodom — both young and old — surround the house and demand that Lot bring out his guests so that they could "know" them. Lot goes outside and, shutting the door behind him, tells them not to do this (Gen 19:4-8). Because of the visit of the strangers, the situation becomes stressful and Lot does not know what he should do about the Sodomites. He is worried about the fate of the strangers and is prepared to go quite far: "Look, I have two daughters who have never slept with a man. Let me bring them out to you, and you can do what you like with them. But don't do anything to these men, for they have come under the protection of my roof" (Gen. 19:8). In the Qur'anic account Lot says: "This is a terrible day. Here, people, are my daughters. They are purer for you than are my guests. Fear God and do not bring any shame on me because of my guests." They reply: "You know that we have no right to your daughters. And you know what we want" (Q 11:77-79; cf. 15:71). Lot thus makes a desperate attempt to keep the inhabitants of Sodom from violating his hospitality. But, in doing so, does he

---

5. By Al-Tha'labî, cited by Martin Bauschke, *Der Spiegel des Propheten: Abraham im Koran und im Islam* (Frankfurt am Main: Lembeck, 2008) 128.

6. D. S. Attema, *Arabië en de Bijbel* (The Hague: Van Keulen, 1961) 57.

find the rape of his daughters less terrible than the rape of his guests? But the Sodomites say: "Get out of our way." They then add: "This fellow came here as a foreigner, and now he wants to play the judge! We'll treat you worse than them." They keep pressuring Lot and move forward to break down the door. "But the men inside reached out and pulled Lot back into the house and shut the door. Then they struck the men who were at the door of the house, young and old, with blindness so that they could not find the door" (Gen 19:9-11).

The Flight of Lot and His Family

The messengers ask Lot if he has any more family members in the city. "Do you have anyone else here — sons-in-law, sons or daughters, or anyone else in the city who belongs to you? Get them out of here, because we are going to destroy this place. The outcry to the LORD against its people is so great that he has sent us to destroy it." Lot informs his sons-in-law: "Hurry and get out of this place, because the LORD is about to destroy the city!" But they laugh at him (Gen 19:12-14). Lot prays for God to save his family from what the Sodomites are doing (Q 26:169). The angels, who are concerned, then say to Lot: "Fear not and do not be dismayed. We will save you and your relatives, except for your wife. She is one of those who remain behind" (Q 29:33; cf. Gen 19:26). Then Lot and his family flee at the instigation of the angels. God brings those in the city who believe out before the judgment begins. No righteous person is found in the city, apart from one family (Q 51:35-36). Lot comes very close to being included in the destruction of Sodom, barely escaping. Thus, only the righteous who were in Sodom were evacuated and saved in the early dawn (Q 54:34).

As soon as the sun has risen, the Lord rains fire and brimstone down on Sodom and Gomorrah. He destroys the cities and the entire area, with all its inhabitants and everything that grows (Gen 19:25). The cities are destroyed by the rain of stones and clay bricks (Q 11:82; 15:74; cf. 7:84; 26:173). God sends a terrible judgment (Q 29:34), raining both fire and brimstone down on the evildoers, stones are launched from the air, and the city is overthrown. According to another description, the punishment consists of a scream, a sandstorm, or an eruption from the sky (Q 51:33; 11:82; 15:74; 27:58). When Abraham goes back in the morning to the place where he had previously seen the stranger standing, the heights at Hebron, he looks down at the cities on the plain and sees smoke rising from the earth, like smoke from a furnace (Gen 19:27-28).

177

Lot's wife, who is walking behind him, looks back, however, and is changed into a pillar of salt (Gen 19:26). God saves Lot, who had received strength from God to judge and is given knowledge, from the city in which loathsome things are done, a population of evildoers. God admits him to his mercy, for he is one of the righteous (Q 21:74-75). Those who are saved go to the city of Zoar, which means "small," on the southeastern coast of the Dead Sea (Gen 13:10; Deut 34:3) in Moab. On account of Lot, that city is spared (Gen 19:20-23).

The saving of the righteous Lot and the destruction of his surroundings is used as a type: "He did not spare the people with whom Lot lived; he abhorred them, rather, for their pride" (Sir 16:8). "She [Wisdom] it was who, while the godless perished, saved the upright man as he fled from the fire raining down on the Five Cities [Pentapolis: Sodom, Gomorrah, Adma, Zeboim, Zoar]" (Wis 10:6-7; Luke 17:29, 32; 2 Pet 2:7), with the apparent exception of Zoar.

Why Was Sodom Destroyed?

What is the actual reason for the destruction of these cities? That destruction is usually connected with "sodomy." This term is defined as the "carnal copulation with a member of the same sex or with an animal" (Merriam-Webster). Several sources, such as the Dutch Van Dale dictionary and the Dutch Wikipedia entry, associate it with sexual acts that are "contrary to nature" or "unnatural," formerly specified as homosexuality. Is that the nature of Sodom's sin? It is usually explained that it must be homosexuality in this story of men wanting to have sex with men (Gen 19:4ff.). Formerly? Still many today, and not just Muslims, link the sin of Sodom with homosexuality. That holds true for traditional Jewish, Christian, and Muslim understandings.[7]

The term "homosexuality" does not appear in the Bible or the Qur'an. Muslim scholars and writers hold various and diverging opinions and arguments on this. Some contend that because the phenomenon indicated by that term does not occur in the Qur'an it thus cannot be discussed in ethics. Others argue that homosexuality does correspond to the description of the men of Lot's people who look at one another lasciviously (Q 27:55; 7:81; 29:29; 26:165-66). Traditional Muslim exegesis holds that the people of Lot

---

7. *EQ* and *EI, s.v.* "Liwât."

were destroyed because of their sexual misdeeds. The act viewed as perverse can be linked to a term *liwât, lûtiyya,* which is derived from the name Lot. The allegedly reprehensible act concerns a "cutting of the way," meaning that a homosexual cannot reproduce and thus interrupts and cuts off the natural way of ancestors and descendants. This act is rejected, and the person and the act are singled out. The homosexual is not automatically excluded from salvation, although sanctions in the hereafter are indicated. Retroactive intentions are thus ascribed to a natural disaster. Only one passage in the Qur'an determines the legal position of two people who have committed immoral acts. The guilty parties must then both be punished, but they must be left alone if they show remorse (Q 4:16).[8]

According to a later tradition, *lûtiyya* merits the death penalty for both partners. Homosexuals are stoned, just as the people of Lot are stoned. A founder of one of the Islamic law schools[9] taught that the perpetrators were to be thrown down from a high place and then stoned, a punishment that makes one think of the story of the inhabitants of Nazareth wanting to throw Jesus down from a cliff (Luke 4:29).

Was this truly the great sin of Sodom, the outcry against which was heard by God? Was that what the Sodomites had done that had to be punished so terribly? Is that what it really says in the Bible and the Qur'an? One must listen carefully to what the text(s) actually say(s). God clearly destroyed and overthrew Sodom (Deut 29:23; Isa 13:19; Amos 4:11) because of the sin of its inhabitants (Q 9:70; 53:54; 69:9; cf. 9:70; 53:54) and the outcry reaching to heaven (Gen 18:20). The misdeeds of Lot's people are the refusal to believe and the stubborn persistence in vices such as a lack of hospitality. The sin that is condemned is Sodom's deliberate humiliation of the stranger, which can, of course, also be sexual sin. It is not that a person, man or woman, is homosexual, lesbian, or heterosexual. Talk of sin arises when justice and love are violated in whatever situation or relationship. The actual sin is the violation of the rights of the guest. Sodom and Gomorrah were overthrown because they themselves turned social relationships on their head. That is why what they have done is "brought down on their own heads," doing injustice against themselves by doing the opposite of what God wills. While the story seems to refer to homosexuality, the prophets focus on the violation of law, drunkenness, adultery, lying, and unremorseful self-assurance (Isa 1:10; 3:9; Ezek 16:46; Jer 23:14). This merits closer examination.

8. Abdulwahid van Bommel, *Islam, liefde en seksualiteit* (Leuven: Bulaaq, 2003) 127.
9. Abû Ḥanîfa (d. A.D. 767).

"The Overthrown Cities":
Sodom and Gomorrah in the Prophets' Tales

The theme of divine punishment is often recorded and discussed, both elaborately and briefly, in the Qur'an. A list of such punishments often begins with the story of Noah and the flood:[10] how God destroyed many a city that did wrong and then raised up another people (Q 21:11), how God brought to ruin many cities for doing wrong, so that they now lie in ruins, and how many a well was no longer used and many a fine fortress abandoned by its inhabitants (Q 22:45). All of this is held up to the inhabitants of Mecca: "Have they, the Meccans, not seen how many generations God destroyed before them?" (Q 36:31).

The story of Lot and the destruction of his countrymen is a main theme in the Qur'an (Q 11:74-83). It accompanies the preceding stories of Noah and his contemporaries (Q 11:25-49) and those of Arab prophets such as Hûd of the people of 'Âd (Q 11:50-60), Sâlih of the people of Thamûd (Q 11:61-68), and the tales that follow of Jethro/Shu'ayb and the people of Midian/Madyan (Q 11:84-95), and Moses and Pharaoh (Q 11:96-99). The story of Lot and Sodom is of a piece with those tales. These conclude: "That belongs to the tales of the cities. We tell them to you. Some cities still exist; others have disappeared from the face of the earth" (Q 11:100-102).

These same stories are also connected elsewhere in similar fashion: the story of Lot forms a unity with those of Noah (Q 7:59-64), Hûd (Q 7:65-72), Sâlih (Q 7:73-79), and the story of Shu'ayb (Q 7:85-93) that follows. God tells the tale of these cities. Messengers are sent to these cities with clear signs. But the inhabitants of the cities are not able or willing to believe in what they have until then declared to be a lie (Q 7:101). Thus, the cities are repeatedly warned.

From ancient times until Muhammad, prophets have prophesied against wickedness in cities. But it should be noted, those cities could also be Jerusalem and Mecca. These shocking examples are given of what happened previously to cities that refused the warnings of the prophets. Lot, mentioned explicitly among the prophets (Q 6:86), is, as it were, a prefiguration of Muhammad's own activities as someone who came into conflict with his fellow inhabitants at whom his message was directly addressed.[11]

Moses calls the people, the present and later generations, to observe

10. Rudi Paret, trans., *Der Koran* (Stuttgart: Kohlhammer, 1966) on Q 17:17.
11. *EI, s.v.* "Lût."

the stipulations of the covenant, the Torah, and to perform them. If they do not, they will suffer the same fate as Sodom and Gomorrah: "Your children who follow you in later generations and foreigners who come from distant lands will see the calamities that have fallen on the land and the diseases with which the LORD has afflicted it. The whole land will be a burning waste of salt and sulfur — nothing planted, nothing sprouting, no vegetation growing on it. It will be like the destruction of Sodom and Gomorrah, Admah and Zeboyim" (Deut 29:22-23). (Admah was a member of the coalition of five Canaanite city-states [Gen 14:2]). The prophets come back time and again to this theme. Sodom and Gomorrah serve as a warning example for other cities that fear punishment in the future (Deut 32:32; Isa 1:9; Zeph 2:9; Luke 17:29; Rom 9:29; 2 Pet 2:6; Jude 7). It will turn out even worse, Jesus says, for the enemies of the kingdom of God than for Sodom and Gomorrah (Matt 10:15; 11:23).

Amos, a shepherd and fig tree farmer from Tekoa in Judah, somewhat south of Jerusalem, was called to leave his sheep and become a prophet. He preached against Jeroboam II, king of Israel, about 760 B.C. At that time the common people were being trampled by those in power. Amos denounces the social abuses, condemning the worship of those whose heart is proud and whose hands are full of injustice (Amos 4:4-5; 5:21-24): "But let justice roll on like a river, righteousness like a never-failing stream" (Amos 5:24). He then compares Israel to Sodom: "'I overthrew some of you as I overthrew Sodom and Gomorrah. You were like a burning stick snatched from the fire, yet you have not returned to me,' declares the LORD" (Amos 4:11).

In 735 B.C. Isaiah, who was called to be a prophet in the temple in Jerusalem (Isa 6:1), proclaims a "woe" over a sinful nation: "Your country is desolate, your cities burned with fire; your fields are being stripped by foreigners right before you, laid waste as when overthrown by strangers. . . . Unless the LORD Almighty had left us some survivors, we would have become like Sodom, we would have been like Gomorrah" (Isa 1:7-9). Isaiah condemns, possibly during a major liturgical ceremony at the beginning of his prophetic activity, the hypocrisy of the people who do bring sacrifices but are guilty of social injustice. He then addresses the leaders of Jerusalem like the leaders of Sodom and asks the people of Gomorrah to listen to the instruction, the Torah, of God. Their hands, which bring sacrifices to God, are full of the blood of the innocent oppressed: "Learn to do right; seek justice. Defend the oppressed. Take up the cause of the fatherless; plead the case of the widow" (Isa 1:10-17). They put their sins on display just as Sodom did — they do not hide a single one (Isa 3:9). Isaiah prophesies that the city of Babylon, the jewel of all kingdoms, the pride of the Chaldeans, will suffer the same fate as Sodom and Gomorrah, which God destroyed: "Her time is at hand, and her days will not be prolonged" (Isa 13:19, 22). Just like Isaiah before him, Jeremiah prophesies the fall of Babylon and the land of the Chaldeans as well, the Neo-Babylonian Empire: "As I overthrew Sodom and Gomorrah along with their neighboring towns, declares the LORD, so no one will live there; no people will dwell in it" (Jer 50:1, 40). In 539 Babylon would be captured by the Persians and in 320 by the Greeks, Alexander the Great.

The prophet Jeremiah (ca. 645-587 B.C.) was instructed to walk through the streets of Jerusalem and look around and search the squares to see if he could find someone who dealt honestly and sought the truth. Then the city would be forgiven (Jer 5:1), just as Sodom might have been saved if at least ten righteous people could have been found in it. But, when asked why God was doing all this to the people — letting them be carried away into captivity — Jeremiah was to answer: "As you have forsaken me and served foreign gods in your own land, so now you will serve foreigners in a land not your own" (Jer 5:19). That happened because they cared nothing at all about the law, about the Torah that God had given them, and had not obeyed him and observed the law. Rather, they stubbornly went their own way and followed the Baals (Jer 9:11-16; cf. 16:10-13). Then many peoples who passed Jerusalem would say to one another: "Why has the LORD done such a thing to this great city?" And the answer would be: "Because they have forsaken the covenant of the LORD their God and have worshipped and served other gods" (Jer 22:8-9). The whole city of Jerusalem has become a Sodom to the Lord and the whole population a Gomorrah (Jer 23:14). In the book of Lamentations, by the prophet Jeremiah, the guilt of the people, the sin of Zion, was called greater than that of Sodom, which had suddenly been destroyed without people's intervention (Lam 4:6).

Israel's "brother nation" as well, Edom, which was viewed as having descended from Jacob's/Israel's brother Esau, also receives a similar judgment from Jeremiah: "Edom will become an object of horror; all who pass by will be appalled and will scoff because of all its wounds. As Sodom and Gomorrah were overthrown, along with their neighboring towns . . . so no one will live there; no people will dwell in it" (Jer 49:17-18).

The prophet Ezekiel, who was deported together with an elite of ten thousand in 597 B.C. to live in exile in Babylon, lived and worked in a district called Tel-abib, which may mean "mound of the deluge." For the city of Jerusalem, he used the image of an adulterous woman or prostitute because of Jerusalem's rejection of God (Ezek 16:15; cf. Isa 1:21; Jer 2:2; 3:6-7; Ezekiel 23;

Hos 1:2; 2:4). He compares Samaria, the capital city of Israel, with Sodom (Ezek 16:46), her younger sister. Both Samaria and Sodom are presented as settlements dependent on Jerusalem, both known for their wickedness (Ezek 16:46, 61). But according to Ezekiel, the cities of Sodom and Gomorrah are still better than Jerusalem: "As surely as I live, declares the Sovereign LORD, your sister Sodom and her daughters never did what you and your daughters have done. Now this was the sin of your sister Sodom: She and her daughters were arrogant, overfed and unconcerned; they did not help the poor and needy. They were haughty and did detestable things before me. Therefore I did away with them as you have seen" (Ezek 16:48-50). It is said, one should note, that Samaria did not commit half the sins Jerusalem did: "You have done more detestable things than they, and have made your sisters seem righteous by all these things you have done" (Ezek 16:51). And then the prophet says in the name of God: "However, I will restore the fortunes of Sodom and her daughters and of Samaria and her daughters, and your fortunes along with them, so that you may bear your disgrace and be ashamed of all you have done in giving them comfort" (Ezek 16:53-54). All three, Samaria, Sodom, and Jerusalem, will be restored to their previous state (Ezek 16:55).

The prophet Zephaniah, an older contemporary of Jeremiah, recalls the jeering by Moab, the descendants of Lot through his daughter, how they cursed Israel and did not respect its borders. "Therefore, as surely as I live, declares the LORD Almighty, the God of Israel, surely Moab will become like Sodom, the Ammonites like Gomorrah — a place of weeds and salt pits, a wasteland forever" (Zeph 2:8-9).

Sodom and Gomorrah and Jesus

Jesus spoke in the same vein as the earlier prophets. When he sent the twelve disciples out, he said that if they were not received and their words not heeded they were to leave that house or town and shake its dust from their feet: "Truly I tell you, it will be more bearable for Sodom and Gomorrah on the day of judgment than for that town." He pronounces a "woe" over the cities of Galilee: "Woe to you, Chorazin! Woe to you, Bethsaida! For if the miracles that were performed in you had been performed in Tyre and Sidon, they would have repented long ago in sackcloth and ashes. But I tell you, it will be more bearable for Tyre and Sidon on the day of judgment than for you. And you, Capernaum [one of the most important places for Jesus' activity, called his own town after he left Nazareth (Matt 9:1; 4:13)], will you be lifted to the heavens? No, you will go down to hades. For if the miracles that were performed in you had been performed in Sodom, it would have remained to this day. But I tell you that it will be more bearable for Sodom on the day of judgment than for you" (Matt 10:15; 11:21-24).

When Jesus speaks about the coming of the kingdom of God and the day of the Son of Man, he draws comparisons with the time of Noah until he went into the ark and draws parallels with the time of Lot as well. In those times, they ate and drank, bought and sold, planted and built, but on the day that Lot left Sodom, it rained fire and brimstone from heaven, destroying all. That is precisely what it will be like on the day that the Son of Man, Jesus, will reveal himself (Luke 17:27-30).

The last book of the Bible speaks of the "beast" that rises up out of the abyss (Rev 11:7), goes to war against the saints, and overpowers them — the embodiment of the antidivine power of Satan on earth. His abhorrent dominion was, for the prophet Daniel, the prelude to the dawning of the kingdom of God (Dan 7:21-22).[12] The first appearance of the beast[13] leads to a deadly conflict. The witnesses suffer and die for the truth. The two martyrs are blood witnesses. Even after their death they are still subject to indignities. People from all races see their bodies lying there and will not allow them to be buried. They are objects of scorn and derision (Ps 79:4; Jer 16:4). The stage for the ignominy is Jerusalem, but in a figurative sense as a symbol of extreme wickedness and depravity (Ps 79:3-4; Jer 16:4; Isa 14:19). The city is called "Sodom" and "Egypt." The martyrs' bodies will lie on the plain of the great city, which is symbolically called Sodom and Egypt, where their Lord was crucified. Sodom and Egypt are constant examples of depravity and the oppression of God's people. Here Jerusalem is meant (Rev 11:8).

Sodom and the Violation of Hospitality

Sodom is the epitome of sin (Isa 1:9ff.; Ezek 16:46ff.). Egypt stands for hardening and enmity toward the community of God. Sodom and Egypt are also alluded to side by side in the book of Wisdom. The Sodomites did not want, after all, to include the unknown men, the strangers, who came to them in

---

12. Johannes Behm, *Das Neue Testament Deutsch: Die Offenbarung des Johannes* (Göttingen: Vandenhoeck and Ruprecht, 1949) 60.

13. This refers to the wicked tyrant Antiochus Epiphanes (175-164 B.C.).

their community; but the Egyptians had originally admitted foreigners, the children of Israel who were their benefactors — through Joseph's sparing them from a seven-year famine — first as guests, but later turned them into slaves. A certain judgment would also be pronounced on those others, given their hostile reception of foreigners. The Sodomites renounced their duty to show hospitality (Gen 19:5). In contrast, the Egyptians first received them with a celebration and then, when the children of Israel had already shared in the rights of Egyptians, they tormented them with hard labor. They were struck with blindness — just like the others at the door of the righteous Lot (Gen 19:6, 9-11) — when they were surrounded by an impenetrable darkness and everyone had to find the way to their own door (Wis 19:14-17). The biting irony is that it is the "holy city" that killed the prophets and crucified Jesus.[14]

The Ruins of the City of Iram

In his proclamations Muhammad called his hearers to pay attention to their environment and to observe it. Just like every traveler in a caravan, as Muhammad himself had been in his youth, he had done that often. Muhammad later also passed by the Nabatean ruins on the way to the campaign at Tabûq in A.D. 631. His soldiers could not refresh themselves at the wells because the place was cursed.[15] That place, called Madâ'in Sâlih ("cities of Sâlih"), located in the south of what is now Jordan, was indeed the most important city after Petra. According to the Qur'an, this area was inhabited by the wicked Thamûd, who carved their homes out of the rocks (Q 7:74) and to whom Sâlih was sent as a prophet. They were judged and punished by means of an earthquake (Q 7:77-78).[16] In the territory of 'Ad, the city of Iram ("full of pillars") was unequalled, cut from the rocks (Q 89:6-9). It is said that the city was built near Aden as an imitation of paradise and that the city was punished for its pride, being destroyed by a tornado. The people of Thamûd were accused of using their buildings to guarantee their immortality through fame (Q 26:128-29).

The city of Iram was discovered during the reign of the first Umayyad caliph of Damascus Mu'âwiyya (602-80) by a man searching for his lost

---

14. Behm, *Das Neue Testament Deutsch*, 60-61. Wis 19:14 KBS.

15. Alfred Guillaume, *The Life of Muhammad: A Translation of Ishâq's Sîrat Rasûl Allâh* (repr. New York: Oxford University Press, 1967) 605.

16. *EI*, s.v. "al-Hidjr."

camel in the Yemen desert. According to the story, Shaddâd was a son of 'Ad who read about paradise in books and decided to build an earthly version of it in his own kingdom over a period of twenty years. It was a city of gold and silver, rubies and pearls, with columns of jewels and lanes of fruit trees. When the city was ready, Shaddâd wanted to visit it. But when he was one day's journey away, God sent upon him and the stubborn unbelievers with him a loud cry from heaven and killed them all by the violence of the cry. Neither Shaddâd nor any of those with him reached the city or ever came within sight of it, and God destroyed all traces of the road leading to it. But the city would remain there, as it were, until the day of judgment. It is written on Shaddâd's grave:

> Be admonished, O thou who art deceived by a prolonged life!
> I am Shaddad the son of 'Ad, the lord of the strong fortress;
> The lord of power and might and of excessive valor.
> The inhabitants of the earth obeyed me, fearing my severity and
>   threats;
> And I held the east and west under a strong dominion.
> A preacher of the true religion invited us to the right way;
> But we opposed him, and said, Is there no refuge from it?
> And a loud cry assaulted us from a tract of the distant horizon;
> Whereupon we fell down like corn in the midst of a plain at harvest;
> And now, beneath the earth, we await the threatened day.

The lost paradise of Iram is sometimes viewed as a precursor of a contemporary Muslim city. Al-Mas'ûdî (896-956), an Arab historian and geographer, known as the "Herodotus of the Arabs," relocates this marvelous city and its inscriptions to the future site of Alexandria. It is said that Alexander the Great found some ruins of a large building with marble pillars and an inscription that said that it was built as a replica of the first Iram.[17]

The Lessons of the Ruins of Cities

There are, of course, all kinds of ruins of places or cities to which one can refer and to which a tale can be attached about why this civilization and these

---

17. *EI*, *s.v.* "Iram"; Richard Stoneman, *Alexander the Great: A Life in Legend* (New Haven: Yale University Press, 2010) 163. Cf. Brannon M. Wheeler, *Mecca and Eden: Ritual, Relics, and Territory in Islam* (Chicago: University of Chicago Press, 2006) 113-14.

cultures declined. "Have they not seen how many generations before them we have destroyed, to whom we gave as much power on earth as we now give you?" (Q 6:6). Some of those cities are still standing, whereas others have disappeared from the face of the earth. It is not blind fate that overcomes them. Humans can only blame themselves, for it is not God who was unjust to them; they themselves have done injustice (Q 11:100-101). God's messengers came to these cities as well, such as Sodom and Gomorrah, with the proof. God did not do them any injustice; they had done that injustice to themselves (Q 9:70). This is a constantly recurring theme in the Qur'an. The human being remains personally responsible for his or her deeds: "And have they not traveled around so they could see the final end of those who lived before their time? They were even greater than them in strength and left more traces on the earth. Then God came with a judgment to punish their guilt and there was no one who could protect them from God" (Q 40:21; cf. 40:82; 35:44; 30:9).

There is thus no punishment without a justified cause. How many cities that boasted in their abundant livelihood has God destroyed? Their houses are abandoned and hardly occupied anymore. But God never destroyed those cities without first sending a messenger to them, to the capital (Q 28:58-59). God reports the tales of these cities. Their messengers have come to the cities with proofs, signs of revelation, but the inhabitants are unable to believe in what they previously declared to be a lie (Q 7:101). God has not destroyed any city without a proclamation in the language of that people or their being in possession of the Scripture (Q 15:4). Everyone has acquired the knowledge of good and evil, for God had already — before any descendants of Adam were born — made a covenant with the children of mankind, whereby they testified that God was their Lord, so they could not claim later as as excuse "We did not know it" (Q 7:172). All people have a conscience for distinguishing between good and evil (Q 91:7-10). God had always sent a messenger so the inhabitants could distinguish between good and evil (Q 28:59). Doing good entails following the way *(shari'a)* that God shows on earth, as laid down in Scripture and the example of the prophet. Thus, there is no punishment without a messenger or without revelatory Scripture. God will not exterminate any city whose inhabitants do what is just (Q 11:117). The Qur'an often refers to people who do good as the "upright," the *salihûn* (Q 21:105; 22:14). The prophet who is sent to the people of Thamûd is called "upright," Sâlih (Q 7:73-79; 11:61-68; 26:141-59; 27:45-53), which can be translated as "the one who does good." God has bestowed his pleasure on the prophets, the just *(siddîqûn),* the martyrs *(shuhadâ'),* and the upright *(sâlihîna)* (Q 4:69). Zechariah, the father of John the Baptist, and John/Yahyâ himself, Jesus, and Elijah are included among the upright *(sâlihîna)* (Q 6:85).[18]

Prayer for the City and the World, *Urbi et Orbi*

Just like Jesus, Abraham was a proclaimer of the truth *(sadîq)* (Q 19:41; 33:7-8), a righteous man *(sâlih)* (Q 16:122). He was a humble man *(halîm)* as well (Q 9:114; 11:75). Someone who is *halîm* "is kind and gentle, who patiently bears everything that happens and occurs and is grateful, someone who never loses hope and is continually full of trust that the bad things that happen make sense and have a purpose and can be turned to good." The Qur'an ascribes this attribute, in addition to God (Q 3:155), to Abraham and his son.[19] God made Abraham his "friend" *(Khalîl)* (Q 4:125; Isa 41:8; Jas 2:23). The famous mystic Ibn al-'Arabî' (d. A.D. 1240) sees this title of friend as expressing a "mutual penetration" between Abraham and God.[20] Abraham prayed for Sodom. Just as it is said of Abraham that he prayed an intercessory prayer for Sodom, so the Qur'an speaks about such a prayer (Q 11:74-75). The intercession belongs to God (Q 39:44). Who would make intercession at the last judgment without his permission (Q 2:255; cf. 10:3)?[21] The angels pray for forgiveness for those who believe (Q 40:7) and for those who are on earth (Q 42:5).

The intercession will be successful only with God's permission (Q 53:26; 20:109; 34:23).[22] The patriarch, the father of all believers, is the model of the true "muslim," an example, the Qur'an says, for Jew, Christian, and Muslim (in the sociological sense of the word) (Q 2:140; 3:67), an example thus for everyone, for the community. Just as this intercessor stands his ground before the face of the Eternal, the "children of Abraham" become an intercessory *qahal, ecclesia,* or *umma,* those who hear the call of the prophets for every city. And then the community must, like Abraham, not turn its heart into a murderers' den. God wants to hear from the mouth of the praying community what goes on among people, what goes wrong: injustice, the violation of human rights. Abraham steps in on behalf of the Sodomites.

18. *EQ, s.v.* "Good Deeds"; "Good and Evil."
19. Bauschke, *Der Spiegel des Propheten,* 55.
20. Bauschke, *Der Spiegel des Propheten,* 57.
21. *EI, s.v.* "shafâ'a."
22. *EQ, s.v.* "Intercession."

This task of the "father of all believers" is apparently also the task of his believing descendants: praying for our cities, for the city, and for the world *(urbi et orbi)*. Prayer also means working at the same time *(ora et labora,* "pray and work"). Abraham shows that he also did that by actually attempting to liberate his nephew Lot and Sodom (Gen 14:13-16). The city and the world can continue to exist because of this kind of prayer and work.

The cities must continue to be prayed for and worked on so that their Sodomite character disappears — the rape of law and love, in the literal and figurative sense. There are many people living in cities who are strangers, strangers to one another. If there is inhospitality that cannot tolerate any stranger, if that happens in our cities, then they start to resemble Sodom. Once, on his way to Jerusalem, Jesus is not welcomed in a Samaritan village because of the hostile relations between Jews and Samaritans, and his disciples, James and John, propose calling down fire from heaven to destroy the people in the village (Luke 9:54). But Jesus reprimands these "sons of thunder" (Boanerges, Mark 3:17) severely (Luke 9:55): that is not the answer to inhospitality. For the city and for the world *(urbi et orbi)* one must continue to pray and work; otherwise these cities will really go the way of Sodom, which God forbids.

"The kingdom of God is this world turned inside out" (Huub Oosterhuis) — turned completely around, completely transformed. That is the true overthrow of the cities that God wants to bring about.

CHAPTER IX

What Threatens the City? Gog and Magog: Mammon and Moloch

During preparations for invading Iraq, former American president George W. Bush remarked in a conversation with the former French president Jacques Chirac that Gog and Magog were active in the Middle East and needed to be defeated: "This confrontation is willed by God, who wants to use this conflict to erase his people's enemies before a New Age begins."

Introduction

Among the various voices one can hear in the Qur'an is foremost the apocalyptic voice in passages featuring dramatic images of hell and paradise, scenes of the last judgment and the end of the world.[1] In all three Books, certain apocalyptic passages on the last days also stand in the context of a "tale of two cities," the time in which everything will come to a head. In all three cases, an apocalypse, a revelation or interpretation of that time, is set in a critical period that can be applied to later history, right up to the present:

> Babylon and Jerusalem were opponents during the time of King Nebuchadnezzar, who was responsible for the occupation and destruction of Jerusalem in the sixth century B.C. This is treated in the books of the prophets Ezekiel and Daniel.

1. Tarif Khalidi, *Images of Muhammad: Narratives of the Prophet in Islam across the Centuries* (New York: Doubleday, 2009) 22.

Jerusalem and Rome were opponents at the end of the first century
B.C. In the last book of the Bible, the Revelation of John (*Apocalypsis* in Greek), Babylon stands for Rome, the center of the powerful
Roman Empire.

Constantinople and Ctesiphon were opponents at the beginning of the
seventh century A.D., the time of the prophet Muhammad's active
ministry.

Apocalyptic texts, which figure in the understanding and interpretation of what happens and will happen, originate in times of crisis and war.
The first to hear the message of the Qur'an were already acquainted with
certain apocalyptic images, and this would continue to be the case during
the first centuries of the expansion of Islam and later in the Middle East.
Jewish, Christian, and Muslim communities that coexisted in those areas
shared similar expectations and visions. There were all kinds of scenarios
about the end times.[2] In the early eighth century there was a wide circulation
of apocalypses in Byzantium and the Latin West, in various areas and in different cultures and languages.[3]

In this chapter we will first look at how certain depictions in the Bible
and the Qur'an are used today to explain the tensive relationships that exist
between people. Where do these depictions come from and what do they
mean? What do the apocalyptic texts in the books of Daniel and Revelation
that are concerned with the expectations of what will happen in the end
time mean? According to Muslim legend, Daniel/Dâniyâl is a revealer of the
future and mysteries about the last days, the beginning of the end. It is said
that Muslim soldiers stumbled on the book of Daniel by accident during the
Muslim conquest of Tustar in southwest Persia under the second successor
of Muhammad, Caliph Umar (A.D. 634-44). The book was in a casket that
was thought to contain Daniel's remains. At the caliph's command the book
was buried anew with Daniel's body.[4]

Jewish, Christian, and Islamic tradition point to the figures of Gog and
Magog, who are hostile to God and who come on the scene in the penulti-

---

2. Hayzettin Yücesoy, *Messianic Beliefs and Imperial Politics in Medieval Islam: The
'Abbâsid Caliphate in the Early Ninth Century* (Columbia: University of South Carolina
Press, 2009) 28.

3. Yücesoy, *Messianic Beliefs and Imperial Politics*, 34. Cf. David Cook, *Studies in Muslim Apocalyptic* (Princeton: Darwin, 2002).

4. *EI, s.v.* "Dâniyâl"; Yücesoy, *Messianic Beliefs and Imperial Politics*, 33. Cf. Cook,
Studies in Muslim Apocalyptic.

mate period preceding the final divine judgment in the end time. In the Qur'an they are called Yâjûj and Mâjûj. In the Jewish and Christian explanation, these events are connected with the end time. Their appearance is one of the signs of the last hour, and they are released to perform their evil pending the return of Jesus/'Îsâ, who has knowledge of the last hour or is himself a portent of the last hour (Q 43:61; cf. Acts 1:6). Because the Qur'an links Gog and Magog to the story of the "man with the two horns," that is, Alexander the Great, as we will see, the latter is also connected with them in both the Bible and the Qur'an. We must look at the so-called *Alexander Romance*, which dates to the third century A.D., and the *Alexander Legend*, from the seventh century. The latter dates to the time of Muhammad's activity as a prophet, when the Byzantine emperor was preoccupied with war against Persia and when the first direct confrontation between the Muslims and the Byzantines occurred. Thus, it is a "tale of two cities" during the life and activity of Muhammad: Byzantium and Ctesiphon.

Contemporary Wars and Armageddon

In this time of war and crisis there are some individuals and groups, Jewish, Christian, and Muslim, who have radical ideas inspired by texts from the three Books. They use them to explain and clarify what is happening or about to happen. Apocalyptic depictions, such as those about the coming of the thousand-year reign of peace, are then applied to the present. The thousand-year reign that is expected (Rev 20:1-6) is a temporary earthly messianic kingdom that will precede the eternal, universal kingdom of God.[5]

The American author, playwright, essayist, and political activist Gore Vidal relates in a 1987 essay how the U.S. president Ronald Reagan, who fought against the "Evil Empire," as he characterized the Soviet Union, was convinced that Armageddon was just around the corner. The name Armageddon is probably derived from the Mount of Megiddo (2 Kgs 23:29-30), the place in Palestine where many wars had been fought in the past (Judg 5:19; 2 Kgs 9:27; 23:29; 2 Chr 35:22). Depictions of the end of history are connected with Armageddon as the place where a final violent battle will take place (Rev 16:16). The Christian "madness" of some American presidents is, according to Vidal, terrifying. In his view, it comes from an American Puritan messianism with its expansionistic politics based on the clear "manifest destiny" that they saw re-

---

5. KBS on Rev 20:1-6.

served for America or the idea of having been chosen for that by Providence: the United States of America as the promised land for a people chosen for divine purposes, given that "God blessed this undertaking; a new order for the ages." A sizeable part of the American political elite is deeply convinced that the United States, as the New Israel, will bring back universal justice and thus the world will be reborn. God and humankind will finally be reconciled.

A similar way of thinking is also present in the twenty-first century. In November 2002, the American president George W. Bush was busy lobbying to form a "Coalition of the Willing," an alliance that was willing and ready to go to war against Iraq because of the presupposed and claimed weapons of mass destruction in Saddam Hussein's Iraq. Bush long used this label for those countries that offered military or political support, a group that included the Netherlands but not France and Germany. At that time Bush told the French president Jacques Chirac that the biblical figures of Gog and Magog were active in the Middle East and must be defeated. He believed that the time had come for that struggle, for that conflict was willed by God who wanted to use it to wipe away the enemies of his people before a New Age could begin.[6] According to reports, Chirac was flabbergasted and irritated by Bush's appeal to biblical prophecies to justify the war in Iraq and is said to have wondered "how someone could be so superficial and fanatic in his beliefs."

In the same year that this conversation with Chirac took place, Bush is also said to have told the Palestinian minister of foreign affairs that, with his invasions of Iraq and Afghanistan, he was on a divine mission and had received orders from God himself. *GQ Magazine (Gilbert Magazine)* revealed that Donald Rumsfeld, then Secretary of Defense, embellished strictly secret war memos with quotes from the Bible, which raises the question of why he thought he could influence Bush in this way. It was obviously because the president had chiliastic ideas, that is, he believed in the expected advent of the thousand-year reign of peace: "When the thousand years are over, Satan will be released from his prison and will go out to deceive the nations in the four corners of the earth — Gog and Magog — and to gather them for battle. In number they are like the sand on the seashore. They marched across the breadth of the earth and surrounded the camp of God's people, the city he loves. But fire came down from heaven and devoured them" (Rev 20:7-9).

---

6. The report of this conversation came out because the "Élysée Palace," astonished by Bush's words, sought advice from a professor of theology at the University of Lausanne. The story was confirmed by Chirac in a book by the journalist Jean-Claude Maurice, *Si vous le répétez, je démentirai* (Paris: Plon, 2009). Cf. n. 7 below.

There was obviously no doubt that the reason behind the American president starting a war in Iraq, at least for himself, was fundamentally religious in nature. He was driven by the belief that an attack on the Iraq of Saddam Hussein was the fulfillment of a biblical prophecy in which Bush himself was chosen to conduct the war as the instrument of God. Many thousands of Americans and Iraqis died in a campaign directed at the destruction of Gog and Magog. That the American president saw himself as a vehicle of God can only strengthen the suspicion in the Middle East that the United States is conducting a crusade against Islam.[7]

Apocalyptic visions can be found in the past and present in Islam, with similar references to the tales of Gog and Magog. The radical Islamist activist born in Aleppo in 1958, better known by his *nom de guerre* Abû Musab al-Sury ("the Syrian"), quoted a dozen Qur'anic texts for his "Call for Global Islamist Resistance" and talks about the return of the Messiah or the struggle with Gog and Magog.[8]

Apocalypses: The Book of Daniel

Apocalyptic books first appeared after the exile of the Jews in Babylon. The book of Daniel is an example, as are a few chapters from the book of the prophet Ezekiel (38 and 39) as well as the book of Revelation, the last book of the Bible written at the end of the first century A.D. These books contain revelations about the events of the end time; they begin with contemporary facts and seek to call people to be loyal to their faith and to have courage to the death in the event of trials and persecutions. I will first look at the book of Daniel. In the Christian canon, following the Greek Septuagint (LXX) of the second century B.C., Daniel is included among the prophetic books and immediately follows the book of Ezekiel. In the Hebrew Bible, the Tanakh, Daniel is placed among the Writings *(Ketubim)* and is found toward the end of the Jewish canon. Apocalyptic literature builds on the heritage of the prophets. The hero in the book of Daniel is a young Jew who was deported under King Nebuchadnezzar (ca. 605-561 B.C.) along with others in exile to

---

7. There is a curious side to this story. When he was a senior at Yale University, George W. Bush was a member of the exclusive Skull & Bones Society, just as his father and grandfather had been. Initiates into Skull & Bones are given nicknames, and Bush's was Magog. Cf. under Bush, God and Magog, www.alternet.org/news/140221.

8. Gilles Kepel, *Beyond Terror and Martyrdom: The Future of the Middle East* (Cambridge, MA: Belknap, Harvard University Press, 2008) 110, 169.

Babylon (2 Kings 25) and stayed with companions at Nebuchadnezzar's court. Not only was Daniel a prophet and interpreter of dreams, but he also responded with grace and patience to the whims of kings. Nebuchadnezzar is seen in his book not only as a tyrant and oppressor but also as a king who respects Daniel's wisdom and the might of his God.[9]

The main character in the book is an example of wisdom, belief, and faith under the worst trials. The various stories and visions fit chronologically into the time of this king and his successors. It is not certain, but it is indeed possible that there was a historical person in exile called Daniel at the end of the Babylonian era and the beginning of the Persian. The names of historical persons were often used in apocalyptic literature as cover.

In these visions historical events have the function of describing in a concealed way the development of the last times before the kingdom of God comes, the time in which God will reign. In Babylon Nebuchadnezzar saw in his dream a large statue: its head was of pure gold, the chest and arms of silver, his stomach and loins of copper, and his feet partly of iron and partly of clay. These different metals are explained as representing the Babylonian, Persian, Greek, and Roman Empires. He then sees a rock that, without the intervention of any human hand, is separated from the statue and strikes the statue on its feet of iron and clay. The rock smashes to bits the statue of iron, clay, copper, silver, and gold.

Daniel interprets Nebuchadnezzar's dream, which has greatly disturbed the king, as follows: The golden head refers to Nebuchadnezzar and the Babylonian Empire. Then four other empires follow: the chest and arms of silver symbolize the Mede Empire, the stomach and loins the Persian Empire, and the feet of iron and clay the Greek empire of Alexander the Great. The rock is the kingdom of God that will finally prevail. God will allow this kingdom to arise, one that will never be destroyed. It will shatter all those empires and will last forever (Dan 2:19-45).

Daniel later has a dream of his own, and he sees all kinds of images: powerful rulers of great empires, often adorned with the horns of strong animals (cf. Dan 7:8, 24). He sees a ram standing before a canal with two horns, the one greater than the other, a symbol of the power of the Medes and Persians. How the horns grow recalls that first the Medes reigned and then the Persians. Then Daniel sees a goat coming which has a prominent horn between its eyes. The horn refers to Alexander the Great (336-323 B.C.), who in

---

9. Irving L. Finkel and Michael J. Seymour, *Babylon: Myth and Reality* (London: British Museum Press, 2008) 157.

331 defeated the Persians and King Darius III (reigned 336 to 330), the last king of the Achaemenid dynasty. At the height of its power, the great horn of the goat breaks off, and four other horns appear in its place. Those are the kingdoms of Alexander's successors, the Diadochi: the Ptolemies in Egypt; the Seleucids in Mesopotamia and northern Syria; the Attalids in Asia Minor; and Antigonids in Macedonia, Alexander the Great's home country. Between the horns Daniel sees a small horn emerge that refers to Antiochus IV Epiphanes (175-164) who would threaten the Jews' existence once more. The book of Daniel dates back to the time of this king (cf. Dan 8:1-12).

The Horn and Power

The image of the horn refers to the power of the king. God gives strength to his king and exalts the horn of his anointed king, the Messiah (1 Sam 2:10). God himself gives the horned heroes power, chooses them to be his servant, like the Persian king Cyrus the Great (559-529 B.C.). Cyrus leaves the religion of the peoples subject to him alone, including the Hebrew religion. In 538 he gave the Jews who were in exile leave to return to Jerusalem and to rebuild the temple with the return of the stolen temple treasures (Ezra 1:1-11). Cyrus is called God's "shepherd," a royal title, who accomplishes God's will (Isa 44:28), his anointed king or Messiah, and the righteous one (Isa 45:1), whom God called from the east and whom he loves (Isa 41:2; 48:14-15). In the hymn of Zechariah, the father of John the Baptist/Yahyâ, a sketch is given of what John will do: "He has raised up a horn of salvation [in the Greek text] for us in the house of his servant David" (Luke 1:69), in other words, "a saving power." In the final book of the New Testament, the lamb, a reference to Jesus, has seven horns and seven eyes, images of power (cf. Deut 33:17) and omniscience. Those are the seven spirits of God sent out over the whole earth (Rev 5:6). The Satanic dragon, in contrast, has seven heads, the counterpart of the seven spirits, and ten horns, a sign of great power, and on his heads he had seven crowns (Rev 12:3). In Christian iconography, the devil is depicted as having goat's horns.

Expectations of the Last Day

The Bible and the Qur'an speak of the coming of the "last day," but only God knows when that will be: "Heaven and earth will pass away, but my words will never pass away. But about that day or hour no one knows, not even the angels in heaven, nor the Son, but only the Father" (Matt 24:35-36; cf. Acts

196

1:7). This notion is confirmed by the Qur'an: "People will ask you about the Hour [of judgment, the last judgment], Say, 'Verily only God knows that. Perhaps the Hour is near'" (Q 33:63; cf. 7:187; 79:42; 51:12; 75:6).

Certain events are said to precede the last hour. All kinds of cosmic events will occur, including the breaking free of Gog and Magog (Q 18:94; 21:96). The beast is inspired by or borrowed from Daniel's vision of the four animals. The beast rises up out of the sea, which is, after all, the domain of mythological monsters (Daniel 7). The first three of the four animals Daniel sees are the lion, a symbol for Nebuchadnezzar, a bear for the Mede Empire, the leopard for the Persian. The fourth is terrifying, frightening, and very strong, with great iron teeth with which it crushes and devours its victims and tramples underfoot whatever was left. It differs from the other animals and has ten horns (Dan 7:7) and represents the empire of Alexander the Great. The seer John sees two beasts rise up, the one out of the sea and the other out of the earth (Rev 13:1, 11). The second beast is also called the "false prophet" (Rev 16:13; 19:20; 20:10). These two beasts symbolize the religious and political power of the Roman Empire, which was unacceptable for believers because of the emperor cult, in other words, the worship of power. What is cited in Daniel (ch. 7) and the book of Revelation (13:11) is stated in the Qur'an as follows: "When the announced judgment will overcome the unbelievers, God will cause a beast *(dabba)* to arise from the earth; it will speak that the people were not convinced by God's signs in their earthly life. They will not be able to produce anything to justify themselves" (Q 27:82, 85). In Muslim tradition the beast is also called al-Dajjâl, al Masîh al-Dajjâl, "the deceitful Messiah, the antichrist" (1 John 2:18, 22; 4:3; 2 John 7), one of the evil figures that will deceive the people in the last days and whose coming will be one of the signs that the last hour is imminent. The antichrist usurps the place of God and the Messiah (2 Thess 2:1ff.; Revelation 13). He acts as a pseudomessiah and pseudoprophet (Mark 13:4-23). Jesus/'Îsâ is expected to return (cf. Q 43:61) and defeat the antichrist. The Mahdî is also mentioned in that context as the one who will do so.[10] He will be guided by God's justice and will come at the end time to bring justice and righteousness on the earth. Jesus and the Mahdî are identified with each other: "There is no other Mahdî than Jesus."[11] According to Ephraim the Syrian (ca. A.D. 306-73) the antichrist will come out of Khurâsân. In the Syrian Peshitta, the (Old) Syriac translation of the Old Testament, the Greek words

---

10. The year 200 in the Islamic calendar *(Anno Hijra)* is called the "deadline" of his advent. Yücesoy, *Messianic Beliefs and Imperial Politics,* 55-56.

11. *EQ, s.v.* "Eschatology"; "Apocalypse." Cf. KBS on Daniel and Revelation.

for liar and antichrist are translated as *daggâlâ* and *mashîhâ daggâlâ*. The antichrist will be released after a six- or seven-year war between the Arabs and the Byzantines, which will reach its high point in the capture and occupation of Constantinople. His coming will be one of the ten signs that precede the last hour. The recitation of the ten first or last verses of chapter 18 of the Qur'an will provide protection against the antichrist.

> On that day, we shall abandon them, to swarm one against another. And the trumpet shall be sounded, and we shall herd them altogether.
>
> On that day, we shall open hell to the unbelievers' view, all in one view. It is they whose eyes were veiled from my remembrance, and who were incapable of hearing.
>
> Did they who disbelieved imagine that they could adopt my servants as protectors instead of me? To the unbelievers, we have prepared hell as a resting place.
>
> Say: "Shall we inform you who are the greatest losers in works? It is they whose manner of living in this present world has strayed far, while all the time imagining that they are acting righteously.
>
> It is they who blasphemed against the revelations of their Lord, and the encounter with him. Their works are voided, and on the day of resurrection we shall consider them of no weight. Thus, their reward is hell for their blasphemy, and for having taken my revelations and messengers as a laughing matter.
>
> But they who believed and performed good deeds, to them the gardens of paradise shall be a resting place. There they will remain forever, seeking no departures from it."
>
> Say: "If the sea were ink for the words of my Lord, the sea itself would run dry before the words of my Lord had run dry, even if we provided its like to replenish it."[12]
>
> Say: "I am but a human being like you, to whom inspiration is sent. Your God is in truth One God. Whoso hopes to meet his Lord, let him perform deeds of righteousness, and associate none with the worship of his Lord." (Q 18:99-110)[13]

There is little doubt that the prophet and his companions were worried about the coming of the antichrist.[14]

---

12. John 21:25.
13. Tarif Khalidi, *The Quran: A New Translation* (New York: Viking, 2008).
14. *EQ, s.v.* "Antichrist."

Gog and Magog, Yâjûj and Mâjûj

Gog is the king of the land of Magog, the personification of the hostile powers from the north (Ezek 38:2–39:15). Which actual people is intended in connection with the names of Gog and Magog? It is sometimes proposed that the Scythians are in view here. The first-century A.D. Jewish historian Flavius Josephus (ca. 37-103) and the Christian church father Jerome (ca. 347-420) do so, for example. They identify Gog and Magog with this nomadic people that in 626 invaded western Asia, going as far as Egypt, which led to great dismay in Syria and Palestine. They rode on horses, were belligerent and technologically advanced. They came originally from Central Asia and established a kingdom in that area that stretched from what is now Bulgaria to the Caucasus (700-200 B.C.). Magog also occurs as the name of an individual (Gen 10:2), a son of Japheth, one of the three sons of Noah who survived the flood (Gen 10:1-2; 1 Chr 1:5). Jewish tradition regarded Magog as a second apocalyptic king alongside Gog. Gog is thought to be the ancestor of the Turks.[15] He was a son of Semaiah, a son of Joel (1 Chr 5:4). Both names recur in Ezekiel's vision: "Son of man, set your face against Gog, of the land of Magog, the chief prince of Meshek and Tubal" (Ezek 38:2). Meshek and Tubal were two other sons of Japheth. But in Ezekiel the reference is to regions. Meshek is a Caucasian mountain people living in Asia Minor southeast of the Black Sea. The name Gog reminds one of King Gyges of Lydia, who reigned from 680 to 650 and played an important role in western Asia. He received acknowledgement from the Delphic oracle for his assumption of power: the pythia declared itself in favor of his kingship. Herodotus reports that Gyges therefore sent gifts to Delphi.[16] Because Meshek and Tubal are mentioned in the same context, it seems that the prophet Ezekiel included these enemies among the Scythians.

Gog and Magog are two figures in the descriptions of the last days in the Bible and the Qur'an. The enemy is said to come in the end time from the north, just as the hostile Babylonians came from the north (Jer 6:22). "North" referred especially to empires such as Assur (Zeph 2:13) or Babylon (Zech 2:6; 6:6, 8). In these apocalyptic texts the north is the place where judgment begins (Isa 14:31; Jer 1:13; 4:6; 6:1; 13:20). While the north is usually the land of destruction, there is also a report of the mountain of God in the

15. Tabari; see *EQ, s.v.* "Gog en Magog."
16. Herodotus, *The Histories,* trans. Aubrey de Sélincourt, rev. A. R. Burn (Harmondsworth: Penguin, 1972) I, 13-14 (p. 46).

extreme north (Isa 14:13, Ezek 28:14; cf. Ps 48:2). God comes from the north (Ezek 1:4).[17] "North" reflects the marching route from Mesopotamia to the Levant (Jer 1:13-15; 3:18; 4:6-7; 6:1; 10:22; 13:20).[18]

The prophet Ezekiel is one of the Jews who was banished to Babylon from Judah. He ends up in the colony of exiles in Babylon, Tel-abib (Ezek 3:15), which probably means "mound of the deluge." In the fifth year of his exile Ezekiel was called in a vision to be a prophet (Ezek 1:1–3:15). He was active for more than twenty years among the exiles in Babylon, and his prophetic authority was accepted in a hard struggle against the fanatical resistance of his compatriots (Ezek 18:1; 14:1; 20:1). He continued the message of the earlier prophets in a radical way. According to Ezekiel, Gog stands at the head of a great invading army from the north moving against the people of Israel. He is accompanied by the allies from Persia, Cush (Nubia), and Put (possibly Libya), equipped with shields and helmets (Ezek 38:5) — an international army of allies. From the far north, with his allies, Gog would attack Israel, the people who lived at the center of the world (Ezek 38:12). Jerusalem was seen as the "navel of the world." But God would destroy the powers and rain fire down on Magog: "and they will know that I am the LORD [YHWH]" (Ezek 38:1–39:16).

Ezekiel and the Revelation of John

The book of Revelation uses the stories of Gog and Magog from Ezekiel and applies an *aggiornamento,* "a bringing up to date," namely, the end of the first century A.D., the time of the Roman Empire. In Revelation it is the "tale of two cities," that of Jerusalem and Babylon, although Babylon here refers to Rome. "Babylon" serves as a symbol for the power hostile to God and humankind in every period. John sees in the war of Satan and those who follow him against the saints an expansion of the old struggle of Gog and Magog against the people of Israel. The Roman Empire was a slave-owner society or, in the words of the church father Augustine, a great gang of robbers.[19] Because the kings of the earth are already destroyed with their armies (Rev 19:19-21), Satan turns to the peoples at the four corners of the earth with the

---

17. *BW, s.v.* "Noorden."

18. Gwendolyn Leick, *The Babylonian World* (New York: Routledge, 2007) 552.

19. Augustine, *The City of God,* IV, 4, trans. Marcus Dods. *The Nicene and Post-Nicene Fathers,* 1st ser. vol. 2, ed. Philip Schaff (repr. Grand Rapids: Eerdmans, 1983) 66.

mythical names of Gog and Magog taken from Ezekiel. After the fall of Babylon or Rome, the following enemies of God still remain: Satan, the beast, and the false prophet, with their followers. These are "the kings of the world," the unjust powerful people of the world. The false prophet or prophet of lies refers to the deceitful propaganda, the propaganda machine of the emperor cult, the idolization of power that the rulers always need in order to make use of such power.

John the seer sees an angellike star descend from heaven with the heavy chains of the abyss, thus like a guard or a jailor of the dungeon underground. The angel seizes the serpent — the devil, Satan, the dragon, whatever he is called — by the scruff of his neck. Satan is the opponent of God and the declared enemy of the believers, the one who deceives people. The guard binds him with the chains and casts him into the abyss, locking and sealing the hatch above him. The dragon is thus imprisoned in such a way that he can no longer mislead the people, at least not for a certain, if long, period of time — a thousand years. For a period of history the devil can no longer have his way with people, which therefore means that he can no longer indulge himself. The idea here is that world history is divided into seven periods of a thousand years each. It will then end with a sabbath, a messianic sabbath of a thousand years, followed on the eighth day by a timeless new cosmic period. John believes the Messiah will found a kingdom of peace, justice, and righteousness, and he sees it all happening before his eyes. Only witnesses who sometimes die for their faith, thus becoming "blood witnesses" or martyrs, share in this thousand-year reign through the first resurrection, and they will reign as kings and priests with God's anointed, the Messiah. The souls of those who were beheaded come to life, and they rise from the dead. The martyrs who are resurrected judge the world (Matt 19:28; Luke 22:29-30; 1 Cor 6:2). Why are they granted this privilege? Because they have died for the faith. John calls the saints and martyrs "happy, blessed."

Then the seer sees thrones.[20] Thrones are a symbol of divine dominion. A judgment can be issued from a throne. But by whom? Who sits on the throne, and who is authorized to issue judgments? The martyrs are. They become judges, the souls of those who had been beheaded because of their witness to Jesus and the word of God, the ones who did not worship the beast. They are those who did not "howl with the wolves in the forest," who did not receive the mark of the beast on their foreheads or his stamp of ownership on their hands, who followed Jesus, went after him, stayed loyal to him. They

20. Cf. Chapter VI.

form the high council of the Most High, the supreme court, that now pronounces judgment over the beast and those who have followed him. They, the saints, then reign with the anointed king, the Messiah. Now the reign is finally truly one of justice being done by a true, messianic king, the caliph, a king as God intended. Not everything about being a king is corrupt. The saints did not live for nothing. An honest human existence is possible in this earthly life here and now. The seer wants to say: it is good to be part of that, to take an active role in that because, behold, it turns out good on earth, and they share in the first resurrection after their death: "Blessed are those who share in the first individual resurrection" (Rev 20:6). The first death is the individual departure at the end of one's earthly life; the second comes at the end of that thousand years. The second death, the eternal death over against the physical death, is the definitive and decisive death: it is not an earthly passing, but an ultimate and irrevocable destruction in the lake of burning sulfur. These words are the basis for the later explanation of the specter of hell. But the second death does not refer to hell any more than the new Jerusalem refers to the hereafter.

When the thousand years have been completed, the devil will have to be released for a short period. It seems as if all hell has now broken loose. That must be so, apparently — it cannot be stopped. And then the texts that are taken from Ezekiel about Gog and Magog follow: "[he] will go out to deceive the nations in the four corners of the earth — Gog and Magog — and to gather them for battle. In number they are like the sand on the seashore. They marched across the breadth of the earth and surrounded the camp of God's people, the city he loves. But fire came down from heaven and devoured them. And the devil, who deceived them, was thrown into the lake of burning sulfur, where the beast and the false prophet had been thrown. They will be tormented day and night for ever and ever" (Rev 20:8-10).[21]

The Alexander Romance

Conflict with the Byzantines in the northwest of the Arabian Peninsula arose in the final years of Muhammad's life. The Qur'an alludes to this, and here the Gog and Magog figures come into view. The "man with two horns" arises in that context as well and refers to Alexander the Great, who is also depicted

---

21. T. J. M. Naastepad, *Geen vrede met het bestaande: Uitleg van het Boek Openbaring* (Baarn: Ten Have, 1999) 217-23.

with a horn in the apocalyptic text of Daniel discussed above. That gives us reason to look at the figure of Alexander the Great in a more detailed way.

Alexander became a legend already during his life, but especially after. He appears in many folkloric elaborations right up to modern-day Baghdad, where mothers frighten their naughty children with the threat that the "man with two horns" will come to get them.[22] Traces of this legend can be found in Mediterranean and European cultures. In a series of lectures organized by the British Library in 1996, "The Mythological Quest," five examples of such a quest were cited: that of Gilgamesh, the quest for the Holy Grail, Jason and the Golden Fleece, Sinbad the Sailor, and that of Alexander. The English poet James Elroy Flecker weaves the Greek and Oriental legends of Alexander together in "The Ballad of Iskander," turning him into a kind of "flying Dutchman."[23]

One version of the *Alexander Legend* is the late-Hellenistic *Alexander Romance*. Formerly attributed to the historian Callisthenes from Alexander's retinue, in actuality it belongs to the folk literature of the city of Alexandria and arose in the third century A.D. This romance was read a great deal in the Middle Ages and is said to be the work that was printed the most after the Bible. The Arabs were familiar with the *Alexander Romance* through a Syriac edition that circulated among Syrian Orthodox Christians. This Syriac edition from the seventh century influenced the Qur'an.[24] Many versions of this *Romance* exist in various languages, including Dutch. Around 1260, Jakob van Maerlant (ca. 1223-88), poet, writer, and translator from the southern Netherlands, wrote the first Dutch version: *Alexanders geesten [Alexander's Heroic Deeds]* (from *gesta*, "heroic deeds"). Van Maerlant puts the primary emphasis on the marvelous and spectacular events in Alexander's life, such as when he visits holy oracle trees of the sun and the moon in India, asking them what the future holds for him. Van Maerlant describes how Alexander held his own against Darius III, the king of the Medes and Persians. Leading a small army with an immense drive, Alexander joined battle

22. Richard Stoneman, *Alexander the Great: A Life in Legend* (New Haven: Yale University Press, 2010) 144; *The Greek Alexander Romance* (London: Penguin, 1991).

23. Stoneman, *Alexander the Great*, 229. Cf. also the medieval Spanish epic poem about Alexander the Great: *De Libro de Alexander*. Jerrilynn D. Dodds, Maria Rosa Menocal, and Abigail Krasner Balbale, *The Arts of Intimacy: Christians, Jews, and Muslims in the Making of Castilian Culture* (New Haven: Yale University Press, 2008) 217-20.

24. Patrick de Rynck, trans, *Avonturen van Alexander de Grote: De Alexander Roman* (Amsterdam: Athenaeum Polok & Van Gennep, 2000) 9. Cf. Anton Wessels, *Islam in Stories*, trans. John Bowden (Leuven: Peeters, 2002) 243-44.

with Darius. When he died at the age of thirty-three, he was the ruler of an empire, but he had also become arrogant. Van Maerlant portrays Alexander for his audience of the elite as a star in the knightly heaven, who already managed to perform great deeds as a young man, thanks to his talent and good upbringing (Aristotle was his teacher, just as Seneca was Nero's). That knightly environment should have been impressed by this prince "so small of stature but so great in deeds." Alexander was presented as a role model for Floris V (1254-1296), count of Holland and Zealand, who was called "God of the Peasants" by the common people. Van Maerlant wanted to use Alexander's life as a mirror for Floris's. The book was to serve as a "Mirror of Princes," a guide for monarchs, in this case an orientation for life in the world for the young Floris and his retinue. The biography of Alexander is both a heroic epic and a lesson in humility. At the end of Alexander's life, however, pride seemed to go before the fall. A philosopher said at Alexander's grave: "When Alexander was alive, the world was too small; now a coffin of a few feet is enough."[25]

Moses and the Stranger, Khidr

The story of the man with two horns is preceded in the Qur'an immediately by a story that, in certain respects, is connected to the *Alexander Romance* just discussed. The story is about Moses, who, together with his servant, also goes on a quest. The goal of their quest is to travel to the place where the two seas meet. When they arrive there, they discover that the fish that they brought with them to eat on the journey suddenly miraculously comes to life and, when it comes into contact with the water, swims away. The two travelers also meet a stranger. Moses says to this "servant of God" that he will follow him because he can teach him the right path. He thus asks him for permission to go with him wherever he goes. Moses' request is granted, but on one condition. He is not allowed to ask any questions of the stranger nor demand any explanations about his behavior. They agree on this, but the servant of God tells Moses from the beginning that Moses will not understand his way of acting and will not be able to appreciate it. Nevertheless, Moses agrees to the conditions.

25. Fritz van Oostrum, *Stemmen op schrift: Geschiedenis van de Nederlandse literatuur vanaf het begin tot 1300* (Amsterdam: Bakker, 2006) 516-17. Michael Wood, *In the Footsteps of Alexander the Great: A Journey from Greece to India* (repr. London: BBC, 2004).

It quickly becomes apparent that when push comes to shove Moses cannot keep his part of the agreement. This servant of God does three terrible things. He drills a hole in the boat of poor fishermen, which prevents them from fishing and catching their daily haul. He kills the son in a house where they had been hospitably received, and finally he helps people who treat them inhospitably by building a wall for them. Unable to hold himself in at any of those times, Moses protests vehemently and each time asks for an explanation. But that is contrary to the agreement. Accordingly, the servant of God answers: "Did I not tell beforehand that you would lose patience with me?" The stranger leaves Moses and, at his departure, explains why he acted as he did in those three cases, for which, according to him, there were good reasons. The boat belonged to poor people who used it to earn a living on the sea. He wanted to damage it because they were being pursued by a king who wanted to appropriate the boat through violence. The boy's parents were believers, but he was not. It was feared that they would suffer under his lack of respect and belief. God wanted to give them a son instead who would be more pious and more affectionate. The wall belonged to two orphan boys in the city, and there was a treasure underneath it that belonged to them. Their father had been a righteous man, and that is why God, Moses' Lord, wanted them to grow up and retrieve their treasure. All this happened through the mercy of God: the stranger did not do it on his own authority. That is the explanation of the acts that Moses could not bear (Q 18:60-82).

In later Islamic exegesis, this stranger, this servant of God, would be called Khidr, the "Green Man." This narrative makes use of preexisting stories. The element of the story of the journey to the place where the two seas meet is borrowed from the Sumerian-Akkadian Gilgamesh epic, which was composed ca. 2500 B.C. Gilgamesh was the legendary king of the Sumerian city of Uruk in southern Babylonia (Erech, Gen 10:10), one of the cities that is thought to be the birthplace of Abraham.[26] Gilgamesh is the main character in the epic named after him, the most important literary creation of Mesopotamia. According to the epic, Gilgamesh went to the place where the two rivers come together.

Another element from this Qur'anic narrative is connected with the *Alexander Romance*.[27] There we read how Alexander the Great, together with his cook, went to the place where the two rivers come together and at the water of life dead fish came to life in a miraculous way:

26. *BE*, s.v. "Erek"; *EI*, s.v. "al-warka'."
27. Stoneman, *Alexander the Great*, 154.

"We came to a place where there was a clear well, of which the water glittered like lightning and where there were a great many other wells. The air at this place also smelled nice and it was not entirely dark there. I became hungry and wanted something to eat, so I summoned the cook, who was called Andreas, and said to him: 'Make some food ready for us.' He took a salted fish and went to the clear water of the well to wash it. But the fish had hardly touched the water before it came to life again and slipped out of the cook's hands. Because the cook was frightened, he did not tell me what had happened. He took some water himself, drank it, and put some in a silver jar to keep it. There was an abundance of wells there, and we drank from all of them. But, ah, unfortunately it was not given to me to drink from the immortal well that brings the dead back to life. My cook did have the good fortune to do that."[28]

•

That story of Moses and the stranger in the Qur'an expresses the fact that, although there was no greater hero than Gilgamesh, no greater prophet than Moses, and no greater king than Alexander the Great, Alexander, despite his unimaginable power and fame, had to be made aware by the stranger how fleeting life was, just like earthly wealth.[29]

The *Alexander Legend*

In A.D. 628-29 — possibly just after 628 — a work was composed in Syriac called *The Glorious Deeds of Alexander*. In the course of the war against the Persians, the Byzantine emperor Heraclius (ruled 610-41) employed religious propaganda to get his allies behind him and to strengthen or boost the Byzantine morale.

This writing was intended, not long after the war ended, to further the emperor's political cause, to reestablish Byzantine authority over the provinces that for some time had been under Persian authority. After almost thirty years of demoralizing war and unparalleled military losses, Heraclius needed to regain the loyalty of the reconquered areas of the Byzantine Empire and their inhabitants and to consolidate those areas as quickly as possible. In those areas certain views held by Syrian Orthodox Christians were dominant which differed from those held by Byzantine Orthodox, who were

---

28. De Rynck, *Avonturen van Alexander de Grote*, 92.
29. Wessels, *Islam in Stories*, ch. 10.

connected with the power of Byzantium. This led for a long time to strained relations between the groups, both religiously and politically.

It is probable that Muhammad's followers knew something of the content of the *Alexander Legend*. This is apparent from the question Muhammad is asked: "And they will tell you about the one with two horns" (Q 18:83). They may have heard of the legend during a military expedition. In September 629 an expedition of three thousand men went to the border of the Byzantine Empire, and for the first time Muslim troops penetrated that empire. Their opponents were themselves from the border area of Palestine, the region of Edom, southeast of the Dead Sea. Thus it was reported by a Byzantine historian — the first time, by the way, that use can also be made of a non-Muslim source for a story from the life of Muhammad. Muhammad's foster son, Zaid ibn Haritha, was the commander of this expedition. According to the Arab reports, these three thousand men faced a superior force of one hundred thousand Byzantine solders and bedouin. It was even suggested that Emperor Heraclius himself was involved with gathering the troops. This is considered improbable.[30] The bloody Battle of Mut'a in 629 was the first battle between Arabs and a Byzantine garrison. Ruins of a mosque of martyrs, set up to commemorate the Muslims who died at Mut'a, still exist. Zaid himself is said to have died. This battle occurred just a few months after the Persians retreated and a few months before Heraclius's triumphant return to Jerusalem with the relics of the true cross of Jesus.

The Syriac *Alexander Legend* now tells how Alexander the Great summons his court to ask about the farthest reaches of the world, for he wants to know and see with his own eyes what it is that surrounds this world. One should not forget that at that time the world was still thought to be flat. His advisors warn him that a smelly ocean surrounded the earth and coming into contact with the ocean could mean death. Alexander is not impressed and wants to explore, traveling to the ends of the earth, where he finds a sea filled with deadly water and crosses a pass that the sun went through every night. He prays to God, whom he addresses as the one who planted horns on his head, which means power over the whole world. Along the way, Alexander hires from the Egyptian king seven thousand copper and ironsmiths to accompany his large army. He then sets out on a voyage for four months and twelve days and reaches a distant country. There Alexander asks if they had any prisoners condemned to death. When these criminals are brought to him, he sends them to the sea to test the poisonous water. When they die, Al-

---

30. *EI, s.v.* "Mut'a."

exander sees how deadly the water is and abandons the plan to cross the sea. Instead, he goes to a place with clear water, to the "window of heaven," which the sun enters when it sets and where there is a way that leads through the heavens to the place where it rises in the east. Alexander then travels to the headwaters of the Euphrates and the Tigris. He goes on to the mountains in the north, apparently the Caucasus, until he comes to a place under Persian rule where he discovers a new pass. The local population complain about the savage Huns on the other side of the pass, a group of peoples with different languages and backgrounds, such as Turkish, Mongolian, Iranian, and possibly other Central Asian peoples. In the fourth century they were driven from the east, after which they migrated west.

The names of the kings mentioned here are Gog and Magog, and a lively description of the barbarism of the Huns is given. The people complain to Alexander that the barbarian trips of these savages are not punished, and they hope that Alexander's rule will be established. Alexander then builds a copper and iron wall to stop the Huns, using the Egyptian smiths he brought with him. On the gate in this wall Alexander places a prophecy about the things that will happen after his death. After 826 years the Huns will break through the gate, come through the pass, and plunder the lands they invade. Then, after 940 years an era of sin will break out, and there will be an unparalleled worldwide war. God will gather the kings and their armies. He will give a sign to tear down the wall, and the armies of the Huns, the Persians, and Arabs will engage each other. So many troops will come through the gate that this pass will become wider and wider. The earth will melt because of the blood and dung of men. Then the kingdom of the Byzantines will be caught up in a terrible war, and they will conquer everything, right up to the borders of heaven. Finally, Alexander cites the text, "From the north disaster will be poured out on all who live in the land" (Jer 1:14). The legend ends with Alexander establishing his throne in Jerusalem at the end of his life.

The Alexander Legend is an apocalyptic text, one about the last days, the end of the world. The Byzantine Empire will conquer the Persian Empire, and a Christian empire will be established worldwide. Alexander is portrayed as someone who foretells coming events, but those future events are also linked to what is happening in his own time. Alexander's prophecy, written on the wall he himself built, gives two dates for the invasion by the Central Asian nomads. The first is when the Huns will break through the great wall and reach the Tigris, important signs of the final conflict that will precede Jesus' return and the end time. The second date refers to the years

628 and 629. This coincides with the end of a long and extremely difficult war between Persia and the Byzantines (603-30), in which Jerusalem was laid waste and the relic of the true cross was stolen from the city. The date that Alexander's prophecy indicates must refer to the devastating wars of that time and their successful conclusion for the Byzantines. The author of the *Alexander Legend* wanted to create an Alexander-Heraclius typology so his contemporaries would recognize a new Alexander in Emperor Heraclius, who went to the east and fought the Persians.

What is the point of having Alexander travel first to the west, then to the east, and then to the north, finally returning to the south? We would see the answer readily enough if we looked at a map of the journey. Alexander's travels make the sign of the cross over the whole world. For the Christian empire, the cross is the sign of conquest, and the prophecies in the legend indicate the imminent rule of the Christian empire. It can be assumed that this crosslike journey is intended to refer symbolically to Heraclius's return of the relics of the true cross at the beginning of the year 630 to Jerusalem, the city where Alexander establishes his throne, according to the legend. Alexander's travels describe the symbol of the Christian (Eastern) Roman or Byzantine power. At the end, the legend includes a prediction that a Byzantine emperor will speedily establish Christian dominion worldwide, followed by the return of the Messiah.[31]

The Man with Two Horns

After giving this explanation and context, we will now look at the Qur'anic passage that speaks about Gog and Magog in connection with the story of the man with the two horns. It can be understood better against the background of the above.

The Qur'an answers the question posed by Muhammad's followers on the story of the "man with the two horns," of whom they had heard, as follows:

> You are asked about the man with the two horns. Say: "I will tell you a tale or story about him." We, God, gave him power on earth and gave him access to everything. He then took a certain path. Finally, he reached the place where the sun sets and discovered that it set in the "Black Sea." And there he encountered a people.

31. Kevin van Bladel, "The Alexander Legend in the Qur'an 18:83-102," in *The Qur'an in Its Historical Context,* ed. Gabriel Said Reynolds (New York: Routledge, 2007) 175-203.

God said: "You, man with the two horns! Either you punish them or you treat them well." He said: "We will punish whoever does injustice. Then, on the last day, he will be brought before his Lord and he will punish him with an evil punishment. But whoever believes and does what is right can expect the very best of rewards. And we will speak to him kindly."

Then he, the man with the two horns, went in a different direction until he reached the place where the sun rises. He discovered that it rose over people to whom we had not offered protection against it before. That was how it was. And we know all about how it is with him, the man with the two horns.

He then went in yet another way between the two barriers. When he arrived between the two barriers, he encountered people who were hardly capable of understanding a word.

They said: "O you man with the two horns. Gog and Magog are spreading destruction on the earth. Shall we pay you to construct a wall or barrier between us and them?" He said: "The power that my Lord has given me is worth more than what you can offer. So help me well so that I build a protective barrier between you and them. Bring me pieces of iron!" And when he had made the barrier as high as the two mountain cliffs between which it was built, he said: "Blow on the fire." And when the iron became red hot, he said: "Bring me liquid metal to pour over it." And they, Gog and Magog, could not traverse the barrier nor breach it. He, the man with the two horns, said: "That is proof of the mercy of my Lord. But when the promise of my Lord is fulfilled, then he will level it to the ground. And the promise of my Lord will come true." (Q 18:83-98)

Alexander is called "the man with the two horns" (Q 18:83, 94). A horn symbolizes strength and power (1 Sam 2:10; Job 16:15). Horns belong to the headdress of eastern gods, and horns can be found as an attribute of gods that are presented and depicted in human form. In ancient Egypt the sky-goddess Hathor, "Mansion of Horus," an earlier form of the goddess Isis, had a disk of the sun between her horns. After visiting Hathor's shrine, Alexander the Great, as a son of Zeus Ammon, had himself depicted with rams' horns. The root of the Arabic word *al-Qarnayn* is cognate with Hebrew *qeren*. The latter occurs in the Bible when Moses comes down from Mount Sinai with the two tables of the law that he received from God. Moses does not know that his speaking with God has made his face radiant (Exod 34:29-30, 35). This Hebrew word can mean both "shine" and "provided with horns." The Greek translation by the Jewish proselyte from the second century, Aquila, thus reads "horned," and the Latin translation by Jerome around A.D. 400 also speaks of "horned" *(cornutus)*. It is striking that the famous statue of Moses by Michelangelo in the church of San Pedro in Vinculo ("Peter in Chains") in Rome has two horns.

When Alexander comes to a people and at their request erects an iron wall between them and Gog and Magog to prevent their bringing destruction on the earth, that use of iron makes one think of the characterization of the kingdom of Alexander as iron in the book of Daniel.

Gog and Magog in Exegesis throughout History

How has this tale been exegeted, and how should it be understood? At the beginning of this chapter we spoke about the use still made today of apocalyptic figures like Gog and Magog. Every age has attempted to understand and interpret the crisis it is confronted with in this way. Throughout the centuries, Jews, Christians, and Muslims have read these stories about Gog and Magog and applied them to their own time. Usually, they use them — as still today — against one another! A Flemish Franciscan monk, Willem van Ruysbroeck (ca. 1210–ca. 1270), wrote one of the earliest reports about the Mongols. He took part in the Seventh Crusade of Louis IX the Pious to Palestine and there heard about the Mongols. He connects the Tartars with Gog and Magog.[32] The nomadic invasions of the Scythians, the Huns, the Mongols, and Turks were so many examples of the breaches of Alexander's "wall" by Gog and Magog.

Jewish Application

According to Martin Buber, in the nineteenth century Hasidic Jews connected Gog and Magog with the wars of conquest and the Napoleonic wars against Russia, with all they entailed in terms of their meaning for Europe. Some "righteous people" *(tsadikim)* attempted by means of a Jewish mystical teaching, the Kabbalah, to turn Gog from the land of Magog into "Napoleon." The coming of the Messiah would follow the Napoleonic wars. But

32. Brett Edward Whalen, *Dominion of God: Christendom and Apocalypse in the Middle Ages* (Cambridge, MA: Harvard University Press, 2009) 298, n. 50.

some other "righteous people" warned, in contrast, that the dawning of the time of redemption would be signaled only by the repentance of all humankind, rather than such acts.[33]

Christian Application

Toward the end of the seventh century a collection of prophecies were compiled under the name of Methodius, who died as a martyr around A.D. 300.[34] This Syriac work, the *Apocalypse of Pseudo-Methodius,* was written in response to the conquest of the Middle East by Islam and shaped the Christian imagination during the Middle Ages. This apocalypse contains familiar themes on the last days: the rise and dominion of the antichrist/Dajjâl, the invasion of Gog and Magog, and the catastrophes that precede the end of the world. The number of the savage hordes from Gog and Magog that attack Christian believers in the end time is like the sand of the sea (Rev 20:8). According to medieval legend, Gog and Magog were captured long ago and locked up behind a wall in the Caspian Mountains by Alexander the Great, where they have been since that time. But it is expected in the last days that Gog and Magog will break out from behind the wall to fight against the saints under the leadership of the antichrist.[35]

In the twelfth century, Joachim of Fiore, an Italian mystic and apocalyptic thinker, believed that the persecutions of Christians were signs of the end time prophesied in the book of Revelation. He refers regularly to the Islamic threat as a prominent factor in the events that led to the end time. Joachim, who provided an exegesis of Revelation, identified the fourth, fifth, and sixth heads of the great red, seven-headed dragon with ten horns with specific adherents of Islam, who, in his view, were forerunners of the antichrist, who was himself represented by the seventh head. He sees the seven-headed dragon with ten horns as representing concrete historical persecutions throughout history (Revelation 12). The fourth, fifth, and sixth heads represent, respectively, Muhammad, Mesomothius (a Saracen tyrant), and Saladin, the Islamic leader who retook Jerusalem from the Crusaders in 1187 and who preceded the seventh head: the antichrist. Viewed as threatening,

33. Martin Buber, *Werke,* vol. 3: *Schriften zum Chassidismus* (Munich: Kösel, 1963) 1257.

34. De Rynck, *Avonturen van Alexander de Grote,* 168.

35. Debra Higgs Strickland, *Saracens, Demons, and Jews: Making Monsters in Medieval Art* (Princeton and Oxford: Princeton University Press, 2003) 228-29.

these representatives of Islam pursued the woman clothed with the sun with the intention of devouring her child. Because the woman is seen to be the Virgin Mary or the church, a persecution of the church by Islam is immediately suggested. The heads represent the worst persecutors of the Christian church from the beginning until Joachim's time. Joachim believed that, as soon as the antichrist would be defeated, the Jews and other unbelievers would convert to Christianity.[36]

Gog and Magog in England

In the Guildhall in London are two gigantic images of Gog and Magog. Geoffrey of Monmouth (ca. 1100–ca. 1154), a clergyman and scholar and important British historian, wrote a history mixed with legends of the British kings before the Saxon invasion. According to Geoffrey, Geaemot or Gaemagot, a bastardization of the names Gog and Magog, was a giant who, together with his brother Gorineous, tyrannized the western horn of England before being defeated by foreign invaders. It is possible that in ancient times the Angles or Saxons had contact with the Scythians or with other tribes that lived north of the Caucasus or the Black Sea.

A survey of how peoples could be seen as monsters in Christian medieval art leads to the conclusion that, if the texts and the images are evaluated together, they embrace both negative and positive Christian attitudes and beliefs. In literary as well as pictorial works, monsterlike races are portrayed as signs of both sin and virtue, Ethiopians as irreproachable and demonic, Jews as virtuous witnesses and Christ's killers, Saracens as respectable knights and as Satan's executioners, Tartars as allies of the Crusaders and agents of the antichrist. This can be seen in the treatment of individuals such as Alexander the Great, who is sometimes seen as demonic, sometimes as pious, and Saladin, who is sometimes seen as a noble knight and sometimes as a follower of the antichrist. The Christian view of non-Christians is not simply blind hate, but complex and ambivalent, and it changes over time.[37] In the fifteenth century, Mehmed, the conqueror of Constantinople, was compared with the beast from the book of Revelation, as was Hitler in the twentieth century.

---

36. Strickland, *Saracens, Demons, and Jews,* 224-26.
37. Strickland, *Saracens, Demons, and Jews,* 242.

Islamic Application

The last days are marked in some Islamic exegesis by figures like Gog and Magog/Yajûj and Mâjûj, the coming of the Mahdî (a messianic figure), the antichrist/Dajjâl, and Jesus. Gog and Magog, the two peoples, will be released to work their evil in the expectation of the descent of Jesus to earth. The connection of the two names with entire peoples instead of individuals corresponds with postbiblical Jewish and Christian traditions.[38]

Accordingly, in the twelfth and thirteenth centuries, Muslims, just like European Christians, identified Gog and Magog with the Mongolian invaders. The Mongols had not yet converted to Islam. They were a nomadic people who rode horses and carried out atrocities that ended in destruction, as when Baghdad, the center of the kingdom of the Abbasids, was destroyed.[39] Gog and Magog were seen as clear representatives of the nomadic peoples who lived beyond the mountains of Caucasus and Transoxiana, whose coming was accompanied by fear and terror breaking out among the established people of the area, Persia in particular. What would happen if they would ever violently engage in invasion, as the Seljuks, Turks, and Mongols eventually did? Gog and Magog represent the fears of the established peoples of northern Persia with respect to the mountain peoples in areas that were never conquered by the Muslims. It was advantageous for everyone to paint them in as terrible a way as possible to allow the repugnance and fear of these "half-human" creatures to grow.[40]

Jewish communities seem to have greeted the Muslim conquerors as liberators and saw the Muslim government as an instrument for the redemption of the Jews from Byzantine persecution and a sign of the coming of the Messiah.[41]

In the explanation given by the Ahmadiyya movement, a Muslim group that arose in the Indian subcontinent in the last decades of the nineteenth century, reference was made to Muslim traditions when speaking about the release of Gog and Magog. They would rule over the whole world: "No one will have the strength to fight them." "They will drink the water of the whole world." "No one but I, God, can destroy them." The Slavic and Teutonic races were thought to be the ancestors of Gog and Magog, and the

---

38. *EQ, s.v.* "Apocalyps"; *EI, s.v.* "Yadjûdj wa — Madjûdj."

39. D. S. Attema, *De Mohammedaansche opvattingen omtrent het tijdstip van den jongsten dag en zijn voortekenen* (Amsterdam: Noord-Hollandsche Maatschappij, 1942) 135.

40. Cook, *Studies in Muslim Apocalyptic,* 182-86.

41. Yücesoy, *Messianic Beliefs and Imperial Politics,* 31.

world domination of Gog and Magog referred, in their view, to the domination of the European nations over the whole world. The prophecy was fulfilled in our time, the end of the nineteenth century and the beginning of the twentieth. Given that the whole world was subject to Gog and Magog, identified with the European nations, the conflict has taken on global proportions. Islam is then viewed as that which would bring the people together (Q 18:99). It would truly then be the only religion in the world to be successful in uniting people of different nations and banishing discrimination of race and color.[42]

Gog and Magog: Moloch and Mammon

What do the three Books really have to tell us today on this issue of apocalyptic depictions? It is essential here that we do not read and exegete these apocalyptic texts against one another, as is done so often. If we want to understand the three Books on this point, then we must state at the beginning that it does not make much difference if Gog and Magog ever referred to the Scythians, the Mongols, or Turks, or even if Gog and Magog were actual individuals or peoples. That is not what these stories are about essentially. What the prophets Ezekiel and Daniel and the seer John and also the Qur'an want to do is not so much to interpret what is happening or to predict what will happen — murder and death, people and peoples that want to kill one another. That is just life, and anyone can write such a tale. What the prophet or apocalyptic seer wants to say, just like what the seer John dreamed, is to give insight into the heart of history, what it is all about in the end, what the final meaning of the events is. The Bible and the Qur'an are concerned with revelation, apocalypse, the unmasking of history. These stories can also be understood in this way in our time, as clarification, as an unmasking of our contemporary history. By "the land of Magog" one should not think so much of territorial areas as of areas of life where the devil, the preeminent enemy of humankind, still vehemently resists because those areas are his last hope. It is precisely that area of life in which all peoples today, perhaps more than ever before, seem to have found one another: world trade and world power. In the Bible Moloch and Mammon are used to refer to those aspects of life. They are the Gog and Magog of our time: the personification of ava-

---

42. Maulana Muhammad Ali, *The Holy Qur'ân* (Dublin, OH: Ahmadiyya Anjuman Isha'at Islam Lahore, 2002) 649-50, 652 on Q 18:98.

rice. Jesus said: "No one can serve two masters. . . . You cannot serve both God and money" (Matt 6:24; Luke 16:9-13). The word "Mammon" derives from Aramaic *mamon;* it refers to that in which one places one's trust, one's faith. Mammon represents money, the money bag. Money is the antidivine power. Mammon is the personification of avarice: "For where your treasure is, there your heart will be also" (Luke 12:34).

In today's terminology, Moloch is "the military industrial complex"[43] in service to the destruction of the children of mankind. To be able to destroy, Moloch needs Mammon, money. To the first area of life, Moloch, belong the tales of the unjust kings, like Nimrod and Pharaoh, as well as the prophetic tales of the unjust kings of the kingdoms of Judah and Israel, or the caliphs who are not rightly guided. With Mammon, as well as with Baal as the god of possessing, of having, it has to do with the evil power of money, as is apparent in the story of Korah/Qârûn. The Qur'an poses the rhetorical question to Korah: Does he not know that, before him, God destroyed generations that were more powerful and had more wealth than he (Q 28:78)? Moloch stands for power; Mammon for money. Both Moloch and Mammon are served by the false prophet, the deceitful prophet, the media propaganda, as it is called today.

What, according to the prophet Ezekiel and the seer John (Revelation 20) and the Qur'an, is the real threat by Gog and Magog? They are a threat for believers who are called by God, the *qahal,* the *ecclesia,* the community, the *umma* — all who build and keep the earth, those who observe the Torah, who are true representatives of God on earth, caliphs, and who do not bring destruction and shed blood on earth. The continued existence of the earth is at stake. The powers surround the camp of the saints, the beloved city, Jerusalem, Medina, the city that is a symbol of the city of justice and light, as the center of the earth where God's people live in peace.

The true community is threatened and hated because they, the saints and the martyrs, do not believe in Mammon and Moloch and oppose them intensely. The "Mammon service" does not want to be bothered by anyone, especially by the true community of God. The seer sees it all happen, that final and decisive struggle of the community, those who follow the prophets, those who do not bow the knee to Baal (1 Kgs 19:18). He sees that the worldly powers are finished. The optimism of the victory is grounded in the witness

43. This is the term the American president Dwight Eisenhower used to refer to the system behind the military of the United States in his farewell address on 17 January 1961. But it can certainly apply to any country with a similarly developed infrastructure.

of the saints who do not bear the mark of the beast and the false prophet. It goes contrary to all doom-mongering, against all the "cads and the crooks" of the world powers of today. It comes, it will happen, says the Lord! Then the inhabitants of the land or the earth will come from their cities. They belong to the community, inhabitants of the actual "Jerusalem," the true "Medina," to make firewood of the weapons. The prophet reports humorously that they will burn those weapons: bows, arrows, clubs, and spears. They can feed their fires for seven years with that wood. They do not have to gather wood from the field or cut wood in the forest. For all that time they can fuel their fires with those weapons. Thus, they plunder those who plundered them and loot those who looted them, says the Lord (Ezek 39:9-10). The seer John sees it as already happening. Satan cannot and will not succeed in the end. The evil power will be consumed by fire and thrown into the lake of fire, in which the beast and the false prophet belong as well: into the oven of fire that glows with sulfur. They are finished. The curtain has fallen. The battle has been fought. Now something new will really begin. The community, the *ecclesia,* the *umma* can and may trust in God, who calls out from "Jerusalem," "Zion," "Medina," "Mecca," from where justice goes out:

> Armed violence bows before God.
> You who snuff out the lightning of war
> and want war no longer. . . .
>
> Those who were equipped for war,
> Unaware of your power,
> You disturbed them in their dreams,
> The proud of heart you discourage,
> Throw in the sea with horse and chariot.
>
> The time will come when every head,
> All who live on earth will praise him,
> And even those who now fight him
> Will tremble before your greatness.
> You will check the angry,
> Yes, all will come to you.[44]

---

44. Translation of a versified version of Psalm 76 in Naastepad, *Geen vrede met het bestaande,* 217-23, 255.

CHAPTER X

How Is the Victory over the Cities Viewed?

It spreads like fire, injustice, it scorches the cities black.
But you live in cooled gardens, with blind walls around
    your heart.
You teach the strong to stalk the weak, you teach them
    to behave unjustly,
like a race apart.

Huub Oosterhuis, "Er schreeuwt een mens, onrecht"
("A Man Cries: Injustice!")

Introduction

In this chapter we will look at a number of striking examples of how the question "To whom does the victory belong?" was answered in the past: the conquests or victory over cities by one party or another, in particular the Christians and the Muslims.

    The chapter concerns the Christian tales about the conquest of Rome by Emperor Constantine the Great in A.D. 312 and the occupation of that city in 410 by the Germanic leader Alaric I and the way in which the church father Augustine (d. 430) responded in his famous "tale of two cities," *De Civitate Dei (The City of God):* the city of God and the city of man. In that work Augustine also provides important insights into the previous "tale of two cities": Rome and Carthage. At the time of Muhammad there is also a "tale of two cities," Byzantium and Ctesiphon. How did Muslims view the conquest of Jerusalem in 638 and talk about the occupation of the most powerful Christian city, Constantinople? What expectations were there when the Muslim conquest had not yet occurred, and what was the attitude when the Turks did succeed in capturing the city in 1453? To whom does the victory belong?

Constantine the Great: "In This Sign You Will Conquer"

Constantine the Great (ca. A.D. 285-337) was the first Roman emperor to convert to Christianity. In 312 he engaged his predecessor, the Emperor Maxentius (ca. 278-312), in battle, defeating him after a long civil war at the Milvian Bridge. Maxentius's army was put to rout, and Maxentius himself, in the confusion that arose, fell into the river Tiber and drowned. Although Constantine was not baptized until he was on his deathbed, his conversion was certainly motivated by political factors. He wanted to put an end to the conflict between the Christian church, which was slowly gaining influence, and the Roman state. Without persecuting pagans, he openly favored the church. In 313 Constantine, together with his fellow emperor Licinius (ca. 265-325), issued the Edict of Milan, whereby Roman citizens were given the freedom to choose their own religion. This edict put an end to the persecution of Christians and gave them freedom of religion. How is the conquest of Rome now viewed and explained? Constantine is said to have seen, prior to the battle, a cross in the sky and the Latin words *In hoc signo vinces* ("In this sign you will conquer").

The church father Eusebius (ca. A.D. 263–ca. 339), bishop of Caesarea, the Roman capital of Palestine, was Constantine's advisor. He later wrote a biography of the latter's life. Eusebius suggests that Constantine entered Rome after the battle in 312 as a Christian emperor. His report speaks of the formation of the *labarum* or monogram of Christ, usually formed by the Greek letters *chi* and *rho,* the first two letters of the name *Christos.* The redacted version of Constantine's vision views it as a parallel to Moses' vision at the burning bush (Exodus 3). Constantine's upbringing in the palace is compared to that of Moses in Pharaoh's court, and he was destined just like Moses to free his people. Eusebius portrays Maxentius as a tyrant who oppressed the people of Rome. He drowns in the Tiber, just as Pharaoh drowns in the Red Sea (Exod 15:4). For Constantine, Christianity is the religion of victory. That was demonstrated at the Milvian Bridge, but it became clear to him only twelve years later. On 18 September 324 another battle took place at Chrysopolis near Chalcedon, an ancient Greek port in Anatolia across from what is now Istanbul, between two emperors: Constantine and Licinius, a battle that Constantine also won. While Eusebius recognizes the importance of this ultimate victory, he shows little interest in how Constantine defeated Licinius. In his *Life of Constantine* the whole campaign is presented purely as a counterpart to the victory at Milvian Bridge. Instead of Maxentius, Licinius is now presented as a "hater of God" and of course as a tyrant. To mark the victory, Constantine founded his own "victory city" *(nikopolis)* that was named after him: Constantinople (although it is disputed whether he himself did the naming). The city became his residence from 11 May 330 until his death in 337. According to legend, Constantine first considered making Troy, which was Rome's antecedent, his new capital. However, Byzantium was chosen because of its proximity to the battlefield of Chrysopolis. An ancient Greek city founded in the seventh century B.C., it had been named after its king, Byzas (Byzantos in the genitive).[1] Byzantium was a brilliant choice, the point where Europe and Asia meet, representing a challenge for the Old Roman world in the west and a stronghold against threats to Roman authority from the east, barbarians or otherwise.[2] Regarded as a lasting testimony to Constantine's most recent and magnificent victory, it was linked to other "victory cities" *(nikopoleis)* founded by his predecessors. Constantinople was compared to Rome and was regarded as the "New Rome."[3] Constantine attempted to make this city a Christian capital, the center of a more Christian empire. By putting it on the same level as Rome, he prescribed by law that this city would be called "the second Rome," *altera Roma.* It is also known as the second Jerusalem.[4]

Among Constantine's most splendid buildings is his own mausoleum in Constantinople, which he dedicated to the holy apostles. His primary concern here was to assure that his remains would rest next to those of the apostles of Christ that he had brought to this city for that purpose.[5]

---

1. Paul Cartledge, *Ancient Greece: A History in Eleven Cities* (Oxford: Oxford University Press, 2009) 167-76.

2. Cartledge, *Ancient Greece,* 186.

3. Paul Stephenson, *Constantine: Unconquered Emperor, Christian Victor* (London: Quercus, 2009) 209-10, 182, 9.

4. Martin Goodman, *Rome and Jerusalem: The Clash of Ancient Civilizations* (New York: Viking, 2008) 554, 556.

5. Stephenson, *Constantine,* 203.

Constantine and Jerusalem

Constantine wanted to promote visits to holy places. He thus made the region around Jerusalem a Christian holy land. Until that time Jerusalem had been an insignificant city. The destruction of Jerusalem was accomplished by the Roman emperor Hadrian (reigned A.D. 117 to 138), who built a new city on top of it in 131 and named it after himself, Colonia Aelia Capitolina. The first part, Aelia, comes from the family name of Emperor Hadrian; the second refers to Jupiter Capitolinus. Jews were forbidden to enter the city. The temple square became an insignificant ruin, and only a small number of Christians lived there. The bishop of Jerusalem, however, directed Constantine's attention to the city during the first ecumenical council of Nicea in 325, and he returned home with a plan to build a church. Under the Capitolinian sanctuary of Jupiter in Jerusalem, built by Hadrian, were found the exact place of Christ's crucifixion and the tomb in which Jesus was laid.[6]

Constantine had ordered the excavation and exhibition of the place where Jesus was killed and buried, which was outside the city walls during King Herod's time but had become included within the limits of the Roman city. Not only was the place found, but during the excavations even the three crosses were discovered. It was determined in miraculous fashion that one of them had been the cross of Christ.[7]

In 325, in honor of the newly discovered grave of Jesus and Golgotha, Constantine ordered a new basilica to be built. The populace, primarily pagans and Jewish Christians, saw this as an imposition by Byzantine Christians, Christians who were connected with the imperial Melkite church, and therefore they did not support the project.

Eusebius describes the building of the Church of the Holy Sepulchre. Through Constantine's wealth and piety, under imperial patronage, Jerusalem became an important religious center, a magnet for pilgrims, but emphatically not intended for the Jews, whose temple it was claimed had been destroyed because of the murder of the Lord Jesus. After his plans had been implemented, however, Constantine himself never visited the holy land. His mother-in-law, Eutropia, and his mother, Helena, did go there. Accord-

6. Diarmaid MacCulloch, *Christianity: The First Three Thousand Years* (New York: Viking, 2010) 193-94.

7. Frank E. Peters, *Islam: A Guide for Jews and Christians* (Princeton: Princeton University Press, 2003).

ing to tradition that arose in the latter part of the fourth century, that was when the wood of the original, "true" cross was found. Eusebius apparently did not yet know the story, which had to have arisen after Constantine's time as a pious imagination.[8] Relics of the cross were distributed quickly and widely after this discovery. They were kept and venerated in special holders, *staurotheke*.[9]

The Fall of Rome in 410 and Augustine's
Tale of the City of God and the City of Man

On 24 (or 14) August 410 at midnight, Gothic hordes under the command of Alaric (ca. 370-410), king of the Visigoths, invaded the city of Rome and plundered it for three days. The fall of this imperial city occurred 1163 years after it had been founded, having made subjects of such a large part of humankind and bringing "civilization." The city was handed over to the wild rage of tribes from Germany and Scythia. Rome had fallen! For people in that time it was as if the end time had come. "The most radiant light on the whole earth was extinguished," wrote the church father Jerome, translator of the Bible into Latin, the Vulgate. He heard the news in Bethlehem: "When the Roman empire was decapitated, and, to speak more correctly, the whole world perished in one city, I became dumb and humbled myself, and kept silence from good words, but my grief broke out afresh, my heart glowed within me. I felt pain. Who could believe that Rome, built by the conquest of the entire world, had suddenly collapsed, that the mother of the nations had also become their tomb?"[10]

Augustine wanted to contradict the Roman pagans who suspected that the old gods, who had become angry, were behind the barbarian attacks because they had been abandoned by the Romans who had become Christians. He responded by saying that the Romans suffered such disasters long before the coming of Christianity. According to Augustine, it was paganism and its vices that led to the collapse of the Roman Empire. Alaric had shown respect for the treasures of the church and persons, saying that he was at war with

8. Goodman, *Rome and Jerusalem*, 560, 564-66; Stephenson, *Constantine*, 201.

9. Yuri Piatnitsky, et al. *Pilgrim Treasures from the Hermitage: Byzantium, Jerusalem* (Amsterdam: Humphries, 2005) 37-40.

10. *Commentary on Ezekiel*, Preface to Book I, trans. W. H. Fremantle. *The Nicene and Post-Nicene Fathers*, 1st ser., vol. 2, ed. Philip Schaff (repr. Grand Rapids: Eerdmans, 1983) 499.

the Romans and not with the apostles, and because of the Christians, Rome, unlike Sodom, was not completely destroyed.[11]

Virgil had predicted in the *Aeneid* that the Romans would rule forever. The city was called the Eternal City. Some church fathers saw the hand of Providence in the rise of the Roman Empire. Caesar Augustus (27 B.C.–A.D. 14) and Jesus were contemporaries, and the Roman Empire seemed in the meantime to have become the bulwark of the Christian faith. The church father Tertullian (160-230), born in Carthage as the son of a Roman officer, justified Christian prayers for the health of the Roman emperors. But for the "pagan" party in Rome, it was precisely the Christians who were the cause of the fall of Rome.

The occasion that led Augustine (d. 430) to write *De Civitate Dei* was this plunder of Rome in 410 by the Christian Alaric and the reaction of the Romans to this event. Alaric adhered to Arianism, a Christian teaching considered to be heretical. The fall of the city made an immense impression on the peoples of the Roman Empire; it could be compared with the shock caused by the destruction of Jerusalem by the Romans in A.D. 70 and of Constantinople in the fifteenth century by the Turkish Muslims. The Romans claimed after the plunder of the city that the gods had turned away from Rome because the atheists who called themselves Christians had invaded the city and suppressed or disposed of the worship of the heathen gods.

Augustine, a Roman citizen who lived and worked in Hippo in northern Africa, modern Tunisia, and who grew up with the works of Virgil and Cicero, was not insensitive to the grandeur and excellence of Rome. That was his principal motive for writing his "tale of two cities": the city of God and the city of man. Augustine divided human reality into two: Babylon, the city of man that necessarily ended in ruin and death, and the new Jerusalem, the city of God, "that would remain forever beyond all dispute, all quarrel, and strife." Augustine worked on this book for thirteen years (413-26) and created a new genre of apologetics for the new religion.

Augustine's "Tale of Two Cities"

Augustine desired to write a discourse on the origins, further development, and final end of the two cities, the earthly and the heavenly, that exist tempo-

---

11. For the summary, see Daniel J. Boorstin, *The Creators: A History of Heroes of the Imagination* (New York: Random House, 1992) 59-60.

rally in mutual entanglement and commingling with this world.[12] The actual struggle in history, which is universal because it is guided toward a unique goal, is that between the city of God *(civitas Dei)* and the earthly city *(civitas terrena)*. These kingdoms are not identical to the visible church and the state, but to two mystical communities that have arisen through opposing forms of human existence. The earthly city began on earth with the fratricide Cain and the city of God with Abel. Cain is the citizen of this age, who through his crime becomes the founder of earthly kingdoms. Abel is the stranger in this age, on a pilgrimage to a supermundane goal. The spiritual descendents of Abel do live in this age in the kingdom of Cain, but are not the founders and citizens of that kingdom. That is why the history of the city of God cannot be coordinated with the city of mankind: the only truly salvific event and the historical course of the city of God are made up of a pilgrimage. The progress is nothing other than a tireless pilgrimage to the final, ideal goal. As a citizenship of pilgrimage, the church is connected with the events of the world, insofar as it promotes the lofty goal of building the house of God. Judged by its own norms, the earthly city allows itself to be led, however, by considerations of usefulness, comfort, and ambition, whereas the city of God in contrast is led by sacrifice, obedience, and humility. The former considerations are vanity, the latter truth. The earthly city exists through natural generation, the city of God through supernatural rebirth. The one is inspired by love for God to the denial of oneself, and the other is inspired by self-love, which leads to the contempt of God.[13]

Rome and Carthage: A "Tale of Two Cities"

It is fascinating to note how Augustine also refers to an earlier "tale of two cities": Rome and Carthage. In his first book of *The City of God*, Augustine takes up the notorious war fought between these two cities. He writes that Scipio Nascia, consul in 162 and 155 B.C., who, according to the whole senate, was judged to be the best citizen in the Roman Empire, did not want Carthage, the former rival of the Roman Empire, to be destroyed. In this important respect Nascia opposed Cato (234-149), Roman soldier, statesman,

---

12. Augustine, *The City of God*, XI, 1, trans. Marcus Dods. *The Nicene and Post-Nicene Fathers*, 1st ser., vol. 2, ed. Philip Schaff (repr. Grand Rapids: Eerdmans, 1983) 205.

13. Karl Löwith, *Wereldgeschiedenis: Wijsgerig en Bijbels gezien* (Utrecht: Aula, 1960) 150-5; *Meaning in History: The Theological Implications of the Philosophy of History* (Chicago: University of Chicago Press, 1957).

and writer. Cato did, after all, end each speech with the words *"Ceterum censeo Carthaginem esse delendam"* ("I am convinced, for that matter, that Carthage must be destroyed"), a saying that every student of Latin learns in order to understand and remember the use of a particular grammatical construction, the Latin gerundive. Cato and other leading senators ask that an army be sent immediately to North Africa, but Nascia holds firm in his view that Carthage did not provide any reason for war.[14]

Between the Second and the Third Punic Wars, Cato insisted again on the destruction of Carthage, which was constantly growing stronger. Nascia feared the feeling of security to be an enemy of weak emotions. According to him, fear was the proper guardian for his immature fellow citizens. According to Augustine, he was not wrong: the facts proved him sufficiently right. When the Roman community was definitively liberated from its greatest fear through the destruction of Carthage in 146 B.C., prosperity immediately caused some disasters. Concord was affected, and fierce and bloody riots and civil wars broke out, in which much was destroyed and much blood shed: "such lawless and cruel proscription and plunder, that those Romans who, in the days of their virtue, had expected injury only at the hands of their enemies, now that that virtue was lost, suffered greater cruelties at the hands of their fellow-citizens."[15] The thirst for power in the proud hearts of a few dominant men was never satisfied until they had attained, by continually extending the term of office, the power of a king. The people were avaricious and eager for the abundance against which the great Scipio Nascia wanted to protect them through his farsighted wisdom when he opposed wiping out the greatest, most powerful, and richest enemy city. Nascia was squarely opposed to Cato's urging to destroy Carthage because he thought that the existence of Carthage was itself a stimulus for Rome.[16] He wanted the Romans' search for pleasure to remain tempered by fear, so that that limitation of the search for pleasure would fend off excess and that, through the bridling of excess, avarice would also be destroyed. Sallust (86-35 B.C.), a Roman historian whom Augustine cites, wrote:

> Yet, after the destruction of Carthage, discord, avarice, ambition, and the other vices, which are more commonly generated by prosperity, more than ever increased.[17]

14. Brian Caven, *The Punic Wars* (New York: St. Martin's, 1980) 268.

15. Augustine, *The City of God*, I, XXX, p. 20.

16. *Grote Winkler Prins: Encyclopedie in 25 delen*, ed. R. C. van Caenegen et al. (8th ed.; Amsterdam, 1979), *s.v.* "Scipio."

17. Augustine, *The City of God*, II, 18, pp. 32-33.

Byzantium, Rûm, and Ctesiphon

A "tale of two cities" can also be told for the time of the prophet Muhammad, the beginning of the seventh century. Two great world powers were engaged in a long-standing conflict: the Eastern Romans or Byzantines, on the one hand, and the Persians during the Sassanid dynasty, on the other. The name that the Qur'an uses for Byzantium is Rûm, which refers to Rome. Constantinople, Byzantium, now Istanbul, is the "second Rome."

In A.D. 602 the Byzantine emperor Flavius Mauricius Tiberius (582-602) was deposed by Phocas (emperor from 602-10), who initiated a reign of terror. Chosroes II Parwîz of Persia (591-628) declared war on Phocas, and the Byzantine defenses collapsed. The widely-hated Phocas was himself deposed in 610 by Heraclius (610-641) and put to death in horrible fashion. Heraclius was declared emperor. In the following decade the Persians conquered Byzantine Syria, Palestine, and Egypt, as well as Anatolia. Finally, Constantinople itself was attacked. Already in 613 the Persian army had set up camp on the other side of the Bosporus with Constantinople in view. But the greatest crisis for the Byzantines came in 626 when the Persians, along with the nomadic Avars and the Slavs, who attacked from the north, besieged the city. In the absence of Heraclius, who was away on campaign, the Orthodox patriarch called upon the populace to carry icons, and a woman, identified as the Virgin Mary, was seen at the head of the defenders. This was an important stimulus for the already vibrant cult of Mary in the Eastern church.[18] In 614 the Byzantines had suffered a severe blow through the occupation of Jerusalem and the relic of the true cross being removed from the Church of the Holy Sepulchre, the Church of the Resurrection *(Qanîsat al-Qiyâma)*.

All this took place while Muhammad was active in Mecca as a prophet. The Qur'an predicted, precisely when the Byzantines lost Jerusalem, that the Persians themselves would be defeated in a few years. The text mentions the land that was closest, probably an allusion to Palestine, which could point to the fact that these verses were revealed not long after the Persian conquest of Jerusalem in 614. "On that day when the Byzantines will be victorious, the believers will rejoice over the victory of God" (Q 30:4-5). The term "believers" undoubtedly refers to the Muslims. What emerges from this is that the believing Muslims shared in the loss that the Byzantines suffered, and one can detect a confidence that ultimately the Byzantines would triumph. It is

---

18. MacCulloch, *Christianity,* 435.

clear that at that time the Muslims had sympathy for the Christian Byzantines.

In 622, however, Heraclius began a counteroffensive against the Persians. He conducted a series of campaigns and managed to retake Armenia, Syria, Palestine, and Egypt from the Persian ruler and carried out forays in the rich domains around the Persian capital, Ctesiphon. The tide turned after another series of campaigns, in which the Persians were decisively defeated at Nineveh in 627.[19] The Persian armies withdrew in 629, and in 630 Heraclius personally brought the relic of the true cross back to Jerusalem in a formal celebration.

However, very quickly afterwards, from around 629/630, the Byzantines became the target of Muslim attacks that led to a great deal of hostility for the next seven centuries.

What was the reason of this change in attitude on the part of the Muslims with respect to the Byzantines during Muhammad's lifetime? Initially, the expectation was that the defeated Byzantines would be victorious in the future (Q 30:3), and Christians were seen as those who are nearest to the Muslims in love (Q 5:82). That changed later. The first military clashes between the Muslims and Byzantines occurred in the northwest of the Arabian Peninsula on the Palestinian border at the Battle of Mut'a in August 629.[20]

That change regarding the Byzantine Christians is thought to be connected to the triumphal return of the true cross by the Byzantine emperor Heraclius and the equating of Christians with polytheists, worshippers of several gods, whereas they had previously been seen as monotheists. It is important to note that Heraclius used a great many treasures of the churches in Mesopotamia and Syria to finance his war efforts. The war of the Byzantines and Sassanids, which was political in nature, also had a religious side. Heraclius gathered the troops to save the "Christian empire" and to return the true cross to Jerusalem, "perhaps the first example of a religiously justified imperial war."[21]

During his visit to Jerusalem to return the true cross, Heraclius carried it himself along the Via Dolorosa. The Battle of Mut'a can be seen as a response to the return of the true cross.[22] This return was triumphantly re-

19. *EQ*, *s.v.* "Byzantines."

20. Cf. Chapter IX.

21. Fred M. Donner, *Muhammad and the Believers: At the Origins of Islam* (Cambridge, MA: Belknap, Harvard University Press, 2010) 24.

22. David Cook, "Why Did Muhammad Attack the Byzantines?" in *Political Islam from Muhammad to Ahmadinejad: Defenders, Detractors, Definitions,* ed. Joseph Morrison Skelly (Santa Barbara: Praeger Security, 2010) 27-28.

ported by later Christian authors who lived under Muslim dominion, and they must have known how offensive that veneration of the cross would have been to Muslims. It can be documented that hostile relations developed very early on the part of Muslims in Syria and Egypt with respect to the symbol of the cross.

When the Qur'an speaks of Christians as those who are nearest in love to the believing Muslims, it is explained that there were priests and monks among them and they were not proud (Q 5:82), referring to an instance when a group of Christians were in the company of Muslims who were returning from Egypt around 628. The primary contacts Muhammad had with Christians in the Arabian Peninsula were not those connected with Byzantium but the Syrian Orthodox Christians and the Nestorian or Assyrian Christians. The spirituality of the latter was far removed from the triumphalistic pomp that characterized the entry of Heraclius into Jerusalem, where it was reported that "everyone worshipped the true cross." The cult of the cross, promoted by the Byzantine imperial church, had to appear strange to the Muslims, and to them it looked like polytheism.[23]

Heraclius, one of the greatest but also one of the most maligned Byzantine heroes, began an imperial dynasty in 610 that would last for the whole of the following seven centuries. But he was so busy fending off enemies in the east and west that he missed the opportunity to see the importance of the forays by the Muslim Arabs in the south. After the defeat of the Byzantine army in 636, the southern provinces, including Jerusalem, were quickly lost to the Muslims.[24]

The message of the Qur'an about the initial loss of the Byzantines and their later conquest fits explicitly these words: "It is God who decides, as it was in the past, so it shall be in the future. On that day the believers, ultimately all believers, will rejoice in God's victory, for he gives the victory to whomever he wills. He is mighty and merciful" (Q 30:4-5).

The Muslim Conquest of the City of Jerusalem

Shortly after Muhammad's death, the Arab Muslims conquered the areas that the Byzantines had taken not long before from the Persians and about

---

23. Cook, "Why Did Muhammad Attack the Byzantines?" 30-32; Robert G. Hoyland, *Seeing Islam as Others Saw It: A Survey and Evaluation of Christian, Jewish, and Zoroastrian Writings on Early Islam* (Princeton: Darwin, 1997) 549, 596-97.

24. MacCulloch, *Christianity*, 435.

which the Qur'an had rejoiced would happen (Q 30:1-4). After the prophet's death, they quickly took the place of the Persians by capturing Syria, Palestine, and Egypt from Byzantium. Particularly important was their capture of Jerusalem.

The Umayyad caliph 'Abd al-Malik (d. A.D. 705) ordered construction of the Dome of the Rock/*Qubbat as-Sahrah* in Jerusalem, a project that began in 685 and was completed in 691. The prophet Muhammad was said to have set his foot on that rock before his journey to heaven, the Mi'râj. Plans for the building had already existed at the time of Mu'âwiyya, the first caliph of the Umayyad dynasty. It is almost certain that the builders and designers were Christians from Syria and Palestine. The lack of depiction of any human figures points to a deliberate assent to Islamic principles. Apart from commemoration of Muhammad's night journey (Isrâ') and heavenly journey (Mi'râj), the building's original purpose could also be connected with the intention of presenting the new faith in the city of Judaism and Christianity. By choosing this place, Islam manifested itself as the heir of both, a triumphal declaration of the superiority of Islam over Judaism and Christianity.[25]

The Dome of the Rock was clearly intended to rival the Church of the Holy Sepulchre and to surpass it in beauty. In that respect it was to be a celebration of the triumph of Islam over Christianity. The Dome of the Rock thus played a role in the symbolic appropriation of the land by Islam. Its inscriptions betray this intention of bringing a clear Islamic message to Christians. As in many mosques, this text is inscribed there: "He has not begotten, nor was he begotten" (Q 112:3). Although this passage was originally directed against Arabic paganism, against the notion that God could have children, especially daughters, it was also thought to express the denial that God could have a son, more specifically, that Jesus was the son of God. It stressed that Jesus was a prophet and denied that he was son of God (Q 2:116; 19:35). The phrase "God has no partner" is repeated five times inside the Dome of the Rock. The following prayer is also repeated: "Pray for your prophet and servant *('abd')*," which is explained as indicating that Jesus is not a son of God. These texts emphasize that there is one God. For that matter, the Bible and the Qur'an confess the oneness of God and see Jesus as a prophet. 'Abd al-Malik (ruled A.D. 685-705) attempted to make Jerusalem a center of the Muslim cultus, declaring that one could make the pilgrimage (Hajj), one of

25. Carole Hillenbrand, "Some Medieval Muslim Views of Constantinople," in *World Christianity in Muslim Encounter,* ed. Stephen R. Goodwin (London: Continuum, 2009) 2:71-83.

the five obligations of every Muslim, to Mecca or to Jerusalem. One of the rites involved here, the circumambulation *(tawâf)* around the Ka'ba, the "house of God," in Mecca, could be replaced by circumambulation of the Dome of the Rock. However, this was disputed.[26]

Constantinople and Islam

The conquest of Constantinople or Byzantium was indeed at the top of the agenda for Muslims. It is hardly surprising that the Umayyads wanted to include Constantinople among their possessions, the great city, the symbol of Christianity and of the Christian imperial tradition.[27] Byzantium had been the center of a world culture and a bridge between East and West for twelve hundred years.

The means initially chosen for achieving the conquest was an invasian by sea. At various times fleets were sent out to set up a blockade against Constantinople in preparation for an attack. It is quite probable that the early caliphs, in particular the Umayyads after the ascension of Mu'âwiyya in A.D. 661, saw their empire as the natural successor of Byzantium. Their coins and their administrative system and state symbols resembled those of the Byzantines. Nevertheless, relations between them and the Byzantines were not always hostile.

The first Umayyad caliph, Mu'âwiyya, was at conflict with the Byzantines. Twice he even threatened to recite the confession of faith "There is no god but God" *(shahâda)* and "God is great" *(takbîr)* until the walls of Constantinople collapsed, like those of Jericho (Joshua 6).[28] There were two specific attacks on Constantinople. A companion of the prophet Muhammad, Abu Ayyûb al-Ansâri, took part in the siege led by Yazîd ibn Mu'âwiyya; he died there of dysentery and was buried at his own request under the walls of Constantinople.

Al-Walid I ibn 'Abd al Malik (A.D. 668-715), who ruled from 705 to 715, conquered al-Andalus, as well as other places. He renovated the mosque of the prophet Muhammad in Medina and built the great mosque of Damascus

---

26. D. S. Attema, *De Mohammedaansche opvattingen omtrent het tijdstip van den jongsten dag en zijn voortekenen* (Amsterdam: Noord-Hollandsche Maatschappij, 1942) 90; *The Umayyads: The Rise of Islamic Art* (Amman: Arab Institute for Research and Publishing, 2000) 44-45.

27. Hillenbrand, "Some Medieval Muslim Views of Constantinople," 73.

28. Attema, *De Mohammedaansche opvattingen*, 88, 92.

on the place where stood the Basilica of John the Baptist/Yahyâ, whose head has been preserved there up to the present time. He also built various desert castles, one of which is the bathhouse Qusayr ʿAmra, 80 kilometers from Amman, the capital of Jordan. As illustration that relations with the Byzantines were not always hostile, when Caliph Walid decided to replace the mosque of Muhammad in Medina (707-9), the Byzantine emperor sent men, money, and materials to help rebuild it. Greek and Coptic architects built the mosque out of stone, with marble and mosaics. The Dome of the Rock in Jerusalem and the Umayyad mosque reflect something of a cultural fusion between Byzantium and Islam in the arts. The frescoes in Qusayr ʿAmra testify to that. There is a painting of six kings: the Umayyad ruler surrounded by other rulers identified as the Byzantine, Persian, and Chinese emperors, the Visigothic king of Spain, the ruler of Abyssinia, and a Hindu or Turkish ruler. The painting was intended to portray the family of kings of which the Umayyads saw themselves part. Here the caliph accepts the honor paid to him by other important rulers of the world.[29]

Caliph Sulaymân b. ʿAbd al-Malik (ruled A.D. 715-17) sent his brother Masalam on a campaign to Constantinople, because a tradition *(hadith)* of the prophet predicted that the city would be captured by a caliph called Sulaymân. On 25 August 716 Masalam began a siege that would last a year, but he had to withdraw when it became clear that the city would not be taken in a short time.[30] This last siege of Byzantium meant a turning point for both empires. The expectation both in Byzantium and at the Umayyad court was that world history was ending and a new era was beginning. The conquest of Constantinople, which the Muslims hoped for, and the approach of the one hundredth year A.H. (*After Hijra*, the Muslim calendar), gave rise to apocalyptic expectations. Sulaymân was seen as the expected Mahdî, the rightly guided leader who would bring justice back to earth after the period of oppression. His name is associated with a mosque that he allegedly built in Constantinople, although it is more probable that it was actually erected by the Byzantines for the Muslims who lived there as prisoners, exiles, merchants, and travelers. Early historians report that in the time of the pious caliph ʿUmar ibn ʿAbd al Azîz (d. 720), a man once asked a scholar of that time: "Is ʿUmar the Mahdî?" His answer was: "He is a Mahdî but not the Mahdî."[31]

29. *The Umayyads*, 120-21, 123; Attema, *De Mohammedaansche opvattingen*, 90.

30. Hillenbrand, "Some Medieval Muslim Views of Constantinople," 73.

31. Cyril Glassé, *The Concise Encyclopaedia of Islam* (rev. ed.; London: Stacey International, 2001), *s.v.* "al-Mahdî."

The Arabs did call the Greeks or Byzantines the "Yellow Ones" *(Banû 'l Asfâr)*. This was explained as deriving from the name of one of Esau's grandsons, an ancestor of Rûm, which meant "sons of Esau/Edom."[32] The phrase "the kings of the Banû 'l Asfâr" was used to refer to the Christian Byzantine rulers. Yellow is the color of flight and cowardice. The eyes of prejudice, religious differences, propaganda, and lack of first-hand knowledge made the Byzantine rulers seem like tyrants. Both the "house of Islam" *(dâr al-islâm)* and Byzantium felt superior to each other; both believed they possessed the truth. The Abbasid caliphs (A.D. 750-1256) thought it necessary to conduct an annual *jihâd* campaign at the Byzantine border. For several centuries, Byzantium was the primary enemy of the Muslim world and was seen as the "house of war" *(dâr al-harb)*. The long conflict between the house of Islam and the Eastern Christian empire was portrayed in an ode by the famous Arab poet al-Mutanabbî (915-965), in which he celebrates the capture of the Byzantine border post of al-Hadath in 954 by Hamdanid Sayf al-Dawla:

> You were not a relative who drives away an equal
> But monotheism that drives out polytheism.

Constantinople manifested an abundance of imperial power, by which the Muslim rulers could measure their own greatness. Damascus, Baghdad, Cordoba, and Cairo measured their prestige through diplomatic contacts with the kings of western Europe. The failure to take the city had far-reaching consequences. The ambition to conquer Constantinople shifted to a distant messianic future. The decline of the Sassanid Empire and the rapid success of Muslim armies everywhere left the Byzantine Empire as a stubborn enemy that still survived. It had not had this status of enemy during Muhammad's lifetime. "Which of the two of us was created to bring the other to ruin?" The conquest of Constantinople appeared to be a cosmic event in an eschatological tradition.[33]

In later Muslim accounts, which developed around the theme of the last day, omens for the last hour, beginning with the death of Muhammad, were followed by the conquest of Jerusalem and ended with the violent struggle between the Muslims and Byzantines. The sign that preceded the last hour was the conquest of the city of Constantinople.[34]

---

32. Even though Esau/Edom is associated with the color red, the color of the earth.

33. *EQ, s.v.* "Byzantines."

34. Hillenbrand, "Some Medieval Muslim Views of Constantinople," 73-75; Attema, *De Mohammedaansche opvattingen,* 87-89; *EI, s.v.* "Asfâr"; "al-Sa'a, Sulaymân b. 'Abd al- Malik."

The Conquest of Constantinople

On 29 May 1453, the Ottoman Turkish sultan Mehmed II (1451-81) finally succeeded in conquering Constantinople. Accordingly, Mehmed was given the nickname *al-Fâtih* ("the Conquerer"). This fulfilled the Muslims' long-cherished objective, one that had existed for seven centuries. Something had occurred that no Muslim conqueror had ever before managed to achieve.

Mehmed II saw himself as the successor of the Arab caliphs and the Byzantine emperors. He called himself emperor and laid claim, as the holder of the imperial city, to all areas of the Byzantine Empire: the Balkans, the southern coast of the Crimea, and Italy. He claimed that Byzantium held supremacy above Rome. Immediately after the conquest, Mehmed appropriated the famous Aya Sophia church, which still dominates the cityscape of Istanbul, to have it turned into a mosque, and the first call to prayer was soon heard. The Christian emperor Justinian I (482-565) had started building the Aya Sophia in 532 and completed it five years later. For centuries, this was the largest of all Christian churches. Justinian himself was so impressed by his own creation that he is said to have stated at the church's dedication on 26 December 537: "Praised be God who chose me to carry out such a work. O Solomon, I have surpassed you" (cf. 1 Kings 8). The costs of the building were very high because of his attempts to restore the final glory of Rome through conquest and building. Because of that, however, he left behind an impoverished and vengeful population, an empty treasury, and weakened armies.[35]

The work to turn the Aya Sophia into a mosque began almost immediately. A high minaret for the call to prayer was quickly raised, and the figurative mosaics were whitewashed, except for the four guardian angels under the dome, which Mehmed considered to be the spirits of the place. On 2 June 1453, the Friday prayers were heard for the first time in what is now called the Aya Sophia mosque, and the Islamic invocation was read in the name of Sultan Mehmed Khan Ghâzi. Mehmed the Conqueror added several minarets to the Aya Sophia. Regarding his claim to the caliphate, in addition to the name of God (Allah), plates in the Aya Sophia name the first caliphs, Abû Bakr, 'Umar, 'Uthmân, 'Alî, and both of 'Alî's sons, Hassan and Husayn, the second and third imams, the grandchildren of the prophet Muhammad. The practice of depicting names was also taken over in other mosques in Turkey.

35. Donner, *Muhammad and the Believers*, 7.

Mehmed collected money for the building of mosques, including the Fâtih Mosque in Constantinople, on the site of the Church of the Holy Apostles *(Hagion Apostolon)*. This church was the burial place of most of the Byzantine emperors and contained the mausoleum of Constantine. Mehmed removed the tombs of the Christian emperors and demolished the building, its ruins serving as a quarry for building materials for the new mosque. The Fâtih Mosque, the "mosque of the conqueror," now became the mausoleum for the new rulers of the Ottoman Turks. The Church of Holy Wisdom (Aya Sophia) inspired the construction of the Fâtih Mosque, which became an important symbol of the transition. Nevertheless, the new mosque with its dome still suggests a building that was clearly Christian. If one approaches Istanbul by sea, the Sultan Ahmed Camii appears, known as the Blue Mosque because of the color of its tiles, as a rival of the Aya Sophia, built a thousand years earlier. But because the Blue Mosque is situated somewhat lower on the hill, it is overshadowed by its great prototype.[36]

Mehmed's conquests realized the imperial ambitions of the Byzantine Empire and the Muslim *jihâd*. Mehmed gave a new name to the city: Islambol, a play on its Turkish name, "people of Islam," but the name did not strike the Turkish ear. The tomb of Ayyûb, Muhammad's standard-bearer who died in 669 and whose death had been a powerful motive for the holy war against the city, was discovered shortly after.

The fall of Constantinople caused an enormous reaction in Europe. Mehmed was portrayed as the beast of the Apocalypse that rose out of the sea (Rev 13:1). The report of the fall of the city was heard not only in palaces and castles but also at intersections, markets, and in inns. It reached the farthest corners of Europe and the most humble people. In the Lutheran prayerbook in Iceland God is asked to save the people from the wiles of the pope and the terror of the Turk.[37]

A Century after the Conquest of Constantinople

A century after the conquest, one of the most famous Ottoman historians, Sa'd ed-Din, ended his long literary description of the conquest with these words:

---

36. Judith Herrin, *Byzantium: The Surprising Life of a Medieval Empire* (Princeton: Princeton University Press, 2008) 60.

37. Roger Crowley, *Constantinople: The Last Great Siege 1453* (London: Faber and Faber, 2005) 237, 239; Stephenson, *Constantine,* 190.

That wide region, that strong lofty city . . . from being the nest of the owl of error, was turned into the capital of glory and honor. Through the noble efforts of the Muhammedan sultan, for the evil-voiced clash of the bells of the shameless misbelievers was submitted the Muslim call to prayer, the sweet five-times repeated chant of the Faith of glorious rites, and the ears of the people of the Holy War were filled with the melody of the call to prayer. The churches which were within the city were emptied of the vile idols, and cleansed from their filthy and idolatrous impurities; and by the defacement of their images, and the erection of the Islamic prayer niches and pulpits, many monasteries and chapels became the envy of the Gardens of Paradise. The temples of the misbelievers were turned into mosques of the pious, and the rays of the light of Islam drove away the hosts of darkness from that place so long the abode of the despicable infidels, and the streaks of the dawn of the Faith dispelled the lurid blackness of oppression, for the word, irresistible as destiny, of the fortunate sultan became supreme in the governance of this new dominion.[38]

To Whom Is the Victory?

Is claiming victory over and capturing cities what the three Books inspire? Is it a question of victories that belong either to Christians or Muslims? To whom does the victory actually belong? Is there a common message given by the three Books, or do they have different messages? Was Constantine the Great's conquest in the sign of the cross in 324 in line with the Bible, thus allowing him to build Constantinople, his "victory city," later that year? Were both victories Christian victories? According to Eusebius, they were. Did the Umayyads triumph in the spirit of the Qur'an through which the Dome of the Rock could be built in Jerusalem in the seventh century as a symbol of the Muslim victory over the city after the conquest in 638 under the second Caliph 'Umar? Was it God who gave the victory to the Turkish sultan over Constantinople, which was sealed by his taking possession of the largest of all Christian churches, the Church of Holy Wisdom? Could Mehmed II call himself Fâtih according to the Qur'an and build a mosque with that name? Is that *al-Fath* (the "success)" that the Qur'an intends when the conquest of

---

38. Bernard Lewis, *Istanbul and the Civilization of the Ottoman Empire* (Norman: University of Oklahoma Press, 1963) 9.

Mecca takes place? Is that the victory *(nasr)* of God that the Qur'an speaks of (Q 110)? Is that the point of the story of the man with two horns, Alexander the Great, even though it is now Muslims rather than Christians who are the victors?[39]

In the course of history, the texts have usually been read in opposition to each other: in an anti-Jewish or anti-Semitic, anti-Christian or anti-Muslim way. Is that the spirit of the Torah, the Gospel, and the Qur'an? Should the prophets be read and understood in this way? That will the topic of the final chapter.

39. Cf. Chapter IX.

CHAPTER XI

To Whom Does the Victory Belong?

Nevertheless, there was a time when those grand words, God, Heaven, Holy, hallowed life instead of destroyed it, honored the human partner and did not belittle him. And their influence was not negative either at a later period. They gave form and direction to desire; they grounded community. I think it must be possible to reconstruct them in that sense, and, in my view, that is needed as well, for one could perhaps get rid of those grand words but not of the desire that gave them life.

Frans Kellendonk, "Grote Woorden"

Introduction

How does the one tale of the two cities, Jerusalem and Babylon, actually present victory, and what does that say to us today?

I will look at how the prophets Zephaniah and Jeremiah present the "tale of two cities." Zephaniah talks about two cities (Jerusalem and Nineveh), and Jeremiah presents another "tale of two cities" (Jerusalem and Babylon). Then we will see that Muhammad presents yet another "tale of two cities" (Medina and Mecca).

For whom is the city intended?

The Prophet Zephaniah and a "Tale of Two Cities": Jerusalem and Babylon

The prophet Zephaniah came on the scene during the time of King Josiah, between 640 and 620 B.C. He can be seen as the one who prepared the reforms under Josiah. The thread running throughout all his prophecies is the "day of the Lord," "the day of judgment," "the last day," which is near and approaching quickly. God will punish sin, which is essentially viewed, very harshly, as pride. At that time, Judah was strongly under the influence of Assur (2 Kings 21). Zephaniah denounced unbelief most of all, which came to expression in the religious imitation of a foreign power. Josiah strove for a reform whose goal was spiritual and political independence.[1]

The prophets proclaim the day of the Lord on which the Lord will come to judge the nations (Joel 2:11). Nowhere is that day so explicitly announced as by the prophet Joel (Joel 1:15; 2:11, 31; 3:14). That day is directed at all that is arrogant and proud (Isa 2:6-22). God will judge righteously. Every human being who does evil can expect trouble and distress, the Jew in the first place, the Apostle Paul writes, but also the Greek — for God does not show any partiality (Rom 2:5, 9-11). The prophet Muhammad will also later warn explicitly about the day of (the last) judgment. Faith in God and the last day is what characterizes a believer (Q 2:8; cf. 2:662, 127, 228, 264).[2]

Who was Zephaniah? There was something noteworthy about him, for we are told two things. He has a double origin. On the one hand, he has royal blood. He is a descendant of King Hezekiah of Judah, thus also a descendant of King David. Hezekiah was one of the few good kings after David.

But on the other hand, he is also called a son of Cush. Cushites were viewed as nomads who lived near the Arabs (2 Chr 21:16).[3] Cush was called a brother of Egypt and Canaan. He is also said to be the father of Nimrod, an unjust king at the time of Abraham, as we have seen.[4] Nimrod is known to be an extremely violent king. So Cush is connected to two powerful kingdoms: Assyria and Babylon, the two other major threats to Israel throughout its whole existence (Gen 10:8-12). Zephaniah is thus descended from two peoples with whom Israel had a great deal to do throughout its whole history. Both peoples blocked Israel's journey to the promised land and opposed their stay in the land, the new land where justice would reign.

---

1. KBS. *BW, s.v.* "Sefanja, boek van."
2. KBS on Joel 1:15.
3. D. S. Attema, *Arabië en de Bijbel* (The Hague: Van Keulen, 1961) 29.
4. Cf. Chapter III.

The prophet Zephaniah, with his dual background, was therefore a descendant of two different kinds of kings: one good and one bad, a caliph and a king, to use the language of the Qur'an. How do we determine if someone else is good or evil? As soon as a king, a prince, or, in contemporary terms, a government, a president, no longer understands that dominion, kingship, belongs to God alone, the government becomes tyrannical. Then the king (*mèlèk, malik*) becomes a Moloch, someone to whom people, primarily children, are sacrificed.

What was the situation when this prophet appeared? It was the time in which Judah was very much under the sway of Assyria, with Nineveh as its capital. One should note that, at that time, the mention of the name Assyria was enough to send shivers down people's spines. The Assyrians were cruel rulers; depictions from that time show how they waged war and the kind of destruction they brought. The spiritual and political leaders of the small city-state Judah, Jerusalem, had to take orders from this world power. Zephaniah appeared in the time that Josiah became king but did not really have any power (2 Kgs 21:19–22:2). He was only eight years old, a child put on the throne. Only later would he implement reforms in the spirit of the Torah.[5]

Zephaniah was active in Jerusalem, whose leaders hung on every word of the superpower Nineveh. The descendant of the just King David "who did justice in the eyes of the Lord," on the one hand, and the unjust King Nimrod, on the other, Zephaniah addressed his audience, primarily the leaders of Jerusalem:

> You Cushites, too,
> will be slain by my sword.
> He will stretch out his hand against the north
> and destroy Assyria,
> leaving Nineveh utterly desolate
> and dry as the desert.
> Flocks and herds will lie down there,
> creatures of every kind.
> The desert owl and the screech owl
> will roost on her columns.
> Their hooting will echo through the windows,
> rubble will fill the doorways,

---

5. Cf. Chapter III.

the beams of cedar will be exposed.
This is the city of revelry
that lived in safety.
She said to herself:
"I am the one! And there is none besides me."
What a ruin she has become,
a lair for wild beasts!
All who pass by her scoff
and shake their fists.
Woe to the city of oppressors,
rebellious and defiled!
She obeys no one,
she accepts no correction.
She does not trust in the LORD,
she does not draw near to her God.
Her officials within her
are roaring lions;
her rulers are evening wolves,
who leave nothing for the morning.
Her prophets are unprincipled;
they are treacherous people.
Her priests profane the sanctuary
and do violence to the law.
The LORD within her is righteous;
he does no wrong.
Morning by morning he dispenses his justice
and every new day he does not fail,
yet the unrighteous know no shame.   (Zeph 2:12-3:5)

Zephaniah was speaking here at a time when the Assyrian kingdom was still supreme and the city of Nineveh had not yet fallen. Assyria still had hegemony over Judah and Jerusalem. Nevertheless, he still mocked both Assyria and Nineveh: Assur would be razed, the capital city would become a wilderness, deserted, only comfortless ruins would remain, and wild animals would make their homes there: "All who see you will flee from you and say: 'Nineveh is in ruins — who will mourn for her?' Where can I find anyone to comfort you?" (Nah 3:7). In the future, whoever passed by would whistle, making a mocking gesture with his hand, and ridicule it (Zeph 2:15). *Sic transit gloria mundi.* That is what would be left of the exuberant, overconfident capital city that was so secure, so detached, that imagined itself master of the whole world and said in its heart: "I am the one! And there is none besides me."

These words from the prophet must have seemed like boasting in the ears of his hearers, for at the time Nineveh was exceptionally powerful. But that is what prophets do: Zephaniah gives insight and understanding about the true situation. He looks straight through outward appearance and exposes everything. He produces, as it were, an x-ray, showing his listeners what they cannot see with the eye alone. He wants his hearers to see that only the skeleton of the city will be left standing. Its true form is a world of death, a no-man's-land, a ghost town, stripped of heart and soul, cold, waste, and empty.

One should pay attention to where Zephaniah speaks these words, where he sings this mocking song. He does not walk around Nineveh as that other prophet, Jonah/Yûnus (Q 10, titled Yunus/Jonah; 37:139-48, 10:98), would. He addresses the leaders of town and country in Jerusalem.

"You Cushites!" Zephaniah calls. His listeners know, of course, that this prophet is also a Cushite, in addition to being a descendant of David. When he addresses them as Cushites, he is also addressing himself! And his contemporaries understand perfectly well what he is talking about: "Whatever you say applies to yourself." He addresses his own people in Jerusalem, probably in the temple, as Cushites. He is not concerned so much with informing them about the situation in Nineveh as about their situation in Jerusalem. Those leaders whom he addresses are under Nineveh and follow its orders. "You Cushites!" thus has the sense of "If the shoe fits. . . ." Zephaniah indicates what is really going on in Jerusalem. By calling them Cushites, he made it clear that the leaders of Jerusalem were actually creating a kind of Nineveh themselves and doing what Nineveh represents: injustice and abuse of power. God thus speaks through the prophet Zephaniah, the son of the Cushite. Prophets liked to bring their messages across by using names. They walked around like the word of God embodied. "Yes, you Cushites!" Zephaniah points — and that is what is so shocking — to the common background they and his people share. This is not, therefore, a simple black-and-white tale: there is no unambiguous "they" and no unambiguous "we," Nineveh on the one side and Jerusalem on the other, the city of justice and peace on the one side and the city of injustice on the other, the kingdom of democracy on the one side and the kingdom of oppression on the other. "It takes one to know one" takes us to the root of evil, which is also in oneself. An evil spirit hovering over Jerusalem has turned Jerusalem into a Nineveh.

The city of Nineveh, which was reproached for its wickedness and seems to be at such a comfortable distance, begins to take on a terrifying form within Jerusalem. The community that has gathered on the temple square had to feel addressed more and more — their chickens had come home to roost. The prophet addresses his own leaders.

Three categories of people are addressed: rulers, prophets, and priests. He says to the rulers, the officials and ministers: You are like roaring lions, who enact measures that only lead to the ruin of ordinary people. You judges are evening wolves because you pronounce justice as if you were jackals. And you prophets as well, the leaders of the Jerusalem cultural planning bureau, are gossipmongers. They are wolves in sheep's clothing, symbol of the "false prophets" (Matt 7:15). Wolves were seen as horrible, bloodthirsty animals (Isa 11:6; 65:25) that shed blood and tear apart their prey primarily in the evening or at night (Zeph 3:3; Hab 1:8). The wolf symbolizes people who gather plunder (Gen 49:27) or engage in destruction: "Her officials within her are like wolves tearing their prey; they shed blood and kill people to make unjust gain" (Ezek 22:27).[6] And finally you priests, the temple clique, you defile all that is holy, you violate the Torah.

Where, after all, does the problem lie in Nineveh and Jerusalem? Nineveh — which seems so large, magnificent, flamboyant, and teeming and so full of activity with its unassailable position, secure, built on its own security system, self-assured — trusted in its own alleged unassailability, its divinity. Nineveh, and thus also its allies, such as the leaders of Jerusalem, made themselves God's competitors: "I am the one! And there is none besides me." "There is no power besides mine." "There is no other God than I," as Pharaoh would state it. When leaders start to speak in this way, they lay claim to divinity. And then it really becomes dangerous for ordinary people: men, women, and children. That is a kind of language that continues to be spoken right up until the present on both sides, both in the West and in the East. But that is not the language of the Bible or the Qur'an. That is not the language of the prophets; it is "Babylonian," "Ninevese."

Woe to the City of Oppressors, Rebellious and Defiled!

The prophet addresses the leaders, judges, false prophets, and priests in Jerusalem, who play the same nasty game as Nineveh. The high political state of-

---

6. *BW,* *s.v.* "wolf"; Hans Biedermann, *Prisma van de symbolen* (4th ed.; Utrecht: Spectrum, 1993), *s.v.* "wolf."

ficials oppress the people, the judges violate justice, the priests defile everything that is holy, the false prophets are windbags and gossipmongers. The city Jerusalem itself has become an oppressive city; it does not want to listen to God's voice, does not accept rules and discipline: this rebellious, filthy, violent, oppressive city.

The Hebrew text uses the word *yanah* here, which is translated in the NIV as "city of oppressors." If that word is given different vowels one immediately recognizes the word "Jonah," the proper name of the prophet Jonah/Yûnus, who was told to call the city of Nineveh to repentance. And that did happen, to Jonah's great dismay and amazement as he contemplates under the tree, quietly waiting in the hope that the city will be destroyed as quickly as possible. But Nineveh repents! It becomes a city of repentance: "everyone turned from his evil way, and from the violence that was in his hands" (Jonah 3; Q 10:98; 37:147-48)!

There is still a third meaning of the word *yanah,* namely, "dove." The Spirit of God is symbolized on earth by the dove. This dove of God incubates the world, just as the spirit of God once hovered above the waters of the chaos of creation (Gen 1:2), and hatches new life as from an egg. When the dove of God comes, a new creation is on the way! Then a truly new holy city will be hatched, a new Jerusalem that descends from heaven to earth (Rev 21:2, 10).

What is the way out? What is the solution? How can one be liberated from that serious situation, from the lack of spirituality, that destruction, that oppression and violation of justice? That can only be driven out by the "sword of God," the weapon of God's Spirit. For over against those who violate justice is God himself. And the righteous person, the one who does Torah, is unable to be an unjust ruler or an oppressive person.

The judges commit their injustice at night. They do it in the evening, for then the sun of justice sets. The opposite is the case with respect to God: he pronounces justice in the morning (cf. 2 Sam 15:2). In Israel, justice was pronounced in the morning like a liturgy, for all justice that was spoken was an echo of God's pronouncement of justice. That is why justice was always pronounced in the morning, for then the sun rises, the time of resurrection. The sun of righteousness (Mal 4:2) rises at the same time as the sun in the east.[7]

What is the prophet's message? It has to do with a spiritual battle, the sword of the spirit. Is this not the language of war that Zephaniah is speak-

---

7. There is a wordplay between the "Name" *(shem)* and the "sun" *(shemesh).*

ing, rather than a call to holy war, a *jihâd* or a just war *(bellum justum)*? It can be read that way perhaps, and certainly has been read that way. But that language is not there. It is a spiritual battle, the *jihâd al-akbar*, the "Greater Holy War." The destruction, injustice, and violence can be driven out only by the sword of God, by the weapon of his Spirit.[8]

The Prophet Jeremiah and a "Tale of Two Cities": Jerusalem and Babylon

In 587 B.C. Jerusalem and the temple were destroyed by the Babylonian king Nebuchadnezzar. This event marked an important transitional phase, just as, since the second half of the twentieth century, we have spoken of before and after the Second World War. It meant the end of the Davidic kingship and the deportation of the leading citizens from Judah and Jerusalem to Babylon. It was the end of the world as it had existed before that time.

What was the answer to the situation of exile? Various prophets appear to speak in the name of God on this question, but Jeremiah stands alone. He experienced the unstoppable rise of the Neo-Babylonian Empire. A sober analysis of the political situation brought him to the understanding that it was meaningless and foolish to attempt anything political or military against the mighty Babylon. For him, the destruction of Judah and Jerusalem was a settled affair.

But Jeremiah did not find an audience for this insight with the kings of Judah, Joiachim (608-597 B.C.) and Zedekiah (597-587), who would be the final king, nor with their advisors. Other prophets opposed him. Jeremiah was alone. Like any true prophet, he did not curry favor with anyone nor did he confirm what others already thought. Despite Jeremiah's warnings, Judah's king Zedekiah, who had sworn loyalty to the king of Babylon, broke his oath and so realized all of the expected consequences. He was taken captive, deported, and came to a horrible end. His sons were killed in front of him, and he was blinded and brought to Babylon, where he would quickly die (2 Kgs 25:7; cf. Jer 39:6-7). If one thing is clear, it is that critical commentary by a prophet does not represent some kind of hobby but is an essential calling. Jeremiah was a reluctant, unwilling prophet, having become one against his will, and later he would himself be stoned to death in Egypt.

Jeremiah wrote the following letter to the exiles in Babylon:

8. Hans van Leeuwen, *Zefanja: Verklaring van een Bijbelgedeelte* (Kampen: Kok, 1979).

This is the text of the letter that the prophet Jeremiah sent from Jerusalem to the surviving elders among the exiles and to the priests, the prophets and all the other people Nebuchadnezzar had carried into exile from Jerusalem to Babylon. . . .

This is what the LORD Almighty, the God of Israel, says to all those I carried into exile from Jerusalem to Babylon: "Build houses and settle down; plant gardens and eat what they produce. Marry and have sons and daughters; find wives for your sons and give your daughters in marriage, so that they too may have sons and daughters. Increase in number there; do not decrease. Also, seek the peace and prosperity of the city to which I have carried you into exile. Pray to the LORD for it, because if it prospers, you too will prosper." Yes, this is what the LORD Almighty, the God of Israel, says: "Do not let the prophets and diviners among you deceive you. Do not listen to the dreams you encourage them to have. They are prophesying lies to you in my name. I have not sent them," declares the LORD. This is what the LORD says: "When seventy years are completed for Babylon, I will come to you and fulfill my good promise to bring you back to this place. For I know the plans I have for you," declares the LORD, "plans to prosper you and not to harm you, plans to give you hope and a future. Then you will call on me and come and pray to me, and I will listen to you. You will seek me and find me when you seek me with all your heart. I will be found by you," declares the LORD, "and will bring you back from captivity. I will gather you from all the nations and places where I have banished you," declares the LORD, "and will bring you back to the place from which I carried you into exile." (Jer 29:1, 4-14)

The first text I ever read by the famous Swiss theologian Karl Barth was his "Brief an einen Pfarrer in der DDR" ("Letter to a Pastor in the German Democratic Republic [East Germany]"), which he wrote during the time of the Cold War. The Berlin wall had not yet been erected, and many East Germans, including many pastors, left for the free West. That could be done relatively easily at that time. In his letter, Barth called on pastors to remain where they were and to work for the peace of East German communist society. This was questionable advice at that time. It seemed to some that Barth had become a "fellow traveler" who collaborated with communism whereas he had previously so clearly resisted national socialism.

In writing this letter, Barth was inspired by Jeremiah's letter to the exiles in Babylon. His advice at that time was no less disputable. Was Jeremiah not collaborating with the enemy? Did he not speak too positively about the archenemy — who, after all, was responsible for the deportation?

Jeremiah's preaching took the form of a letter, for a considerable number of the people to whom he directed his message were personally unaccessible to him. They had been carried away into exile, whereas he himself had been left behind in Jerusalem. The exiles were not imprisoned there, were not put into a refugee camp or asylum center. Rather, land had been given to them on which they could settle. They had their own leaders, elders, and these were the first addressees of this letter.

The content of the letter shows that the exiles found themselves in a curious dilemma. On the one hand, they felt themselves incapacitated, yet on the other, they lived with high expectations. Each feeling could lead to very different circumstances. In our society as well there are many migrants who would like to return to their country as soon as possible. The exiles felt helpless because they could not understand why God allowed things to come so far that they, members of a chosen people, were taken away to this foreign land. They were homesick, like all people facing a similar plight who have become acquainted with the "anatomy of loneliness." The exiles in Babylon had much the same feelings. Their greatest distress was that they had to live in a strange, unclean land and would have to die there as well (Amos 7:17; cf. Hos 9:3).

Nevertheless, these exiles harbored high expectations. They hoped to return quickly and to be able to pick up the thread of their lives again — the happiness they lost for which their hearts were yearning, would soon return, or so they hoped. They were inclined to view the exile as merely temporary. An exile, just like a prisoner, is interested in the present only to the extent that it would pass. That was also true for the exiles in Babylon. In their view, their lives had been rich and fulfilling until they were exiled, and their lives would become meaningful again when they would be allowed to return. The time between the deportation and the return was nothing, only an interruption in their lives. They could see no sense in it; they did not want to say "yes" to life in exile. They were consumed on the one hand by the past and on the other by a passionate hope for a future that was not yet.

It is that way of thinking, that attitude, that Jeremiah opposes. He takes a different approach and wants to make clear to them that God is the one who had put them in this situation: "I have carried you into exile." It is God himself who has handed the people over to the Babylonian Empire. Their exile is not coincidental but has been arranged by God himself: "Now I will give all your countries into the hands of my servant Nebuchadnezzar king of

Babylon" (Jer 27:6). Jeremiah recommends that the exiles accept the new circumstances: "Build houses and settle down; plant gardens and eat what they produce" (29:5). "Marry and have sons and daughters. . . . Increase in number there; do not decrease" (29:6; Gen 1:28). The goal of all this is not only one's own happiness as husband and father, as wife and mother, but also the continued existence of the people. Otherwise, the people would decrease and die out (Jer 30:19). What Jeremiah wanted to make clear to them is precisely this: every place is God's place; every time is God's time. In whatever situation one finds oneself, recognize the present hour as the hour of God and use it (Eph 5:16). He is telling the exiles: work and live in a way directed to the long term. For after all, however long it lasts, it will not end before the fruit tree planted today bears fruit. If one says: "Start a family, and let your children do the same," then one is thinking in terms of generations.

"Build houses, plant gardens" pays only if one is counting on staying for a long time. That means that the Jews in Babylon had to try to find their place, had to sink down roots. For how long? Seventy years. What Jeremiah means is: Judah and the other small states would have to serve the Babylonian world power for the full extent of a person's life. A human life at its maximum spans three generations. The seventy years that Jeremiah cites means that even newborns would die before salvation comes. The adults who were taken to Babylon would never see their homeland again.

Jeremiah's recommendations are at odds with what other — in Jeremiah's eyes — false prophets and soothsayers assert. The other prophets were apparently strongly convinced that God did not want things to come to that, that this exile would not last long, and that God would soon lead them out of Babylon with his strong hand and outstretched arm (Jer 28:2-4). Jeremiah contradicts that directly: "Do not listen to the words of the prophets who say to you, 'You will not serve the king of Babylon,' for they are prophesying lies to you" (27:14).

The opposition between this word of God that Jeremiah brings and the false prophecy is that between the short and the long term. The message is that it will last a long time. Jeremiah takes from the exiles any possible illusion that they will awaken very soon out of this bad dream. He calls them back down to earth. God takes detours. They need to expect to persevere for a long time. Nor does the difference between Jeremiah and his opponents lie in the fact that Jeremiah preaches only disaster while his opponents preach salvation. Jeremiah is also a prophet of salvation. Rather, the difference lies in the question of when salvation will become reality.

But those words come across in Babylon like swearing in church — or, rather, the synagogue. "How can we sing the songs of the LORD while in a foreign land? If I forget you, Jerusalem, may my right hand forget its skill" (Ps 137:4-5). Jeremiah does not deny the latter, but he attempts to curb premature enthusiasm: that road only leads to disappointment. That his intervention is not appreciated and people would rather keep dreaming is proven in a letter that came back from Babylon: "He has sent this message to us in Babylon: It will be a long time. Therefore build houses and settle down; plant gardens and eat what they produce" (Jer 29:28).

But this is quite something that Jeremiah asks of them. Franz Kafka once wrote: "Oh, unendlich viel Hoffnung, aber nicht für uns" ("plenty of hope, an infinite amount of hope — but not for us"). To know that such a hope exists but will not be achieved for us makes the desperation in our lives even worse, for "hope deferred makes the heart sick" (Prov 13:12). If we desire someone or something, that longing can make us ill.

The exiles will not only have to resign themselves to their fate in Babylon but make the best of it at the same time. They will have to seek peace for the city. They will have to be directly involved in a constructive way, for in the peace of the city Babylon lies their own peace. Their fate has been bound by God to that of Babylon: standing up loyally for the interests of Babylon. What is new and unprecedented in Jeremiah's recommendation to the exiles is that they become active residents in their place of exile. And the high point is the paradoxical task of praying for the well-being of Babylon. That must have looked to his contemporaries like treason and sounded like blasphemy in their ears.

Even prayer alone is not sufficient. The exiles cannot stop there. It is a matter of *ora et labora* ("prayer and work"). They are also, they are told, to promote Babylon's prosperity. They are to seek the best for the city and to pray for it. They are given a priestly role (Jer 29:12). Certainly, Babylon has a government against which there are many objections, and God will have and speak the last word about Babylon: "But when the seventy years are fulfilled, I will punish the king of Babylon and his nation, the land of the Babylonians, for their guilt" (Jer 25:12-14). But, in the meantime, they are to seek the peace, the salvation, of the city. They are to devote themselves to that. Just as the Jewish exiles had to pray for Babylon, so the Christian *ecclesia* was later advised to pray for the government, beginning with the Roman emperors and governments (1 Tim 2:2). It still holds true today that the peace of the *qahal*, *ecclesia*, *umma* depends on the peace of the world.[9]

---

9. Gottfried Voigt, *Der Helle Morgenstern* (Göttingen: Vandenhoeck & Ruprecht, 1961) 151-55.

Muhammad and a "Tale of Two Cities": Medina and Mecca

As indicated at the beginning, the Qur'an also tells a "tale of two cities": Mecca, the city of injustice, and Medina, the city of justice. There was hostility between both cities that intensified after the emigration from Mecca to Medina in A.D. 622 until Mecca finally opened itself in 630 to the true surrender to God ("islam").

In "the chapter of the victory" *(sûra an-nasr),* the Qur'an speaks as follows of the capture of Mecca in 630: "When God's help *(nasr)* comes, and success *(fath)* and you [Muhammad] see the people entering the religion of God in droves, then praise the glory of your Lord and ask him for forgiveness. He is gracious and willing to forgive your sins" (Q 110:1-3).

What is the character of that victory? To whom must the victory be ascribed, and what is God's role in it? To be able to answer that question, we must look at how the peace of God, God's presence, is talked about and how the words "victory" *(nasr)* and "success" *(fath)* must be explained in this context.

The "presence of God" is defined by the term *shekinah, sakîna,* which indicates God's "indwelling."[10] *Shekinah,* which means "living," is a name for God that allows Jews to avoid speaking God's name, YHWH. Jerusalem, which God chose as a dwelling for his Name (Deut 12:11), is described in that way. The verb *shakan,* from which this word is derived, means "go down, settle, rest, live." It is used for the glory of God and for the people as a sign of God's presence (Exod 24:16; Num 9:17). God lives on Mount Zion (Isa 8:18).[11] This expression alludes to the invisible armies that God sends down from heaven. God sent Muhammad help when the unbelieving Meccans drove him out of Mecca at the time of the Hijra: when Muhammad and Abû Bakr, his friend and supporter, later his first successor or caliph, found refuge in a cave during their flight, Muhammad says to him: "Don't be worried! God is with us." Then God sent his "peace of God" on him and strengthened him with armies from heaven that he did not see (Q 9:40; cf. 2 Kgs 6:16-17; Matt 26:53).[12]

God showed Muhammad in a dream that the prophet would pray in Mecca (Q 48:27). In March 628 he went with a thousand men, unarmed and

10. *EQ, s.v.* "Shekhinah."

11. *Christelijke Encyclopedie,* ed. F. W. Grosheide and G. P. van Itterzon (2nd ed.; Kampen: Kok, 1956), *s.v.* "Schechina."

12. Cf. Chapter VII on the prophet Elisha and the city of Samaria.

dressed as a pilgrim, to perform the pilgrimage (Hajj) to the Ka'ba in Mecca. When he neared the city, he was stopped by Meccan troops. The Meccans began negotiating at about a distance of 16 kilometers from the city at the well of al-Hudaybiyya, and Muhammad concluded a treaty with them that was named after that place. The Muslims saw the treaty as humiliating, but Muhammad explained to his followers that the treaty was in fact a *fath*, a "success" (cf. Q 48:1). God is the one who sent the "peace of God" down into the hearts of the believers so that they would be strengthened in their faith. God alone has the armies of heaven and earth at his disposal. He is all-knowing and wise (Q 46:4). That is said after God brought about or opened *(fatahna)* a clear success *(fathan mubînan;* Q 48:1) and helped them to a great victory *(nasr;* Q 48:3). That means that the treaty (of al-Hudaybiyya) opens (the original meaning of the word) the victory over Mecca for them (i.e., Islam). God was pleased with the believers when they swore faithfulness under the tree at al-Hudaybiyya so that God saw what kind of ideas they had in their hearts. Then he sent the peace of God on them and gave them the prospect of a victory in the near future *(fath qarîb)*[13] as a reward (Q 48:18; cf. 48:26).

The Muslims concluded a peace treaty with the Meccans, a truce for ten years, whereby Muhammad and his followers were not permitted to perform the pilgrimage that year but were allowed to do so in A.D. 629. They did, in fact, complete this pilgrimage the following year. Shortly after, in 630, Muhammad used the breaking of the treaty by Mecca as a reason to advance against the city, which did not offer any real resistance. Precisely a few months before the Byzantine emperor Heraclius arrived in Jerusalem, so the tradition goes, the inhabitants of Mecca surrendered peacefully to Muhammad and subjected themselves to his authority. The city surrendered practically with no resistance. Muhammad wanted to become reconciled with the Meccans rather than crush them with violence. Fourteen days after the conquest, the Battle of Hunayn occurred a day's march from Mecca (Q 9:25-26). A large group of nomads had gathered there. The troops in total numbered twelve thousand under Muhammad's command, ten thousand of whom had accompanied Muhammad from Medina and had participated in the conquest of Mecca. The other two thousand were from the Quraysh, which had recently converted to Islam, and were under the command of Abu Sufyân.[14] The battle ended in a decisive victory for the Muslims, although the Muslim

13. A reference to the conquest of Khaybar, a Jewish settlement.
14. *EI, s.v.* "Hunayn."

soldiers had initially been routed; that changed as soon as God "sent down the peace of God" on his messenger and the believers and "an army of angels you did not see" (Q 9:25-26). The peace of God was sent down to show God's support for his chosen instrument, Muhammad, in the face of unbelief, including sometimes even that of his followers.[15]

A young Muslim was appointed governor of Mecca, but Medina remained the capital. The Ka'ba, which for years had indicated the direction of prayer *(qibla)* was stripped of its idols following the conquest.[16] The city that had symbolized injustice and oppression was now purified and became a city of justice.

The Qur'an calls the capture of Mecca by Muhammad a "success" *(fath)* and "victory" *(nasr;* Q 110). Is that a victory like the ones the Persian prince achieved in 614 and later the Byzantine emperor in 629, both in Jerusalem? What, the question arises again, is the meaning and character of victory?

Nasr, "Help"

To get a better understanding of the terms *nasr* ("help" or "victory") and *fath* ("conquest" or "success"), one should look more closely at the specific contexts in which the words occur in the Qur'an: God gave "help" *(nasr)* to Noah/Nuh — he and his family were saved from the disaster, the deluge (Q 21:76-77; 37:75-76). When Jesus detected unbelief and asked who would be God's "helpers," his disciples answered that they would be his helpers *(ansar)* on the way to God (Q 3:52). The prophet Muhammad was encouraged by the fact that messengers who preceded him were considered liars but did stay patient until God's help *(nasr)* came (Q 6:34). Muhammad also receives that *nasr,* "help," "support," or "victory" from God in the spring of 624 at the Battle of Badr despite their small number (Q 3:123; cf. 8:26; 3:13). That is true also for the help that God gave at the Battle of Hunayn after the conquest of Mecca (Q 9:25). After all, the kingship of the heavens and earth belongs to God. He gives life and causes death, and apart from him there is no Protector *(wali)* or Helper *(nasir;* Q 9:116; cf. 9:74). The *ansar,* the helpers who stood by Muhammad in Medina (Q 9:117), are called such, but in a more general sense the term covers all those who progress on God's way by

15. *EQ, s.v.* "Shekhinah." Frants Buhl, *Das Leben Muhammads* (repr.; Darmstadt: Wissenschaftliche Buchgesellschaft, 1961) 311-14.

16. *EI, s.v.* "Makka."

choosing the side of Jesus and the other prophets. "You who believe be the 'helpers' of God, just as 'Isa/Jesus, the son of Maryam/Mary, said to the apostles: 'Who are the helpers to God?' The apostles said: "We are the helpers of God.' Then a group of the children of Israel became believers, but another group did not believe, and God strengthened the believers against their enemies so that they had the upper hand" (Q 61:14).

Fath, "Success"

Muhammad's triumphal entry into Mecca is seen as the greatest *fath* ("success"). But what is the character of that *fath?* It is incorrect to understand the use of the word *fath* in Muhammad's time in its later sense of "conquest." Here it has to do with victory that is given by God to the believers. Indeed, the word was used by the next generation in connection with their trampling of the Persian and Byzantine empires. The word acquired the meaning of "conquest," literally, "opening," namely, the expansion of Islam,[17] and thus the later conquests that the Muslims would achieve for the expansion of Islam were called *"conquests of the lands" (futûh al-buldân).* But it is obvious, according to the Qur'an, that the attainment of the conquest and victory and the use of violence, however minor, entail dirty hands. That is why forgiveness must be continually sought: "When God's help *(nasr)* comes, and success *(fath),* and you [Muhammad] see the people entering the religion of God in droves, then praise the glory of your Lord and ask him for forgiveness" (Q 110:1-3; cf. Q 40:55; 71:10). The prophet was made aware of how quickly human beings can make themselves guilty whenever they exercise power and dominion. The success and the victory belong to God alone. The prince, caliph, or imam derives his power only from God and deserves the exalted position of authority if he exercises that authority in accordance with the way God indicates. As Kenneth Cragg remarks, the clemency that he offers to the city of Mecca indicates that the whole Medinan enterprise was not a matter of the perverted enjoyment of power or uncontrolled aggression. Rather, it was a disciplined campaign to attain a religious goal.[18] That

---

17. Cf. "The LORD will open the heavens, the storehouse of his bounty, to send rain on your land in season and to bless all the work of your hands. You will lend to many nations but will borrow from none" (Deut 28:12); "Therefore I will expose [open] the flank of Moab, beginning at its frontier towns — Beth Jeshimoth, Baal Meon and Kiriathaim — the glory of that land" (Ezek 25:9).

18. Kenneth Cragg, "Islam Hostage to Itself?" In *World Christianity in Muslim En-*

the fall of Mecca is called a *fath* as such is explained more in terms of salvation history than in a military or legal sense.[19]

If we have understood properly what is meant by "success," "help," and "victory" in the Qur'an, then it is not a question here of using it to see the building of the Dome of the Rock in Jerusalem as a symbol of the triumph of Islam over Judaism and Christianity. Nor is it in the spirit of the Qur'an to celebrate the conquest of Christian Constantinople in a triumphalistic way by the building of the Fâtih mosque. Were that so, the warning that the Qur'an gives Muhammad would not be heeded: when you see this happen ask for forgiveness (Q 110:3).

The cross cannot be used either, in the spirit of the Bible, as a sign of victory or employed to explain the capture of Rome by Constantine the Great in the sense of a God who would bless weapons, nor may or can it serve to legitimate crusades centuries later.

It is not a question of the victory of one party or the other: Jew, Christian, or Muslim. Every human being is, after all, confronted with a choice right from the start: will he or she be a caliph or a king? Of the party of God *(hizbollah)* or of the party of Satan *(hizb al-shaytân)*? The party of Satan will lose (Q 58:19; 4:119). If someone joins the side of God, his messenger, or those who believe, he has made the right choice. Those who are on God's side are of his party and will be the true conquerors *(al-ghâlibûn,* Q 5:56).[20] The victory belongs to God alone.

For Whom Is the City Jerusalem, Mecca, Medina Intended?

The inclination often arises to see the holy cities, especially Jerusalem and Mecca, as the exclusive possession of one of the three groups, Jews, Christians, or Muslims. This has happened in exegesis throughout the centuries, especially in the time of the conquests.[21]

Jerusalem became the city of David after the conquest of the fortress of Jebus, its pre-Davidic name (the southwestern slope was called the "slope of the Jebusites"; Josh 15:8; 18:16), and remained so until the capture and destruction of the city by King Nebuchadnezzar in 586 B.C. Control of the city

---

counter: Essays in Memory of David A. Kerr, ed. Stephen R. Goodwin (London: Continuum, 2009) 2:135.

19. *EQ, s.v.* "Conquest."
20. *EQ, s.v.* "Victory, Apostle."
21. Cf. Chapter X.

was returned to the Jews after their return from exile under Cyrus (Kores), the Persian king (559-529). Periods then follow in which the successors of Alexander the Great, the Seleucids, especially Antiochus IV Epiphanes, exercised dominion, interrupted by the era of the Maccabees. Then various Herods ruled under the supervision of the Romans. In A.D. 70 the Romans razed the Jerusalem temple, and the consequences of Jewish resistance in the second century proved disastrous for the city. After the defeat of the Bar Kokhba rebellion (132-35), the Jews were forbidden to live in the city. This lasted until the fourth century. Since that time it came under Byzantine Christian authority, briefly interrupted by the rule of the Persians (614-29). In the seventh century, during the time of 'Umar, the second successor of Muhammad, Jerusalem was conquered by the Arab Muslims. Jerusalem remained under Muslim rule for fourteen centuries, interrupted only during the time of the Crusades (1099-1286). In our time, the state of Israel claims the entire city as an indivisible capital of the state, and the Palestinians make the same claim on East Jerusalem as the capital of the Palestinian state.

During the first period of Muhammad's activity as prophet, Mecca was the city of injustice (A.D. 610-22). That is the reason for the first emigration *(hijra)* to Ethiopia and later in 622 to Medina. But circumstances did not remain that way. The situation in Mecca slowly changed, and thus also the attitude of Muhammad and the Muslims toward the city. The desire for Mecca as the essential destination of the exiles in Medina surfaced scarcely two years after the emigration. The prayer orientation, the direction in which prayers were made, the *qibla* Jerusalem, changed in response to the negative experiences Muhammad had with most Jews in Medina: "The fools among the people say: 'What turned the Muslims away the prayer direction *(qibla)* they had followed until then?' Say: Both east and west belong to God. He guides whomever he wills on a 'straight' path *(sirât al-mustaqîm)*. And thus we have made you a community of the middle way" (Q 2:142-43). The focus must now be directed to the devoted house of prayer *(al-masjid al-haram)*, the Ka'ba in Mecca. Wherever one is, it is in that direction one must face when praying.

Does that mean that from that moment on Jerusalem was written off or replaced by Mecca? We must look foremost at the symbolic meaning of what the cities, Jerusalem and Mecca, represent. In the dedication prayer of the Ka'ba by Abraham, the shrine is not only seen as a place of pilgrimage for a certain group but also as a sign for the whole of humanity: "And then Abraham said: 'Lord, make this area of the Ka'ba a safe place, a sanctuary, and give its people fruits, those of them who believe in God and the last day!" (Q 2:126-27). "And when Abraham was laying the foundations with Ishmael, he prayed to God: 'Accept it from us. You hear all and know all. And make us both submissive and our descendants into a community that submits to you in full trust'" (Q 2:127-28).

Therefore, the question is not if Mecca replaces Jerusalem. Rather, it has to do with an appeal to Abraham so that Mecca or Jerusalem could be or become "the true Jerusalem" or "the true Mecca." In this prayer the Ka'ba appears as the monument of a new or renewed divine establishment. It originated as Bakkah, the first monotheistic "house of God" established for the blessing and guidance of all people (Q 3:96),[22] for all of Abraham's "descendants."

This is not the place nor is it my intention here to discuss the historical and political circumstances, causes, or explanations about the possession and ownership of the actual cities Jerusalem and Mecca. Rather, the question that will be posed is: What, essentially, is in keeping with these three Books? Is there one tale with respect to the question: "To whom does the city belong?"

As far as Mecca is concerned, the general Muslim view is that it is not a place for non-Muslims, meaning it is not for Jews and Christians. According to a tradition *(hadith),* no two religions can exist next to each other in the Arabian Peninsula. Muhammad is said to have proclaimed this on his deathbed, but that seems improbable. The fact is that in A.D. 640 the second successor of Muhammad, 'Umar, drove the Jews out of Hijâz and the Christians from Najrân, even though Muhammad had concluded a treaty that allowed them to stay. In the time of Mu'âwiyya, the first caliph of the Umayyads, a group of two hundred Christians constituted the police in Medina, and for a long time there was a cemetery for "unbelievers" in Mecca.[23] Whatever the case may be, it is well known that the city of Mecca today and for centuries has not been accessible to non-Muslims. Signs have been posted on the roads leading to Mecca announcing this. For that reason, a road leading around Mecca is popularly known as the "Christian" road.

Daniel van der Meulen (1894-1989), a Dutch diplomat, explorer (Hadramut, Yemen), and writer, worked for the Dutch government in the later days of the Dutch East Indies/Indonesia. He served as a consul for the Netherlands in Jeddah in Saudi Arabia. Jeddah was an important consulate

---

22. *EQ, s.v.* "Geography."

23. Youssef Courbage and Philippe Fargues, *Christians and Jews under Islam,* trans. Judy Mabro (London: Tauris, 1997).

because of the many Islamic pilgrims who came from the Dutch East Indies to Arabia. Quite a number of Indonesian Muslims came originally from Hadramaut. Van der Meulen wrote a biography on the founder of the current ruling dynasty, Ibn Saud (1876-1953). He once asked the king if he would give him permission to go to Mecca. The king refused, however, because he was not a Muslim. Van der Meulen then asked the king: "If it would be possible to ask Muhammad himself if he would give a true believer, whether Jew, Christian, or Muslim, permission to go to Mecca, do you not think the prophet would permit him to go?" The king's answer was, "Yes, I think he would. But I will not permit you to go to Mecca."

For all kinds of historical, traditional, and political reasons, it is probably understandable why Jews and Christians were excluded from Mecca, but is it in accordance with the Qur'an and even with the Sunna or custom of the prophet Muhammad? With respect to the latter, in October 632 a delegation of Christians led by a bishop from the Christian city of Najrân in southern Arabia paid a visit to the prophet in Medina.[24] A conversation that has become famous took place, to which the Qur'an alludes (Q 3:61), and Muhammad allowed the Christians to pray in his own mosque.

Why can Mecca, which is connected with Abraham, not be a city open to all believers?

The One City of God and Humankind

To read and to understand the Bible and the Qur'an as a "tale of two cities" shows precisely how it can be with cities. Sometimes the unjust cities come to insight and repent. That happened with Nineveh, the city that repented because of the message of Jonah. The Ninevites sought support with God and proclaimed a fast, and everyone, from great to small, man and beast, donned sackcloth as a sign of repentance. And God saw what they did; he saw that they gave up their evil ways, and God relented and did not bring on them the destruction he had threatened. He did not carry out his judgment (Jonah 3:5; cf. Q 37:147-48). God appeared to be sympathetic toward "the great city of Nineveh, in which there are more than a hundred and twenty thousand people who cannot tell their right hand from their left — and also many animals" (Jonah 4:11).

However, the reverse can also be the case. Thus, Jerusalem, the city of

---

24. *EQ, s.v.* "Najrân"; "Curse."

righteousness and peace, can become a city of injustice (just like Mecca and Medina) and be equated with Sodom and Gomorrah (Isa 1:9).

But the future perspective that the prophets have in mind up until the seer John is a new Jerusalem. John's "tale of two cities," the book of Revelation, is about Jerusalem and Babylon. Just as Jesus was brought by the devil to a high mountain and shown all kingdoms of the earth (Matt 4:8), so God shows John the new Jerusalem, the holy city that descended out of heaven, radiating from God's glory (Rev 21:2). The description of that city is very striking and salient: a city on both sides of the river with many trees (chs. 21–22). Everyone who has ever been in Jerusalem knows that the earthly city in Israel, Palestine, does not look at all like that. It is not a city situated on a river. But what city is? Babylon! Babylon is the model for the new Jerusalem. Jerusalem can become a city of injustice as in Jesus' day, and Babylon can be used as an image for the new Jerusalem. Babylon can repent, just like wicked Mecca, and can become or become again *Mekka al-Mukarrama,* the "noble city." In the Bible Jerusalem is not the geographical center, so one cannot say: the new city will be located there or even anywhere in the Middle East. John dreamed of a global capital city, where all the peoples are at home and of which the gates will be wide open to all corners of the earth on a permanent basis. This new Jerusalem is not yet anywhere but can be expected everywhere. This new Jerusalem must be dreamed of everywhere — in New York, Belfast, Sarajevo, Baghdad, Ramallah, but especially also in Jerusalem, even in Amsterdam.

Ultimately it concerns one city of God and humankind.

Amsterdam, Rome, and . . . Bethlehem

The seventeenth-century Dutch poet Joost van den Vondel (1587-1679) was asked to write a play for the opening of the new theater in Amsterdam. He called it *Gijsbrecht van Aemstel, d' onderganck van zijn stadt en zijn balling-schap* (Gijsbrecht van Amstel, the Destruction of His City and his Exile). Vondel based his play on a short report in a medieval chronicle and worked it up into a tragedy. He was filled with the certainty that the destruction would be the necessary condition for a brilliant future:

> Although the city lies destroyed, it will not shudder at that: it will rise with a greater sheen from ashes and dust.

Vondel wanted to write a Christian counterpart to the national epic of the Romans, Virgil's *Aeneid,* the story of the destruction of Troy from which the cosmopolitan city Rome would triumphantly arise. Does Vondel do the same as this Roman poet? Is this not just a nationalist pep talk? A proud heroic epic about Amsterdam? To understand Vondel's answer properly, it is important to look at which cities play a role in Vondel's play. There are three: Amsterdam, Troy, and Bethlehem!

The play takes place against the background of the events in Bethlehem at Christmas. The first performance of *De Gijsbrecht* was on Boxing Day. The play presents the opposition between the barbaric decline of earthly greatness and the permanent significance of eternal values such as humility and trusting surrender to God — *islam* in the deepest meaning of the word, the actual surrender to God. Over against the rich, scintillating, glittering cosmopolitan city, we see in Bethlehem the simplicity of the child Jesus and his mother. Vondel had understood that not Jerusalem but Bethlehem was the city of God. Jerusalem is elsewhere called the city of David (2 Sam 5:7), but ultimately it is Bethlehem that is a "city of David," an idea that was influenced by the prophet Micah: "But you, Bethlehem Ephrathah, though you are small among the clans of Judah, out of you will come for me one who will be ruler over Israel, whose origins are from of old, from ancient times" (Mic 5:2; Matt 2:6; cf. 1 Sam 17:12). There the true messianic king would be born — David in the sense of a true caliph, just like Jesus, who could resist the devil's temptation as the second Adam (Matt 4:1-11). The destruction of the proud earthly city occurs on Christmas night, in which the humble child is born. The small rock that represents the kingdom of God shatters the proud image of Nebuchadnezzar (Dan 2:45). The "small" is what is chosen by heaven, for whoever is reborn in humility is born of heaven (van den Vondel).

This is the One Tale that the Three Books tell about, and is directed towards the One City on the Hill.

Glossary

Aaron Hârûn, brother of Moses and Miriam.

Abbasids The third dynasty of caliphs (A.D. 750-1256), with Baghdad as its capital.

Abd Allah ("servant of God"). Muhammad's father (died before the prophet was born).

'Abd al-Malik See Walid I ibn 'Abd al-Malik, Al-.

Abel ("breath," "triviality," "vanity"). Hâbîl, second son of Adam and Eve. He represents the shepherd culture over against the agricultural culture of Cain.

Abraham Ibrâhîm, the father of the "believers," Jews, Christians, and Muslims. Abraham was a "muslim."

Absalom Son of David.

Abû Bakr Friend of Muhammad, and his first successor or caliph.

Abû Jahl Opponent and enemy of the prophet Muhammad.

Abû Lahab ("father of the flame," i.e. "hell"). A violent opponent of Muhammad, leader of the boycott against him in Mecca.

Abû Sufyân Rich merchant who led the opposition to the prophet Muhammad.

Abû Talib Uncle, supporter, and protector of Muhammad; father of his cousin 'Ali.

Abyssinia See Cush.

Achaemenids Royal dynasty of the Persian Empire (538 to 332 B.C.). Palestine came under this empire founded by Cyrus the Great.

Achilles Son of Peleus and Thetis (a sea nymph); a hero of the Trojan War.

Acropolis The hill of Ares/Mars in Athens.

Actium Site of battle on 2 September 31 B.C. off the coast of Greece, where the fleet of Mark Antony and Cleopatra fought against the fleet of Octavian (later Caesar Augustus).

ʿÂd A powerful Arab tribe to which the prophet Hûd was sent.

Adam The first human being.

ʿAdn Garden of Eden.

Adonijah Son of David.

Adoniram Head of the department of forced labor under the kings David, Solomon, and Rehoboam.

Aeneid Epic poem by the Roman poet Virgil (70-19 B.C.).

Aeschylus Playwright, author of *The Persians* (ca. 525-456 B.C.).

Agag King of Amalek. The name Gog has been associated with Agag.

Agamemnon King of Mycenae, brother of Menelaus.

Ahab King of Israel (ruled ca. 873-851 B.C.), son of Omri.

Ahashverosh Xerxes I, king of Babylon; Biblical Ahasuerus. He repudiated his wife and chose Esther as his new queen.

Ahijah A prophet from Shiloh at the time of King Solomon. He appointed Jeroboam I as king.

Ahl al-Dhikr People of the Memory; alternative term for people of the Book (ahl al-Kitâb).

Ahl al-kitâb People of the Book: Jews, Christians, and Muslims.

Ahriman The entity of evil that is opposed to Ahura Mazda and all his creatures.

Ahura Mazda Zoroastrian deity, the one God, creator of heaven and earth, worshipped by Darius. Lord of light and wisdom, this god represents all that is good.

Alaric King of the Aryan Visigoths (West Goths; ca. A.D. 370-410) who sacked Rome in 410.

Alba Longa City in the Albanian hills southeast of Rome, head of the Latin League prior to its defeat by Rome in the seventh century B.C.; founded by the son of Aeneas. Romulus and Remus were descended from the kings of Alba Longa.

Alexander Legend *The Glorious Deeds of Alexander*. Syriac work from the time of Muhammad.

Alexander Romance Late Hellenistic version of the *Alexander Legend* from the third century A.D. A popular Syriac edition circulated among Orthodox Christians and influenced the Qur'an.

Alexander the Great Alexander III, king of Macedon (356-323 B.C.). Creator of one of the largest empires of antiquity, contributing to the rise of Hellenism.

Alexandria City west of the Nile Delta founded by Alexander the Great in 332-331 B.C. A major center of Hellenism.

'Alî The fourth caliph, cousin and son-in-law of Muhammad.

Allah Possibly a compilation from *al-Ilâh*, "the God," a name for God already in use before Islam.

Amalek 'Amâlîk, a nomadic people living in the area of Kadesh, related to the Edomites; preeminent enemies of the children of Israel.

Ammon A neighboring people to the east of Israel.

Amorites West Semitic people living in Palestine before the arrival of the Israelites.

Amos A prophet from Tekoa, who prophesied ca. 760 B.C. against Jeroboam II in Bethel.

Amram 'Imrân, father of Moses, Aaron, and Miriam.

Anak 'Anaq, a giant, ancestor of the Anakim.

Anakim (lit., "long-necked people"). A tall or giant people among the original inhabitants of Canaan.

Ansâr "Helpers" of the prophet Muhammad from Medina; also a term for Jesus' disciples.

Antiochus Epiphanes Antiochus IV, Seleucid king (175-164 B.C.), also called *Theos Epiphanes* (The "God Who Appeared").

Apocalyptic texts Writings concerning visions or prophecies of the end time (e.g., Ezekiel 38–39, Daniel, the Revelation of John, the *Alexander Legend*).

Apostle ("One sent [out]"). A disciple of Jesus.

Arameans A nomadic people descended from Nahor, brother of Abraham, who engaged in war with Saul, David, and Solomon.

Ard (Arabic "earth, land"). Also refers to "city."

Ares Mars, god of war and conflict.

Argonauts Greek heroes under the leadership of Jason in a quest to retrieve the Golden Fleece from Colchis; a reflection of trade expeditions to the rich East.

Arianism Christian movement from the beginning of the fourth century that did not accept the doctrine of the Trinity.

Aristotle Greek philosopher (384-322 B.C.), student of Plato and teacher of Alexander the Great.

Arius Presbyter in Alexandria (A.D. 256-336) who viewed Christ as subservient to God (Arianism).

Ark A portable shrine (Arabic *tâbût*). The Israelites took the ark of the covenant (the dwelling place of God) with them on their journey through the desert. It was with Joshua during the crossing of the Jordan, the entry into the land, and the blessing on Mount Ebal.

Âsîya Pharaoh's wife, who raised Mûsâ/Moses. In the Bible it is Pharaoh's daughter who does so.

Assur Oldest city of Assyria and from the beginning of the second millennium B.C. capital of the empire (later replaced by Nineveh). Named after its chief deity; also the name of the country. The Assyrians were known for their cruelty in war.

Astarte Canaanitte goddess of fertility, the queen of heaven; identical with Akkadian Ishtar. Patron goddess of the cities of Ashkelon, Tyre, and Sidon. Solomon had sacrifices made to the "goddess of the Sidonians" for political reasons (1 Kgs 11:5).

Atonement, Day of Yom Kippur, an annual day of fasting and penitence on the tenth day of the New Year, five days before the Feast of Tabernacles. Muhammad arrived in Medina after the *hijra* from Mecca in 622 on the Day of Atonement.

Atreus King of Mycenae; father of Agamemnon and Menelaus.

Augustine Latin church father (A.D. 354-430) from the West Roman province of Africa (northeastern Algeria, northern Tunisia). Author of *De Civitate Dei (The City of God)*.

Âya (*âyât* pl.) "Sign" or verse of the Qur'an.

Ayyûb See Job.

Âzar Name for the father of Abraham in the Koran. Called Terah in the Bible.

Azîz Name in the Qur'an for Potiphar, a "person of power" in Egypt.

Baal Ba'l ("Lord," "Possessor"). A deity viewed as an idol, regarded as parallel to the Mesopotamian god Baal and his three daughters who were worshipped as "daughters of God."

Babel, Tower of According to tradition, built by Nimrod or by Haman on Pharaoh's orders. See ziggurat.

Bâbil See Babylon.

Babylon Bâbil, city on the river Euphrates; the world's largest city between 1770 and 1670 B.C.

Babylonian Empire Mesopotamian empire of the second millennium B.C., with its capital at Babylon.

Babylonian Exile The deportation to Babylon by Nebuchadnezzar II in 598 B.C. of much of the population of Judah (2 Kgs 24–25; 2 Chr 36), lasting until the edict by Cyrus in 538 (2 Chronicles 36; Ezra 1). Also called the Babylonian Captivity.

Badr Site of battle in March A.D. 624 resulting in victory by Muslim followers of Muhammad over the Meccans. It was the "Day of Distinction" *(furqân),* the separation between the spirits of good and evil. Badr is the "Muslim Exodus."

Bakkah A name for Mecca.

Balaam A pagan prophet, a seer, at the time of the conquest of Canaan.

Banû al-Asfâr The "Yellow Ones," a name used by Arabs for the the Byzantines.

Banû Isrâ'îl "Children of Israel."

Bar Kokhba Leader of the Jewish rebellion against the Romans A.D. 132-35.

Beast Designation of world powers in Daniel's vision of the four animals and in Revelation for enemies of the ecclesia.

Bel A name or title ("Lord") for Marduk, cognate to Baal.

Bethel Site of the Israelite national sanctuary established by Jeroboam.

Bethlehem Birthplace of David and Jesus.

Bilqîs Islamic name for the queen of Sheba (Balkis in Christian tradition).

Briseis Daughter of a priest at Lyrnessus near Troy, taken by Achilles to be his slave.

Bukht-Nassar See Nebuchadnezzar II.

Byzantines People of the Eastern Roman Empire.

Byzantium Capital of the Eastern Roman Empire; later called Constantinople.

Cain Kâbîl, eldest son of Adam and Eve. He killed his brother Abel.

Caleb Faithful follower of Moses, one of the twelve spies sent into the promised land.

Caliph Representative of God on earth; successor of the prophet Muhammad.

Caliphate Political and religious administration following the death of Muhammad, initiated with the first four "rightly guided caliphs" (Abû Bakr, 'Umar, 'Uthmân, and 'Alî).

Caphtor Land of origin of the Philistines, probably Crete.

Carmel Mountain ridge in northern Israel. Elijah challenged the prophets of Baal and Asherah on Mount Carmel and demonstrated the power of Yahweh (1 Kings 18).

Carthage "New city" on the Gulf of Tunis founded by the Phoenicians in the ninth century B.C., a commercial and cultural center that rivalled Rome.

Cato the Elder Roman stateman and orator (234-149 B.C.), opponent of Hellenization who fought as an officer in the Second Punic War.

Chaldea(ns) A people who settled southern Babylonia around 1000 B.C. The name became synonymous with Babylonia under the Chaldean dynasty, the last to rule Babylonia (626-539 B.C.).

Chosroes I Kisrâ (Persian Khusrau) Anûshirwân, considered the greatest of the Sassanid kings (A.D. 531-79), called the Pious or the Just. Although a Zoroastrian, he supported Christianity in Persia. He built numerous churches and monasteries in and around Ctesiphon at the instigation of his wife, a Christian. Chosroes himself had adopted a Christian patron saint, Sergius the Martyr, to whom he ascribed his successes.

Chosroes II Kisrâ Aparwîz, Sassanid king of Persia (A.D. 591-628), called Parwîz ("Conqueror"). He declared war on the Byzantine usurper Phocas after the fall of the Byzantine emperor Mauritius, conquered Persian Armenia, and destroyed Jerusalem in 614.

Colchis In antiquity the area on the eastern coast of the Black Sea (modern Georgia).

Constantine I Roman emperor (ca. A.D. 280-337). Declared imperator and Augustus by his troops; in 324 became the sole ruler of the entire empire. In 313 he declared himself in favor of Christianity. He and his mother Helena are included in the Byzantine calendar as saints. In Western church tradition he is honored as "the Great."

Constantinople Byzantium, refounded in A.D. 330 as Nova Roma or Konstantinoupolis ("City of Constantine"); capital of the Byzantine Empire.

Croesus King of Lydia (561-542 B.C.) in western Asia Minor. He subdued the Asian Greeks and made them pay tribute. His wealth was legendary.

Ctesiphon A Persian city near Baghdad, capital of the Parthian Empire, later the Sassanid Persian Empire. It was captured a number of times by the Romans. Following the destruction of the Jerusalem temple in A.D. 70, it became a powerful Jewish center. Conquered by the Arabs following the battle of Qâdisîyah in 637, the city came to an end in 751 when the new capital of Baghdad was founded.

Cush Oldest son of Ham, son of Noah. A designation for Ethiopia, Abyssinia. He is regarded as the father of the Assyrian king Nimrod and father of the Arab tribes. The prophet Zephaniah is a descendent of Cush.

Cyrus the Great Cyrus II, king of Persia (559-529 B.C.). He toppled the powerful Median Empire (553), subdued the Greek cities of Ionia (546), and conquered Babylon (539), thereby founding the Persian Empire. In 538 he allowed the Jewish exiles to return home.

Dabba The beast of the earth, a sign of the coming of the last day.

Dagon The national god of the Philistines, adopted when they moved into the coastal areas of Canaan. A temple of this god still existed in Ashdod at the time of the Maccabees.

Dajjâl ("liar," derived from Syriac). The antichrist.

Daniel Dâniyâl, a young Jew, deported together with others to Babel at the time of King Nebuchadnezzar. In Muslim legend, a revealer of the future and mysteries surrounding the last things.

Dâr al-Harb "House of War," post-Qur'anic expression for areas outside Muslim observance. Byzantium was so named as an enemy of Islam.

Dâr al-islâm "House of Peace," post-Qur'anic expression for areas of Muslim dominance. Also dâr al-salâm, a name for paradise.

Darius I Darius the Great, king of Persia (522-486 B.C.), the most important Persian ruler in antiquity. He is associated with the rebuilding of the temple by the returning exiles.

Darius III The last Achaemenid king (336-330 B.C.; 1 Macc 1:1). Although a talented ruler, he was defeated by Alexander the Great in 333 at Issus and in 331 at Gaugamela and was murdered in 330.

Dathan and Abiram Brothers who joined Korah's rebellion against Moses during the journey of the children of Israel through the desert. As punishment they were swallowed up by the earth.

Datis Median admiral at the time of the Battle of Marathon.

David Dâwûd, second king of Israel (ca. 1010-970 B.C.). Called caliph in the Qur'an.

Deutero-Isaiah Second Isaiah (chs. 40–55), active in the last ten years of the exile.

Dhikr Memory.

Dhû Nûwâs Last Jewish king of Sabâ' (ruled A.D. 515-25), known for his persecution of Christians in the city of Najrân.

Diadochi "Successors," the generals of Alexander the Great's army who took over and divided his immense empire.

Dragon Mythical monster of chaos, Leviathan, sea monster; not sharply distinguished from the serpent.

Ecclesia (Greek "called"). Community. See *Qahal, Umma*.

Edom A nation and region south of Moab and east of the Arabah. "The red one," nickname for its ancestor Esau because of his red or ruddy color.

Egypt One of the earliest and greatest civilizations, situated along the Nile River. It can be called a paradise, a land of refuge (Abraham, Jesus), as well as a land of oppression and slavery.

El "God," Semitic name for the supreme God.

Eliezer Abraham's most trusted servant.

Elijah Ilyâs/Yâsîn, a major Yahwist prophet, whose name means "The Lord is my God."

Elisha Al-Yasa', the "man of God" who succeeded Elijah as prophet.

Enûma Elish Babylonian epic of the creation of the world.

Ephraim Second son of Joseph who received the blessing of the firstborn instead of his older brother Manasseh. Also the name given the tribe and the entire northern kingdom of ten tribes.

Eretz Hebrew "land, earth."

Esau Jacob's twin brother, son of Isaac and Rebecca. Also called Edom ("red"). Esau represents the hunter culture.

Esther A young Jewish exile after whom the biblical book is named, the foster child of Mordecai, chosen as queen by Ahashverosh.

Ethiopia See Cush.

Eusebius Church father, bishop of Caesarea (ca. A.D. 263–ca. 339). Advisor of Constantine the Great.

Eve Hawwâ', the first woman, "Mother of all living."

Exodus "Departure."

Ezekiel Judean prophet who was deported in 597 B.C. as exile to Babel.

Ezra 'Uzayr, scribe and priest considered to be the reformer of Judaism after the Babylonian captivity.

Fasâd "Doom," the bringing of ruin and destruction upon the earth.

al-Fath ("victory," divine "gift"). The conquest of Mecca by Muhammad in A.D. 630. A sura of the Qur'an.

Fâtih "Conqueror," nickname of Ottoman Turkish sultan Mehmed II.

Fâtih Mosque "Mosque of the Victory" in Istanbul, founded by Mehmed II.

Fâtima Daughter of Muhammad and Khadija. Wife of 'Ali, Muhammad's cousin.

Fir'awn See Pharaoh.

Fitna Civil war.

Fitra *Din al-Fitra,* "natural religion," the original religion or service to God in contrast to particular religions that arose later.

Furqân A term meaning "distinction," "separation," "liberation," "salvation," "escape," "redemption," "criterion." It can also mean "Revelation."

Gabriel Jibrîl ("Strength of God"), one of the foremost angels who brought messages to the prophets. He explained visions to Daniel and announced the birth of John the Baptist and Jesus.

Gehenna Jahannam, "hell." The valley of Hinnom, where human sacrifices were brought.

Giants Jabbarîn, children of Anak/ʿAnaq.

Gideon An Israelite judge, renowned for expelling Midianite invaders.

Gilgamesh Legendary king of the Sumerian city of Uruk in southern Babylonia. The Gilgamesh Epic is a Mesopotamian account (ca. 2500 B.C.) of the flood as told by the hero Utnapishtim.

Gog and Magog Yâjûj and Mâjûj. Two figures who appear in the last days. A classic example of nomadic invasions, symbols of oppressive powers.

Goliath Jâlût, a giant, champion of the Philistines.

Gospel Injîl, New Testament accounts of the life and teachings of Jesus: Matthew, Mark, Luke, John.

Gyges King of Lydia (685-644 B.C.), identified with Gog.

Hâbîl See Abel.

Hadîth Traditions and sayings of the prophet Muhammad, an important Muslim source after the Qur'an.

Hadrian Publius Aelius Trajanus Hadrianus, Roman emperor (A.D. 76-138). He adored Greek culture and was thus called "the little Greek."

Hagar Egyptian slave woman of Sarah, mother of Ishmael.

Haggadah Jewish narrations that embellish the biblical stories with various sagas and legends. Haggadah can be learned from the midrashim, a commentary on the Old Testament or its particular books. The oldest is the book of *Jubilees* from the second half of the second century B.C.

Haggai Prophet at the time of the Persian king Darius I (522-486 B.C.); commented on events in 520.

Hajj Pilgrimage to Mecca

Halakah ("way to travel"). Interpretation of divine and rabbinic law based on the Torah (613 regulations); juridical-casuistic interpretation of legal prescripts.

Haman Hâmân, the vizier of King Ahashverosh; a descendant of King Agag.

Hammurabi King of Babylon (ca. 1792-1750 B.C.), famous for his law code.

Hanging Gardens of Babylon One of the seven ancient wonders of the world.

Hanîf ("Seeker of God," "monotheist"). One who follows the true religion, over against the polytheist, idolater. Abraham is called a *hanîf.*

Hannibal Army commander from Carthage (247-183 B.C.). During the Second Punic War he marched an army, which included war elephants, from Iberia over the Pyrenees and the Alps into northern Italy.

Haran City in northern Mesopotamia where Abraham and his father lived after leaving Ur and from which Abraham and Lot departed for Canaan.

Hârûn See Aaron.

Hârût and Mârût Two angels sent by the council of angels to judge the earth. They taught sorcery in Babylon.

Hasmoneans Priestly family that revolted against Antiochus IV Epiphanes in 167 B.C. Flavius Josephus so named the Maccabean dynasty after their ancestor, Hasmon.

Hawwâ' See Eve.

Helen Wife of Agamemnon, king of the Greek city of Sparta.

Helena Mother of Constantine the Great.

Hell Hebrew Gehenna, Arabic Jahannan.

Hellenism The political and cultural expansion of Greek civilization from the time of Alexander the Great in the third century B.C. to the triumph of Rome in the first century B.C.

Heraclius Byzantine emperor (A.D. 610-41) who fought against Chosroes II. His rule was characterized by constant military campaigns: the Roman-Persian wars and later the Byzantine-Arab wars.

Herod Antipas Tetrarch of Galilee and Perea (4 B.C.–ca. A.D. 39), son of Herod the Great. He founded Tiberias as his capital, which he named after the emperor, and married his Hasmonean sister-in-law Herodias. Antipas ruled during the time of John the Baptist and Jesus.

Herod the Great Herod I, king of Judea (ca. 73-4 B.C.). Of Edomite or Idumean ancestry, he converted to Judaism.

Herodias Wife of Herod Philip, Herod Antipas's half-brother. Antipas wanted to marry her, which led to the death of John the Baptist, who criticized the act. Mother of Salome.

Herodotus The "father of historiography" (ca. 485-425 B.C.). He visited Babylon.

Hezekiah King of Judah (d. 687 B.C.), one of the few good kings.

Hijâz Region in the western Arabian Peninsula, modern Saudi Arabia, where the holy cities of Mecca and Medina are situated.

Hijra ("migration"). The emigration of Muhammad and his followers from Mecca to Medina in A.D. 622.

Hikma Arabic "Wisdom."

Hinnom Valley near Jerusalem where children were sacrificed to Moloch.

Hirâ' The "mountain of light," location of the cave near Mecca where Muhammad received his first revelation from God.

Hizb shaytân The party of Satan.

Hizbollah Party *(hizb)* of God (Allah).

Hokmah Hebrew "Wisdom."

Homer Greek author of the *Iliad* and the *Odyssey.*

Horeb Sinai, the mountain of God.

Horn Bull's or ram's horn. Symbol of power associated with the king, the Messiah, the apocalyptic enemy.

Hosea Prophet to northern Israel (ca. 750-722 B.C.) during the flourishing of the kingdom and its decline.

Hubris Pride, overconfidence.

Hûd Arab prophet sent to the people of ʿAd.

Huns Nomadic Central Asian peoples, including the Turks and Mongols, who made many raids into Europe, mostly in the western Roman Empire. The empire of Attila (d. 433) extended from the Caucasus to the Rhine.

Iblîs A name for Satan or the devil, the sower of division. A derivative of Greek *diabolos.*

Ibrâhîm See Abraham.

Icarus Mythic figure who attempted to escape Crete but flew too close to the sun and his wax wings melted.

Idumea Hellenistic name for Edom, the territory south of Judea, part of the kingdom of Herod the Great.

Ilyâs See Elijah.

Imam Leader "in the land," a spiritual guide, later used as an alternate title to caliph as successor to Muhammad.

Immanuel "God with us."

Incense Perfumes from southern Arabia.

Injîl See Gospel.

ʿÎsâ Ibn Maryam, Jesus the son of Mary.

Isaac Ishâq, son of Abraham and Sarah, brother of Ishmael.

Isaiah Prophet, called in the Jerusalem temple in the year King Uzziah of Judah died (740 B.C.). See Deutero-Isaiah.

Ishmael Ismâʾîl, son of Hagar and Abraham, older brother of Isaac. Ancestor of the prophet Muhammad.

Ishtar Mesopotamian goddess of war and love, Canaanite Astarte.

Ishtar Gate Eighth gate of Babylon, built by Nebuchadnezzar II ca. 575 B.C. and dedicated to the goddess. Glazed with blue, it was considered one of the wonders of the world. The royal palaces were close to the gate.

Islâh The restoration of order.

Isrâʾ See Night journey.

Istanbul Later name of Byzantium/Constantinople.

Jacob Ya'qûb, younger son of Isaac and Rebekah, Esau's brother. Another name for Israel. Jacob represents the shepherd culture.

Jacob's ladder In Jacob's dream, a ladder or stairway that reached to heaven from earth (Gen 28:10-19).

Jahannam See Gehenna.

Jahiliyya ("time of ignorance"). The era that preceded the advent of Islam.

Jâlût See Goliath.

Japheth One of the three sons of Noah, along with Shem and Ham, all of whom survived the flood. His descendants are mentioned only in the books of Isaiah and Ezekiel.

Jason High priest (174-171 B.C.) appointed by Antiochus IV Epiphanes.

Jehoiakim King of Judah (608-597 B.C.), deposed when Nebuchadnezzar besieged Jerusalem.

Jehu King of Israel (845-818 B.C.). He overthrew the dynasty of Omri and Ahab and started a new dynasty that lasted one hundred years.

Jeremiah Prophet from Anathoth. He had respect for King Josiah and agreed with his politics.

Jeroboam King of Israel (ca. 927-907 B.C.) over the ten northern tribes following Solomon's death.

Jeroboam II King of Israel (787-747 B.C.). His long rule was the last high point in the political history of Israel.

Jerome Latin church father (ca. A.D. 348-420) who translated the Bible into Latin (the Vulgate).

Jerusalem al-Quds, capital of Judah and the united monarchy; according to Pliny (A.D. 23-79) "by far the most famous city of the East." In the fourth century A.D. it was a primarily Christian city. In 614 Jerusalem was conquered and plundered by the Persians. Heraclius reconquered it in 628, and the Christians took revenge on the Jews. Ten years later Sophronius had to hand the city over to Caliph 'Umar.

Jesus 'Isâ, Jesus of Nazareth.

Jethro Shu'ayb, priest in Midian/Madyan; the father-in-law of Moses.

Jewish wars Jewish revolt against Rome fought from A.D. 66 to 70 and the Bar Kokhba rebellion from 132 to 135.

Jezebel Queen in Israel (d. 845 B.C.) from Sidon, wife of Ahab.

Jibrîl See Gabriel.

Jihâd (Lit., "make an effort," that is, on the way of God [*fî sabîl Allah*]). A broad term: "struggle," "striving," "effort." Radical groups see jihâd as "holy war."

Job Ayyûb, a righteous man of Uz, focus of the biblical book that recounts his trials and suffering.

John the Baptist Yahyâ, forerunner of Jesus. Named among the prophets, he is called the returned Elijah.

Jonah Yûnus, one of the Minor Prophets.

Joseph Yûsuf, one of the twelve sons of Jacob. Sold by his brothers into slavery in Egypt, he rose to power in Pharaoh's court.

Josephus, Flavius Jewish historian (A.D. 37-100).

Joshua Yûsha', a helper ("the young man") of Moses. He accompanied Moses on his journey (Q 18:60-64) and was his successor; one of the spies sent into Canaan.

Josiah King of Judah (640-609 B.C.). He was one of the few good kings, used by the prophet Jeremiah as an example. He died in battle against Pharaoh Necho II.

Jubilees Also called "Lesser Genesis," a postbiblical book paralleling Genesis and Exodus. Emphasis is on precise observance of the Sabbath and other cultic laws, and the patriarchs are idealized as ethical examples.

Judah One of the twelve sons of Jacob, ancestor of the tribe and nation. After the division of the monarchy upon the death of Solomon, the name designated the southern kingdom with Jerusalem as its capital.

Judges Saviors and liberators, active in the period following Joshua and before the kingship in Israel. A book of the Bible among the Former Prophets.

Justinian I Byzantine emperor (A.D. 527-65), "the Great." In 529 he closed the Academy of Athens, which still promoted Neo-platonism. Most famous for rebuilding the Hagia Sophia, he also built St. Catherine's Monastery at the foot of Mount Sinai.

Ka'ba Shrine dedicated to God *(al-bayt Allah)* in Mecca, built by Abraham together with his son Ishmael. "The dedicated place of prayer" *(al-masjid al-harâm)* refers to the Grand Mosque, the location of the Ka'ba.

Kâbîl See Cain.

Kâfir Unbeliever, lit., "ungrateful."

Ketubim Writings, the third part of the Tanakh.

Khadija Muhammad's first wife, mother of Fâtima.

Khidr ("Green man"). A companion of Moses.

Kir Land of origin of the Arameans. The location is unknown, perhaps in the northeast of the Syrian Arabian desert.

Kisrâ Anûshirwân See Chosroes I.

Kisrâ Aparwîz See Chosroes II.

Kitâb Arabic "book."

Korah Qârûn, leader of rebellion against Moses during the wilderness wanderings. He was characterized by wealth about which he brags and by pride.

Laban Brother of Rebecca, Isaac's wife, and father of Leah and Rachel, both of whom Jacob married.

Labarum Monogram of Christ: the Greek letters *chi-rho.*

Lamech Lamak, descendant of Cain.

al-Lât "The Goddess," pre-Islamic mother goddess; daughter of Baal.

Lavinium City in Latium (west-central Italy) that Aeneas named after his wife.

Law of the king Prescriptions for a king; "Mirror of Princes."

Leonidas I King of Sparta who led a Greek alliance against the Persians at Thermopylae.

Leviathan Dragon that embodies chaos and other powers hostile to God.

Leviticus Third book of the Torah, in Hebrew called *Wayyiqra* ("And he called").

Livy Livius, Roman historian (ca. 59 B.C.-A.D. 17) who wrote a monumental history of Rome from 753.

Lot Lût, Abraham's nephew and son of Haran.

Lucifer An archangel, proud and greedy for status; medieval name for Satan.

Lût See Lot.

Maccabees Hasmonean dynasty that rebelled against Antiochus IV Epiphanes (ca. 167-135 B.C.).

Madyan See Midian.

Mahdî "Guided one," a leader whose arrival in the end time will return justice to the earth, a messiah figure sometimes connected with the return of Jesus. He does not appear in the Qur'an.

Maimonides A foremost medieval Jewish philosopher and Torah scholar (A.D. 1135-1204).

Mâjûj See Gog and Magog.

Makôm (Hebrew "place"). A name for Jerusalem.

al-Mala' Prominent people, leaders, notables, counselors. These are the unjust leaders of the peoples and the preeminent opponents of the prophets. They stand over against the weak and oppressed.

Malik Arabic "king."

Mammon The personification of avarice.

Man with two horns Dhû al-Qarnayn, symbol for Alexander the Great (Daniel 8).

Manasseh King of Judah (696/687-642 B.C.), son of King Hezekiah whom he succeeded.

Manât Pre-Islamic goddess of fate or time; daughter of Baal.

Manna "Bread from heaven" that the children of Israel were given during their journey through the desert.

Marathon Battle in 490 B.C. in which the Athenian Greeks ended the first Persian invasion of Greece under Darius I.

Marduk The chief Babylonian god. He defeated Tiamat, the monster of chaos. His main temple in Babylon had a tower (ziggurat).

Mark Antony Roman politician and general (ca. 83-30 B.C.). After the death of Julius Caesar he formed a triumvirate with Lepidus and Octavian to govern the Roman Empire.

Mars Ares, god of war and conflict. Regarded as the father of Romulus and Remus. Wolf is dedicated to him; *fuga* ("flight") and *timor* ("fear") follow after him.

Mârût See Hârût and Mârût.

Mary Maryam, the mother of Jesus.

Masîh See Messiah.

Mecca al-*Mukarrama* ("The Blessed City"), Umm al-Qurrâ "Mother of the cities" ("metropolis"). The birthplace of Muhammad. Also called Bakkah.

Meccan chapters Chapters of the Qur'an revealed between A.D. 610 and 622.

Medina Madîna, "City," namely of the prophet Muhammad; originally Yathrib. The second holiest city in Islam and burial place of the prophet. Also called *al-Madînat al-munawarra,* the "city of light."

Medinan chapters Chapters of the Qur'an revealed between A.D. 622 and 632.

Mehmed II Ottoman Turkish sultan (A.D. 1451-81), "the Conqueror." He defeated Constantinople in 1453, ending the Byzantine Empire.

Melchizedek ("king of righteousness"). King of Salem and a priest whom Abraham met.

Melek Hebrew "king."

Melkites Christians who supported the ruler of Byzantium and the Council of Chalcedon.

Menelaus King of Sparta, brother of Agamemnon.

Merciful See Rahmân.

Messiah "Anointed," the king or Christ. Arabic Masîh.

Midian Madyan, region in the northwestern Arabian Peninsula. The oldest known tribe of camel nomads.

Midrash (Hebrew "ask" or "investigate"). Explanations of the Tanakh by Jewish religious leaders.

Milk and honey Attribute of the promised land. Necessities of life for nomads.

Mi'râj The ascension (heavenly journey) of the prophet Muhammad from Jerusalem.

Miriam Maryam, sister of Moses and Aaron.

Mirror of Princes Nasîhat al-muluk, a "mirror" that is held up to the ruler and whose strictures he must follow; Law of the King.

Misr, Misraïm Egypt.

Mithras Roman deity, called "the invincible sun" *(Sol invictus)*, based on the ancient Persian god of light, Mithra.

Moab A neighboring people of Israel, situated in the Transjordan between Ammon and Edom, descended from Lot and his older daughter.

Moloch Canaanite god (from *melek*, "[unjust] king"), to whom children were sacrificed.

Moses Mûsâ, Israelite liberator and lawgiver.

Mu'âwiyya II Caliph (reigned A.D. 661-80), the first Umayyad caliph in Damascus; son of Aû Sufyân.

Muhadjirûn ("emigrants"). Those who left Mecca with Muhammad for Medina.

Muhammad The Messenger of God (ca. A.D. 570-632); the prophet (al-nabî). He saw himself as Abraham's descendant through Ishmael.

Mulk Arabic "kingship" (secular).

Mûsâ See Moses.

Muslim One who submits to God in complete trust.

Mut'a The first battle in A.D. 629 between Arabs and a Byzantine garrison in which Muhammad's forces were defeated.

Nahum Prophet from southern Judah. He predicted that Nineveh, capital of the Assyrian Empire, would fall (612 B.C.), just as had Thebes, the Egyptian city laid waste by the Assyrians.

Najrân The first place where Christianity took root in southern Arabia.

Namrûd See Nimrod.

Nâmûs Arabic "law."

Nasîhat al-mulûk "Advice for kings, rulers"; Mirror of Princes.

Nasr Arabic "help," "victory" given by God.

Nebo Mountain from which Moses could see the promised land without being able to enter it.

Nebuchadnezzar II Bukht-Nassar, king of Babylonia (604-562 B.C.). He conquered Jerusalem in 597 and again in 587, deporting much of the populace to Babylon.

Negus Title of the rulers of Ethiopia, descended from the union of King Solomon and the Queen of Sheba.

Nemesis Greek goddess of retribution, the personification of avenging justice.

Neo-Babylonian Empire Mesopotamian empire from 612 B.C., following the decline of Assyria.

Nestorians Assyrian Christians, a branch of the church deriving from schism over the divine and human nature of Christ.

New Year's Feast Babylonian spring (March) feast during which the king saw his power as representative of God on earth renewed.

Night journey Isrâ', the journey of Muhammad from Mecca to Jerusalem, from which he ascended to heaven.

Nimrod Namrûd, king of Assur and Babylon, said to have built the tower of Babel.

Nineveh Capital of the Assyrian Empire, conquered by Medes and Babylonians in 612 B.C.

Ninus According to Hellenistic Greek historians, the legendary Assyrian founder of Nineveh.

Noah Nûh, commanded by God to build an ark that would save him from the flood. Father of Ham, Shem, and Japheth.

Nomos Greek "law," which through the influence of the Torah has come to mean instruction for one's life.

North Point of origin of enemies representing divine judgment.

Nûh See Noah.

Og 'Uj, Amorite king of Bashan; considered to be one of the Rephaim, the legendary original population of the land of Canaan. Several legends occur in the Haggadah and Islamic tradition.

Omri King of Israel (878-871 B.C.), father of Ahab.

Palace Residence of the king; in the ancient Near East, located next to the temple, the most important center of civilization.

Palestine In the Qur'an called "the land whose borders God has blessed" for all peoples.

Palladium Image of Pallas Athena in Troy that protected the city.

Paris Son of the Trojan king Priam, he abducted Helen.

Parwîs See Chosroes II.

Passover The Feast of Unleavened Bread, commemorating the Israelites' haste when leaving Egypt, thus the exodus itself. The feast celebrates their liberation from Egypt and the hope of the coming redemption.

Pentapolis The five cities: Sodom, Gomorrah, Adma, Seboim, and Soar, a coalition of five Canaanite city-states.

Pentateuch The five books of Moses: Genesis, Exodus, Leviticus, Numbers, Deuteronomy.

People of the Book Adherents to received Scripture: Torah/Tawra and Gospel/Injîl, namely Jews and Christians.

Persepolis Achaemenid ceremonial royal capital. Greek name of Parsa, founded ca. 520 B.C. by Darius I. In Persian called "the throne of Jamshid."

Pharaoh Fir'awn, ruler of Egypt.

Philistines Aegean people who migrated from Caphtor (Crete) to the southern coast of Palestine in the thirteenth-twelfth centuries B.C.

Pilate Pontius, appointed procurator of Judea by the Emperor Tiberius (A.D. 26-36).

Pilgrimage See Hajj.

Potiphar Azîz, Pharaoh's captain of the guard.

Priam King of Troy, father of Hector and Paris.

Pride Arrogance, "making oneself great." Only God is great *(Alluhu akbar)*.

Ptolemy Macedonian dynasty that ruled Egypt after the death of Alexander the Great. Under Ptolemy I Soter (323-285 B.C.), general under Alexander, the country became a Hellenistic kingdom in which Hellenistic Judaism grew. Between 274 and 168, six wars occurred between the Ptolemies and the Seleucids. Cleopatra VII was the last of the dynasty, which ended with conquest by Rome in 30 B.C.

Punic Wars Three wars (Bella Punica) between Rome and Carthage (founded by Phoenicia, hence the name Punic) 246-146 B.C. In the First Punic War (264-241), the Romans encountered the seafaring Carthaginians over control of Sicily. The Second Punic War (218-201) was a land war fought primarily in Italy and on the Iberian Peninsula, during which Hannibal led his army over the Alps. The Third Punic War (149-146) involved no more than the siege of Carthage and ended in the city's complete destruction.

Purim Jewish feast on 14 Adar commemorating the salvation of the Jews under Ahashverosh.

Qâdisîyah Site of battle in which the Sassanid Persians, led by Chosroes, were defeated in A.D. 637 by Arab Muslims, after which they captured the capital city of Ctesiphon.

Qahal Hebrew "community." The Jewish people who are "called."

Qarn See Man with two horns.

Qârûn See Korah. Also a symbol for a wealthy person.

Qarya Arabic "city, village, place where people live and meet." Cf. Phoenician *qart-hadasht*, Carthage; Hebrew Qiryat Arba', Hebron.

Qaysar Arabic name for the Byzantine emperor, mentioned alongside the king of Persia and the negus of Ethiopia.

Qibla Prayer direction, initially Jerusalem but later Mecca and the Ka'ba.

al-Quds "The Holy," Arabic name for Jerusalem.

Queen of Sheba Bilqîs/Balkis, "Queen of the South."

Qur'an The Scripture of Islam (derived from *'iqra*, "recite"), revealed to the prophet Muhammad through the archangel Gabriel/Jibrîl. Divided into 114 named chapters *(suras)* and more than 6000 verses *(ayât)*. Part of the Qur'an was revealed in Mecca and the rest in Medina, thus the Meccan and Medinan division of chapters.

Rabb Arabic "Lord," name of God in the Qur'an.

Rabbi ("my master"). Title of respect for Jewish teacher of Scripture. Jesus rejected this title but was so called by the people.

Rahab Sea monster, the primeval dragon of chaos defeated by God in creation. A metaphor for Egypt.

Rahmân The "Merciful," an important name for God in the Qur'an. This name appeared already in the pre-Islamic era, namely in inscriptions at Saba.

Ramadân Month of fasting, in which the Qur'an was revealed and also when the Battle of Badr occurred.

Rasûl A messenger, apostle.

Rehoboam King of Judah (926-910 B.C.), son and successor of Solomon and against whom the ten northern tribes revolted.

Rightly guided caliphs The four original caliphs: Abû Bakr, 'Umar, 'Uthmân, 'Alî.

Rome "The new Troy" (Virgil), name for both the capital and the empire. Christianity was officially sanctioned under Constantine in A.D. 312. The fall of Rome may be traced to the Visigoth sack of the city in 410.

Romulus and Remus Twins, mythical founders of Rome. On the site where Rome would be built they were suckled by a she-wolf. Romulus killed his brother Remus.

Rûm Name in the Qur'an for Byzantium, the "second Rome."

Sabâ' See Sheba.

Sakîna Shekinah, the divine "presence" of God, "God's peace."

Saladin Muslim ruler (A.D. 1137-93) who recaptured Jerusalem from the Crusaders in 1187 and seized the "true cross" that had been taken by the bishop of Akko in the battle of Hattin. Saladin's name is sometimes preceded by the phrase "the victorious king" *(al-malik al-nâsir)*.

Salamis Site of sea battle between an alliance of Greek city-states and the Persian Empire in 480 B.C., in the straits between the island and the mainland.

Salât and zakât Prayers to be offered five times daily and 2.5 alms tax on wealth, the religious and social obligations that have become two of the five pillars of Islam.

Salem ("peaceful," "safe"). Residence of the priest-king Melchizedek, identified with Zion. A symbolic and religious name for the holy city, Jerusalem.

Sâlih Messenger to the people of Thamûd.

Salman the Persian A companion of the prophet Muhammad, so close he was called a member of the family. On his advice, a defensive moat was dug around Medina in A.D. 625 as a defense against the Meccan opponents.

Salome Daughter of Herodias who persuaded her to ask for the head of John the Baptist.

Samaria Capital of the northern kingdom of Israel after King Solomon.

Samarra Capital of the Abbasid caliphate, ca. 100 km north of Baghdad. Caliph al-Mutawakkil had a minaret built for the great mosque in Samarra ca. A.D. 850, its form inspired by the Babylonian ziggurats.

Samuel Shamwil, "the one prayed for from God." A prophet, the last of the Israelite judges.

Sanhedrin The "high council," the central Jewish judicial authority in Jerusalem during the Greek-Roman period.

Sardis City in Asia Minor, capital of the kingdom of Lydia.

Sassanids Persian dynasty that reigned over the last pre-Islamic empire, from A.D. 224 to 651.

Satan Shaytân, enemy and tempter of human beings; Greek *diabolos*.

Saul Tâlût, the first king of Israel.

Scipio Nascia Roman general and politician (236-183 B.C.) who in the Second Punic War defeated Hannibal. He had to withdraw from political life under pressure from Cato the Elder.

Scythians A nomadic people, probably of Iranian origin. Reliant on horses, characterized as belligerent and wild but also technically advanced. They came from Central Asia and founded a kingdom in the area of the Danube and the Don (700-200 B.C.). Conducting raids as far as Egypt, they became a cause for concern in Syria and Palestine: the people from the north mentioned by Jeremiah.

Seir (Hebrew "forested"). Central mountain range of Edom, a place of divine revelation and judgment.

Seleucids Dynasty whose empire encompassed the fertile crescent, from the death of Alexander the Great until 120 B.C. The most important Seleucid rulers were Seleucus I, Antiochus II, and Antiochus IV (175-164). Under the conqueror Antiochus III (223-187), called the Great, the empire reached its greatest dimensions, including Mesopotamia, Syria, and Phoenicia. The Seleucids greatly spread the influence of Hellenism, including the deconsecration and rededication of the Jerusalem temple.

Semiramis Legendary Assyrian queen, spouse of King Ninus, founder of the city of Nineveh.

Septuagint ("seventy," LXX). Greek translation of the Hebrew Scriptures (end of the second century B.C.), the word of Revelation for the Greek-speaking Jews. The ancient church adopted and used this translation.

Shadrach, Meshach, and Abednego Daniel's companions in the Babylonian court, thrown into a fiery furnace by King Nebuchadnezzar.

Shafa'a Intercession.

Shamwil See Samuel.

Sharî'a Often translated as Islamic "law" (cf. Torah), its primary meaning is "way."

Shaytân See Satan.

Sheba Sabâ', a people and kingdom in southwestern Arabia known for its wealth that was based on trade. In ancient times the area was called Arabia Felix, "Happy Arabia." The last kings of the kingdom converted to Judaism.

Shemaiah Prophet at the time of Rehoboam.

Shepherd A divine or royal title, e.g., a "shepherd for his people."

Shu'ayb Jethro, prophet to the inhabitants of Midian.

Sign A verse (âya) of the Qur'an.

Sin Moon-god worshipped in Ur.

Sinai Sînâ, the mountain of God where Moses and Elijah encountered God.

Sodom and Gomorrah Cities in the vicinity of the Dead Sea that were "overthrown" through divine judgment.

Sol Invictus ("invincible sun"). Sun-god of the later Roman Empire. His feast was celebrated on December 25.

Solomon Sulaymân, the son and successor of David as king of Israel (970-930 B.C.).

Song of Songs Collection of love poems attributed to Solomon.

St. Catherine's Monastery Orthodox monastery at the foot of the traditional mountain of Moses in the Sinai Peninsula, built by the Byzantine emperor Justinian.

Strabo Greek historian, geographer, and philosopher (64 B.C.–A.D. 19).

Stranger Greek *xenos*, also "guest" (cf. *hostis*, "enemy"), occasional term for God.

Sulayha Potiphar's wife.

Sulaymân See Solomon.

Sumerians The first major civilization in Mesopotamia (third millennium B.C.), whose rich culture influenced later Babylonian, Israelite, and even Greek civilizations.

Sura A chapter of the Qur'an.

Sûrat al-Fâtiha The opening chapter of the Qur'an.

Susa Ancient capital of Elam. After conquest by Cyrus II, it became the residence of the Achaemenids and the stage for the book of Esther. Conquered by Alexander the Great in 331 B.C., it declined under his successors, the Seleucids. Alexander organized a mass wedding in Susa (324) in the guise of cultural collaboration between peoples.

al-Tabarî Muslim historian from the ninth century A.D.

Tabor Mountain in the plain of Jezreel, according to Origen the location of the transfiguration.

Tahrîf Twisting of Scripture, an accusation made of the "people of the Book" (i.e., Jews and Christians).

Talmud Compendium of Jewish law, legend, and wisdom. The Babylonian Talmud is the normative collection of the oral Torah.

Tâlût "The tall," a name for King Saul. In Arabic, wordplay between Tâlût and Jâlût (Goliath).

Tanakh Acronym for the Jewish Scriptures: Torah (Law), Nebi'im (Prophets), Ketubim (Writings).

Tawra Holy Scripture revealed to Moses after Abraham.

Tel-abib Colony of Jews, including the prophet Ezekiel, along the River Chebar in Babylon.

Temple In 586 B.C. the Babylonian king Nebuchadnezzar II (605-562) destroyed Jerusalem, including the temple of Solomon. Rebuilding began in 520 through the initiative of the prophet Haggai, who associated its completion with the promise of the dawn of the messianic salvific age. The prophet Zechariah connects eight night visions of successive preparation phases of the era of salvation with resumption of building of the temple.

Terah Hebrew name for the father of Abraham according to the Torah. See Âzar.

Tertullian Latin church father (A.D. 160-230).

Tetragrammaton (Greek "four letters"). The sacred name of God represented by the Hebrew consonants.

Thamûd A people of central Arabia to which the prophet Sâlih was sent as a messenger. They disappeared before the time of Muhammad.

Themistocles Athenian statesman and admiral.

Thermopylae Battle in 480 B.C. between an alliance of Greek city-states under Leonidas I and the Persians commanded by Xerxes I.

Tiamat Mythical primal figure in the *Enuma Elish* that, with the powers of the deep, rebelled against the higher gods; depicted as a kind of dragon.

Tiberius The second Roman emperor (A.D. 14-37).

Titus Roman emperor (A.D. 79-81). As general, he laid siege to Jerusalem in 70, lacing the ground around the city with salt, making it infertile, and razing the temple to the ground.

Topheth Place in the valley of Hinnom where children were sacrificed, dedicated to the service of Moloch by fire.

Torah Hebrew "law," but more accurately "instruction," "way," or "signpost." The first division of the Hebrew canon, the "Five Books of Moses."

Troy Greek Ilion, city in the northwest of Asia Minor, close to the Hellespont. According to tradition, the Trojan War took placce in the twelfth century B.C.

True cross Relic found by Helena, mother of Constantine the Great.

al-Tûr (Arabic and Aramean "mountain"). Mount Sinai/Sînâ.

Tuwâ According to the Qur'an the valley where Moses was called. Also the name of the area surrounding Mecca, where Muhammad halted during his triumphal entry into the city in A.D. 630.

Tyre (*ṣûr,* "rock"). Phoenician port and kingdom.

ʿUj See Og.

ʿUmar Ibn ʿAbd al-Azîz Umayyad caliph (A.D. 717-20) known to be pious.

ʿUmar ibn al-Khattâb The second caliph (d. A.D. 644).

Umayyads The second dynasty of caliphs (A.D. 661-750), with its capital in Damascus.

Umm al-Qurrâ See Mecca.

Umma Arabic "community," which can refer to the totality of the Jewish, Christian, or Muslim communities.

Ummî "Unlettered," in the sense of having not received Scripture.

Unbeliever See Kâfir.

Unlettered prophet *al-nabi al-ummî,* namely Muhammad, the prophet for those who have not received the written revelation.

Ur A major Sumerian and later Babylonian-Chaldean city, Abraham's hometown and place where the moon-god Nanna (Sin) was worshipped. The ziggurat of Ur (twenty-first century B.C.) is one of the best preserved.

Uruk Erech, city in southern Babylonia founded by Nimrod. Home of the legendary king Gilgamesh.

'Uthmân The third caliph (A.D. 644-56), successor of the prophet Muhammad.

Utnapishtim ("He who found life"). In Tablet XI of the Gilgamesh Epic, the hero who survived the flood.

'Uzayr See Ezra.

Al-'Uzzâ "The Strong," "The Powerful," a pre-Islamic goddess. Muhammad destroyed her shrine after the conquest of Mecca in A.D. 630.

Al-Walid I ibn 'Abd al-Malik Umayyad caliph in Damascus (A.D. 668-715). He conquered Andalusia and built the great mosque of Damascus on the spot where the Basilica of John the Baptist stood, as well as various desert places including the bathhouse Qusayr 'Amra. He was famous for his piety.

Waraqa ibn Nawfal Christian cousin of Khadija, the prophet Muhammad's wife.

Wisdom Hebrew *hokmah,* Arabic *hikma.*

Wolf Symbol of the evil that constitutes a threat for the herd (the believers). "Wolf in sheep's clothing" is a symbol for false prophets.

Xerxes I Achaemenid king of Persia (486–ca. 446 B.C.); biblical Ahashverosh/Ahasuerus. He destroyed Athens and was defeated at the Battle of Salamis in 480.

Yahweh The God of Israel, who appears on Mount Sinai to Moses and Elijah. YHWH represents the name of God that is not pronounced by Jews. In the LXX, it is translated as *kyrios,* "Lord."

Yahyâ See John the Baptist.

Yâjûj See Gog and Magog.

Ya'qûb See Jacob.

al-Yasa' See Elisha.

Yâsîn See Elijah.

Yathrib See Medina.

Yellow Ones Banû Asfâr, Arab name for the Byzantines.

Yûnus See Jonah.

Yûsha' See Joshua.

Yûsuf See Joseph.

Zabûr (*zubur* pl.). The holy book of David/Dâwûd, writing(s) revealed before the Qur'an, often identified with the biblical book of Psalms.

Zealots Jewish national freedom fighters, against not only enemies but also moderate elements among their own people.

Zechariah (1) Prophet (ca. 520-518 B.C.) who, together with the prophet Haggai, argued for completion of the rebuilding of the temple. (2) Zakariyyâ, a priest, father of John the Baptist/Yahyâ.

Zedekiah The last king of Judah (597-587 B.C.).

Zephaniah Prophet whose warning of a world disaster gave stimulus for the reforms by King Josiah. A contemporary of the prophet Jeremiah and a descendant of King Hezekiah.

Zerubbabel Leader of a group of Jewish exiles who, together with the high priest Joshua, was in charge of the returning exiles. His name means "offspring of Babel," because he was born in the exile.

Ziggurat ("built up high"). Sumerian, Assyrian, and Babylonian terraced-step pyramidal towers or temple towers, a Mesopotamian symbol for a mountain. The building of such, namely the tower of Babel, was occasion for the confusion of language. Sumerians viewed high mountains as the dwelling place of the gods.

Zion Jebusite fortress of Zion, captured by David. Another name for Jerusalem, the city of David.

Zoroaster Zarathustra, prophet who believed in one almighty God, Ahura Mazda. He saw the world as a theater of merciless war between good and evil.

Bibliography

English Translation of the Bible

New International Version (unless otherwise indicated)

Translations of the Qur'an

Ali, Maulana Muhammad. *The Holy Qur'ân*. Dublin, OH: Ahmadiyya Anjuman Isha'at Islam Lahore, 2002.

Arberry, Arthur J. *The Koran Interpreted*. Repr. Oxford: Oxford University Press, 2008.

Complete English Translation of the Noble Quran: http://www.dar-us-salam.com/TheNobleQuran/index.html.

Khalidi, Tarif. *The Qur'an: A New Translation*. New York: Viking, 2008.

Kramers, J. H. *De Koran*. Repr. Amsterdam: Arbeiderspers, 2005.

Leemhuis, Fred. *De Koran*. Repr. Houten: Wereldvenster, 1990.

Paret, Rudi. *Der Koran*. Stuttgart: Kohlhammer, 1966.

Other Works

Ali, Kecia. *Sexual Ethics and Islam: Feminist Reflections on Qur'an, Hadith, and Jurisprudence*. Oxford: Oneworld, 2006.

Ali, Tariq. *Bush in Babylon: The Recolonisation of Iraq*. London: Verso, 2003.

Almon, Ian. *The New Orientalists: Postmodern Representations of Islam from Foucault to Baudrillard*. London: Tauris, 2007.

Armstrong, Karen. *Jerusalem: One City, Three Faiths*. New York: Knopf, 1996.

Attema, D. S. *Arabië en de Bijbel*. The Hague: Van Keulen, 1961.

———. *De Mohammedaansche opvattingen omtrent het tijdstip van den jongsten dag en zijn voorteekenen*. Amsterdam: Noord-Hollandsche Maatschappij, 1942.

————. *Het oudste Christendom in Zuid-Arabië.* Amsterdam: Noord-Hollandsche, 1949.

Audah, Ali. *Konkordansi Qur'an.* Jakarta: AntarNusa, 1991.

Auden, W. H. *Selected Poems.* Ed. Edward Mendelson. New York: Vintage, 1979.

Augustine, Aurelius. *The City of God.* Trans. Marcus Dods; ed. Philip Schaff. *The Nicene and Post-Nicene Fathers.* 1st ser. Vol. 2. Repr. Grand Rapids: Eerdmans, 1983.

Balthasar, Hans Urs von. *Herrlichkeit: Eine theologische Aesthetik.* Vol. 3/2: *Theologie.* Pt. 1: *Alter Bund.* 2nd ed. Einsiedeln: Johannes, 1989. Eng. *The Glory of the Lord.* Vol. 6. Edinburgh: T. & T. Clark, 1991.

Baricco, Alessandro. *An Iliad: A Story of War.* Trans. Ann Goldstein. New York: Knopf, 2006.

————. *De Ilias van Homerus.* Breda: De Geus, 2004.

Bartelink, G. J. M. *Klassieke letterkunde: Overzicht van de Griekse en Latijnse literatuur.* Utrecht: Spectrum, 1989.

Bauschke, Martin. *Der Spiegel des Propheten: Abraham im Koran und im Islam.* Frankfurt am Main: Lembeck, 2008.

Behm, Johannes. *Das Neue Testament Deutsch: Die Offenbarung des Johannes.* Göttingen: Vandenhoeck and Ruprecht, 1949.

Ben-Chorin, Schalom. *Kritik des Esther-buches: Eine theologische Streitschrift.* Jerusalem: "Heatid," Salingré, 1938.

Biedermann, Hans. *Prisma van de symbolen.* 4th ed. Utrecht: Spectrum, 1993.

De Bijbel uit de grondtekst vertaald: Willibrordvertaling. 2nd rev. ed. 's-Hertogenbosch: Katholieke Bijbelstichting, 1996.

Bijbels-historisch Woordenboek. Ed. Bo Reicke and Leonhard Rost. Vols. 1-6. Utrecht: Spectrum, 1969.

Blachère, Régis. *Le Coran: Traduction selon un essai de reclassement des Sourates.* Paris: Maisonneuve, 1951.

Bladel, Kevin van. "The Alexander Legend in the Qur'an 18:83-102." In *The Qur'an in Its Historical Context,* ed. Gabriel Said Reynolds. New York: Routledge, 2007, 175-203.

Blom, Amélie, Laetitia Bucaille, and Luis Martinez, eds. *The Enigma of Islamist Violence.* New York: Columbia University Press, 2007.

Boer, Dick. *Erlösung aus der Sklaverei: Versuch einer biblischen Theologie im Dienst der Befreiung.* Münster: ITP-Kompass, 2008.

Bommel, Abdulwahid van. *Islam, liefde en seksualiteit.* Leuven: Bulaaq, 2003.

Boorstin, Daniel J. *The Creators: A History of Heroes of the Imagination.* New York: Random House, 1992.

Borgman, Erik, et al. *Mohammed onder de profeten? Als Christen de Koran lezen.* Leuven: TGL, 1993.

Brinner, William M., trans. *The History of al-Tabarî.* Vol. 2: *Prophets and Patriarchs.* New York: SUNY Press, 1987.

Brockelmann, Carl. *History of the Islamic Peoples.* Trans. Joel Carmichael and Moshe Perlmann. London: Routledge, 2000.

Brueggemann, Walter. *Theology of the Old Testament: Testimony, Dispute, Advocacy.* Minneapolis: Fortress, 1997.

Buber, Martin. *Het geloof der profeten.* Wassenaar: Servire, 1972.

―――. *Voordrachten over opvoeding: en autobiografische fragmenten.* Utrecht: Bijleveld, 1970.

―――. *Werke.* Vol. 2: *Schriften zur Bibel.* Munich: Kösel, 1964.

―――. *Werke.* Vol. 3: *Schriften zum Chassidismus.* Munich: Kösel, 1963.

Buhl, Frants. *Das Leben Muhammads.* Repr. Darmstadt: Wissenschaftliche Buchgesellschaft, 1961.

Burrow, John. *A History of Histories: Epics, Chronicles, Romances and Inquiries from Herodotus and Thucydides to the Twentieth Century.* New York: Knopf, 2008.

Burton, Richard F. *Personal Narrative of a Pilgrimage to al-Madinah & Meccah.* 2 vols. New York: Dover, 1964.

Caenegen, R. C. van, et al. *Grote Winkler Prins: Encyclopedie in 25 delen.* 8th ed. Amsterdam: Elsevier, 1979.

Cartledge, Paul. *Ancient Greece: A History in Eleven Cities.* Oxford: Oxford University Press, 2009.

Cary, George. "Alexander the Great in Medieval Theology." *Journal of the Warburg and Courtauld Institutes* 19 (1954): 98-114.

―――. *The Medieval Alexander.* Ed. D. J. A. Ross. Cambridge: Cambridge University Press, 1956.

Caven, Brian. *The Punic Wars.* New York: St. Martin's, 1980.

Chugg, Andrew Michael. *Alexandre le Grand: Le Tombeau Perdu.* London: Periplus, 2004.

Collins, Owen, comp. *Speeches That Changed the World.* Louisville: Westminster John Knox, 1999.

Cook, David. *Studies in Muslim Apocalyptic.* Princeton: Darwin, 2002.

―――. "Why Did Muhammad Attack the Byzantines?" In *Political Islam from Muhammad to Ahmadinejad: Defenders, Detractors, and Definitions,* ed. Joseph Morrison Skelly. Santa Barbara: Praeger Security, 2010, 27-34.

Courbage, Youssef, and Philippe Fargues. *Christians and Jews under Islam.* Trans. Judy Mabro. London: Tauris, 1997.

Cragg, Kenneth. "Islam Hostage to Itself?" In *World Christianity in Muslim Encounter: Essays in Memory of David A. Kerr,* ed. Stephen R. Goodwin. London: Continuum, 2009, 2:128-44.

Crowley, Roger. *Constantinople: The Last Great Siege 1453.* London: Faber and Faber, 2005.

Dalby, Andrew. *Rediscovering Homer: Inside the Origins of the Epic.* New York: Norton, 2006.

Dickens, Charles. *A Tale of Two Cities.* Ed. George Woodcock. Harmondsworth: Penguin, 1970. Repr. 1985.

―――. *In Londen en Parijs.* Utrecht and Antwerp: Het Spectrum, 1952.

Dijk, Bertus, Kees Samhoffer, and Klaas Wellinga, eds. *Stem van Alarm; Stem van vuur: Geëngareerde poëzie uit Latijns Amerika, Afrika en Azië*. Bussum: Wereldvenster and The Hague: Novib, 1981.

Dijk, P. van, A. Houtepen, and H. Zeldenrust. *Geloof en geweld: De vrede van God en de oorlogen der mensen*. Kampen: Kok, 1988.

Dodds, Jerrilynn D., Maria Rosa Menocal, and Abigail Krasner Balbale. *The Arts of Intimacy: Christians, Jews, and Muslims in the Making of Castilian Culture*. New Haven: Yale University Press, 2008.

Donner, Fred M. *Muhammad and the Believers: At the Origins of Islam*. Cambridge, MA: Belknap, 2010.

Duran, Bunyamin. "Salomo als rolmodel voor een harmonieus leven: een moslimperspectief." In *Bijbelse figuren in de islamitische traditie*, ed. Martha Fredriks. Zoetermeer: Meinema, 2007, 108-18.

Elmarsafy, Ziad. *The Enlightenment Qur'an: The Politics of Translation and the Construction of Islam*. Oxford: Oneworld, 2009.

Empereur, Jean-Yves. *Alexandria: Jewel of Egypt*. New York: Abrams, 2002.

Encylopaedia of Islam. New ed. Ed. P. J. Bearman et al. 12 vols. Leiden: Brill, 1960-2005.

Encylopaedia of the Qur'ān. Ed. Jane Dammen McAuliffe. 6 vols. Leiden: Brill, 2001-6.

The Epic of Gilgamesh. Trans. N. K. Sanders. Harmondsworth: Penguin, 1972.

Erasmus, Desiderius. *Erasmus: Een portret in Brieven*. Trans. and ed. Jan Papy, Marc van der Poel, and Dirk Sacré. Amsterdam: Boom, 2001.

Esack, Farid. *On Being a Muslim: Finding a Religious Path in the World Today*. Oxford: Oneworld, 1999.

Esposito, John L. *The Oxford History of Islam*. New York: Oxford University Press, 1999.

Farrokh, Kaveh. *Shadows in the Desert: Ancient Persia at War*. New York: Midland House, 2009.

Finkel, Irving L., and Michael J. Seymour. *Babylon: Myth and Reality*. London: British Museum Press, 2008.

Firestone, Reuven. *Journeys in Holy Lands: The Evolution of the Abraham-Ishmael Legends in Islamic Exegesis*. New York: SUNY Press, 1990.

Frembgen, Jürgen Wasim, and Hans Werner Mohm. *Lebensbaum und Kalaschnikow: Krieg und Frieden im Spiegel afghanischer Bildenteppiche*. Bieskastel: Gollenstein, 2000.

Frör, Kurt. *Biblische Hermeneutik*. Munich: Kaiser, 1961.

Gabrieli, Francesco. *Arab Historians of the Crusades: Selected and Translated from Arabic Sources*. Trans. E. J. Costello. Berkeley: University of California Press, 1969.

Geiger, Abraham. *Was hat Muhammad aus dem Judenthume aufgenommen?* 2nd ed. Leipzig: Kaufmann, 1902.

Gibb, H. A. R., and J. H. Kramers. *Shorter Encyclopaedia of Islam*. Leiden: Brill, 1961.

Gills, Anton. *The Rise and Fall of Babylon: Gateway of the Gods*. London: Quercus, 2008.

Glassé, Cyril. *The Concise Encyclopaedia of Islam*. Rev. ed. London: Stacey International, 2001.

Goodman, Martin. *Rome and Jerusalem: The Clash of Ancient Civilizations.* New York: Vintage, 2008.

Goodwin, Stephen R. *World Christianity in Muslim Encounter: Essays in Memory of David A. Kerr.* Vol. 2. London: Continuum, 2009.

Groetelaers, Remco, and Jan van Laarhoven. *De waanzin ten top: Driezuidend jaar toren van Babel.* Nijmegen: SUN, 1998.

Grosheide, F. W., and G. P van Itterzon, eds. *Christelijke Encylopedie.* 2nd ed. 6 vols. Kampen: Kok, 1956-61.

Grosheide, F. W., et al., eds. *Bijbelse Encyclopaedie.* Kampen: Kok, 1950.

Guillaume, Alfred. *The Life of Muhammad: A Translation of Ishâq's* Sîrat Rasûl Allâh. Repr. New York: Oxford University Press, 2001.

Hagen, Rose-Marie, and Rainer Hagen. *What Great Paintings Say: From the Bayeux Tapestry to Diego Rivera.* Vol. 1. Cologne: Taschen, 2005.

Hammarskjöld, Dag. *Markings.* London: Faber and Faber, 1964.

Hansen, Mogens Herman, and Frits Naerebout. *Polis: An Introduction to the Ancient Greek City State.* Oxford: Oxford University Press, 2006.

Hayek, Michel. *Le Mystere d'Ismaël.* Paris: Maison Mame, 1964.

———. *Les Arabes: Ou, le baptême des larmes.* Paris: Gallimard, 1972.

Heering, G. J. *Fall of Christianity: A Study of Christianity, the State, and War.* Trans. J. W. Thompson. Repr. New York: Garland, 1972.

Heimert, Alan, and Andrew Delbanco, eds. *The Puritans in America: A Narrative Anthology.* Cambridge, MA: Harvard University Press, 1985.

Herodotus. *The Histories.* Trans. Aubrey de Sélincourt. Rev. A. R. Burn. Harmondsworth: Penguin, 1972.

Herrin, Judith. *Byzantium: The Surprising Life of a Medieval Empire.* Princeton: Princeton University Press, 2008.

Hillenbrand, Carole. "Some Medieval Muslim Views of Constantinople." In *World Christianity in Muslim Encounter: Essays in Memory of David A. Kerr,* ed. Stephen R. Goodwin. London: Continuum, 2009, 2:71-83.

Hinze, Bradford E., and Irfan A. Omar, eds. *Heirs of Abraham: The Future of Muslim, Jewish, and Christian Relations.* Maryknoll: Orbis, 2005.

Hitti, Philip K. *History of the Arabs.* 8th ed. New York: St. Martin's, 1964.

Hoet, Hendrik. *De weg van Paulus: Leven en brieven van de Apostel der volkeren.* Tielt: Lannoo, 2008.

Hogenelst, Dini, and Frits van Oostrom. *Handgeschreven Wereld: Nederlandse Literatuur en Cultuur in de Middeleeuwen.* Amsterdam: Prometheus, 1995.

Holland, Tom. *Persian Fire: The First World Empire and the Battle for the West.* New York: Doubleday, 2005.

Homer. *The Iliad.* Trans. E. V. Rieu. Harmondsworth: Penguin, 1950.

———. *The Odyssey.* Trans. E. V. Rieu. Harmondsworth: Penguin, 1946.

Houtepen, Anton. *Geloven in gerechtigheid: Bijdragen tot een oecumenische sociale ethiek.* Zoetermeer: Meinema, 2005.

Hoyland, Robert G. *Seeing Islam as Others Saw It: A Survey and Evaluation of Christian, Jewish, and Zoroastrian Writings on Early Islam.* Princeton: Darwin, 1997.

Hussein, Muhammad Kāmel. *City of Wrong: A Friday in Jerusalem.* Trans. Kenneth Cragg. New York: Seabury, 1966.

————. *De stad des verderfs: Een vrijdag in Jeruzalem.* Amsterdam: De Brug-Djambatan, 1991.

Izutsu, Toshihiko. *Ethico-Religious Concepts in the Qur'an.* Montreal: McGill University Press, 1966.

————. *God and Man in the Koran: Semantics of the Koranic Weltanschauung.* Tokyo: Keio Institute of Cultural and Linguistic Studies, 1964.

Jaffé, Dan. *Le Talmud et les origines juives du Christianisme: Jésus, Paul et les judéo-chretiens dans la littérature talmudique.* Paris: Cerf, 2007.

Jeffery, Arthur. *The Foreign Vocabulary of the Qur'ān.* Baroda: Oriental Institute, 1938.

Josephus, Flavius. *Jewish Antiquities.* Ware: Wordsworth Editions, 2006.

Kasimow, Harold, and Byron L. Sherwin, eds. *No Religion Is an Island: Abraham Joshua Heschel and Interreligious Dialogue.* Maryknoll: Orbis, 1991.

Kean, Roger Michael. *Forgotten Power: Byzantium, Bulwark of Christianity.* Ludlow: Thalamus, 2006.

Kedourie, Elie, ed. *The Jewish World: Revelation, Prophecy, and History.* London: Thames & Hudson, 1979.

Kepel, Gilles. *Beyond Terror and Martyrdom: The Future of the Middle East.* Cambridge, MA: Belknap, Harvard University Press, 2008.

Khalidi, Tarif. *Images of Muhammad: Narratives of the Prophet in Islam across the Centuries.* New York: Doubleday, 2009.

Kotkin, Joel. *The City: A Global History.* New York: Modern Library, 2005.

Küng, Hans. *Islam: Past, Present and Future.* Repr. Oxford: Oneworld, 2008.

Lassner, Jacob. *Demonizing the Queen of Sheba.* Chicago: University of Chicago Press, 1993.

Lazarus-Yafeh, Hava. *Intertwined Worlds: Medieval Islam and Bible Criticism.* Princeton: Princeton University Press, 1992.

Leaman, Oliver. *Islamic Aesthetics: An Introduction.* Notre Dame: University of Notre Dame Press, 2004.

Leaman, Oliver, ed. *The Qur'an: An Encyclopedia.* London: Routledge, 2006.

Leemhuis, Fred. "From Palm Leaves to the Internet." In *The Cambridge Companion to the Qur'ân,* ed. Jane Damme McAuliffe. Cambridge: Cambridge University Press, 2006, 145-61.

Leeuwen, Hans van. *Zefanja: Verklaring van een Bijbelgedeelte.* Kampen: Kok, 1979.

Leeuwen, Richard van. *Shahrazaad.* Amsterdam: Bulaaq, 1999.

Leick, Gwendolyn. *The Babylonian World.* New York: Routledge, 2007.

Lewis, Bernard. *Istanbul and the Civilization of the Ottoman Empire.* Norman: University of Oklahoma Press, 1963.

Löwith, Karl. *Meaning in History: The Theological Implications of the Philosophy of History.* Chicago: University of Chicago Press, 1957.

———. *Wereldgeschiedenis: Wijsgerig en Bijbels gezien.* Utrecht: Aula, 1960.

Lyons, Jonathan. *The House of Wisdom: How the Arabs Transformed Western Civilization.* New York: Bloomsbury, 2009.

MacCulloch, Diarmaid. *Christianity: The First Three Thousand Years.* New York: Viking, 2010.

Manguel, Alberto. *The City of Words.* London: Bloomsbury, 2008.

———. *Homer's the Iliad and the Odyssey: A Biography.* New York: Grove, 2007.

Marzahn, Joachim et al. *Babylon: Myth and Truth.* 2 vols. Munich: Hirmer, Staatliche Museen zu Berlin, 2008.

Merchant, Peter. "Introduction." In Charles Dickens, *A Tale of Two Cities.* London: Wordsworth Classics, 1999.

Meulen, Daniël van der, and Hermann von Wissamann. *Hadramaut: Some of Its Mysteries Unveiled.* Leiden: Brill, 1932.

———. *The Wells of Ibn Sa'ud.* New York: Praeger, 1957.

Milstein, Rachel. *La Bible dans l'art islamique.* Paris: Presses Universitaires de France, 2005.

Mommsen, Katharina. *Goethe und der Islam.* Frankfurt: Insel, 2001.

Moormann, Eric M., and Wilfried Uitterhoeve. *Van Achilles tot Zeus: Thema's uit de klassieke geschiedenis in literatuur, muziek, beeldende kunst en theater.* Nijmegen: SUN, 1997.

———. *Van Alexandros tot Zenobia: Thema's uit de klassieke geschiedenis in literatuur, muziek, beeldende kunst en theater.* Nijmegen: SUN, 1989.

Naastepad, T. J. M. *Geen vrede met het bestaande: Uitleg van het Boek Openbaring.* Baarn: Ten Have, 1999.

———. *Salomo: Verklaring van een Bijbelgedeelte.* Kampen: Kok, 1975.

———. *Van horen zeggen: Uitleg van het boek Deuteronomium.* Baarn: Ten Have, 2001.

Nagel, Tilman. *Der Koran und sein religiöses und kulturelles Umfeld.* Munich: Oldebourg, 2010.

Neuwirth, Angelika. *Studien zur Komposition der Mekkanischen Suren.* Berlin: De Gruyter, 1981.

Oosterhuis, Huub, and Alex van Heusden. *Het Evangelie van Lukas.* Vught: Skandalon, 2007.

Oostrom, Frits van. *Maerlants Wereld.* 3rd ed. Amsterdam: Prometheus, 1996.

———. *Stemmen op schrift: Geschiedenis van de Nederlandse literatuur vanaf het begin tot 1300.* Amsterdam: Bakker, 2006.

Pagden, Anthony. *Worlds at War: The 2,500-Year Struggle between East and West.* New York: Random House, 2008.

Paret, Rudi. *Der Koran: Kommentar und Konkordanz.* Stuttgart: Kohlhammer, 1971.

Partner, Peter. *God of Battles: Holy Wars of Christianity and Islam.* London: Harper-Collins, 1997.

Peters, Frank E. *Islam: A Guide for Jews and Christians.* Princeton: Princeton University Press, 2003.

Phillips, Wendell. *Qataban and Sheba: Exploring the Ancient Kingdoms on the Biblical Spice Routes of Arabia.* New York: Harcourt, Brace, 1955.

Piatnitsky, Yuri, et al. *Pilgrim Treasures from the Hermitage: Byzantium, Jerusalem.* Amsterdam: Humphries, 2005.

Pines, Shlomo. "The Jewish Christians of the Early Centuries of Christianity According to a New Source." In *Proceedings of the Israel Academy of Sciences and Humanities* 2/13 (1967).

————. "Notes on Islam and on Arabic Christianity and Judaeo-Christianity." *Jerusalem Studies in Arabic and Islam* 4 (1984): 135-52.

————. "Studies in Christianity and in Judaeo-Christianity Based on Arabic Sources." *Jerusalem Studies in Arabic and Islam* 6 (1985): 107-61.

Pollard, Justin, and Howard Reid. *The Rise and Fall of Alexandria: Birthplace of the Modern Mind.* New York: Viking, 2006.

Presser, Jacob. *Napoleon: Historie en legende.* Amsterdam: Elseviers, 1978.

Pritchard James B., ed. *Solomon and Sheba.* London: Phaidon, 1974.

Rad, Gerhard von. *Wisdom in Israel.* Nashville: Abingdon, 1972.

Renard, John. *Seven Doors to Islam: Spirituality and the Religious Life of Muslims.* Berkeley: University of California Press, 1996.

Revius, Jakobus. *Selected Poems.* Trans. Henrietta ten Harmsel. Detroit: Wayne State University Press, 1968.

Reynolds, Gabriel Said. *The Qur'ân and Its Biblical Subtext.* London: Routledge, 2010.

Riley-Smith, Jonathan. *The First Crusade and the Idea of Crusading.* Philadelphia: University of Pennsylvania Press, 1986.

Rodinson, Maxime. *Muhammad.* Trans. Anne Carter. New York: Pantheon, 1971.

Roggema, Barbara, Marcel Poorthuis, and Pim Valkenberg, eds. *The Three Rings: Textual Studies in the Historical Trialogue of Judaism, Christianity, and Islam.* Leuven: Peeters, 2005.

Rubin, Uri. *The Eye of the Beholder: The Life of Muhammad as Viewed by the Early Muslims: A Textual Analysis.* Princeton: Darwin, 1995.

Runciman, Steven. *A History of the Crusades.* Vol. 2: *The Kingdom of Jerusalem and the Frankish East (1100-1187).* Harmondsworth: Penguin, 1965.

Rynck, Patrick de, trans. *Avonturen van Alexander de Grote: De Alexander Roman.* Amsterdam: Athenaeum Polok & Van Gennep, 2000.

Schimmel, Annemarie. *Mystical Dimensions of Islam.* Chapel Hill: University of North Carolina Press, 1975.

Schneemelcher, Wilhelm, ed. *New Testament Apocrypha.* Trans. R. McL. Wilson. Vol. 1. Rev. ed. Louisville: Westminster John Knox, 1991.

Schuman, N. A. *Gelijk om gelijk: Verslag en balans van een discusie oer goddelijke vergelding in het Oude Testanment.* Amsterdam: VU Uitgeverij, 1993.

Schwarz-Bart, André. *The Last of the Just.* Trans. Stephen Becker. New York: Atheneum, 1960.

Serafin, Steven R., ed. *Encyclopedia of American Literature.* New York: Continuum, 1999.

Simpson, St John, ed. *Queen of Sheba: Treasures from Ancient Yemen.* London: British Museum Press, 2002.

Sims, Eleanor. *Peerless Images: Persian Painting and Its Sources.* New Haven: Yale University Press, 2002.

Skelly, Joseph Morrison, ed. *Political Islam from Muhammad to Ahmadinejad: Defenders, Detractors, and Definitions.* Santa Barbara: Praeger Security, 2010.

Speyer, Heinrich. *Die Biblischen Erzählungen im Qoran.* Darmstadt: Wissenschaftliche Buchgesellschaft, 1962.

Stauffer, Ethelbert. *Christ and the Caesars: Historical Sketches.* Philadelphia: Westminster, 1955.

Steiner, George. "Homer and the Scholars." In *Language and Silence.* London: Faber, 1985.

Stephenson, Paul. *Constantine: Unconquered Emperor, Christian Victor.* London: Quercus, 2009.

Stern, S. M. "New Light on Judaeo-Christianity?" *Encounter* 28/5 (May 1967): 53-57.

Stobart, J. C. *The Grandeur That Was Rome.* 4th ed. New York: St. Martin's, 1987.

Stoneman, Richard. *Alexander the Great: A Life in Legend.* New Haven: Yale University Press, 2010.

————. *The Greek Alexander Romance.* London: Penguin, 1991.

Stowasser, Barbara Freyer. *Women in the Qur'an, Traditions, and Interpretation.* New York: Oxford University Press, 1994.

Strickland, Debra Higgs. *Saracens, Demons, and Jews: Making Monsters in Medieval Art.* Princeton: Princeton University Press, 2003.

Strootman, Rolf. *Gekroonde Goden: Hellenistische vorsten van Alexander tot Kleopatra.* Amsterdam: Amsterdam University Press, 2005.

Thyen, Johann-Dietrich. *Bibel und Koran: Eine Synopse gemeinsamer Überlieferungen.* Cologne: Böhlau, 1989.

Toorn, K. van der, and P. W. van der Horst. "Nimrod before and after the Bible." *Harvard Theological Review* 83 (1990): 1-29.

Tottoli, Roberto. *Biblical Prophets in the Qur'an and Muslim Literature.* Richmond: Curzon, 2002.

Ullendorff, Edward. *Ethiopia and the Bible.* Schweich Lectures 1967. Oxford: Oxford University Press, 1968.

The Umayyads: The Rise of Islamic Art. Amman: Arab Institute for Research and Publishing, 2000.

Van Dale Groot Woordenboek der Nederlandse Taal. 's Gravenhage: Nijhoff, 1961.

Virgil. *The Aeneid.* Trans. F. Jackson Knight. Harmondsworth: Penguin, 1968.

Voigt, Gottfried. *Der Helle Morgenstern.* Göttingen: Vandenhoeck & Ruprecht, 1961.

Vondel, Joost van den. *De Gijsbrecht van Aemstel.* Repr. Amsterdam: University of Amsterdam Press, 1994.

Wadud-Muhsin, Amina. *Quran and Woman.* 2nd ed. New York: Oxford University Press, 1999.

Wansbrough, John. *Quranic Studies: Sources and Methods of Scriptural Interpretation.* Amherst, NY: Prometheus, 2004.

Watt, W. Montgomery. *Companion to the Qur'an: Based on the Arberry Translation.* London: Allen and Unwin, 1967.

————. "The Queen of Sheba in Islamic Tradition." In *Solomon and Sheba,* ed. James B. Pritchard. London: Phaidon, 1974, 85-103.

Wessels, Anton. *Arab and Christian? Christians in the Middle East.* Kampen: Pharos, 1995.

————. *Gelukkig in de Akbarstraat.* Kampen: Ten Have, 2004.

————. *Islam in Stories.* Trans. John Bowden. Leuven: Peeters, 2002.

————. *Islam verhalenderwijs.* Repr. Amsterdam: Nieuwezijds, 2002.

————. *Moslim in Mokum.* Amsterdam: Vrije Universiteit Press, 2002.

————. *Muslims and the West: Can They Be Integrated?* Trans. John Bowden. Leuven: Peeters, 2005.

————. *Twee watermeloenen in één hand: De acteurs in het Libanese drama.* Amstelveen: Luyten, 1986.

Whalen, Brett Edward. *Dominion of God: Christendom and Apocalypse in the Middle Ages.* Cambridge, MA: Harvard University Press, 2009.

Wheeler, Brannon M. *Mecca and Eden: Ritual, Relics, and Territory in Islam.* Chicago: University of Chicago Press, 2006.

————. *Prophets in the Quran: An Introduction to the Quran and Muslim Exegesis.* London: Continuum, 2002.

Wielenga, Bas. *It's a Long Road to Freedom: Perspective of Biblical Theology.* Madurai: Tamilnadu Theological Seminary, 1981.

Wigoder, Geoffrey. *Joodse Cultuur: Oorsprong en bloei.* Baarn: Ambo, 1994.

Wilken, Robert L. *The Land Called Holy: Palestine in Christian History and Thought.* New Haven: Yale University Press, 1992.

Wood, Michael. *In the Footsteps of Alexander the Great: A Journey from Greece to India.* Repr. London: BBC, 2004.

Worthington, Ian. *Alexander the Great: A Reader.* 2nd ed. New York: Routledge, 2012.

Wullen, Moritz, and Günther Schauerte, eds. *Babylon: Mythos.* Berlin: Staatliche Museen, 2008.

Wytzes, J. *De Vergilius: De Dichter van het imperium.* Kampen: Kok, 1951.

Yücesoy, Hayrettin. *Messianic Beliefs and Imperial Politics in Medieval Islam: The 'Abbâsid Caliphate in the Early Ninth Century.* Columbia: University of South Carolina Press, 2009.

Zeitlin, Irving M. *The Historical Muhammad*. Cambridge: Polity, 2007.

Ziegler, Konrat, and Walther Sontheimer, eds. *Der Kleine Pauly: Lexikon der Antike in fünf Bänden*. Stuttgart: Druckenmüller, 1979.

Index